BENJAMIN

BENJAMIN

Philosophy, Aesthetics, History

Edited by Gary Smith

The University of Chicago Press
Chicago and London

The University of Chicago Press, Chicago 60637

The University of Chicago Press, Ltd., London

98 97 96 95 94 93   5 4 3

Library of Congress Cataloging-in-Publication Data

Benjamin—philosophy, aesthetics, history / edited by Gary Smith.
    p. cm.
    Most of this material is reprinted from Fall-winter 1983–84
    issue of the Philosophical forum, vol. XV, nos. 1–2.
    Includes bibliographical references.
    ISBN 0-226-76512-1 (cloth).—ISBN 0-226-76514-8 (paper)
    1. Benjamin, Walter, 1892–1940—Philosophy. I. Smith, Gary
(F. Gary)
    B3209.B584B46   1989
    193—dc20   89-5178
                                                       CIP

The translations of texts by Walter Benjamin, Theodor W.
Adorno, and Rolf Tiedemann are printed with the kind
permission of Suhrkamp Verlag, Frankfurt am Main.
Sources are as follows:

"N [Re the Theory of Knowledge, Theory of Progress],"
    from Walter Benjamin, *Das Passagen-Werk,* ed. Rolf
    Tiedemann (Frankfurt am Main: Suhrkamp, 1982), pp.
    570-611 (*Gesammelte Schriften,* V).

"On the Program of the Coming Philosophy," from Walter
    Benjamin, *Gesammelte Schriften* II, ed. Rolf
    Tiedemann and Hermann Schweppenhäuser (Frankfurt
    am Main: Suhrkamp, 1977), pp. 157-71.

"Progress," from Theodor W. Adorno, *Stichworte.*
    Kritische Modelle 2 (Frankfurt am Main: Suhrkamp,
    1969), pp. 29-50.

"Historical Materialism or Political Messianism? An
    Interpretation of the Theses 'On the Concept of
    History'," from Rolf Tiedemann, *Dialektik im
    Stillstand. Versuche zum Spätwerk Walter Benjamins*
    (Frankfurt an Main: Suhrkamp, 1983), pp. 99-142.

Contents

THINKING THROUGH BENJAMIN:
AN INTRODUCTORY ESSAY

GARY SMITH

> *In memory of Gershom Scholem (1897-1982)*
>
> Benjamin was a philosopher. He was one through all the phases and in all the fields of his activity. On the face of it he wrote mostly about subjects of literature and art, sometimes also about topics on the borderline between literature and politics, but only rarely about matters conventionally considered and accepted as themes of pure philosophy. Yet in all these domains he derives his impulse from the philosopher's experience [. . .] of the world and its reality. He was a metaphysician [. . .] pure and simple.
>
> *Gershom Scholem*[1]

I

Hannah Arendt, echoing an ambition Benjamin had once expressed himself, made it commonplace in the English-speaking world to refer to Benjamin as "the most important critic of [his] time."[2] This did not do his reputation as a philosopher any good—if anything, she was damning him with great praise. Whereas on the Continent an efflorescence of studies of philosophical themes in Benjamin's thought soon ensued, this aspect of his thinking was to receive little attention in the United States and Great Britain.[3] There, literary critics and art historians lionize Benjamin's aesthetics, while philosophers seem oblivious even to this aspect of his work. The influence in the United States and Britain of Arendt's brilliant portrait of Benjamin as one of the last *hommes de lettres* has scarcely waned in the more than two decades since she first set forth her view. As a result, there has been no productive tension of competing images or paradigms such as that which her essay, first published in *The New Yorker,* would ironically generate in Germany. The present collection, which builds upon a special double issue of *The Philosophical Forum,* represents an attempt to remedy this shortcoming by introducing the central philosophical features of Benjamin's thought, without making an attempt to claim it for philosophy alone.

For those who knew Benjamin, the attempt to articulate the exceptional features of his manner of thinking became a sort of perennial project. Arendt's characterization of the nature of Benjamin's thought as *poetic* met with reservations in Germany, most directly from Theodor W. Adorno and Gershom Scholem, administrators of Benjamin's literary estate and co-editors of a selected edition of Benjamin's letters published the year before.[4] Arendt foresaw the controversy her view would engender, a fact that is documented by a remarkable, unpublished exchange of letters between her and Adorno. In a letter from Adorno, whose introduction to the two-volume edition of Benjamin's *Schriften*[5] in 1955 remains the most influential and resolute reading of Benjamin as a philosopher, Arendt cautiously forewarns of the disapproval she expects her forthcoming portrait to evoke. The text of her letter is brief and general:

> I hope very much that I do not become entangled in a controversy, no matter on which side. I think very highly of your introduction to Benjamin's *Schriften,* but nonetheless do not have the same image of Benjamin that you do. It could possibly turn out that neither you nor Scholem[6] will be satisfied with me.[7]

Arendt offers no details of her differences with Adorno and Scholem. Nonetheless, her allusion is unambiguous. Arendt, whose own thought is a study in tensions between the writer and the philosopher, intended to challenge the primacy of the philosophical in Benjamin's thinking. In her view, Benjamin's works resist classification. Just as he could not be properly described as a scholar, a translator, or an historian, he "was neither a poet nor a philosopher."[8] The source of the significance and singularity of Benjamin's work is his "gift of *thinking poetically.*"[9] This apparent paradox of the poetic thinker who is neither poet nor philosopher, however, already suggests that this opposition might not be categorical.

In Adorno's answer, which followed six weeks later, he correctly perceives the locus of contention and defends the view of Benjamin's thought as quintessentially philosophical:

For me, what defines Benjamin's significance for my own intellectual existence is axiomatic: the essence of his thought as philosophical thought. I have never been able to see his stuff from another perspective, and it even seems to me that its entire weight is due to this alone. Just how far it distances itself from every traditional conception of philosophy is something I am aware of, of course, as I am, moreover, that Benjamin did not make it easy for one to retain this view of him. For all that, I think, judging from our contact, the outwardly so very abrupt changes in Benjamin's position were in truth much less drastic. He would not have been the great figure that he was, had this been otherwise.

Adorno's statement summarizes the central contention of his 1955 introduction, in which he endeavors to reconcile Benjamin's philosophical motives with the latter's literary and historical motifs, or, to put it differently, the primacy of Benjamin's *philosophical* project with the fact that Benjamin almost invariably addressed historical and literary material.

But does thought which "distances itself from every traditional concept of philosophy" warrant the label "philosophy?" Adorno contends that it does, because despite Benjamin's deliberate, "stark opposition to all modern philosophy,"[10] his writings represent the singular expression of a philosophical "consciousness." Adorno can therefore project a linear perspective over the whole of his production, *id est*, in order to posit a coherence between texts which seem utterly dissimilar in mode and motive. Adorno's perspective casts light on the theoretical filiation between the two seemingly unlike texts published here in English translation: Benjamin's early, programmatic philosophical statement "On the Program of the Coming Philosophy"[11] and his late methodological *bricolage* "N. [Re the Theory of Knowledge, Theory of Progress]."[12]

Scholem sees the nature of Benjamin's thought in a similar vein. He defines its impetus as a metaphysical one. (If we follow Carnap, who insisted that all metaphysics is poetry, then Scholem and Arendt would seem to see eye to eye.) In Benjamin's generation, Scholem pointed out in 1965, it had been more common to apply metaphysics to "subjects which would seem to have little or no bearing on metaphysics."[13] Simmel's work, which itself is not without direct resonance in Benjamin's works,[14] exemplifies this approach. Benjamin and Simmel are allied, *inter alia,* in their attempts "to lead philosophy out of the 'frozen wasteland of abstraction' and carry thought over into concrete historical images."[15]

Adorno's position must finally be compared to a view published twenty-seven years earlier by Siegfried Kracauer, who first introduced

Adorno to Benjamin in the 1920s. Kracauer articulated these same exceptional aspects of Benjamin's thinking—his philosophical resourcefulness combined with an adamant anti-traditionalism—in a masterful review essay (one of only a handful of notices Benjamin received in his lifetime) published in 1928. That was the same year Benjamin published two entirely dissimilar works: *Ursprung des deutschen Trauerspiels,* a difficult tractarian study of the German lamentation play, and *Einbahnstraße,* a work thoroughly modern in its textual fragmentation and even in its design.[16]

Kracauer attributes the strangeness of Benjamin's manner of thinking to his procedure, which rests in part upon the imbricated relationship Benjamin proposes between ideas, concepts, and phenomena. Benjamin's procedure is antithetical to "the philosophical system which wants to secure its grasp of the world by means of universal concepts; [it is] the counter-position to abstract generalisation as a whole."[17] The observer who comprehends a phenomenon "as the realization of some abstraction" is misled into thinking that such an "immediate encounter reveals [. . .] something of the essentialities [*Wesenheiten*] that it [the phenomenon] contains." For Benjamin, the form experienced by the observer is ephemeral. (Benjamin makes light of Husserl's belief, at least espoused in the *Cartesian Meditations,* that knowledge of essences can be gained through the analysis of intentional consciousness.) In this brief sketch of Benjamin's position—which is actually an account of what is original in the "Prologue to a Critique of Knowledge" ["Erkenntniskritische Vorrede"] to Benjamin's *Trauerspiel* book[18]—Kracauer refers to Platonic, Scholastic, Husserlian, and Leibnizian allusions embedded in Benjamin's procedure. Yet this dense fabric of philosophical allusions should not obscure the fact that Benjamin's thinking presumes a fundamental reorientation of the philosopher's task. The crucial difference between Benjamin's way of thinking and "the usual abstract thinking" is thus described by Kracauer in the following way:

> Whereas the former drains the concrete plenitude of the objects, the latter burrows itself into the material thicket in order to unfold the dialectic of the essentialities. It accepts no generalities whatsoever, pursuing instead the course of specific ideas through history. But since for Benjamin every idea is a *monad,* every representation of such a monad seems to him to provide access to the world.[19]

The great astuteness of Kracauer's review shows itself in his attempt to pin down Benjamin's conception of the nature of philosophy and the role of the philosopher: While "in Benjamin philosophy regains the determinateness of its contents; the philosopher is placed into the 'elevated middle between researcher and artist'."[20]

II

Benjamin never once acknowledged the boundary taken for granted by all modern thought: the Kantian commandment not to trespass into unintelligible worlds or, as Hegel riposted, to where there are "houses of ill repute." [. . .] For Benjamin everything habitually excluded by the norms of experience ought to become part of experience to the extent that it adheres to its own concreteness instead of dissipating this, its immortal aspect, by subordinating it to the schema of the abstract universal.

Theodor W. Adorno[21]

There is no doubt that Benjamin thought of much of his own production in philosophical terms. Numerous passages in which he articulates philosophical ambitions can be found in his various curricula vitae. In one submitted to the fledgling Hebrew University of Jerusalem in 1928, Benjamin describes his doctoral thesis as the expression of a growing interest in "the substantial philosophical contents of literary works" and his *Trauerspiel* book as an attempt to address "the philosophical content of a lost and misjudged artform, the allegory."[22] He expands upon this project, in another autobiographical statement, written at about the same time:

Just as Benedetto Croce lay open the way to the individual work of art by demolishing the doctrine of art forms, my attempts to date endeavor to clear the way to the artwork through the demolition of the doctrine of art's territorial character. Their common programmatic aim is to further the integration process of *Wissenschaft,* which increasingly abandoned the rigid barriers between the disciplines, such as marked the concept of *Wissenschaft* during the previous century, through an analysis of the work of art which recognizes in it an integral expression—territorially limiting to no side—of the religious, metaphysical, political, [and] economic trends of an epoch [. . .] In this respect the eidetic contemplation of phenomena stands nearer to it than the historical.[23]

Even in his early, expressly philosophical work, Benjamin seldom fails to exemplify his theorizing in the philosophy of art through an outstanding work of art. He declares his intention to make a principle of this practice in the autobiographical statement prepared for the University of Frankfurt in 1925. Here Benjamin presents his *Ursprung des deutschen Trauerspiels* in part as an attempt to give certain thoughts about theory of language "concrete literary-historical" form. To the extent that this approach closely identifies "aesthetic questions" with "the great works of German literature," it foreshadows "the method of my subsequent works."[24]

Such is the case in his study of the German *Trauerspiel,* which is prefaced by reflections on the critique of knowledge; in Benjamin's interpretation of "Zwei Gedichte von Friedrich Hölderlin" (1914-1915);[25] in his translation of a group of poems by Baudelaire, "Tableaux parisiens" (1914-1922),[26] which he precedes with his essay on "The Task of the Translator" (1921);[27] and in his most difficult and brilliant composition, the essay on Goethe's *Elective Affinities.*[28] Moreover, Benjamin confirms this particular confluence of philosophical reflections in a late autobiographical statement, in which he recounts the predominance of his "interest in the philosophy of language next to the theory of art."[29]

In Benjamin's principal early works, then, the literary work of art serves as the measure of philosophical reflection. First of all, this signifies a productive convergence of his theories of art and language, whereby he will seek to ground certain concepts and relations. The centrality of the philosophy of language is especially apparent in Benjamin's valorization of the concept of experience, a principal theme of this volume.[30]

Benjamin's two texts presented here in English translation, "On the Program of the Coming Philosophy" (1917-18) and "N. Re The Theory of Knowledge, Theory of Progress" (1927-1940), are indispensible for any assessment of his philosophical thought.

Indeed, if we think of Benjamin's "Program" essay as a distant conceptual preamble to his late *Arcades Project,* a leitmotif of this volume and Benjamin's thought in general necessarily emerges: *his theory of experience.* In the course of this introductory essay, I shall take these two strikingly dissimilar texts as paradigmatic of Benjamin's philosophical approach.

'Experience' has been heralded by many as Benjamin's great theme. It has been claimed to constitute the true focal point of his analysis of modernity, philosophy of history, and theory of the artwork. Peter Krumme places the theory of experience into "the by no means secret center of all of Benjamin's conceptions."[31] Krista Greffrath considers it the most productive part of Benjamin's philosophy of history.[32] Jürgen Habermas accuses Benjamin of failing in his attempt to mold historical materialism to meet the theoretical demands of his broadly framed theory of experience.[33] For Fredric Jameson, the relationship between experience and narrative is "Benjamin's great theme—the formal unfolding of disintegration of storytelling as a reflex of village society, the great industrial city, and the world of media respectively."[34] Rolf Tiedemann maintains that Benjamin's early ambition to restore validity to theological experience was transformed by the surrealist insight that such experience should properly be transported "into the profane." For Tiedemann, the "epistemic intention" of Benjamin's application of "profane illumination" to history ultimately rests on his theory of experience, because it derives from his theory of mimetic ability.[35]

Benjamin wrote the first of the texts presented here, "On the Program of the Coming Philosophy," from 1917 to 1918, at the age of twenty-five. His preoccupation with the concept of experience, however, reaches back five years earlier, when he published a short essay simply entitled "Erfahrung."[36] This essay remained important enough for Benjamin to refer to it in a note composed in 1929 (if not later), and thereby disclosed the concept's pride of place throughout two decades of the author's thought:

> In an early essay I mobilized all the rebellious forces of youth against the word "experience." And now this word has become an integral element of much of my work. Despite this, I have remained true to myself. For my attack cut through the word without destroying it. It penetrated into the center of the matter.[37]

By 1918, Benjamin focusses his criticism on the ramifications of the Kantian theory of experience. As Michael Jennings has noted, by the time Benjamin was twenty-one (in mid-1913) he was familiar with the fundamentals of Kant's philosophy, having read the first and third *Critiques* as well as the *Prolegomena to the Metaphysics of Morals*.[38] In fact, while studying in Munich from 1915-1916, Benjamin took two Kant seminars with Moritz Geiger, one on Kant's third critique and the other on Kant's teleology.[39] Around 1918 he studied the *Critique of Practical Reason*.[40] Benjamin even originally intended to write his doctoral thesis on Kant's philosophy of history,[41] a plan which led him to the topic of Kant's concept of the "infinite task" [*unendliche Aufgabe*].[42] Even once Benjamin had abandoned such plans and decided to write on the philosophical grounds of early Romantic *Kunstkritik* [art criticism], he expected this topic to lead him back to Kant.[43] All that ultimately remained of this topic, however, was the confluence of the Fichtean and early Romantic concerns with boundlessness of reflection [*Unendlichkeit der Reflexion*].

The context for Benjamin's interpretation of Kant around 1918 can be understood in conjunction with the view of the Marburg School of neo-Kantianism. If a single work can be considered the cornerstone of this school, then it must be Hermann Cohen's *Kants Theorie der Erfahrung*.[44] The third, revised edition, published in 1918, includes a new foreword as well as a programmatic resumé in the form of an afterword. There Cohen presents, in thesis form, nineteen points where Kant's philosophy requires "revision." Cohen's theses follow from his view that the primary task Kant set for himself in the *Critique* was to present a theory of experience.

There are two components of Kant's theory of experience, according to Cohen: the Transcendental Aesthetic and Analytic, which constitutes a "doctrine of experience,"[45] and the Transcendental Dialectic, which constitutes a "doctrine of ideas." Approximately four-fifths of the book is devoted to the doctrine of experience, since the doctrine of ideas is ultimately incorporated into this doctrine.

Cohen proposes a revisionist historical genealogy for the Kantian system, in which Hume's role is greatly reduced. For Cohen, Kant's true lineage includes Plato, Descartes, Galileo, Newton, and Leibniz, all of whom were primarily concerned with the critique and certainty of knowledge. Thus Plato becomes the father of *Erkenntniskritik,* that neo-Kantian term first coined in the early decades of the nineteenth century.[46] Cohen's Kant accentuates the close filiation between mathematics, mathematical physics, and philosophy, since the first two serve as the measure of knowledge's validity.

Cohen's readings of Kant's endeavor was as influential as it was controversial. The great Kant scholar and editor Erich Adickes published a famous challenge in 1897, in which he concedes the importance of the problem of experience in the first *Critique* while disputing its centrality.[47] Indeed, Kant's *Critique of Pure Reason* can only be construed as a theory of experience to the extent that Kant resolves to offer an explanation of the possibility of experience. Yet Cohen's reading downplays other significant aspects of Kant's project: Kant's argument for the objective validity of *a priori* knowledge is just as central to the *Critique*'s overall structure.

The contextual correspondence between Benjamin's aim in "On the Program of the Coming Philosophy" and Cohen's undertaking have led some interpreters to assume Cohen's direct influence on Benjamin's essay. True, Benjamin's reflections are thematically situated squarely within the framework of Cohen's interpretation of the Kantian system. Furthermore, when Benjamin presented the essay to Gerhard Scholem, he recommended that his friend read it in tandem with Cohen's book. Cohen's basic views, however, had been common philosophical knowledge for several decades. His general approach was clearly engrained in Benjamin from the very beginning, even before Benjamin read—and was estranged by[48]—the actual work. Benjamin wrote his essay, in fact, *before* reading Cohen's book; he first studied the book together with Scholem during the summer of 1918, shortly after it appeared in the substantially expanded third edition.

This closeness of context has obscured Scholem's role in bringing Benjamin to the central thoughts contained in the "Program" essay. This point is significant, among other reasons,[49] in light of the trend in recent years to underestimate Scholem's obvious *philosophical* acumen, and to attend only to the philological and historical aspects of his achievements. Scholem, six years younger than the twenty-five year old Benjamin, must have been a precocious philosophical thinker to have attracted and sustained such an intensive intellectual relationship with Benjamin. Benjamin's correspondence with Scholem, who at the time was studying philosophy and mathematics in Jena, records Scholem's influence on the direction of Benjamin's philosophical reflections. Scholem was attending Frege's *Begriffschrift* lectures and Bruno Bauch's lectures on Kant as well as studying Husserl's *Logical Investigations*[50] with Paul Linke.[51] Early in the Winter Semester 1917/1918, Scholem apparently sent Benjamin a detailed letter about Kant, since Benjamin frames his extensive reply as an expression of agreement with Scholem's remarks. Some of the principal thoughts on Kant that Benjamin would develop in the "Program" essay already emerge in this letter. Here Benjamin speaks of his "firm conviction" that the aim of "philosophy and therefore doctrine [. . .] can never become [. . .] a convulsion, an overthrow of the Kantian system." The philosopher must display an adamantine commitment to the Kantian system and strive for its "universal development." Benjamin continues:

> The deepest typology of thought of the doctrine has always become intelligible to me through his words and thoughts up to now, and this typology of his system, which [. . .] can only be compared to Plato's, must be preserved. Philosophy can only become doctrine, or at least become incorporated into it, by following Kant and Plato [. . .] in the course of revising and building upon Kant.[52]

Benjamin is determined to preserve the "essential" in Kantian thought, without yet knowing—as he admits in the letter to Scholem—what constitutes its essence. This adherence to Kantian criteria finally becomes problematic, however, when Benjamin wishes to validate pre-rational thought-forms or "an experience as 'noumenal' as that of nature's mourning" as philosophical experience.[53]

Another unexplored and intriguing point of reference, although not as fully documented, is the relation between Benjamin's modification of Kant and Hans Reichenbach's early departure from Kantian orthodoxy,[54] as set forth in the latter's doctoral thesis, *Der Begriff der Wahrscheinlichkeit für die mathematische Darstellung der Wirklichkeit.*[55] Benjamin and Reichenbach knew each other from their university days in the Free Students Movement,[56] and they corresponded after Reichenbach completed his doctoral thesis.[57] Reichenbach's proposal to add the principle of probability to Kant's inventory of categories addresses an imperfection in the Kantian theory of experience by positing their principle as a necessary condition of experience.

Benjamin's original intention to write his doctoral thesis on Kant and history was grounded in his conviction that "in the philosophy of history, the specific affinity of a philosophy with the true doctrine must most clearly come to the fore; for it is here that the theme of the historical development [*Werden*] of cognition—which dissolves that of the doctrine—must emerge."[58] This preoccupation with the philosophy of history and the historicity of cognition intensified over the years, as attested to by Benjamin's methodological position in the *Arcades Project* as well as by his outright historical epistemology in "The Work of Art in the Age of Its Technical Reproducibility."[59] It is thus no accident that the contributions to the present volume are largely devoted to Benjamin's late philosophies of history and art.

At the time Benjamin wrote his programmatic essay on the "Coming Philosophy," however, he still believed in systematic philosophy, and specifically in the need to build upon the Kantian system.[60] Yet by the time Benjamin wrote his study of the Baroque lamentation play, he would abandon his belief in system in the course of his search for alternative forms of philosophical representation. Such forms generally went unheeded in the nineteenth century, dominated as it was by the concept of system and its flawed universalism. By 1937 Benjamin would harshly attack the "unconscious complicity with positivism"of neo-Kantianism, whose great flaw was above all its belief in system.[61]

At the time of the "Coming Philosophy" essay, though, Benjamin still shared Cohen's desire to build on the Kantian system and, like the neo-Kantians, insisted upon structural emendations inconsistent with the spirit of Kant's original plans. Unlike Cohen, however, Benjamin thought he could rescue metaphysics. He reproved Kant for the narrow scope of his concept of experience; a suitable concept of experience must account for noumenal experience, for religious experience. Consequently, when Scholem moved to Berne from Jena for the following semester, he and Benjamin spent much time discussing the essay and "the scope of the concept of experience" that it demanded:

> It encompassed man's intellectual and psychological connection with the world, which takes place in the realms not yet penetrated by cognition. When I mentioned that consequently it was legitimate to include mantic disciplines in this conception of experience, Benjamin responded with an extreme formulation: "A philosophy that does not include the possibility of soothsaying from *coffee grounds* and cannot explicate it cannot be a true philosophy."[62]

Of the parallels between Benjamin's and Cohen's critiques of Kant, one is of consequence for Benjamin's subsequent work. Like Cohen, who in the third edition of *Kants Theorie der Erfahrung* underscores the place of Kant's doctrine of ideas in his theory of experience,[63] Benjamin makes the broader concept of experience dependent on a reconception of the idea: "the basis of the unity and continuity of that experience which is not vulgar nor merely scientific, but metaphysical must be demonstrated in the ideas,"[64] This problem became a focal point of his subsequent thinking, as attested to by his valorization of a doctrine of ideas in the "Epistemo-critical Prologue" of the *Trauerspiel* book. (Did Benjamin know Goethe's dictum: "Experience is almost always a parody of the Idea?")[65]

Another tenet of Benjamin's Kant critique would also remain of abiding consequence for his subsequent thinking. Benjamin revives Hamann's disagreement with Kant's epistemology[66] and employs it, *mutatis mutandis,* against neo-Kantian *Erkenntniskritik*. It is not surprising, given the role of Hamann's theory of language for Benjamin,[67] that there are striking parallels with Hamann's Kant critique, which rests on Hamann's theory of the historicity of language.[68] According to Benjamin, just as Kant's principles were examined with reference to the principles of Newtonian science, the new concept of experience needed broader orientation, and not just to the most contemporary conception of science. Its touchstone had to be language:

> The great transformation and correction which must be performed upon the concept of experience [. . .] can only be attained by relating

knowledge to language, such as was attempted by Hamann during Kant's lifetime [. . .] all philosophical knowledge has its unique expression in language [. . .] A concept of knowledge gained from reflection on the linguistic nature of knowledge will create a corresponding concept of experience which will also encompass regions that Kant failed to integrate into his system.[69]

The last lines of Benjamin's essay augur the major move that future philosophy will have to make: the concept of knowledge can only be rescued by reconsidering its linguistic nature.

III

The earliest texts we have of Benjamin's attest that his thinking—whether epitomized by the concept of experience in the "Program" essay or by the relation between beauty and semblance as construed in the *Elective Affinities* essay—rely on a highly original theory of language, one focal point of which is a concept of mimetic ability defined in anthropological and historical terms. Benjamin's philosophy of language has been treated extensively in the literature, and productive comparisons have been drawn to the twentieth-century theories of Whorf and Wittgenstein.[70] But one of the most striking and least understood elements of Benjamin's theory of language is the prevalence of the theological. In a passage in the *Arcades Project,* Benjamin notes: "My thinking relates to theology the way a blotter does to ink. It is soaked through with it."[71] In this connection, Stéphane Moses' study of the influence of Franz Rosenzweig's thought on Benjamin's theories of language and history has important ramifications for our understanding of Benjamin's thinking.[72] Moses, author of the standard work on Rosenzweig's philosophy,[73] delves beneath a brief reference Scholem made to Benjamin's early reading of Jewish philosophy and examines the precise parameters of this relation. His underlying concern is to understand "which elements in Rosenzweig's thinking especially attracted Benjamin."[74] Moses shows that certain theological ideas in Benjamin's writings derive not directly from the Bible but are mediated through Rosenzweig's *The Star of Redemption.*[75] Yet Moses resists the temptation to read too much into Benjamin's use of Rosenzweig, since the motifs in question have been characteristically transformed in the course of their appropriation. As a consequence, his study is exemplary for its sober appraisal of Benjamin's transfiguration of such elements, such as Rosenzweig's theory of the tragic hero. In the course of his explication of the philosophical scaffolding of Rosenzweig's thought, Moses also treats a particular confluence of language and experience.[76] The "real structure of human experience," according to Rosenzweig, is formed by three relationships, all of which have been overlooked in classical philosophy:

> *Creation* is man's immediate experience that the existence of the world is good; *relevation* characterizes the experience of the divine word in prayer and ritual; *redemption* is that utopian effort upon which all human action is based.[77]

Each of these concepts plays an important role in Benjamin's philosophies of history, art, and language.[78] In Rosenzweig as well as Benjamin, these relationships are all "immediately present in language," since language, and "not abstract throught, [. . .] is the medium through which human experience is expressed." Hence this distinctively Benjaminian position, whose locus classicus is an essay from 1916 entitled "On Language as Such and on the Language of Man,"[79] "anticipates some of Rosenzweig's most important trains of thought."[80]

IV

Just as *Erkenntniskritik* underlies much of Benjamin's early thinking, epistemological considerations serve to ground some of the most influential ideas in his aesthetics and philosophy of history. The epistemological grounds of Benjamin's aesthetics do not escape Joel Snyder in his reading of Benjamin's essay on "The Work of Art in the Age of Its Technical Reproducibility."[81] Snyder begins by showing how Benjamin's reflections on photography in the "Work of Art" essays challenge "traditional notions of reality" as well as "the reigning standard of depiction."[82] Snyder then endeavors to show why Benjamin is *obliged* to historicize the relationship between perception and depiction. This move makes Benjamin the forerunner of those contemporary philosophers of art who argue that the historicization of perception becomes expressed in artistic praxis.[83]

Historical epistemology, the doctrine that modes of human sense perception and representation change historically, is a central tenet of Benjamin's late work. It receives its most direct statement in his "The Work of Art in the Age of Its Technical Reproducibility" (1936): *"During long periods of history, the perception by the historical collectives changes with the changes in their historical mode of being. The way in which human perception organizes itself—the medium in which it takes place—*

is conditioned not only naturally, but also historically."[84] This assertion alone, Snyder claims, does not suffice to account for "why works of art change stylistically, or [. . .] how the very definition of art can change."[85] Benjamin still needs to establish that changes in the way we see "are expressed in some evident fashion in the formal character of artworks."[86] To this end Snyder takes up Benjamin's reference in the "Work of Art" essay to the work of the Viennese school art historians Alois Riegl and Franz Wickhoff, whom Benjamin claims "were the first to draw conclusions from [the emergence of certain art forms] about the way in which perception was organized in the period of its production."[87]

It is no accident that a review Benjamin wrote in 1929 about four "great works of German scholarship" whose influence endured ("Bücher, die lebendig geblieben sind") includes not only Rosenzweig's *Star of Redemption* but Riegl's *Late Roman Art Industry*[88] as well.[89] Benjamin read Riegl's work as early as 1916, and references to it repeatedly appear at key places in his writings.[90] Accordingly, the significance of Benjamin's attraction to Riegl's thought has recently been the subject of a great deal of attention.[91] Sandor Radnóti, in the course of his broadly cast thoughts on "Benjamin's Dialectic of Art and Society,"[92] sees Benjamin's and Riegl's reflections converge at the problem of experience. Benjamin makes use of "Riegl's experience of perception—the way of seeing as the foundation of the artistic will, of collective reception," even while he recognizes the need to broaden it. Most other discussion of the relation of these two thinkers to date centers around Benjamin's "Rigorous Study of Art,"[93] a review of the first volume of the *Kunstwissenschaftliche Forschungen* in which Benjamin gives the most sustained account of his debt to the Viennese school of art history. For Benjamin, the importance of Riegl's approach derived from its revolutionary methodology.[94] Thus Benjamin's attraction to the thought of the old and new Vienna schools[95] goes hand in hand with his assessment of the failures of Wölfflin's *method* of formal analysis.[96] Given this background, Snyder's argument that Benjamin read "a Wölfflin-like account of artistic development" into Riegl's position[97] is all the more provocative. In the end, Benjamin would regard each of these methods as too narrow as a means of historical analysis. His search for method took place in terms of the prescription that "*philosophical writing* [. . .] must continually confront the problem of (re)presentation."[98]

Each of Benjamin's first three major texts with philosophical ambitions constitutes a confrontation with the problem of forms of philosophical representation, and each in turn seems to present a different solution. These texts are (1) his dissertation for the philosophy faculty of the University of Berne, "Der Begriff der Kunstkritik in der deutschen Romantik," (2) his essay on "Goethes *Wahlverwandtschaften,*" and (3) the work with which he intended to habilitate at the University of Frankfurt, *Ursprung des deutschen Trauerspiels.* The first study is a "problem-historical investigation," the second "exemplary (read "immanent") *Kritik,*" and the third a "philosophical tractatus."[99]

I will only examine the *Trauerspiel* book here in this connection, since Benjamin gives this problem its most direct treatment in the prologue to this work. In considering the problem of representation at the beginning of his study of the German lamentation play, Benjamin is not following Herder and others in the eighteenth century, who employed the term *Darstellung* to translate *mimesis.*[100] His quandary also has little in common with the contemporary problem of representation discussed by Nelson Goodman and others. Benjamin's concern is the broadest one imaginable, a common question before the system-building of the nineteenth century diminished its prominence: "how is philosophy to be presented?"[101] Once presumptions of totality or systematicity are relinquished, this problem of (re)presentation becomes even more intricate.

Benjamin criticizes contemporary mathematics, for example, for holding "the sign of genuine knowledge" to be "the total elimination of the problem of representation." The more mathematics claims to abolish representation, Benjamin maintains, the more "it reveals its renunciation of that area of truth towards which language is directed."[102] "Alternative philosophical forms [. . .] were generally ignored by the nineteenth century," which was dominated by the concept of system and its flawed universalism. Benjamin's general underlying point has become a familiar one recently. Arthur Danto, for instance, has recently argued at length "that the concept of philosophical truth and the form of philosophical expression are internally enough related that we may want to recognize that when we turn to other forms we may also be turning to other conceptions of philosophical truth."[103] Benjamin puts it this way: "for truth [method] is self-representation, and is therefore immanent in it as form."[104]

In the book on *Trauerspiel,* the quintessence of the tractarian method is "(re)presentation as detour."[105] The paratactical montage form that Benjamin later incorporates into his approach in the *Arcades Project* shares several striking features of this early form, so that statements in the *Trauerspiel* book can be seamlessly applied to the latter project. Hence the project's method follows the process of thought "tirelessly [. . .] returning in a roundabout way to its original object." Both forms—tractatus and montage—renounce a discursive flow of arguments which follow a single line of inquiry, a single end or logic [Benjamin's word is "intention."] Benjamin's statement about the tractatus applies to both: each forces a "continual pausing for breath [. . .] For by pursuing different levels of meaning in its examination of one single object, [the tractatus] receives both the incentive to begin again and the justification for its irregular rhythm."[106] The truth becomes accessible in the moment of interruption; in the "Theses on the Philosophy of History" Benjamin notes that "thinking not only involves the flow of thoughts, but their arrest as well." In that moment of cessation the dialectic is crystallized into an image "where thinking suddenly stops in a configuration pregnant with tensions."[107] (The conceptual grammar of this moment also corresponds to that of the "expressionless" (*Ausdruckslose*), which Benjamin equates with "the critical violence of the true" in the *Wahlverwandtschaften* essay.) This thought has its counterpart in sheaf "N" of the *Arcades Project:*

> Thinking involves both thoughts in motion and thoughts at rest. When thinking reaches a standstill in a constellation saturated with tensions, the dialectical image appears. This image is the caesura in the movement of thought.[108]

Benjamin's work on the *Arcades Project,* as we now know, reached a standstill for a time around 1929, in part because he had reached an impasse over the question of representation. Looking back six years later in a letter to Adorno, he speaks of the "rhapsodic naiveté" and "romantic form" of the "carefree, archaic, nature-oriented philosophizing" of his early studies.[109] Thus one formidable obstacle in interpreting Benjamin's *opus postumum*—not the *magnum opus* whose outlines we only believe to be legible—was shared by its author. Even if we discern a strategy of paratactical interruption behind Benjamin's juxtaposition of excerpts, we need to reflect upon the changes Benjamin's method of (re)presentation underwent in the intervening decade and the concomitant shifts in other aspects of his method or thought.

What method of (re)presentation could conceivably be more distant from those of traditional scholarship than the procedure Benjamin contemplated for the *Arcades Project?*[110] "This project," Benjamin submits early in "N," "must raise the art of quoting without quotation marks to the very highest level. Its theory is intimately linked with that of the montage."[111] This endless experimentation with forms of representation is one productive vantage point from which we can judge the whole of his *oeuvre*. In the *Arcades Project*, Benjamin goes further in his lifelong endeavor to solve the problem of representation than he ever had before.

V

I shall not presume to offer yet another introduction to the *Arcades Project* here: its posthumous publication is preceded by an excellent conspectus which details the project's structure, rise, and fall.[112] In the present collection, moreover, Richard Sieburth addresses a number of the project's exceptional conceptual elements (the role of the name, dialectical images, "historiography as exhibit," montage) among other provocative themes (the relation between "Benjamin's passion for the diminutive" and his "tendency toward centrifugal proliferation" in the *Arcades Project;* the debate about the project's eventual form). Sieburth puzzles over the theoretical significance for Benjamin of the practice of scrivening. What methodological impulse lies behind the immense act of copying the roughly 15,000 quotations which constitute the *Arcades Project?* In "N," extracting becomes the rule; consequently, Sieburth inquires into "the ontological and semiotic dimensions of quotation,"[113] and shows that "in the asymptotic distance that separates the original from its literal translation, the document from its handwritten transcription, lies that ontological threshold where 'pure language' may come into being." He further submits that Benjamin's venture represents a reconception of the relationship between author and text.

The introduction to the *Arcades Project* that is most sorely missing, in fact, is the one Benjamin promised to provide. In one of many epistolary comparisons he made with his study of the German lamentation play, Benjamin remarked to Scholem that his new project would require "an introduction dealing with the theory of knowledge, and this time, especially with the theory of the knowledge of history."[114] The fragments of such a text are contained in "N. Re The Theory of Knowledge, Theory of Progress." This incomplete propaedeutic, which "falls in Sternean fashion at the alphabetical middle of his manuscript ,"[115] does largely focus on the theory of history. Even its passages on knowledge concentrate on historical knowledge, "proposing a 'materialist' epistemology based not on concepts but on images that dialectically relate historical subject and historical object, present and past, into what Benjamin terms the *Jetzt der Erkennbarkeit.*"[116] For this reason the present collection devotes particular attention to the topic of Benjamin's theory of history.

We can begin to discern some of the continuities and discontinuities of Benjamin's thinking on history by returning to the theme of experience discussed in the "Program" essay. In the *Arcades Project,* the role of experience is informed by the theory of historical materialism. Here Benjamin addresses the "contemplative and experiential material" of the superstructure. (Benjamin's formulation again presumes the distinction between thinking and experiencing). Benjamin's search in linguistic and especially metaphorical relations for the "material" and "real" led Arendt to observe that Benjamin was even capable of understanding the doctrine of the superstructure as "the final doctrine of *metaphorical* thinking."[117] Moreover, Benjamin's addition of the base-superstructure model to his philosophical inventory provides him with a conceptual framework with which he can rethink the kinds of social and existential experience available in a given social structure.[118] In this sense Benjamin's "theory of experience is ultimately based" on his philosophy of history, as Richard Wolin observes in his conspectus of their relation, "Experience and Materialism in Benjamin's *Passagen-Werk.*"[119] According to Wolin, Benjamin seeks to revise the theory of experience as a means of remedying certain shortcomings of historical materialism.[120] He therefore sees Benjamin's "relevance" in terms of "present attempts to reformulate a historically adequate conception of Marxism."[121]

Benjamin's thinking about the philosophy of history during this period, informed by the theory of historical materialism, clearly diverges from every traditional conception of Marxism. Not the least of his divagations is his specification of *expression* rather than reflection as the nature of the relation between base and superstructure:[122]

> Marx describes the causal connection between economic system and culture. The expressive relationship is what matters here. The expression of an economic system in its culture will be described, not the economic origins of culture. In other words, the point is to attempt to grasp an economic process as a concrete original phenomenon (*Urphänomen*), from which proceed all the vital manifestations of the arcades (and—to that extent—of the nineteenth century).[123]

Benjamin's apparent deviation from traditional Marxism has led Heinz-Dieter Kittsteiner to distinguish Benjamin's position from a Marxist one by calling Benjamin a "materialist historian" rather than a "historical materialist."[124] This suggestion agrees with Benjamin's own description of the *Passagen-Werk* as an attempt to provide a "materialist history of nineteenth century France." Benjamin challenges traditional historiography in his presentation of the traces left by the interaction of society's "collective unconscious" with "the new" "in a thousand configurations of life, from permanent buildings to ephemeral fashions."[125] The historical cases he adumbrates—from technological innovations in iron construction to photography to artificial lighting—exemplify the implications of his approach for a general historiography of technology.[126] The theory of quotation is one cornerstone of this approach. The construction of a historical narrative "means to *quote* history. But the concept of quotation implies that any given historical object must be ripped out of context."[127] Synthesis is achieved through the theory of the dialectical image, "the primal phenomenon of history." It "is that form of the historical object that [. . .] exhibits a true synthesis."[126]

Many of the issues Benjamin raises in his theory of materialist historiography are familiar to us from the "Theses on the Philosophy of History." This is hardly surprising, since the most extreme formulations of his methodological position are often not to be found in the *Arcades Project,* but instead in those more finished works which grew out of it. The claim has even been made, by its editor, that "what survives of this project [. . .] rarely goes theoretically beyond positions that have been formulated more radically in [those] texts."[129] Benjamin implicitly supports this view in a letter he wrote to Scholem on May 2, 1936:

> My last work, whose French version—"L'oeuvre d'art a l'époque de sa reproduction mécanisée"—should be appearing in three weeks time, has also evolved from this planning. It touches on the major project only superficially, but *it indicates the vanishing point for some of its investigations.*[130]

Thus "manifestly autonomous" texts such as the Baudelaire book, the "Work of Art" essay, and the "Theses on the Concept of History," ironically gained in methodological stature through the *Arcades Project*'s publication.

Thus Rolf Tiedemann encounters a number of themes closely related to those in "N" in his reading of Benjamin's theses "On the Concept of History." In his discussion of Thesis XVII, for instance, he inquires into the compatibility of Benjamin's "materialist historiography" and "the method of Marx itself."[131] Tiedemann also takes up what is presumably the most influential aspect of Benjamin's reconception of materialist historiography: his critique of the concept of progress. Tiedemann sums up Benjamin's position as follows: "any concept of progress which makes 'dogmatic claims' is doomed to failure."[132] This leads Tiedemann to equate the angel in the ninth thesis with the historical materialist. The storm that blows from Paradise and which "irresistibly propels him into the future to which his back is turned" is the storm of progress. This repudiation of progress's role in the theory of historical materialism is a methodological ambition of the *Arcades Project* as well. There Benjamin announces his aim to adumbrate a doctrine of:

> historical materialism which has cancelled out the idea of progress in itself. Historical materialism has good cause, here, to set itself off sharply from the bourgeois cast of mind; its basic principle is not progress, but actualization.[133]

The critique of 'progress', the theme where Adorno's debt to Benjamin can be most clearly discerned, is the subject of a celebrated lecture Adorno gave in 1962, and which is published in this volume. Adorno acknowledges his obligation in the early pages of his lecture: "Benjamin's polemic," Adorno observes, is "likely the weightiest thinking toward a critique of the idea of progress which derives from the ranks of those accounted for crudely as political progressives." Here he is alluding to Benjamin's critique of the Social Democratic conflation of two kinds of progress: "the progress of skills and knowledge [and] humankind's progress." Benjamin's critique, Adorno observes, originates in his awareness that a positive concept of 'progress' must depend on a "Kantian universal or cosmopolitan concept" of history, *id est,* on totality.[134] Adorno then explores the antinomies of 'totality', the indefeasible link (and antagonism) between progress and redemption, the social versus the philosophical moments in 'progress', among other aporetic features of the concept. The final thought of Adorno's lecture—his own method precludes calling it a conclusion—defines progress as "resistance." (Hence the storm of the ninth thesis is not true progress but only "what we call progress.") This "resistance at all stages, not capitulation to the mainstream which courses through them,"[135] is the mark of Benjamin's mode of thinking.

VI

Benjamin's inscrutability has caused some readers to suspect him of being more a philosophical initiate than an innovator. Of course, the non-professional philosopher is always vulnerable to the charge of dilettantism. In Benjamin's case, the great breadth of his allusion and formidable difficulty of his form of presentation make such doubts natural and inescapable. The debate on this very point had drastic consequences for Benjamin's own career. His study of the German lamentation play was met with incomprehension by philosophers at the University of Frankfurt, from Hans Cornelius to Max Horkheimer. Cornelius insisted Benjamin retract his *Habilitationsschrift* because, being incomprehensible, it was impossible to discern whether it did indeed make a contribution to aesthetics.[136] The work's doctrine of ideas, set forth in the "Epistemo-critical Prologue," even met with reservations from unexpected quarters.

The eminent Orientalist Hans Heinz Schaeder, when asked by his bene-factor Hugo von Hofmannsthal to review the book, characterized Ben-jamin's method as "Pseudoplatonism [. . .] the most dangerous malady that can befall anyone who deals with historical matters either *ex professo* or out of his own inclination." In a letter to Hofmannsthal, who was an important supporter of Benjamin's career as well, Schaeder explicated the grounds of his dissatisfaction with the new work: "Benjamin [. . .] does not present his subject [. . .] but instead seeks to grasp the suppos-edly ideational content of his subject, eliminating the historical *hic et nunc* [. . .] Only a very small number of readers will have sufficient patience and time to assimilate this altogether personal scholasticism, obscure to the point of incomprehensibility."[137]

Even Adorno voiced similar doubts privately about the prologue to Benjamin's *Trauerspiel* book. In the course of discussing the parameters of his debt to Benjamin's thinking in his Kierkegaard manuscript,[138] Adorno complains to Kracauer that the "famous" prologue to the *Ursprung des deutschen Trauerspiels,* "despite marvelous things like the concept of configuration," does not work because of its "blatant, histor-ically oblivious, and in the end, veritably mythological Platonism, which not by accident must take frequent recourse to phenomenology."[139]

The greatest reservations about Benjamin's thought have addressed his fusion of elements from seemingly incompatible theories. The most pub-licized such charge is presumably Jürgen Habermas' remark that "an anti-evolutionary conception of history cannot be tacked onto historical materialism [. . .] as if it were a monk's cowl."[140] Habermas furthermore charges that Benjamin failed in his ambition to " 'enlist the services' of historical materialism for the theory of experience."[141] On the one hand, this second allegation is implicitly answered in Richard Wolin's afore-mentioned contribution to this volume, "Experience and Materialism in Benjamin's *Passagen-Werk.*"[142] For Wolin, the imbrications of Ben-jamin's theory are made even more complex by the role of theology: historical materialism, Benjamin advises as late as 1940, must "enlist the services of theology" in order to "be a match for anyone."[143] Moreover, in the *Arcades Project,* Benjamin writes of "an experience that 'prevents us from fundamentally understanding history without theology'."[144]

Benjamin's writings reflect an interpenetration of traditions which inform and transform each other. Too little consideration has been given to the great breadth of intellectual traditions—neo-Platonism, neo-Kantianism, early Romanticism, Goethe's aesthetics, Surrealism, Marxism—that compete for prominence in Benjamin's thought. For instance, Benjamin shores up a shortcoming he perceives in the methodology of historical materialism by appropriating the principle of montage from Surrealism and applying it to history.[145] Does this amount to a "personal scholasticism?" The contributors to this volume present strong arguments against such a protestation, either by placing his ideas in context with those of other thinkers (such as Moses' comparison of Benjamin and Rosenzweig; Radnoti's reflections on Benjamin and Gadamer), by endeavoring to employ his ideas in contemporary debates (Snyder on Benjamin's challenge to standard notions of reality and depiction; Todd on the question of the meaning of the work of art and on the efficacy of Benjamin's insights in the debates between conventionalists and deconstructionists; Sieburth on affiliations of Benjamin's project with that of other "romantic or modernist myths of descent" such as Goethe's *Faust,* Eliot's *Waste Land,* Joyce's *Ulysses,* and even Pound's first Canto), or by building upon Benjaminian ideas directly (Adorno's lecture on the idea of progress).

These contributions represent a few of the philosophical contexts and questions to be explored in Benjamin's thought. Many other examples have never been examined, let alone mentioned, in the critical literature. These include the work of Benjamin's teachers and fellow doctoral students in Berne; the institutionalized aesthetic discourse in professional journals such as *Logos, Kant-Studien,* and the *Zeitschrift für Ästhetik und Allgemeine Kunstwissenschaft;* and the ideas of the short-lived, avant-garde "G" group.[146] Further, there are striking parallels between the ambivalences of Benjamin's theories of the origin of language and the name, and Plato's views of the same as set forth in the *Cratylus.* Or again: Benjamin's dissertation advisor, Richard Herbertz, wrote on the philosophy of the Baroque, the problem of truth in Greek philosophy, and the relationship between philosophy and other sciences, all themes important to Benjamin's early work.[147] Finally, a fellow doctoral student of Herbertz's, Paul Köhler, published his dissertation on Leibniz's concept of representation in the same series in which Benjamin's doctoral thesis appeared.[148] This theme becomes crucial for Benjamin in his *Habilitationsschrift,* where he seeks grounds for objective interpretation in the monadic structure of the idea. Here Benjamin asserts that the idea's structure contains the prestabilized image of the world, the "representation of phenomena."[149]

Whereas many interpreters have attempted to gain access to Benjamin's writings by looking for affinities in the works of his friends and acquaintances such as Rang, Klages, Scholem, Brecht, and Korsch, only slight attention has been paid to what Benjamin actually read. This failing has in part been remedied by the recent publication of his "Verzeichnis der gelesenen Schriften,"[150] a catalogue Benjamin made of several thousand books he read from cover to cover. The fact that he read Karl Mannhein's *Strukturanalyse der Erkenntnistheorie*[151] around 1922 indicates knowledge of a certain way of differentiating epistemological typologies which might throw light on epistemological distinctions in the *Trauerspiel* book. At the same time, this list will surely engender as much misinterpretation as insight, if only because it excludes essays as well as books only consulted or partially read. Both were often more consequential for the formation of Benjamin's thought. Benjamin makes repeated mention of articles and journals in his letters; one of many references which exemplify this point is the one to Jean Hering's "Bemerkungen über das Wesen, die Wesenheit und die Idee."[152] Although no title of Husserl's appears in Benjamin's reading list, his reference to Hering's article provides evidence of the parameters of Benjamin's cognizance of the Husserlian tradition[153] (exemplified in his formulation of the relation between idea and essence).

By the same token, some books of profound importance for Benjamin's thought are conspicuously absent from the "Verzeichnis." The most telling example is Aragon's *Paysan de Paris,* about which Benjamin wrote to Adorno that he could not bear to read more than a few pages a night, "because my heart would start pounding with such intensity, that I'd have to put the book down."[154] The place of this avant-garde opus in Benjamin's conception of the *Arcades Project* is testified to by a seminal fragment in section "N," in which Benjamin both asserts the work's centrality and criticizes its ahistorical mythologisation of Paris:

> Setting off the slant of this work against Aragon: whereas Aragon persistently remains in the realm of dreams, here it is a question of finding the constellation of awakening. While an impressionistic element lingers on in Aragon ("mythology")—and this impressionism should be held responsible for the many nebulous philosophemes of his book—what matters here is the dissolution of "mythology" into the space of history. Of course, that can only happen through the awakening of a knowledge not yet conscious of what has gone before.[155]

Richard Sieburth notes that even though Benjamin takes the metaphor of the arcade from Aragon "as a figure for the ephemeral, the passing, the out-of-date, a dense emblem of that particular (capitalist) logic whereby the New is fated [. . .] to fall out of style," he distances himself from Aragon's ahistorical "neo-romantic mythopoeia." Benjamin demands both that myth be historicized and that "history be exposed as myth: the very idea of the 'modern' (or of 'progress') reveals itself to be nothing more than a degraded variant of the archaic, prehistoric myth of the Eternal Return."[156]

Benjamin likens the dialectic of myth and history to that of dreaming and waking up—a principal methodological device in Benjamin's project. For Sieburth as well as for Benjamin, this means that Proust rather than Aragon provides the project's true epistemological paradigm. Indeed, Proust often tips the scale of competing models for Benjamin's project. A few lines from Proust's *Chronique Paris* (1927) weigh heavier than "most of what exists" in the domain of "materialist analysis."[157] Benjamin records his methodological alliance with Proust in two passages in "N":

> Just as Proust begins his life story with the moment of awakening, so every presentation in history must begin with awakening; in fact, it should deal with nothing else. This one deals with awakening from the nineteenth century.

> Can it be that awakening is the synthesis whose thesis is dream consciousness? Then the moment of awakening would be identical with the "Now of recognizability" in which things put on their true—surrealistic—face. Thus, in Proust, the importance of staking the whole of life on its ultimate dialectical breaking point—the moment of awakening[. . .][158]

This valorization of awakening as opposed to dreaming has its antipode in a different, positive methodological role in Benjamin's late work. There, Wolin points out, it serves as "an autonomous source of experience" and "repository of utopian visions."[159] It exhibits another side of the antagonism between experiencing and thinking, for, as Adorno remarks, in Benjamin's works, "the dream becomes a medium of unregimented experience, a source of knowledge opposed to the stale superficiality of thinking."[160]

The "threshold between waking and sleeping" becomes "worn away" by both Breton and Aragon.[161] However Benjamin's method may be informed by the theories of Aragon, Breton, or Freud,[162] one principle for reading the *Arcades Project* emerges. All genealogies that imply more than mere contextualization must be called into question. Benjamin created new contexts for every concept and motif, whether it originated in Riegl or Aragon, Leibniz or Kant.

VII

We are still far from being able to specify what makes Benjamin's thought exceptional. Scholem and Adorno attempt to answer this question by articulating what constitutes his nontraditional approach to philosophy, and this suggests that the answer at least in part hinges on Benjamin's conception of the nature of philosophy. This is the crux of the philosopher Hans Heinz Holz's early investigation of what he terms Benjamin's "prismatic thinking."[163] Even Arendt's formulations suggest that a different conception of philosophy is at issue, insofar as her portrayal of Benjamin draws him toward a Heideggerian conception of the poetic philosopher.[164] Her emphasis on Benjamin's *thinking* foreshadows an account she would give of the enduring fascination with Heidegger's works: "it is not Heidegger's philosophy [. . .] but Heidegger's *thinking* that has shared so decisively in determining the spiritual physiognomy of this century."[165] The above reflections and the essays collected in this volume will begin, I hope, to adumbrate some features of Benjamin's conception of philosophy which have not yet received satisfactory treatment.

Berlin, September 1989

NOTES

1 Gershom Scholem, "Walter Benjamin," in: Scholem, *On Jews and Judaism in Crisis. Selected Essays,* ed. Werner J. Dannhauser (New York: Schocken Books, 1976), pp. 177-8.

2 Hannah Arendt, "Introduction. Walter Benjamin: 1892-1940," in: Walter Benjamin, *Illuminations,* trans. Harry Zohn (New York: Schocken Books, 2nd ed., 1973), p. 14. Arendt's essay first appeared in *The New Yorker,* October 19, 1968, pp. 65-156.

3 There are a number of recent exceptions to this assertion, most notably Michael Jennings' *Dialectical Images: Walter Benjamin's Theory of Literary Criticism* (Ithaca: Cornell University Press, 1987) as well as three essays first published in *Studies in Twentieth Century Literature* 11, 1 (Fall 1986): see Timothy Bahti, "Theories of Knowledge: Fate and Forgetting in the Early Works of Benjamin," pp. 47-68; Rudolphe Gasché, "Saturnine Vision and the Question of Difference: Reflections on Walter Benjamin's Theory of Language." pp. 69-90; and Rainer Nägele, "Benjamin's Ground," pp. 5-24.

4 Walter Benjamin, *Briefe,* ed. Theodor W. Adorno & Gershom Scholem. 2 vols. (Frankfurt am Main. L Suhrkamp, 1966); hereafter cited as *Briefe.* An extensive edition of all of Benjamin's known letters is now being prepared.

5 Theodor W. Adorno, "Introduction to Benjamin's *Schriften*," trans. R. Hullot-Kentor with Tom Levin and Eric Krakauer, in: *On Walter Benjamin: Critical Essays and Reflections*, ed. Gary Smith (Cambridge, MA: MIT Press, 1988), pp. 2-17. The two-volume selected edition of Benjamin's *Schriften* has been superceded by the edition of his collected writings, the *Gesammelte Schriften*, ed. Rolf Tiedemann & Hermann Schweppenhäuser with the cooperation of Theodor W. Adorno & Gershom Scholem, 7 vols. (Frankfurt am Main: Suhrkamp, 1972-1989); hereafter cited as *GS*.

6 The explicit reference here is to Scholem's famous lecture entitled "Walter Benjamin" (cf. Scholem, *On Jews and Judaism in Crisis*, pp. 172-97) as well as to two of Scholem's other published texts on Benjamin: "Erinnerungen an Benjamin," and "Vorrede zu Benjamins *Briefen*" (reprinted in: Scholem, *Walter Benjamin un sein Engel. Vierzehn Aufsätze und kleine Beiträge*, ed. Rolf Tiedemann [Frankfurt am Main: Suhrkamp, 1983], pp. 161-73). The veiled reference is to the controversy with Scholem four years earlier over Arendt's Eichmann book; cf. " 'Eichmann in Jerusalem'. An exchange of letters between Gershom Scholem and Hannah Arendt." *Encounter* 22, 124 (1964), pp. 51-3.

7 Arendt's letter as well as Adorno's reply can be found among Arendt's papers in the Library of Congress, Washington, DC. (All translations are my own.)

8 Arendt, "Introduction. Walter Benjamin: 1892-1940," p. 50.

9 *Ibid*.

10 *Ibid*., p. 4.

11 This volume, pp. 1-12. "N" is but one sheaf of Benjamin's notes for his unfinished *Arcades Project*, which has been published as *Das Passagen-Werk* (*Gesammelte Schriften*. Vol. V, ed. Rolf Tiedemann [Frankfurt am Main: Suhrkamp, 1983]).

12 This volume, pp. 43-83.

13 Scholem, "Walter Benjamin," p. 178. Scholem originally delivered his essay as a lecture at the Leo Baeck Institute in New York.

14 The relation of Benjamin's thought to Simmel's is profound, despite few apparent points of contact. Benjamin's infrequent mention of a thinker is a notoriously inaccurate index of that thinker's significance for Benjamin; Simmel and Erich Auerbach are two of many cases in point. (For documentation of Benjamin's relationship with Auerbach, cf. Karlheinz Barck, "5 Briefe Erich Auerbachs an Walter Benjamin in Paris," *Zeitschrift für Germanistik* [Leipzig] 9, 6 [December 1988], pp. 688-94).

Benjamin surely knew Simmel's pages on the ruin, a celebrated motif in Benjamin's works (cf. Simmel, *Philosophische Kultur. Über das Abenteuer, die Geschlechter und die Krise der Moderne. Gesammelte Essais*. 4th ed. Afterword by Jürgen Habermas. Berlin: Klaus Wagenbach, 1983, pp. 106-12). His direct indebtedness to Simmel's formulation of the Goethean concept of "Urphänomen" is documented in sheaf "N" of the *Arcades Project* and further confirmed in early notes published in Benjamin's *GS*, I, pp. 953-4. Moreover, in a series of rubrics commemorating the 100th anniversary of Goethe's death in 1932, Benjamin would lavish high praise on Simmel's Goethe book as: "The most suspenseful and thought-provoking portrayal Goethe has received to date. If Franz Mehring was the first to collect the sociological material for a future Goethe presentation, then Simmel binds together the most valuable indications of its dialectical structure" (*GS*, III, p. 339). According to Simmel, Goethe considered the artist's primary aim to be to make the "idea" visible in the *Gestalt* (p. 54). *Gestalt* then becomes, in Goethe's idiosyncratic view, something like pure, unmediated sensualness or the pure sensuality of the object.

15 Adorno, "Introduction to Benjamin's *Schriften*," p. 7.

16 Both books came out in Rowohlt Verlag in Berlin. Concerning Benjamin's *Ursprung des deutschen Trauerspiels,* see note 18. A selection from *Einbahnstraße* has been translated in: *idem, Reflections. Essays, Aphorisms, Autobiographical Writings,* ed. Peter Demetz, trans. Edmund Jephcott (New York, London: Harcourt Brace Jovanovich, 1978), pp. 61-94.

17 Siegfried Kracauer, "On The Writings of Walter Benjamin," in: Kracauer, *Ornament of the Masses,* trans. Thomas Y. Levin (Cambridge, MA: Harvard University Press, 1990), forthcoming.

18 I employ this designation for Benjamin's *Ursprung des deutschen Trauerspiels* (1923-1925), translated by John Osborne as *The Origin of German Tragic Drama* (London: New Left Books, 1977); hereafter cited as *OGTD.* The work, which Benjamin wrote for his anticipated *Habilitation* at the University of Frankfurt, is also designated in the present volume as the "Baroque book," the "*Trauerspiel* book," or the "study of the German lamentation play."

19 Kracauer, "On The Writings of Walter Benjamin," forthcoming.

20 Kracauer is quoting a line from Benjamin's prologue to his *Trauerspiel* book, p. 32.

21 Adorno, "Introduction to Benjamin's *Schriften,*" p. 4.

22 *GS,* VI, p. 216.

23 *GS,* VI, pp. 218-9.

24 *GS,* VI, pp. 215-6.

25 *GS,* II, pp. 105-26.

26 *GS,* IV, pp. 7-63.

27 *GS,* IV, pp. 7-21.

28 "Goethes Wahlverwandtschaften," in: *GS,* I, pp. 123-201. I offer an interpretation of this text as a theory of beauty in my dissertation on "Walter Benjamin's Idea of Beauty" (Boston University, January 1989).

29 "Curriculum Vitae Dr. Walter Benjamin" (1939 or 1940), *GS,* VI, p. 227. Benjamin broadens his focus in his late works, where his art-theoretical writings address such non-literary artforms as photography, film, and painting. The "Work of Art" essay (cf. "The Work of Art in the Age of Mechanical Reproduction," in: Benjamin, *Illuminations,* pp. 217-51) and "A Short History of Photography" (cf. "Walter Benjamin's Short History of Photography," trans. Phil Patton, *Artforum* 15, 6 [February 1977]: 46-61) are two obvious documents of this shift. Attention should also be paid to the second "Pariser Brief" on painting and photography as well as to Benjamin's early theoretical contribution to the "G" group (which included Man Ray and Hans Richter), in which he was the only writer involved. Cf. Eckhard Köhn's thoughtful and informative essay, "Konstruktion des Lebens. Zum Urbanismus der Berliner Avant-Garde" (in *Avant-Garde,* Amsterdam, no. 1 [1988], pp. 33-72).

30 Close scrutiny of those texts in which the literary artwork is no longer foregrounded, and in which visual and audial motifs expand the scope of Benjamin's analysis and theory, is also required.

31 Peter Krumme, "Zur Konzeption der dialektischen Bilder," *Text + Kritik,* nos. 31/32 ("Walter Benjamin"), 2d ed., July 1979, p. 80.

32 Krista R. Greffrath, *Metaphorischer Materialismus. Untersuchungen zum Geschichtsbegriff Walter Benjamins* (Munich: Wilhelm Fink Verlag, 1981).

33 See Jürgen Habermas, "Walter Benjamin: Consciousness-Raising or Rescuing Critique," trans. Fred Lawrence, (rev.) in: Smith, *On Walter Benjamin,* pp. 90-128. Habermas was first to recognize that Benjamin's theory of experience follows directly from his theory of language rather than his philosophy of history. But Habermas'

GARY SMITH

analysis hedges in general terms at the point it should provide an analysis of Benjamin's "mimetic" conception of language. He also wrongfully accuses Benjamin of not explicitly coming to terms with effective historical consciousness, with reference to Benjamin's "Theses on the Philosophy of History" (in: Benjamin, *Illuminations*, pp. 253-64). Yet this is a principal point of Benjamin's "The Storyteller. Reflections on the Works of Nikolai Leskov" (*ibid.*, pp. 83-109).

34 Fredric Jameson, "Afterword," in: Jameson, *Sartre. The Origins of a Style,* 2d ed. (New York: Columbia University Press, 1984), p. 206.

35 Rolf Tiedemann, "Dialectics at a Standstill: Approaches to the *Passagen-Werk,*" trans. Gary Smith & Andre Lefevere, in: Smith, *On Walter Benjamin,* pp. 269-70.

36 *GS,* II, pp. 54-6.

37 *GS,* II, p. 902.

38 Jennings, *Dialectical Images,* p. 83.

39 Benjamin's studies in Munich are documented in the archive of the Ludwig-Maximilian-Universität München; cf. register 759 for the Winter Semester 1915/16 and register 908 for the Summer Semester 1916. The philosopher Moritz Geiger (1880-1937), who taught at Vassar College after being forced to emigrate from National Socialist Germany, was a prominent disciple of Edmund Husserl and co-founder of the *Jahrbuch für Philosophie und phänomenologische Forschung.*

40 Cf. entry 547 in his "Verzeichis der gelesenen Schriften," *GS,* VII, p. 441.

41 *Briefe,* p. 151.

42 Benjamin pursued this intention for about half a year. See his letters from October 1917 until May 1918, esp. *Briefe,* pp. 151-152, 158-159, 161-162, 179. Three fragments of Benjamin's study of this topic have survived—"Die unendliche Aufgabe," "Über die transzendentale Methode," and "Zweideutigkeit des Begriffs der 'Unendlichen Aufgabe' in der Kantischen Schule"—and are published in *GS,* VI, pp. 50-3.

43 By May 1918, however, his studies had already advanced far enough for him to recognize the insuperability of the task of bringing the Romantics' "historically fundamentally important coincidence with Kant [. . .] to 'dissertational' realization" (*Briefe,* p. 188). In the end, Fichte would become the principal Idealist figure in the dissertation.

44 First published in 1871, it was revised in 1885 and 1918. The third edition was brought out in Berlin by the publisher Bruno Cassirer.

45 Following his reflection on the Transcendental Aesthetic, Cohen presents Kant as attempting to establish a principle to explain the *possibility* of experience. This principle is understood to be the central feature of Kant's *Critique;* Cohen argues for the pure "erkenntniskritische" character of Kant's works against other views, such as Schopenhauer's "psychologizing" interpretation.

46 Klaus Christian Köhnke addresses the genealogy of the term "Erkenntnistheorie" in his excellent historical study: "Über den Ursprung des Wortes Erkenntnistheorie—und dessen vermeintliche Synonyme," *Archiv für Begriffsgeschichte,* vol. 25 (1981), pp. 185-210.

Cohen's recourse to the term "Erkenntniskritik" is briefly treated by Gert Eedel in his "Einleitung" to the reprint of the 1918 edition of *Kants Theorie der Erfahrung,* 5th ed. (Hildesheim, Zurich, New York: Georg Olms, 1987), p. 23 (Hermann Cohen, *Werke,* vol. 1, part 1.1). Cohen distanced himself from the term "Erkenntnistheorie" in 1883, "since it creates the impression that cognition *as a psychological process* comprises the subject of this investigation, which as the psychological dismantling of the cognitive apparatus" can then achieve the status of a theory (Cohen, *Das Princip der Infinitesimal-Methode und seine Geschichte. Ein Kapitel zur Grundlegung der*

Erkenntniskritik [Marburg: Elwert, 1883], §7). As a consequence, in the second edition of *Kants Theorie der Erfahrung* published two years later, Cohen replaced every mention of "Erkenntnistheorie" with the term "Erkenntniskritik."

47 See Erich Adickes, "Die bewegenden Kräfte in Kants philosophischer Entwicklung und die beiden Pole seines Systems" (part 1), *Kantstudien* 1, 1 (April 25, 1896): 9-59, esp. 48-59. Adickes claims that those interpreters ("Vaihinger, Cohen, Caird etc.") who posit the constitution of experience as Kant's principal endeavor in the first *Critique* fail to account for Kant's neglect of that very problem in the introduction. In his aforementioned conspectus of the history and reception of Cohen's work, Gert Eedel oddly fails to mention Adickes' significant challenge.

48 Scholem provides details of the grounds of Benjamin's as well as his disappointment with Cohen's work in his memoir of Benjamin: *Walter Benjamin: The Story of a Friendship*, trans. Harry Zohn (Philadelphia: Jewish Publication Society, 1981), pp. 59-60.

49 Scholem's influence on the development of Benjamin's thought—usually thought to be confined to the exposure to Judaism and Jewish motifs—has been fundamentally misconstrued by interpreters as diverse as René Wellek and Leo Lowenthal. The decisive steps in Benjamin's coming to terms with both his Jewish self-image and with Zionism took place *before* he first met Scholem; hence a reassessment of their relationship is called for. On this subject, see my essay on "Benjamins frühe Auseinandersetzung mit dem Judentum," forthcoming in: Mauro Ponzi, ed. *Deutsche Literatur und jüdische Tradition* (Rome, 1990) as well as two excellent studies by Anson Rabinbach: "Between Enlightenment and Apocalypse: Benjamin, Bloch and Modern German Jewish Messianism" (*New German Critique* 34 [Winter 1985]: 78-124) and "Introduction," in: *The Correspondence of Walter Benjamin and Gershom Scholem, 1932-1940*, ed. Gershom Scholem, trans. Gary Smith and Andre Lefevere (New York: Schocken Books, 1989), pp. vii-xxxviii.

50 Trans. into English in two volumes by J. N. Findlay (London: Routledge and Kegan Paul, 1970).

51 Cf. Scholem, *Walter Benjamin: The Story of a Friendship*, p. 48.

52 Benjamin's letter of October 17, 1917 is published in *GS*, II, p. 937.

53 Irving Wohlfarth, "On Some Jewish Motifs in Benjamin," in: *The Problems of Modernity. Adorno and Benjamin*, ed. Andrew Benjamin (London & New York: Routledge, 1989), p. 214.

54 Cf. Milic Capek, "Reichenbach's Early Kantianism," *Philosophy and Phenomenological Research* 19, 1 (September 1958): 86-94.

55 *Zeitschrift für Philosophie und philosophische Kritik*, vols. 161, 162, 163 (1916-1917).

56 Concerning Benjamin's role in this movement, cf. Erdmut Wizisla, " 'Die Hochschule ist eben der Ort nicht, zu studieren.' Walter Benjamin in der freistudentischen Bewegung," *Wissenschaftliche Zeitschrift der Humboldt-Universität zu Berlin* ("Gesellschaftswissenschaftliche Reihe") 36, 7 (1987), pp. 616-23.

57 The unpublished correspondence can be found in the Archives for Scientific Philosophy at the University of Pittsburgh.

58 *Briefe*, p. 152.

59 His philosophy of history has been the subject of numerous studies and is the primary subject of the essays in this volume by Tiedemann (pp. 175-209) and Wolin (pp. 210-227). Adorno's "Progress" (this volume, pp. 84-101) is paradigmatic for its reliance on a Benjaminian thematization.

60 Benjamin's trust in system plays an important role in his early thinking. In an unassuming, early talk on "The Life of the Students" which Benjamin first published in *Der*

Neue Merkur (1915), he implicitly associates the concept of critique with the philosophical system: "The only way to deal with the historical place of studenthood and of the University is through system. As long as certain conditions for this are lacking, all that remains is to knowingly free the future from its misshaped form in the present. Critique serves this alone." (Cf. "The Life of the Students: an essay by Walter Benjamin," trans. Ken Frieden, *A Jewish Journal at Yale* 2, 1 (Fall 1984), pp. 46, 51.) The philosophical form of such investigations furthermore raises every such study to universality.

The problem of system is also focal in his argument in an important fragment entitled "Theorie der Kunstkritik" (*GS,* I, pp. 833-5), in which Benjamin continues to seek a solution to a problem underlying the early association between system and the concept of *Kritik:* can artworks, in the course of their *Kritik,* be said to meet the demand of philosophy for truth? In that text, Benjamin first considers that impossibility of a single question which would encompass all philosophical questions—in his estranging formulation, a question which can be asked of the unity of philosophy, by which he means philosophy as system. Were such a question conceivable, then the only imaginable answer would be "the system of philosophy itself."

61 *GS,* III, p. 565. Benjamin makes this comment in the course of a review of Richard Hönigswald's *Philosophie und Sprache. Problemkritik und System* (Basel: Haus vom Falken, 1937) for the *Zeitschrift für Sozialforschung.*

62 Scholem, *Walter Benjamin: The Story of a Friendship,* p. 59.

63 Cohen also attributes the origins of *Erkenntniskritik* to Plato's doctrine of ideas. Cf. for instance, Cohen's brief treatise on *Platons Ideenlehre und die Mathematik* (Marburg: Elwert'sche Verlagsh., 1879), which is reprinted in *Hermann Cohens Schriften zur Philosophie und Zeitgeschichte,* ed. Albert Görland and Ernst Cassirer, vol. 1 (Berlin: Akademie, 1928), pp. 336-66.

64 This volume, p. 9.

65 Johann Wolfgang von Goethe, "Reise in die Schweiz 1797" ("Sammlung einzelner Notizen"), in: Goethe, *Poetische Werke* III (Berlin: Aufbau, 1978), p. 489.

66 Cf. Günter Wohlfart, "Hamanns Kantkritik," *Kant-Studien* 75, 4 (1984): 399-419.

67 Cf. Winfried Menninghaus, *Walter Benjamins Theorie der Sprachmagie* (Frankfurt am Main: Suhrkamp, 1980).

68 Cf. Karlfried Gründer, *Figur und Geschichte. Johann Georg Hamanns "Biblische Betrachtungen" als Ansatz einer Geschichtsphilosophie* (Freiburg, Munich: Alber, 1958) as well as Wohlfart's already mentioned study on "Hamanns Kantkritik."

69 This volume, p. 9.

70 Fredric Jameson interprets Benjamin as extrapolating a Sapir-Whorfian view of linguistic expression onto the domain of narrative: the opposition between language and thinking corresponds to that between *storytelling* and *experience* (Jameson, "Afterword," p. 206). Comparisons with Wittgenstein's theory of language have been frequent. Best known is perhaps Max Bense's "Exkurs über Walter Benjamin und Ludwig Wittgenstein," in his *Programmierung des Schönen. Allgemeine Texttheorie und Textästhetik. aesthetica IV* (Baden-Baden, Krefeld: Agis, 1960), pp. 46-51. Charles Rosen argues that Benjamin's reconception of the Idea anticipates Wittgenstein's "concept of meaning as a 'family' " (Rosen, "The Ruins of Walter Benjamin," in: Smith, *On Walter Benjamin,* p. 160). The relation has also been exaggerated, as in Liselotte Wiesenthal's *Zur Wissenschaftstheorie Walter Benjamins* (Frankfurt am Main: Athenäum, 1973).

71 This volume, p. 61. The passage continues: "If one were to go by the blotter, though, nothing of what has been written would remain."

72 Benjamin's first semester at the University of Freiburg was Rosenzweig's last at that same institution; Rosenzweig was finishing his doctoral thesis on Hegel and the state (*Hegel und der Staat,* 2 vols. [Munich, Berlin: Oldenbourg, 1920]) under the supervision of Friedrich Meinecke, the history faculty's leading light.

Moses is the only interpreter (besides Scholem, of course) with vast knowledge of the history of Jewish philosophy to examine Jewish motifs in Benjamin. The potential hazards of a sketchy grasp of Jewish thought in this regard is exemplified by Ulrich Hortian's comparative reflections on "Zeit und Geschichte bei Franz Rosenzweig und Walter Benjamin," in: Wolfgang Schmied-Kowarzik, ed. *Der Philosoph Franz Rosenzweig (1886-1929),* vol. 2 (Freiburg, Munich: Karl Alber, 1988), pp. 815-27. On the other hand, Irving Wohlfarth's essay "On Some Jewish Motifs in Benjamin," is exemplary in its exploration of how Benjamin appropriates certain Jewish motifs in his philosophy of language.

73 Stéphane Moses, *Système et Révelation. La philosophie de Franz Rosenzweig.* Preface by Emmanuel Lévinas. (Paris: Éditions du Seuil, 1982). German edition, 1985.

74 This volume, p. 230.

75 Trans. by William W. Hallo (Notre Dame: Notre Dame Press, 1985). Benjamin's abiding estimation of this book is attested to in several places in his late work, such as in a letter from June 3, 1926 where he comments on a critique of Martin Buber published by Kracauer in the *Frankfurter Zeitung:* "And, if [. . .] a single regret remains (for which I find no sympathy from Bloch and perhaps even from you), then it is to see Rosenzweig—who to my mind in spite of everything holds a secure place among current writers because of the *Star of Redemption*—forever tarnished by such an association [with Buber]." (Cf. Walter Benjamin, *Briefe an Siegfried Kracauer.* With four letters from Kracauer to Benjamin. Ed. by the Theodor W. Adorno Archive. [Marbach am Neckar: Deutsche Schillergesellschaft, 1987], p. 21).

76 This subject is dealt with at length in an essay by Reiner Wiehl, "Experience in Rosenzweig's New Thinking," in: *The Philosophy of Franz Rosenzweig,* ed. Paul Mendes-Flohr (Hanover, London: University Press of New England, 1988), pp. 42-68. This outstanding anthology also includes a modified, English version of the remarkable memorial address Scholem delivered in Hebrew in 1930: "Franz Rosenzweig and His Book *The Star of Redemption,*" pp. 20-41. According to Professor Mendes-Flohr, Scholem felt "that this essay represented his definitive view of Rosenzweig" ("Introduction," p. 14).

77 Moses, this volume, p. 229.

78 Cf. also Giorgio Agamben, "Language and History in Benjamin," *Differentia* 2 (Spring 1988).

79 In Benjamin, *Reflections,* pp. 314-32.

80 Moses, this volume, p. 237.

81 Translated as "The Work of Art in the Age of Mechanical Reproduction" in *Illuminations,* pp. 217-51.

82 This volume, p. 163.

83 The canonical statement of this view can be found in Marx Wartofsky's "Pictures, Representation, and the Understanding," in: Wartofsky, *Models: Representation and the Scientific Understanding.* (Dordrecht, Boston: Reidel, 1979), p. 175. (Boston Studies in the Philosophy of Science, vol. 48; Synthese Library, vol. 129). A recent historical study founded upon this premise is Peter Galassi's *Before Photography: Painting and the Invention of Photography* (New York: Museum of Modern Art, 1981), which as Henri Zerner and Charles Rosen write, "places the continuity of photography within

the history of perspective and, more generally within the changing conception of vision as it related to the making of pictures." (Cf. C. Rosen and H. Zerner, *Romanticism and Realism. The Mythology of Nineteenth Century Art*. London, Boston: Faber and Faber, 1984, p. 106.)

Jonathan Crary ("Techniques of the Observer," *October* 45, Summer 1988: 20) presents Plateau's Phenkistiscope, which tests "persistence of vision," as a scientific invention which confirms Benjamin's thesis and then considers the crucial role played by the stereoscope in 19th-century debates about the perception. "The stereoscope as a means of representation . . . *[Its] very functioning* . . . *depended on the visual priority of the objects closest to the viewer and on the absence of any mediation between eye and objects viewed*. It was a fulfillment of what Walter Benjamin saw as part of the *visual culture* of modernity: 'Day by day the need becomes greater to take possession of the object—from the closest proximity—in an image and the reproduction of the image'." ("Walter Benjamin's Short History of Photography," p. 49.)

84 The translation is Snyder's, this volume, p. 163. In *Illuminations* the passage appears on p. 222.
85 This volume, p. 165.
86 *Ibid.*
87 The translation of Benjamin's text is from Snyder, p. 163.
88 Trans. Rolf Winkes. (Rome: Giorgio Bretschneider, 1985). (Archaeologica, vol. 36).
89 *GS*, III, pp. 169-71. Benjamin also names Georg Lukàcs' *Geschichte und Klassenbewußtsein* (trans. by Rodney Livingstone as *History and Class Consciousness* [Cambridge, MA: MIT Press, 1971]) and Alfred Gotthold Meyer's *Eisenbauten. Ihre Geschichte und Ästhetik*. [. . .] (Eßlingen: P. Neff, 1907).
90 Benjamin's citation of Riegl is thoroughly documented in Jennings' *Dialectical Images*, pp. 152-63.
91 Besides the excursus in Jennings' *Dialectical Images*, see Thomas Y. Levin, "Walter Benjamin and the Theory of Art History. An Introduction to 'Rigorous Study of Art'," *October* 47 (Winter 1988): 77-83; Rosen, "The Ruins of Walter Benjamin," pp. 134-5, 140-1; Kurt Forster, "Residues of a Dream World, in *On the Methodology of Architectural History*, ed. Demetri Porphyrious (London: Architectural Design, 1981), pp. 69-71; and three texts by Wolfgang Kemp: "Walter Benjamin und die Kunstwissenschaft. Teil I. Benjamins Beziehung zur Wiener Schule," *Kritische Berichte* 1, 3 (1973), pp. 30-50; "Walter Benjamin und die Kunstwissenschaft. Teil II. Walter Benjamin und Aby Warburg," *ibid.*, 3, 1 (1975), pp. 5-25; and "Fernbilder, Benjamin und die Kunstwissenschaft," in *Walter Benjamin im Kontext*, ed. Burkhardt Lindner, 2d rev. ed. (Königstein, Ts.: Athenäum, 1978), pp. 224-57.
92 This volume, pp. 126-57.
93 Translated by Thomas Y. Levin in *October* 47 (Winter 1988): 84-90.
94 Benjamin takes Riegl's book to be "the most decisive proof that every major scholarly discovery . . . signifies a revolution in procedure on its own" (*GS*, III, p. 170).
95 Cf. note 13 in Levin's aforementioned essay.
96 Benjamin's repudiation of Wölfflin's art-theoretical position has its origin in his attendance at Wölfflin's lectures in Munich in 1915. In a letter from December 4, 1915, Benjamin writes to his friend Fritz Radt that Wölfflin is "a by no means overwhelmingly gifted man [. . .] he has a theory which fails to grasp what is essential but which, in itself, is perhaps better than complete thoughtlessness [. . .] He does not see the artwork, he feels obliged to see it, demands that one see it, considers his theory a moral act; he becomes pendantic, ludicrously catatonic, and thereby destroys any natural

talents that his audience may have. For the combination of an underground, surreptitiously obtained concept of refinement and distance, and the brutality with which he obscures his lack of (receptive) genius, has the effect to attracting an audience that clearly has no idea of what is going on: they are getting an understanding of art which is on the same level and of the same purity as their 'normal' understanding of culture." (Quoted from Thomas Y. Levin's translation in his "Walter Benjamin and the Theory of Art History," pp. 79-80. Levin argues persuasively that " in the following years it was [. . .] not Wölfflin but Riegl who served Benjamin as a methodological model" [*Ibid.*, p. 801]).

97 Both positions were of course subjected to strong criticism by Erwin Panofsky, whose affinity to Benjamin has yet to be explored. Cf. Panofsky, "Das Problem des Stils in der bildenden Kunst," *Zeitschrift für Ästhetik und allgemeine Kunstwissenschaft* 10 (1915): 460-7 and "Der Begriff des Kunstwollens," *Zeitschrift für Ästhetik und allgemeine Kunstwissenschaft* 14 (1920): 321-39. Kenneth J. Northcott and Joel Snyder have translated the second essay as "The Concept of Artistic Volition" in: *Critical Inquiry* 8 (Autumn 1981): 17-33.

98 *OGTD*, p. 27.

99 *GS*, I, p. 11; *Briefe*, 281; *GS*, I, p. 209.

100 *Darstellung* later became a significant term in both Goethe's and Schiller's aesthetics. See the source in the following footnote.

101 Jean-Luc Nancy, *Le Discours de la syncope: Logodaedalus* (Paris: Aubier-Flammarion, 1976), p. 26; quote in the translators' introduction to Philippe Lacoue-Labarthe & Jean-Luc Nancy, *The Literary Absolute*, trans. P. Barnard & C. Lester (Albany: State University of New York Press, 1988), p. x. Though Nancy employs the same formulation, he is addressing an entirely different question.

102 *OGTD*, p. 27.

103 Cf. Arthur Danto, "Philosophy as/and/of Literature," in: Danto, *The Philosophical Disenfranchisement of Art* (New York: Columbia University Press, 1986), p. 140.

104 *OGTD*, p. 30.

105 *OGTD*, p. 28.

106 *OGTD*, p. 28.

107 *Illuminations*, pp. 262-3.

108 This volume, p. 67.

109 *GS*, V, p. 117; the translation is from Richard Sieburth's essay in this volume, p. 24.

110 To ascribe the fragmentary form of the *Arcades Project* to biographical happenstance is a fallacy pointed out in 1955 by Adorno, who insisted that "it was implicit from the start in the structure of his thought" (Adorno, "Introduction to Benjamin's *Schriften*," p. 6).

111 This volume, p. 45. This imperative sounds surprisingly close to a description he gives of his method of constructing the *Trauerspiel* book as it neared completion: "The written consists almost entirely of quotations. The drollest mosaic technique one can imagine" (*GS*, I, p. 881).

112 Cf. Tiedemann, "Dialectics at a Standstill," pp. 260-92. Cf. also Irving Wohlfarth's perceptive prefatory reflections to the English translation of a number of contributions to the first international conference on the *Passagen-Werk*, held in Paris in 1983: "Refusing Theology. Some First Responses to Walter Benjamin's Arcades Project," *New German Critique* 39 (Fall 1986): 3-24.

113 This volume, pp. 28-33.

114 *GS*, V, p. 1094. The translation is from Sieburth, this volume, p. 40.

115 Sieburth, this volume, p. 40.

GARY SMITH

116 Sieburth, this volume, pp. 40-1. To the extent that images are permitted into philosophy, they remedy that "stigma of philosophical language, which since Aristotle has almost always been a language of concepts, . . . that it does not extend to mimesis." (Tiedemann, this volume, p. 177.)

117 Cited from Greffrath, *Metaphorischer Materialismus*, p. 9.

118 Fredric Jameson, "Afterword," p. 206.

119 Wolin's contribution to this volume represents a continuation of his work on this topic. Cf. Wolin, "Benjamin's Materialist Theory of Experience," *Theory and Society* 11, 1 (January 1982): 17-42.

120 This volume, p. 222. The fundamental innovation of this theory is Benjamin's concept of "dialectical images." Benjamin's deployment of this concept drew sharp criticism from Adorno, who insisted that the projection of "the dialectical image into consciousness as a dream" divests it of the objectivity "which could legitimate it in materialist terms." (Adorno, "Letters to Walter Benjamin," in: *Aesthetics and Politics* [London: New Left Books, 1977], p. 111.) Benjamin himself, in fact, admits that the fusion of materialism and the dialectical image constitutes the "truly problematic component" of the project: "to give up claim to nothing, to demonstrate that the materialist presentation of history is imagistic in a higher sense than traditional historiography" (this volume, p. 51). History is composed of images rather than stories.

121 *Ibid.*, pp. 223-4.

122 This theme is addressed by both Sieburth and Wolin in their respective contributions.

123 This volume, pp. 46-7.

124 H[ans]-D[ieter] Kittsteiner, "Walter Benjamin's Historicism," trans. Jonathan Monroe and Irving Wohlfarth, *New German Critique* 39 (Fall 1986): 179.

125 Walter Benjamin, "Paris—Capital of the Nineteenth Century," in: Benjamin, *Charles Baudelaire: A Lyric Poet in the Era of High Capitalism,* trans. Harry Zohn (London: Verso, 1983), p. 159.

126 A notable example of this influence is the popular-historical work of Wolfgang Schivelbusch, whose studies of the history of artificial illumination and of train travel build upon Benjamin's approach: cf. *Geschichte der Eisenbahnreise. Zur Industrialisierung von Raum und Zeit im 19. Jahrhundert* (Munich: Carl Hanser, 1977) and *Lichtblicke. Zur Geschichte der künstlichen Helligkeit im 19. Jahrhundert* (Munich: Carl Hanser, 1983).

127 This volume, p. 67.

128 This volume, p. 64.

129 Cf. Tiedemann, "Dialectics at a Standstill," p. 262.

130 *GS,* V, p. 1154.

131 This volume, p. 185.

132 This volume, p. 179.

133 This volume, p. 47.

134 This volume, p. 85.

135 This volume, p. 101.

136 Burkhardt Lindner chronicles Benjamin's ill-fated attempt to habilitate at the University of Frankfurt, based on documents in the university files, in: "Habilitationsakte Benjamin. Über ein 'akademisches Trauerspiel' und über ein Vorkapitel der 'Frankfurter Schule'," in Lindner, *Walter Benjamin im Kontext.*, pp. 324-41. The failure of Benjamin's application was ultimately due to an unenthusiastic report on the *Trauerspiel* book by Cornelius's *Assistenten,* Max Horkheimer and Adhemer Gelb, who confirmed Cornelius's view that the work was incomprehensible.

137 Quoted from Scholem, *Walter Benjamin: The Story of a Friendship*, p. 148.
138 Regarding the terminological and methodological closeness of Adorno's *Kierkegaard* book to Benjamin's thought, see Robert Hullot-Kentor's "Foreword. Critique of the Organic," in Theodor W. Adorno, *Kierkegaard. Construction of the Aesthetic*, trans. Robert Hullot-Kentor (Minneapolis: University of Minnesota Press, 1989), pp. xiv-xvi & 146.
139 Adorno to Kracauer, Cronberg, May 12, 1930. Unpublished letter in Deutsches Literaturarchiv, Marbach am Neckar. Adorno claims that Benjamin conceded these points in a conversation, "after I'd brought him to bay just like the stag on St. Hubert's Day."
140 Habermas, pp. 113-4.
141 *Ibid.*, p. 120.
142 This volume, pp. 210-27.
143 Benjamin, "Theses on the Philosophy of History," p. 253.
144 Tiedemann, this volume, pp. 176, 204.
145 See N 2,6; this volume, p. 48.
146 See note 22.
147 See Richard Herbertz, *Das Wahrheitsproblem in der griechischen Philosophie* (Berlin: G. Reimer, 1913) and also, *Philosophie und Einzelwissenschaften* (Berne: A. Francke, 1913). Cf. also Benjamin's reflections "Zu[m Thema] Einzelwissenschaft und Philosophie" (*GS* VI, pp. 50-1). The decussations between Benjamin's Kant critique and Herbertz's work on Kant have never been considered; see for instance, R[ichard] Herbertz [. . .], *Rede gehalten an der Akademischen Gedächtnisfeier der Universität Bern zum 200. Geburtstage Kants. Kant als Grenzaufrichter.* [. . .] (Bern: P. Haupt, 1924).
148 The series, *Neue Berner Abhandlungen zur Philosophie und ihrer Geschichte*, was edited by Herbertz. Benjamin's *Der Begriff der Kunstkritik in der deutschen Romantik* was number five; Köhler's thesis, *Der Begriff der Repräsentation bei Leibniz*, was number three.
149 *OGTD*, p. 47.
150 *GS*, VII, pp. 437-76.
151 Berlin: Reuther & Reichard, 1922. (*Kant-Studien*. Supplementary volume, no. 57.)
152 Cf. *GS*, I, p. 971; Hering's article appeared in the *Jahrbuch für Philosophie und phänomenologische Forschung* 4 (1921): 495-543. Four years earlier, Benjamin had responded to Linke's attack on Theodor Elsenhans in the *Kant-Studien* (Cf. Paul Linke, "Das Recht der Phänomenologie. Eine Auseinandersetzung mit Th. Elsenhans," in: *Kanstudien. Philosophische Zeitschrift* 21 [August 10, 1916]: 163-221) with a gloss on concept and essence entitled "Eidos und Begriff" (*GS*, VI, pp. 29-31).
153 In a colloquium at the Free University of Berlin in 1968, Scholem asserted that the only text of Husserl's which Benjamin was likely to have read was part of the first volume of the *Logical Investigations*. (The transcript of this colloquium is unpublished.) In a letter from December 4, 1915, Benjamin mentions having read Husserl's *Logos* essay many years before. He later made reference to this work in his important review essay on the sociology of language "Probleme der Sprachsoziologie" (cf. *GS*, III, pp. 467-8).
154 The letter, from May 31, 1935, is published in Benjamin's *Briefe*, p. 663.
155 This volume, pp. 44-5. Concerning Benjamin and Aragon, cf. also Jacques Leenhardt, "Le passage comme forme d'expérience: Benjamin face à Aragon," in *Walter Benjamin et Paris*, ed. Heinz Wisman (Paris: Cerf, 1986), pp. 163-71 and Mauro Ponzi, "Benjamin e Aragon: Mito e Modernità," *Micromégas* 13, 2-3 (May-December 1986): 87-110. Wolin also mentions this relation; see pp. 215-6, this volume.

156 *Ibid.*, p. 18.

157 *GS*, V, pp. 498-9.

158 This volume, pp. 52-3.

159 This volume, p. 217.

160 Quoted by Wolin, this volume, p. 217.

161 *Reflections*, p. 178. [Reprinted in "Postage Illumination".]

162 Concerning Breton and Benjamin, see Margaret Cohen's forthcoming monograph, *Towards a Post-Realist Theory of Ideology: Paris, Surrealism, and Walter Benjamin.* Regarding Benjamin's adherence to Freudian paradigms, see Winfried Menninghaus' argument that Benjamin employs "Freud's analogy between myth and dream [. . .] in the *Arcades Project*" ("Walter Benjamin's Theory of Myth," in: Smith, *On Walter Benjamin*, pp. 301-2) as well as Jutta Wiegmann's doctoral thesis on *Die Bedeutung der Freudschen Theorie für Benjamins späte Geschichtsphilosophie* (Free University Berlin, 1988).

163 Hans Heinz Holz, "Prismatisches Denken" (1956), in *Über Walter Benjamin* (Frankfurt am Main: Suhrkamp, 1968), pp. 62-110.

164 *Poetic Thinking* is the apt title of a recent study of Heidegger by David Halliburton (Chicago, London: University of Chicago Press, 1981).

165 See her excursus on thinking in *The Life of the Mind,* ed. Mary McCarthy, vol. 2: "Thinking." (New York: Harcourt Brace Jovanovich, 1978).

All of the translations published here have been emended especially for this edition. The editor is indebted to Mary Ellen Petrisko, Von Underwood, and Richard Wolin for their generous help in editing several of the translations for the original edition of *The Philosophical Forum* as well as to Matthew Affran and Jeremy Gaines for carefully reading the introduction at various stages of its gestation. But above all, the editor wishes to express his profound gratitude to Professor Marx Wartofsky, editor of *The Philosophical Forum*, and Dr. T. David Brent, senior editor at the University of Chicago Press, for their persistent efforts to make publication of this volume possible and for their indefatigable encouragement over a very long period of time.

ON THE PROGRAM OF THE COMING PHILOSOPHY

WALTER BENJAMIN

The central task of the coming philosophy will be to turn the deepest intimations it draws from our times and our expectation of a great future into knowledge by relating them to the Kantian system. The historical continuity that is ensured by following upon the Kantian system is also the only such continuity of decisive and systematic consequence. For Kant is the most recent of those philosophers for whom what mattered was not primarily the compass and depth of knowledge, but first and foremost its justification, and with the exception of Plato he is perhaps the only one. Both of these philosophers share a confidence that the knowledge of which we can give the clearest account will also be the most profound. They have not dismissed the demand for depth in philosophy, but have found their own unique way of meeting it by identifying it with the demand for justification. The more vastly and boldly the development of future philosophy announces itself, the more deeply it must struggle for certainty, the criterion of which is systematic unity or truth.

The most important obstacle to linking a truly time- and eternity-conscious philosophy to Kant is, nevertheless, the following: the reality with which, and with the knowledge of which, Kant wanted to base knowledge on certainty and truth is a reality of a low, perhaps the lowest, order. The problem faced by Kantian epistemology, as by every great epistemology, has two sides, and Kant only managed to give a valid explanation for one of them. First of all, there was the question of the certainty of knowledge that is lasting, and secondly, there was the question of the integrity of an experience that is ephemeral. For the universal philosophical interest is continually after both the timeless validity of knowledge and the certainty of a temporal experience which is regarded as the immediate, if not the only, object of that knowledge. This experience, in its total structure, had simply not been made manifest to philosophers as something singularly transitory, and that holds true for Kant, as well. Especially in the *Prolegomena,* Kant wanted to take the principles

1

of experience from the sciences, especially mathematical physics, and yet from the very beginning, and even in the *Critique of Pure Reason,* experience itself and unto itself was never identical with the object realm of that science. Even if it had become so for him, as it did for the neo-Kantian thinkers, the concept of experience thus identified and determined would still have remained the old concept of experience, which is distinguished by its relationship not only to pure consciousness but, in addition, to empirical consciousness as well.

But this is precisely what is at issue: the conception of the naked, primitive, and self-evident experience, which, for Kant, as a man who somehow shared the horizon of his times, seemed to be the only experience given, indeed, the only experience possible. This experience, however, as already indicated, was unique and temporally limited. Above and beyond a certain formal similarity which it shared with any sense of experience, this experience, which in a significant sense could be called a *world-view,* was the same as that of the Enlightenment. In its most essential characteristics, however, it is not all that different from the experience of the other centuries of the modern era. It was an experience or a view of the world of the lowest order. The very fact that Kant was able to commence his immense work under the constellation of the Enlightenment indicates that his work was undertaken on the basis of an experience virtually reduced to nadir, to a minimum of significance. Indeed, one can say that the very greatness of his work, his unique radicalism, presupposed an experience which had almost no intrinsic value and which only attained its (we may say) sad significance through its certainty. No pre-Kantian philosopher saw himself confronted with the epistemological task in this sense. Nor did any of them have such a free hand, since an experience whose best aspect, whose quintessence, was Newtonian physics, with all its certainty, could take rough and tyrannical treatment without suffering. For the Enlightenment there were no authorities, not only in the sense of authorities to whom one would have to submit unconditionally, but also of intellectual forces who might have managed to give a higher content to experience. Just *what* the lower and inferior nature of experience in those times amounts to, just where its astonishingly small and specifically metaphysical weight lies, can only be hinted at in perceiving the manner in which this low-level concept of experience also had a restricting effect on Kantian thought. It is obviously a matter of that same state of affairs that has often been mentioned as the religious and historical blindness of the Enlightenment, without recognizing the extent to which these features of the Enlightenment pertain to the entire modern era.

2

It is of the greatest importance for the philosophy of the future to recognize and sort out which elements of the Kantian philosophy should be adopted and cultivated, which should be reworked, and which should be rejected. Every demand for a return to Kant rests upon the conviction that this system, which encountered a notion of experience whose metaphysical aspect had been dealt with by the likes of Mendelsohn and Garve, has, by virtue of its brilliant exploration of the certainty and justification of knowledge, derived and developed a depth that will prove adequate for a new and higher kind of experience that is yet to come. This simultaneously presents the primary challenge to be faced by contemporary philosophy and asserts that it can be met: it is, according to the typology of Kantian thought, to undertake the epistemological foundation of a higher concept of experience. And precisely this is to be made the theme of the expected philosophy—that a certain typology can be demonstrated and clearly drawn out from the Kantian system which can do justice to a higher experience. Nowhere does Kant deny the possibility of a metaphysics; he merely wishes to have criteria established upon which such a possibility can be proven in the individual case. The notion of experience held in the Kantian age did not require metaphysics; the only thing historically possible in Kant's day was to deny its claims, because the demand of his contemporaries for metaphysics was weakness or hypocrisy. Thus it is question of finding, on the basis of Kantian typology, prolegomena to a future metaphysics, and in the process of envisioning this future metaphysics, this higher experience.

But it not only with reference to experience and metaphysics that philosophy must be concerned with the revision of Kant. And methodically considered, that is, as true philosophy should consider it, the revision should begin not with reference to experience and metaphysics, but with reference to the concept of knowledge. The decisive mistakes of Kantian epistemology are, it cannot be doubted, traceable to the hollowness of the experience available to him, and thus the double task of creating both a new concept of knowledge and a new conception of the world on the basis of philosophy becomes a single one. The weakness of the Kantian concept of knowledge has often been felt in the lack of radicalism and the lack of consistency in his teachings. Kant's epistemology does not open up the realm of metaphysics, because it contains within itself primitive elements of an unproductive metaphysics which excludes all others. In epistemology every metaphysical element is the germ of a disease that expresses itself in the separation of knowledge from the realm of experience in its full freedom and depth. The development of philosophy is to be expected because each annihilation of these metaphysical elements in an episte-

3

mology simultaneously refers it to a deeper, more metaphysically fulfilled experience.

There is—and here lies the historical seed of the approaching philosophy—a most intimate connection between that experience, the deeper exploration of which could never lead to metaphysical truths, and that theory of knowledge, which was not yet able to determine sufficiently the logical place of metaphysical research. After all, the sense in which Kant uses the term "metaphysics of Nature," for instance, seems definitely to lie in the direction of the exploration of experience on the basis of epistemologically secured principles. The inadequacies with respect to experience and metaphysics manifest themselves within epistemology itself as elements of speculative metaphysics (that is, metaphysics that has become rudimentary). The most important of these elements are: Kant's conception of knowledge as a relation between some sort of subjects and objects or subject and object, which he was unable to ultimately overcome, despite all his attempts to do so; second, the relation of knowledge and experience to human empirical consciousness, also only very tentatively overcome. Both of these problems are closely interconnected, and even to the extent that Kant and the neo-Kantians have overcome the object nature of the thing-in-itself as the cause of sensations, there remains the subject nature of the cognizing consciousness to be eliminated. This subject nature of this cognizing consciousness, however, stems from the fact that it is formed in analogy to the empirical consciousness, which of course has objects confronting it. All of this is a thoroughly metaphysical rudiment of epistemology, a piece of just that shallow "experience" of these centuries which crept into epistemology. It simply cannot be doubted that the notion, sublimated though it may be, of an individual, living ego which receives sensations by means of its senses and forms its ideas on the basis of them, plays a role of the greatest importance in the Kantian concept of knowledge. This notion is, however, mythology, and so far as its truth content is concerned, the same as every other epistemological mythology. We know of primitive peoples of the so-called pre-animistic stage who identify themselves with sacred animals and plants and name themselves after them; we know of insane people who likewise identify themselves in part with objects of their perception, which are thus no longer objecta, "placed before" them; we know of sick people who do not relate the sensations of their bodies to themselves, but rather to other creatures, and of clairvoyants who at least claim to be able to feel the sensations of others as their own. The commonly shared notion of sensuous (and intellectual) knowledge in our, as well as the Kantian and the pre-Kantian epochs, is very much a mythology like those mentioned.

In *this* respect, as far as the naive conception of the receipt of perceptions is concerned, Kantian "experience" is metaphysics or mythology, and indeed, only a modern and religiously particularly infertile one. Experience, as it is conceived in reference to the individual living human and his consciousness, instead of as a systematic specification of knowledge, is again in all of its types the mere *object* of this real knowledge, specifically of its psychological branch. The latter divides empirical consciousness systematically into the types of madness. Cognizing man, the cognizing empirical consciousness, is a type of insane consciousness. By this, nothing more is meant than that within the empirical consciousness there are only gradual differences between its various types. These differences are simultaneously differences of value, the criterion of which, however, cannot be the correctness of cognitions, and which is never the issue in the empirical, psychological sphere; to determine the true criteria for differentiating between the values of the various types of consciousness will be one of the highest tasks of the future philosophy. To the types of empirical consciousness there correspond just as many types of experiences, which in regard to their relation to the empirical consciousness, as far as truth is concerned, have only the value of fantasy or hallucination. For an objective relation between the empirical consciousness and the objective concept of experience is impossible. All genuine experience rests upon the pure epistemological (transcendental) consciousness, if this term is still usable under the condition that it be stripped of everything subjective. The pure transcendental consciousness is different in kind from any empirical consciousness, and the question therefore arises of whether the application of the term consciousness is allowable here. How the psychological concept of consciousness is related to the concept of the sphere of pure knowledge remains a major problem of philosophy, one which perhaps can only be restored from the age of scholasticism. Here is the logical place for many problems that phenomenology has recently raised anew. Philosophy is based upon the fact that the structure of experience lies within the structure of knowledge and is to be developed from it. This experience, then, also includes religion, as the true experience, in which neither god nor man is object or subject of experience but in which this experience is based on pure knowledge. As the quintessence of philosophy alone can and must think of God. The task of future epistemology is to find for knowledge the sphere of total neutrality in regard to the concepts of both subject and object, in other words, it is to discover the autonomous, innate sphere of knowledge in which this concept in no way continues to designate the relation between two metaphysical entities.

It should be made a tenet of the program of future philosophy that in the course of the purification of epistemology which Kant made possible to pose as a radical problem—while also making it necessary as a next step—not only a new concept of knowledge should be established but also a new concept of experience, in accordance with the relationship Kant has found between the two. Of course, as was said, neither experience nor knowledge may be bound to the empirical consciousness in this process; but here too it would continue to be the case, indeed it would first derive its proper significance to say that the conditions of knowledge are those of experience. This new concept of experience, which would be established, given the new conditions of knowledge, would itself be the logical place and the logical possibility of metaphysics. For Kant had no other reason to make metaphysics a problem and experience the only basis of knowledge than that, proceeding from his concept of experience, the possibility of a metaphysics that would have the importance of previous metaphysics (properly understood, not the possibility of having a metaphysics at all) would have had to appear excluded. Metaphysics does not seem to be distinguished solely by the illegitimacy of its insights, however, at least not for Kant, who would otherwise hardly have written prolegomena to it. Its distinctiveness lies rather in its universal power to tie all of experience immediately to the concept of God through ideas. Thus the task of the coming philosophy can be conceived as the discovery or creation of that concept of knowledge which, by relating the concept of experience *exclusively* to the transcendental consciousness, makes not only mechanical but also religious experience logically possible. This should definitely not be taken to mean that knowledge makes God possible, but that it definitely does make the experience and doctrine of him possible in the first place.

In the development of philosophy called for and considered proper here, one symptom of neo-Kantianism can already be detected. A major problem of neo-Kantianism was to eliminate the distinction between intuition and intellect, a metaphysical rudiment that occupies a position like that of the theory of the faculties in Kant's work. With this—that is, with the transformation of the concept of knowledge—there also began a transformation of the concept of experience. For it cannot be doubted that the reduction of all experience to scientific experience is not intended with such exclusivity by Kant, no matter how much it may belong to the training of the historical Kant in some respects. There certainly existed a tendency in Kant against the division and fragmentation of experience into the realms of the individual sciences. Even if later epistemology has to deny the recourse to experience in the common sense, such as occurs in Kant, on the other hand, in the interest of the continuity of experience, its representation as the system of the sciences as the neo-Kantians have it is still to be found lacking. A way must be found in metaphysics to form a pure and systematic continuum of experience; indeed, it seems that the true meaning of experience is to be sought in this area. But in the neo-Kantian rectification of one of Kant's metaphysicizing thoughts (and not the fundamental one) a modification of the concept of experience occurred, and significantly enough, first of all in the extreme extension of the mechanical aspect of the relatively empty Enlightenment concept of experience. It should by no means be overlooked that the concept of freedom stands in a peculiar correlation to the mechanical concept of experience and was accordingly further developed in neo-Kantianism. But here, too, it must be emphasized that the entirety of the context of ethics can no more be absorbed into the concept of morality held by Kant, the Enlightenment, and the Kantians than the context of metaphysics fits into that which they call experience. With a new concept of knowledge, therefore, not only the concept of experience but also that of freedom will undergo a decisive transformation.

One could actually argue here that with the discovery of a concept of experience that would provide a logical place for metaphysics the distinction between the realms of nature and freedom would be abolished. Yet here, where we are concerned only with a program of research and not with proof, only this much need be said: no matter how necessary and inevitable it may be to reconstruct, on the basis of a new transcendental logic, the realm of dialectics, the realm of the cross-over between the theory of experience and the theory of freedom, it is just as imperative that this transformation not end up in a confounding of freedom and experience, even though the concept of experience may be changed in the metaphysical realm by the concept of freedom in a sense that is perhaps as yet unknown. For no matter how incalculable the changes may be that will reveal themselves to research here, the trichotomy of the Kantian system is one of the great features of that typology which is to be preserved, and it, more than any other, must be preserved. The question may well be raised of whether the second part of the system (quite apart from the difficulty of the third) must still be related to ethics or whether the category of causality through freedom might have a different meaning. The trichotomy, whose metaphysically deepest aspects are still undiscovered, has its decisive foundation within the Kantian system in the trinity of the relational categories. In the absolute trichotomy of the system, which in this threefold aspect is applied to the entire realm of culture, lies one of the reasons for the historical superiority of the Kantian system over that (*sic*) of his predecessors. The formalistic dialectics of the post-

Kantian systems, however, is not based on the definition of the thesis as categorical, the antithesis as hypothetical, and the synthesis as disjunctive relations. But besides the concept of synthesis, another concept, that of a certain non-synthesis of two concepts in another, will become very important systematically, since another relation between thesis and antithesis is possible besides synthesis. This can hardly lead to a four-fold structure of relational categories, however.

But if the great trichotomy must be preserved for the structuring of philosophy, even while the components themselves are still misdefined, the same does not hold true for all the individual schemata of the system. Just as the Marburg school has already begun with the elimination of the distinction between transcendental logic and aesthetics (even though it is questionable whether an analogue of this distinction must not return on a higher level), so must the table of categories be completely revised, as is not generally demanded. In this very process, then, the transformation of the concept of knowledge will begin to manifest itself in the acquisition of a new concept of experience, since the Aristotelian categories are both arbitrarily posed and have been exploited in a very one-sided way by Kant in the light of a mechanical experience. First and foremost must be considered whether the table of categories must remain in their present isolation and lack of mediation, or whether it could not take a place among other members in a theory of orders or itself be built up to such a theory, founded upon or connected to primal concepts [*Urbegriffe*]. To such a theory of orders would also belong that which Kant discusses in the transcendental aesthetic, and furthermore, all the basic concepts not only of mechanics, but also of geometry, linguistics, psychology, the descriptive natural sciences, and many others, to the extent that these concepts had a direct relationship to the categories or the other highest ordering concepts of philosophy. Outstanding examples here are the principles of grammar. Furthermore, one must recall that, with the radical elimination of all those elements in epistemology that provide the concealed answer to the concealed question about the origins of knowledge, the great problem of the false or of error is opened up, the logical structure and order of which must be ascertained just like those of the true. Error can no longer be explained in terms of erring, any more than the true can be explained in terms of correct understanding. For this investigation of the logical nature of the false and the mistaken, the categories are also presumably to be found in the theory of the orders; everywhere in modern philosophy the recognition crops up that categorical and related orders are of central importance for the knowledge of an experience which is multiply gradated and which also is not mechanical. Art, jurisprudence, and history; these and other areas must orient themselves according to the theory of categories with much more intensity than Kant did. But at the same time, one of the greatest problems of the system occurs in regard to the transcendental logic, specifically the question of its third part—in other words, the question of those scientific types of experience (the biological ones) which Kant did not treat on the ground of the transcendental logic and one must also inquire why he did not do so. Further, the question of the relationship of art to this third, and of ethics to the second part of the system. The fixing of the concept of identity, unknown to Kant, will likely play a great role in the transcendental logic, inasmuch as it does not occur in the table of categories, yet presumably constitutes the highest of transcendental logical concepts and is perhaps truly suited to founding the sphere of knowledge autonomously beyond the subject-object terminology. The transcendental dialectic already displays in the Kantian formulation the ideas upon which the unity of experience rests. For the deepened concept of experience, however, as already mentioned, continuity is almost as indispensable as unity, and the basis of the unity and continuity of that experience which is not vulgar nor only scientific, but metaphysical must be demonstrated in the ideas. The convergence of ideas towards the highest concept of knowledge must be shown.

Just as the Kantian theory itself, in order to find its principles, needed to be confronted with a science with reference to which it could define them, so will it be for modern philosophy. The great restructuration and correction which must be performed upon the concept of experience, oriented so one-sidedly along mathematical-mechanical lines, can only be attained by relating knowledge to language, such as was attempted by Hamann during Kant's lifetime. For Kant, the consciousness that philosophical knowledge was absolutely certain and *apriori,* the consciousness of that aspect of philosophy in which it is fully the peer of mathematics, caused the fact that all philosophical knowledge has its unique expression in language and not in formulae or numbers to go almost completely untreated. This fact, however, might well ultimately prove to be the decisive one, and it is ultimately because of this fact that the systematic supremacy of philosophy over all science as well as mathematics is to be asserted. A concept of knowledge gained from reflection on the linguistic nature of knowledge will create a corresponding concept of experience which will also encompass regions that Kant failed to integrate into his system. The realm of religion should be mentioned as the foremost of these. And thus the demand upon the philosophy of the future can finally be put in these words: to create on the basis of the Kantian system a concept of knowledge to which a concept of experience corresponds, of which the knowledge is the doctrine. Such a philosophy in its universal element would either itself be designated as theology or would be superordinated to theology to the extent that it contains historically philosophical elements.

Experience is the uniform and continuous multiplicity of knowledge.

ADDENDUM

In the interest of clarifying the relation of philosophy to religion, the contents of the preceding essay should be repeated to the extent that it concerns the systematic schema of philosophy. It is concerned first of all with the relationship among the three concepts, epistemology, metaphysics, and religion. All of philosophy breaks down into epistemology and metaphysics, or as Kant would say, into a critical and a dogmatic part. This division, however, is not as an indication of content but as a principle of classification not of principal importance. With it, one is only trying to say that upon the basis of all the critical ensuring of cognitive concepts and the concept of knowledge, a theory can now be built up of that upon which in the very first place the concept of knowledge is epistemologically fixed. Where the critical ends and the dogmatic begins is perhaps not clearly demonstrable, because the concept of the dogmatic is only supposed to designate the transition from critique to theory, from the more general to particular fundamental concepts. All philosophy is thus theory of knowledge, but just that—a theory, critical and dogmatic, of knowledge. Both parts, the critical and the dogmatic, fall completely within the realm of the philosophical. Since that is the case, since it is not true that, for instance, the dogmatic part coincides with that of individual sciences, the question naturally arises as to the borderline between philosophy and individual science. The meaning of the term "metaphysical," as introduced in the foregoing, consists precisely in declaring this border nonexistent, and the reformulation of "experience" as "metaphysics" means that so-called experience is virtually included in the metaphysical or dogmatic part of philosophy, into which the highest epistemological, i.e., the critical is transformed. (For the exemplification of this relation for the area of physics see my essay on explanation and description.) If the relationship between epistemology, metaphysics, and the individual sciences are thus very generally outlined, two questions remain. First, that of the relation of the critical to the dogmatic moment in ethics and aesthetics, which we can let alone here since we must postulate a solution in a manner perhaps systematically analogous to that in the domain of physics. Secondly, there is the question of the relation between philosophy and religion. First of all, it is now clear that what is at stake is not the issue of the relationship between philosophy and religion but that between philosophy and the dogma of religion, in other words, the question of the relationship between knowledge in general and knowledge of religion. The question of existence raised by religion, art, etc., can also play a role philosophically, but only on the path of inquiry into the philosophical *knowledge* of such existence. Philosophy always inquires about knowledge, in relation to which the question of the knowledge of its existence is only a modification, albeit an incomparably marvelous modification, of the question of knowledge in general. Indeed, it must be said that philosophy in its questionings can never hit upon the unity of existence, but only upon new unities of various conformities to laws, whose integral is "existence."

The original or primal concept of epistemology has a double function. On the one hand, this concept is the one which by its specification, after the general logical foundation of knowledge, penetrates to the concepts of specific types of cognition and thus to specific types of experience. This is its real epistemological significance and simultaneously the one weaker side of its metaphysical significance. However, the original and primal concept of knowledge does not reach a concrete totality of experience in this context, no more than it reaches any concept of existence. But there is a unity of experience that can by no means be understood as a sum of experiences, to which the concept of knowledge as theory is *immediately* related in its continuous development. The object and the content of this theory, this concrete totality of experience, is religion, which, however, is presented to philosophy in the first instance only as theory. The source of existence lies in the totality of experience, however, and only in theory does philosophy encounter something absolute, as existence, and in so doing encounter that continuity in the nature of experience in the neglect of which the failing of neo-Kantianism can be suspected. In a *purely* metaphysical respect the original concept of experience in its totality is transformed in quite a different sense than with its individual specifications, the sciences: *viz.,* immediately, where the meaning of this immediately *vis-à-vis* the former mediacy remains to be determined. To say that knowledge is metaphysical means in the strict sense: it is related via the original concept of knowledge to the concrete totality of experience, i.e., *existence*. The philosophical concept of existence must answer to the religious dogmatic concept, but the latter to the epistemological original concept. All of this is only a sketchy indication. The basic tendency of this definition of the relationship between religion and philosophy, however, is to meet the demands for, first, the virtual unity of religion and philosophy, second, the incorporation of the knowledge of religion into philosophy, third, the integrity of the tripartite division of the system.

Translated by Mark Ritter

BENJAMIN THE SCRIVENER

RICHARD SIEBURTH

For Irving Wohlfarth

"To great writers," Benjamin observes, "finished works weigh lighter than those fragments on which they labor their entire lives."[1] Conceived in Paris in 1927 and still in progress when Benjamin fled the occupation of the capital in 1940, the text that has come down to us as *Das Passagen-Werk* (or the *Arcades Project*) is in no sense a finished work; its specific gravity, rather, is that of a massive fragment or monumental ruin meticulously constructed over the course of thirteen years—"the theater," as Benjamin explained to his friend Scholem, "of all my struggles and all my ideas."[2] Shrouded by his habitual veil of secrecy, Benjamin's undisclosed magnum opus had long been rumored to exist among his unpublished papers, but it was not until 1982 that the manuscript would finally see the light of print, three and half decades after its rediscovery at the Bibliothèque Nationale where it had been deposited in the safe-keeping of Georges Bataille for the duration of the war. Published as volume five of the Suhrkamp *Gesammelte Schriften* and impeccably edited by Rolf Tiedemann, the two hefty tomes of the *Passagen-Werk* comprise over a quarter of a million words laboriously transcribed from hundreds of tiny folios covered in Benjamin's minuscule hand, the entire manuscript, according to Bataille, standing no more than fifteen or twenty centimeters high.

Benjamin's passion for the diminutive is well-documented; Scholem reports his admiration for two grains of wheat in the Jewish section of the Musée Cluny on which the complete *Shema Israel* had been inscribed.[3] The smaller the object, Hannah Arendt observes, the more likely it seemed to Benjamin that it could contain in the most concentrated form everything else—reduction in size having as its corollary a recovery of primal pattern (as in the Goethean *Urphänomen*) or a distillation of synecdochical cosmic design (as in the Leibnizian monad). The purely *material* dimensions of Benjamin's manuscript—the greatest possible number of words packed into the smallest possible volume—offer a clue to the elusive economy of his enterprise. On the one hand the *Arcades Project* would appear to be governed by a law of infinite expansibility; on the other, this tendency toward centrifugal proliferation is countered by a centripetal impulse toward contraction, toward reduction, toward ascesis—"criticism," Benjamin remarks, "means the mortification of works."[4]

What was at the outset to have been a lapidary essay on the rise and fall of the Paris *passages* widens over the course of the thirties into a virtual encyclopedia of 19th-century Parisian (and, by extension, European) culture—a sprawling *histoire des mentalités*. Every time the project seems to be nearing completion, however, new fields of investigation open up, fresh territories of inquiry invite exploration, requiring months of additional research at the Bibliothèque Nationale—Benjamin complains to Scholem of his ongoing battle to conquer and subjugate his material, to master this "ancient, more or less mutinous, half-apocryphal province of my thoughts" (1086). But even as the scope of his project grows more ambitious, ever enlarging its boundaries, ever accumulating a greater fund of raw data, Benjamin seeks to impose another economy: to reduce the scale of his materials, to miniaturize and abbreviate the archive by a Lilliputian stroke of the pen. Not the sacred *Shema Israel* on a kernel of wheat, but the profane palimpsest of modernity so compressed, so compacted by the pressures of dialectical insight that it becomes capable of releasing the enormous energies of history that lie bonded within it. Breaking with the sweeping, imperial overviews of traditional historicism, Benjamin will therefore focus on the infinitesimal, the overlooked, the transitory, in order "to detect the crystal of the total event in the analysis of the small, discrete moment." (575) If read with sufficient attention, any such moment could reveal itself to be "a muscle strong enough to contract the whole of historical time" (600) into an apocalyptic Now (*Jetztzeit*), providing "the strait gate through which the Messiah might enter."[5] Conversely, if written in small enough hand, his text might just conceivably succeed in telescoping past, present, and future into its monadic script, abridging the entire Library of Babel into a single, redemptive word.

In the beginning was the Name. Commenting on the range of resonances contained in the French word *passage*, Benjamin observes in his preliminary drafts of the *Arcades Project*:[6] "Nothing of them remains but their name: Passages, and: Passage du Panorama (1001) . . . Their name has now become like a filter that only lets through the most inner, bitter essence of the past" (1007). As he charts the cultural topography of 19th-century Paris, Benjamin finds himself entering into a landscape of proper nouns: "Through its street names the city becomes the likeness (*Abbild*) of a linguistic universe . . . It is above all the encounter of two different street *names* that makes up the magic of the 'corner' . . . Link of name and labyrinth in the Métro" (1008). Names endow the city with the features of a face or text; to write a city is therefore to mime its nomenclature, to engage in onomastic inventory. From its initial drafts (1927-1929) through its later elaborations, the *Arcades Project* will maintain as its basic structural and heuristic device the form of a *list,* a paratactic mapping of cultural traffic, a gazetteer of urban signs:

> Marchand de lorgnettes
> Names of the Magasins de Nouveautés (most taken from popular vaudevilles): La fille d'honneur/ la Vestale/ le page inconstant/ le masque de fer/ le coin de la rue/ la lampe merveilleuse/ le petit chaperon rouge/ la petite Nanette/ Chaumière allemande/ Mamelouk
> Shop sign of a confiseur "aux armes de Werther." Gantier au ci-devant jeune homme
> Passage Vivienne, "solid" in contrast to the Passage des panoramas. No luxury shops in the former. Stores in the Passages des panoramas. Restaurant Véron, Marquis, cabinet de lecture, marchand de musique, caricaturiste. Théâtre des Variétés (tailleurs, bottiers, merciers, marchands de vin, bonnetiers)
> Rue Franciade 84 "Passage du désir" menant jadis à un lieu galant (1002-1004)

Meditating on the relation of identity to name ("Am I that which names W. B. or am I simply named W. B.?"). Benjamin remarks in these early drafts that "the name is the object of a mimesis," simultaneously preserving and prefiguring "the habitus of a lived life." Since "the domain of the name is that of similarity" (a name resembles what it names), and since "similarity is the organon of experience" (experience is the rhyme of likenesses), the name "can therefore only come to be recognized through the interrelations of experience." (1038) We live in (or as) a name; it is that which we correspond to, a locus of identity, a configuration of experience, a connecting space . . . a passage.[7]

Just as Benjamin's 1928 study of German baroque drama may be read as an extended mulling over of the rhetorical and metaphysical ramifications of the term *Trauerspiel,* so his *Arcades Project* can be construed as an encyclopedic unfolding of the historical potential that lies dormant within the word *passage*. According to Benjamin's own account, it was Aragon's evocation of the demise and demolition of the Passage de l'Opéra in *Le Paysan de Paris* (1926) that initially provided him with the metaphor of the arcade as a figure for the ephemeral, the passing, the out of date, a dense emblem of that particular (capitalist) logic whereby the New is fated, at an ever accelerating rate, to fall out of style and plunge into eternal oblivion.[8] Following up on the "Préface à une mythologie moderne" that introduces Aragon's excursions into the poetry of obsolescence offered by the *passages*, Benjamin observes that architecture provides the clearest index of the "latent mythology" of a given era (1002). As a *genius loci* that bespeaks both space and time, that defines both an architectural form and a historical process, the *passage* thus allows Benjamin to *name* (or site) the mythology of modernity, to read the glass-and-iron construction of the arcades both as a spatial projection of the bourgeois ideology of technological advance and as a transparent repository of the collective fantasies of 19th-century capitalism.[9]

Benjamin's early drafts describe the arcades as offering a "prehistoric landscape of consumption" (993), animated not by mammoths and ichthyosaurs but by once-fetishized commodities now destined for extinction—an antediluvian clutter of the latest fads and fashion, an oneiric bric-a-brac of luxury goods and novelty items. Benjamin's telling analogy defines the historian's task as a paleontological excavation of the fossilized (or reified) relics of capitalist consumerism (the shift from the analysis of production to the analysis of consumption being, as many critics have pointed out, Benjamin's crucial advance on Marx). To venture into the twilight world of the arcades is therefore somewhat akin to finding oneself in the caves of Lascaux prehistoric sites filled with ritual representations at once utterly exotic in time and sensibility and yet recognizably contemporary. The archaeological impulse of the *Arcades Project* places it squarely among other modernist endeavors to recover the primitive as the New. Benjamin diverges, however, by situating the archaic, the Other, not in some remote place or time but at the very heart of the familiar, in the uncanny passage of modernity into instant antiquity, instant ruins.

"Allegories are, in the realm of thoughts, what ruins are in the realm of things," Benjamin observes in his study of the baroque *Trauerspiel*. [10] Arcades are both: literally in ruin, their sheer semantic potential activates them as allegories, that is, as figures inviting historical (re)construction or (re)interpretation—as Baudelaire phrased it, in an age of Haussmannization, "tout pour moi devient allégorie." As allegories, the very vacancy

of the arcades makes them ideal vessels for the hermeneutic transformations of metaphor. Benjamin's brooding ambles through the pre- and
posthistory of the *passages* lead him into an echo chamber of Baudelairean
correspondances:

> Musée Grevin: cabinet des Mirages. Describe the connection between
> temple, railway station, passage, market-hall where rotten (phos-
> phorescent) meat is sold. The opera in the passage. Catacombs in
> the passage. (1002)

Elsewhere in these notes he likens the arcades to labyrinths (1007), to
mineral springs (1033), to aquariums (1051), to the "inner-most glowing
cells of the City of Light" (1050)—the metaphors all suggest a chthonic,
almost amniotic environment associated with "the deepest strata of
dream" (1009) or the inner recesses of the body (1010). One does not so
much enter a *passage* as sink into it: "The flaneur . . . saunters along the
street; for him every street is a declivity. It leads downwards, if not into
the realm of the Mothers then at least into a past that is all the more
profound because it is not his own personal past while nonetheless remaining some childhood recollection." (1052) Passages: a regression into
the infantile dreams of modern capitalism, a plunge into the collective
unconscious or phantasmagoric innards of the city . . . a descent into a
modern Avernus.

Benjamin's metaphors affiliate his project with a number of romantic or
modernist myths of descent, ranging from Goethe's *Faust* (as the above
allusion to the Mothers makes clear) to the *nekuia* of Pound's first Canto,
the Hades chapter of Joyce's *Ulysses,* the "Unreal City" of Eliot's *Waste
Land,* the "Leidstadt" of Rilke's tenth Duino Elegy—not to mention the
atavistic psychic strata of the "Eternal City" in Freud's *Civilization and
its Discontents* or the buried archetypes of Jung. What distances Benjamin from this tradition, however, is his dialectical reversal of these
myths of descent (or descents into myth). His early notes already show
him at pains to dissociate his project from the neo-romantic mythopoeia
of an Aragon:

> Setting off the slant of this project against Aragon: whereas Aragon
> persistently remains in the realm of dreams, here it is a question of
> discovering the constellation of waking. Whereas an impressionistic
> element lingers on in Aragon (i.e. "mythology") . . . what matters here
> is the dissolution of "mythology" into the space of history. Of course

... can only happen through the wakening of a not yet conscious knowledge of the past. (1014)

Though alert to the mythic energies latent in the arcades (inasmuch as they embody a secularized version of the primal dream of a Golden Age), Benjamin insists on the necessity of *historicizing* such myth, that is, of reading cultural archetypes (or *Urphänomene*) not as timeless essences but as the products of concrete social and economic relations. But if myth is to be thus historicized, then by the same token history must be exposed as myth: the very idea of the "modern" (or of "progress") reveals itself to be nothing more than a degraded variant of the archaic, prehistoric myth of the Eternal Return—the merchandizing of the New merely masks the monotonous recurrence of the Same in the commercial guise of innovative change.[11]

As his critique of Aragon indicates, Benjamin equates this dialectical reversal of myth into history (and vice versa) with the passage from sleep to waking. As much as he admires the possibilities of "profane illumination" promised by Surrealist ventures into heightened or altered states of consciousness, he fears that these could all too easily lend themselves not to the revolutionary transformation of political and historical awareness but merely to private avant-garde narcosis. History, for Benjamin, is a nightmare from which it is imperative to awake. If he chooses to dream his way back into the initiatory labyrinth of the arcades, it is only so that he may more lucidly emerge into the sobering dawn of the here and now. It is therefore not Aragon but Proust who provides the fundamental epistemological model for Benjamin: like *A la recherche du temps perdu,* the *Arcades Project* begins with the efforts of a consciousness (individual? collective? Benjamin never makes it quite clear) to get its bearings in space and time as it hovers between past and present, dreaming and waking.

Speaking of the "Copernican turn" historiography must now take, Benjamin accordingly insists that it be henceforth grounded in "the dialectical structure of awakening" (1058). Instead of positing the past as a fixed point toward which the present must somehow return in order to recover or reconstruct it "as it really was," and conversely, instead of hypostatizing the present as that which has been ineluctably prefigured or predetermined by the past, the historian must make it clear that if there is any knowledge of the past or present to be had, this can only result from the dialectical interchange that occurs when the two meet. The place they meet is what Benjamin (following Proust) calls "awakening" (*Erwachen*) or "remembering" (*Erinnerung*), for just as the moment of waking up

18

provides a precarious synthesis whose thesis is the dream from which it is just emerging and whose anithesis is the state of total wakefulness it has yet to achieve, so what once was and what is still to come momentarily collide to create the Now in which the historian suddenly remembers. The flash of insight (or epistemological "constellation") that arises out of this collision of opposites at once resembles the *dépaysment* provoked by Surrealist metaphor and the shock of recognition brought about by Proustian *mémoire involontaire*. Benjamin names it a "dialectical image" or "dialectics at a standstill," an instant of illumination in which the dreary newsreel of history suddenly snaps, freezes into a frame, then burns away.

Dialectical images, according to Benjamin, define both the form and the content of historical knowledge—indeed, this deliberate blurring of the distinction between (idealist) subject and (materialist) object of knowledge lies at the crux of Adorno's later critiques of the *Arcades Project*. Built as they are on the principle of ambiguity or *Zweideutigkeit* (1050), arcades are Benjamin's privileged example of the dialectical image: their very architectonics make them, as he notes, "buildings, passageways that have no exterior. Like dream." (1006) At once edifice and street, the *passage* converts house into corridor, residence into traffic, permanence into transit.[12] Roofing the external world of the city into a domesticized interior, bathed in a twilight of natural and artificial illumination, the arcade occupies a space that seems to offer both the panoramic openness of natural landscape and the cozy closure of a room (1053). A cross between Leibniz's windowless monad and Plato's cave, it houses reflections of reflections—the shadowy simulacra of desire on display under glass, luring the customer's eye into a gallery of mirrors where commodities stare back with the frozen features of a waxwork or a daguerrotype's hieratic gaze.

The study of this looking-glass world demands what Benjamin terms a *Schwellenkunde,* a science of thresholds (147):[13]

> The threshold is a *zone*. And in fact a zone of passage (*Übergang*). Transformation, passage, flux—all are contained in the word threshold. . . . We have become quite poor as far as threshold experiences go. Falling asleep is perhaps the only such experience that has remained to us. (1025).

Architecturally, an arcade is a perfect realization of such liminal space, articulating as it does a zone that is both inside and outside, open and closed, container and contained. Historically, it also defines a threshold: at once familiarly near and utterly remote in time, it is a place where the preindustrial crosses over into the modern and the new passes away into the old. Like some Surrealist "porte battante" that simultaneously opens onto the dream and the real, the arcade invites the historian to sink into its slumber, to undergo a *rite de passage*,[14] to descend into the nightmare-world of commodity fetishism in order to retrieve from its phantasmagorias the millenial dream-images of a future that has yet to awake—the fallen capitalist world reversed (or redeemed) into classless Utopia as it crosses over the threshold of revolution.[15]

Although he wants to claim it as a modernist version of dialectics, Benjamin's Janus-like "science of thresholds" (each thing capable of reverting into its opposite, each moment seized as lying in between) more resembles the deconstructive indeterminacy of the Derridean *pharmakos* or Mallarméan *pli*—its ludic impulse is evident in his first working title for the project, *Pariser Passagen. Eine dialektische Feerie* (the French word *féerie,* like the old English "faery," suggesting a fairytale world, a universe of enchantment, a magical extravaganza). Indeed, Benjaminian dialectics may be no more (or less) than child's play. In his *Berlin Childhood around 1900* he tells of a treasure (or "dowry") that he believed to be buried in the inner recesses of a rolled sock:

> I wanted to unroll the "treasure" from its woollen pocket. I pulled it
> ever closer toward me until the overwhelming event took place: the
> "treasure" had been completely unrolled from its pocket, and yet had
> utterly disappeared. Over and over again I carried out the test of this
> enigmatic truth: that form and content, container and contained,
> "treasure" and pocket were one and the same. One and the same
> thing—and yet a third thing as well: this sock into which both had been
> transformed.[16]

Fort-Da. A sock, an arcade.

Benjamin's fascination with the *passages,* as he admits in a 1928 letter, is very closely linked to his longstanding interest in toys (1084). A chapter of *One-Way Street* entitled "Construction Site" describes how children salvage the castoff odds and ends of adult labor and metamorphose them into their own private playthings:

> Children are particularly fond of haunting any site where things are
> being visibly worked upon. They are irresistibly drawn by the detritus
> generated by building, gardening, housework, tailoring, or carpentry.

In waste products they recognize the face that the world of things turns directly and solely to them. In using these things they do not so much imitate the works of adults as bring together, in the artifact produced in play, materials of widely differing kinds in new, intuitive relationship. Children thus produce their own small world of things within the greater one.[17]

Emblems of modern capitalism in its childhood, arcades engage in similar play: transforming use-value into exchange-value, they reassemble the disparate products of industry into a magical microcosm whose commercial bric-a-brac is displayed in new, surreal configurations—Lautréamont's chance meeting of an umbrella and a sewing machine on a dissection table.

By the same token, Benjamin's *Arcades Project* is itself an experimental toy constructed on the childish principle of *bricolage,* modern dialectics miming archaic *pensée sauvage:*

Method of this project: literary montage. I need say nothing. Only show [*zeigen*]. I will appropriate no clever turns of phrase nor steal any valuables. But the refuse, the trash: which I will not describe but instead exhibit [*vorzeigen*]. (1030)

The materialist historian, in other words, not only engages in an adult version of child's play but, more specifically, assumes the role of the *Lumpensammler* or Baudelairean *chiffonier,* for his vocation is above all to collect—and recollect. And what he collects are not the monuments and memorabilia of high culture but instead its *Abfall,* it garbage, its surplus waste. As Irving Wohlfarth has argued,[18] this focus on refuse is in itself a strategy of radical refusal: rejecting the value of the cultural heritage that the bourgeoisie wants to preserve, Benjamin will instead carry out a rescue mission whose purpose is to save that which has been excluded, to give voice to that which has been silenced, to revalorize *la part maudite* by alchemically transmuting bourgeois dreck into revolutionary gold. Wohlfarth compares the historian-ragpicker to the dialectician: bending over to pick up chance trash, he imitates an Hegelian *Aufhebung* that simultaneously preserves and cancels the past—history at once annihilated and redeemed.

"Construction presupposes destruction," Benjamin observes of his project (587). Inspired by the revolutionary nihilism of Dada and Surrealism, his early drafts show him determined to rip away the delusive appearance [*Schein*] of harmony and totality from the bourgeois ideology

of culture in order to show it for what it really is: a junkheap of stereotypes and received ideas, fragments shored against ruins. But having
blasted apart the temple of culture, he will ingather the diaspora of its
debris into his arcade: having declared its bankruptcy, he will reinvest it
with value—not the auratic, fetishized cult value traditionally accorded to
the sacred cultural artifacts of the bourgeoisie, but rather that politicized,
demystified "exhibition value" of which he later speaks in "The Work of
Art in the Age of Mechanical Reproduction." The very principle of the
arcade—commodities on display—is therefore turned against itself by a
kind of inspired homeopathy. The writing of history, Benjamin suggests,
can henceforth dispense with description or narration; all it need do is
perform the deixis implied in the German verb *zeigen:* to show, to exhibit,
to indicate, to say by pointing, to silently name.

Benjamin's redefinition of historiography as exhibit (in both the legal
and museological sense) is tied to his desire to achieve "the utmost
concreteness" in his presentation of the physiognomy of an entire era
(1091). Benjamin's "city portraits" of this period—the Berlin of *One-Way
Street* (1928), his essays on Naples (1925), Moscow (1927), and Marseilles
(1929)—offer similar instances of a *Sachlichkeit* intent on pointing only to
the literal signatures of things.[19] He writes Martin Buber in 1927, "I want
to write a description of Moscow at the present moment in which 'all
factuality is already theory' and which would thereby refrain from any
deductive abstraction, from any prognostication and, even within certain
limits, from any judgment."[20] This "materialist" bracketing of theory
becomes even more pronounced in the first drafts of his *Pariser Passagen*. Retreating from the explicitly metaphysical concerns of his earlier,
more philosophical works, Benjamin now espouses a radical "science of
the concrete" (Lévi-Strauss) or "magical positivism" (Adorno):

> Formula: Construction out of fact. Construction with the complete
> elimination of theory. Something only Goethe attempted in his mor-
> phological writings. (1033)

Goethe's "zarte Empirie," his gentle attention to the minute particulars
of plant structure, will be brought to bear not on nature but on history, or
as Adorno puts it, on "constellations of historical entities which do not
remain simply interchangeable examples for ideas, but which in their
uniqueness constitute the ideas as historical."[21] No ideas but in things.
No things but in history.

The "things" or "facts" to be displayed in Benjamin's Arcade will be brought together (or apart) by what he terms "literary montage." (1030) References to film are scattered throughout his early drafts:

> Re the contemporary rhythm that in fact defines this project. It is very characteristic of the movies that the oppositions created by the jerky sequence of the images (which fulfill the deepest exigency of the genre) should be denied by the "flow" of the "development" and gliding musical accompaniment. To rid the image of history of any trace of "development". . . (1013)

Benjamin's reflections on montage (which bear a remarkable family resemblance to the "ideogrammic" methods that Pound and Eisenstein were at the same time developing from their studies of the Chinese character)[22] represent an attempt to move historiography into a more graphic, cinematic mode of presentation whose rapid-fire juxtaposition of "small, fleeting pictures" would serve to unsettle the "professional coziness" of traditional historicism (1034). What draws Benjamin to film is its quality of concrete presence, its proximity; he speaks of applying this "technique of nearness" (1015) to a historiography constructed on that most minimal of narrative frames or images, the anecdote:

> Anecdote brings things closer to us in space, allows them to enter into our lives. Anecdote represents the extreme opposite of history—which demands an "empathy" that renders everything abstract. Empathy amounts to the same thing as reading newspapers. The true method of making things present is: to imagine them in our own space (and not to imagine ourselves in their space). Only anecdote can move us in this direction. (1014)

Anecdotes do not so much tell stories as epitomize situations: genuine nearness is only possible, then, when narrative is condensed into name.

Despite the nostalgia for the traditional narrative modes that informs such essays as "The Storyteller" (1936), Benjamin's predilection for the poetics of parataxis is evident throughout his critical career—from his early work on Hölderlin's "harte Fügung" (1915) and romantic theories of the fragment (1919), through his later investigations into the brittle intermittences of the baroque *Trauerspiel* (1927), the uncanny collages of Surrealism (1929), the apocalyptic mosaics of Karl Kraus (1931), or the didactic discontinuities of the Brechtian stage (1931, 1939):

> Like pictures in a film, the epic theater moves in spurts. Its basic form

is that of the shock with which the single, well-defined situations of the play collide. The songs, the captions, the lifeless conventions set off one situation from another. This brings about intervals which, if anything, impair the illusion of the audience and paralyze its readiness for empathy. These intervals are reserved for the spectator's critical reaction—to the actions of the players and to the way in which they are presented.[23]

"Epic history" in the same sense as Brecht's "epic theater," the *Arcades Project* will not only administer the shock therapy of montage to block the transference projected onto the past by historicist "empathy," but more importantly, by deploying its materials into a rhythm of caesurae it will break the illusion that anything like continuity or causality connects past to present. This is perhaps the most far-reaching intuition of Benjamin's early notes toward the *Pariser Passagen:* history is not a cumulative, additive narrative in which the uninterrupted syntagm of time flows homogeneously from past to future, but rather a montage where any moment may enter into sudden adjacency with another. History as parataxis—time scattered through space like stars, its course no longer taking the form of progress but leaping forth in the momentary flashes of dialectical constellations.

Writing to Scholem in mid-1932, Benjamin observes that although many of his works have assured him "victories on a small scale," these various successes have been offset by "large-scale defeats." Among the projects he defines as "disaster areas whose boundaries I can no longer survey," he includes his study of the Paris arcades, now five years in the making and already a ruin (1096). Benjamin seems to have broken off work on the *Pariser Passagen* in late 1929 after having submitted his first drafts to the criticism of Adorno, Horkheimer and Asja Lacis. The precise upshot of these discussions remains unclear, but Benjamin in later letters refers to them as marking the "end of an era," as provoking a decisive break with the "rhapsodic naiveté" and "romantic form" that had characterized the "carefree, archaic, nature-oriented philosophizing" of his early notes (1117). He informs Scholem in early 1930: "Whereas up to now I had been absorbed on the one hand by documentation and, on the other, by metaphysics, I now see that to complete the project, to give it a solid scaffolding, I will need nothing less than a study of certain aspects of Hegel and of certain parts of *Capital*." (1094) Although his early drafts contain in embryonic form virtually all of the major directions his project would subsequently take, it would appear that Benjamin had now been (tempo-

rarily) convinced that only a rigorous application of dialectical materialism could mediate the gap that had developed between "documentation"
and "metaphysics," between the Surrealist *bricolage* of individual fact
and a more global Marxist philosophy of history. The ongoing gestation of
the *Arcades Project* over the course of the thirties may in a sense be
understood as Benjamin's attempt both to resolve *and* maintain this contradiction.

The various theoretical and methodological aporias identified by
Adorno, Horkheimer, Lacis, and, somewhat later, by Brecht, would keep
the *Pariser Passagen* stalled for the next four years. It was only in early
1934, upon taking up definitive exile in Paris, that Benjamin would return
to the project he had abandoned as a ruin. He orders special note paper
from Berlin, establishes a rigorous reading schedule at the Bibliothèque
Nationale, and speaks of the "fresh face" (1103) that the enterprise has
taken on as a result of "new and far-reaching sociological perspectives."
(1118) At the end of March he reports that he has provisionally divided his
work into chapters (1103), and by November can claim to Horkheimer
that "the clear structure of the book now lies before my eyes." (1105)
Optimistic as these accounts might sound, Benjamin's progress reports
are very much *ad hominem*, addressed as they are to friends and colleagues instrumental in arranging the financial support of his project by
the Frankfurt Institute for Social Research. Other letters show him less
confident; to Gretel Adorno, for example, he cryptically confides that his
Arcade is the "tertius gaudens between myself and fate." (1100) Even
after having bowed to the request of Friederich Pollock to produce a *mise
au point* of the project for the Institute in 1935 (the *exposé* entitled "Paris,
die Hauptstadt des XIX. Jahrhunderts"), Benjamin admits to Scholem
that "countless questions still remain unresolved" and wonders whether
his undertaking will ever manage a dialectical synthesis of its ever-
growing mass of materials (1113).

Reading between the lines of Benjamin's correspondence, one can
sense the tremendous pressures he was working under during the thirties—the professional and financial uncertainties of his emigré life in
Paris, the ongoing need to justify his Institute stipendium by orthodox
publications, the intellectual pressures exerted on his project by his close
associates (exemplified by Adorno's devastating critique of the 1935 *exposé*), and finally the aura of mounting expectation that had for a number
of years surrounded what his friends believed would be the crowning
achievement of his career (1115). Little wonder, then, if Benjamin seems
to retreat into oracular equivocation when pressed to define the precise
stage or vector of his project. Again and again he insists on the "provi-

sional character'' (1159) of his current work, asking that it be merely considered as a ''preliminary investigation'' for a text whose definitive organization still escapes him (1158). Indeed, at one point he writes to Scholem that his project may amount to nothing more than a series of prolegomena and parilipomena—prefaces or addenda to a missing book (1095).

''L'oeuvre est l'attente de l'oeuvre,'' Blanchot observes of Mallarmé.[24] From 1934 to 1940, Benjamin expends much of his time and intellectual energy simply waiting for his work to take shape. He begins, at long last, a serious study of Marx in order to define the central theoretical concept that he hopes will unify the entire project, namely, the notion of commodity fetishism: he compiles the 900 pages of documentation that Tiedemann has gathered under the editorial title ''Aufzeichnungen und Materialien'' (''Notes and Materials''); he shuffles and reshuffles his data into some 36 different cross-referenced *Konvolute* or thematic rubrics; he sketches out two rough groundplans for his edifice (the 1935 and 1939 *exposés* of ''Paris, Capital of the 19th Century''); he quarries his mass of notes to produce, at the Institute's request, collateral studies of Eduard Fuchs (1937) and two essays on Baudelaire (1938, 1939). As Michel Espagne and Michael Werner have argued on the basis of manuscripts recently rediscovered at the Bibliothèque Nationale, Benjamin's Baudelaire studies pinpoint the extremely problematic textual imbrications of the *Arcades Project* in its later stages.[25] Initially intended as the penultimate chapter of this magnum opus (according to the blueprint of ''Paris, Capital of the 19th Century''), Benjamin's 1938 Baudelaire essay gradually becomes, as he informs Horkheimer, a ''miniature model'' of the entire work (1164). In the course of its elaboration, however, this *mise en abyme* of the Arcade increasingly takes on its own life as a full-fledged, independent book which, although not identical to the *Passagen* as Benjamin insists (1167), nonetheless threatens to displace and devour the whole of which it was originally only destined to be a minor part.

But to conclude, as Espagne and Werner do, that the secret architecture or definitive plan of the *Arcades Project* is to be found in Benjamin's notes toward his projected Baudelaire book is to underestimate the radically processual, open-ended nature of his fragmentary work-in-progress. Indeed, it may be a misnomer to speak of it as a *work* at all (except in Blanchot's sense of an ''oeuvre de l'absence d'oeuvre''). Benjamin himself most frequently refers to it simply as his *Passagen* or *Passagenarbeit*, that is, as a passage or project. Tiedemann's title, *Das Passagen-Werk*, is an editorial invention that runs the risk of reifying an exploratory process of writing into an inert textual artifact. Benjamin, by contrast, describes his Arcade not as a work but as an ongoing event, a peripatetic meditation or *flânerie* in which everything chanced upon en route becomes a potential direction his thoughts might take (570, 587). Elsewhere he compares its composition to a slow ascension:

> How this project was written: rung by rung, as chance offered a narrow foothold; and always like someone climbing dangerous heights, not looking around for a second, in order not to get dizzy (but also to save the full power of the panorama stretched before him for the very end). (575)

Characteristically, Benjamin here posits an eventual telos to his labors, but defers this moment of panoramic fulfillment to some as of yet undefined future—very much in the same fashion that Ernst Bloch in his *Geist der Utopie* speaks of works of art as anticipatory images or Messianic promises of a Utopian totality that they cannot in and of themselves embody but that they nevertheless indicate as still to come.[26] Ever in progress, ever in preparation (or ruin), Benjamin's Arcade contains its eventual completion within itself as a faint principle of hope, but like the *flâneur* or gambler or Wandering Jew, his fate is above all to wait—a passenger in time, trusting that at any moment his destination might arrive.

In the meantime, Benjamin spends his days at the Bibliothèque Nationale patiently reading and writing. As he observes in his study of the *Trauerspiel,* "the Renaissance explores the universe, the baroque explores libraries."[27] Tiedemann lists some 850 sources consulted between 1934 and 1940; Espagne and Werner have in turn discovered a list of 400 additional bibliographical references that Benjamin apparently planned to investigate before his death. The sheer volume of preparatory research seems to overwhelm any completion of the project, bogging it down in a "Saturnine tempo" (1115) of archival melancholia:

> These notes, which deal with the Paris arcades, were begun under the open sky—a cloudless blue that arced over the foliage—and yet they are covered with centuries of dust from millions of leaves through which have blown the fresh breeze of diligence, the measured breath of the researcher, the squalls of youthful zeal, and the idle gusts of curiosity. For the painted summer sky that peers down from arcades in the reading room of the Paris National Library has stretched its dreamy, unlit ceiling over them. (571)

27

As he sits taking notes in the dream-arcade of the Bibliothèque Nationale, conjuring up the shades of the past like a necromancer (571), Benjamin is tempted into a phantasmagoria of erudition akin both to the allegorical encyclopedism of the baroque and to that more distinctively modern experience of the fantastic which Foucault locates in Flaubert:

> This domain of phantasms is no longer the night, the sleep of reason, or the uncertain void that stands before desire, but on the contrary, wakefulness, untiring attention, zealous erudition, and constant vigilance. Henceforth, the visionary experience arises from the black and white surface of printed signs, from the closed and dusty volume that opens with a flight of forgotten words; fantasies are carefully deployed in the hushed library, with its columns of books, with its titles aligned on shelves to form a tight enclosure, but within confines that also liberate impossible worlds. . . . Dreams are no longer summoned with closed eyes, but in reading; and a true image is now a product of learning; it derives from words spoken in the past, exact recensions, the amassing of minute fact, monuments reproduced to infinitesimal fragments, and the reproductions of reproductions. . . . The imaginary is not formed in opposition to reality as its denial or compensation; it grows among signs, from book to book, in the interstices of repetitions and commentaries, it is born and takes shape in the interval between books. It is a phenomenon of the library.[28]

But if Benjamin's phantasmagoria of the Library recalls Flaubert's Saint Anthony, the encyclopedic ambitions of the *Arcades Project* more resemble the *sottisier* of *Bouvard et Pécuchet,* a dictionary designed to annihilate the entire 19th century by reducing it to a catalogue of clichés. Like Flaubert's two retired clerks, Benjamin discovers a kind of saintly vocation in the sheer act of copying, day after day, passages culled from the Archive. Of the quarter of a million words that comprise Tiedemann's edition, at least 75 percent are direct transcriptions of texts Benjamin collected over thirteen years. The amount of source material he copies so exceeds anything he might conceivably need to adduce as documentary evidence in an eventual book that one can only conclude that this ritual of transcription is less a rehearsal for his *livre à venir* than its most central *rite de passage:*

> The power of a country road is different when one is walking along it from when one is flying over it by airplane. In the same way, the power of a text is different when it is read from when it is copied out. The

airplane passenger sees only how the road pushes through the land-scape, how it unfolds according to the same laws as the terrain sur-rounding it. Only he who walks the road on foot learns of the power it commands. . . . Only the copied text commands the soul of him who is occupied with it, whereas the mere reader never discovers the new aspects of his inner self that are opened by the text, that road cut through the interior jungle forever closing behind it: because the reader follows the movement of his mind in the free flight of day-dreaming, whereas the copier submits to its command.[29]

Renouncing the panoptic presumptions of traditional historicism, Ben-jamin the scrivener places himself at the eye- or street-level of history. His relation to his material is not one of domination, but one of willing, ascetic submission. Like a religious scribe or halakhist, he will serve his text (no matter how profane) in order to save it by faithful reiteration, by reproducing its likeness. For just as copy mimes original, so the very gesture of writing (according to Benjamin's theories of graphology) re-veals language itself as man's highest mimetic faculty.[30] Like that ideal interlinear translation of which he speaks in "The Task of the Translator" (where "the sentence is the wall before the language of the original [but] literalness is the arcade"), the act of copying involves a repetition of the same, a reduplication of identity—but an identity that contains within itself a crucial, infinitesimal difference.[31] For in the asymptotic distance that separates the original from its literal translation, the document from its handwritten transcription, lies that ontological threshold where, ac-cording to Benjamin, "pure language" may come into being. Foucault:

Because to copy is to *do* nothing: it is to *be* the books being copied. It is to be this tiny protrusion of redoubled language, of discourse folded upon itself; this invisible existence transforms fleeting words into an enduring and distant murmur. Saint Anthony was able to triumph over the Eternal Book in becoming the languageless movement of pure mat-ter; Bouvard and Pécuchet triumph over everything alien to books, all that resists the book by transforming themselves into the continuous movement of the book.[32]

Becoming the arcade of what he copies, giving himself up to the inter-textual passage of language, Benjamin observes a silence that allows the past to speak, to awake, to resurrect as Book—"tout, au monde, existe pour aboutir à un livre." (Mallarmé). But if the act of copying serves to redeem or raise the fallen language of the original into a new (Messianic) light, this *Aufhebung* also observes an opposite impulse—to cancel the original by mimesis, to erase it by repetition. Benjamin's comments on Karl Kraus's satirical personae perfectly define the strategy: "He imitates his subjects in order to insert the crowbar of his hate into the finest joints of their posture . . . he creeps into those he impersonates in order to annihilate them. . . . 'When the age laid hands upon itself, he was the hands.' "[33] Further on in the same essay, Benjamin compares Kraus's impersonations to cannibalism because they demonstrate "the true mystery of satire, which consists in devouring the adversary." In a certain sense, the textual indigestion of the *Arcades Project* also identifies it as a version of satire (and herein its affinities not only to Kraus's *Last Days of Mankind* but also to *Bouvard and Pécuchet, Ulysses,* and *Cantos*). Benjamin himself alludes to the "dietetics" of his project (603) and frequently describes the activity of the collector as a hunting and gathering of nourishment (as in his study of Fuchs, "le monsieur qui mange tout Paris").[34] The years spent copying at the Bibliothèque Nationale resemble a protracted Menippean banquet at which Benjamin feasts on the corpse (or corpus) of the bourgeoisie, hoping, by his sheer appetite for transcription, to ingest the entire 19th century, to devour the enemy that still gnaws on the present—the historian as cannibal, like eating like.

To copy is to place invisible quotation marks around the passage transcribed; excerpted from their original context, the words acquire a new kind of margin that enables them to speak as if italicized. Benjamin's fascination with citation reaches back to his early studies of the romantic fragment and is already exemplified by the critical strategy of his *Trauerspiel* thesis, an assemblage of over 600 quotations arranged in what he calls the "craziest mosaic technique imaginable" in order "to plumb the depths of language and thought . . . by drilling rather than excavation."[35] But it is only in his later essays on Kraus and Brecht that he begins to formulate explicitly the theory of quotation that will guide the textual montage of his Arcade. In Kraus's art of polemical or parodic quotation he discovers the paradoxically creative and destructive power of all language:

In the quotation that both saves and chastises, language proves the matrix of justice. It summons the word by its name, wrenches it destructively from its context, but precisely thereby calls it back to its origin. It appears, now with rhyme and reason, sonorously, congruously in the structure of a new text. As rhyme it gathers the similar into its aura; as name it stands alone and expressionless. In quotation the two realms—of origin and destruction—justify themselves before language. And conversely, only where they interpenetrate—in quotation—is language consummated.[36]

"To quote a word," Benjamin observes, "is to call it by its name," to restore it to its primal identity and autonomy, to reendow it with distance. But a quotation is also a rhyme, an original text and its repetition speaking the same words at different times, each bringing the other into a new proximity, each gathering the other's echo into its voice. As a figure of rhyme, quotation thus resembles the metaphorical structure of the dialectical image—two elements, two perspectives, two eras interpenetrating in juxtaposition: distance and closeness, preservation and annihilation, then and now, the original context in which a word or thing initially appeared and its political repositioning in (or as) the present. As with the dialectical image, the sense of the quotation lies less in the actual words cited than in the very fact of their repetition, for the act of citation institutes a (temporal) gap that transforms the quotation into a sign, each portion of which is reciprocally signifier and signified (just as the 19th century is the signifier of the 20th and vice versa).[37] By heightening texts, by providing them with the invisible majuscules that convert them into names or allegorical insignia, quotation thus fulfills the most crucial calling of language—to render justice, to issue a citation, to summon the world before the tribunal of the word.

Benjamin's essay on Kraus explores the ontological and semiotic dimensions of quotation; his studies of Brecht (particularly the 1939 version of "What is Epic Theater?") extend its tactical implications for historiography. "Epic theater," he notes, "does not reproduce situations, it uncovers them. This uncovering is accomplished by the interruption of sequences."[38] Similarly, the *Arcades Project* cites the past not in order to reproduce it, but in order to reveal it, to literalize it, to lay bare its device by the alienating effect of quotation marks. And like Brechtian theater, it "makes gestures quotable" by interrupting their context, by creating a space around them—as Benjamin observes, "an actor must be able to space his gestures the way a typesetter produces spaced type."[39] Quotation in the *Arcades Project* likewise introduces punctuation into the specious continuum of history, articulating blanks and margins that fundamentally alter its traditional layout. Transformed into a montage of disconnected citations, it offers itself to a new kind of scansion: the text it proposes is so literal it can only be read between the lines.

Although etymologically rooted in verbs of motion (the Latin "ciere" or Greek "kinein"), citation does precisely the reverse in the *Passagen,* for its purpose is not to excite movement (or empathy) but on the contrary to arrest the flow of history, to bring it to a standstill, to petrify it with a Medusan gaze. Directing its mirror at modernity, quotation catches it in the sorry act of repetition, revealing it as a phantasmagoria of *das Immerwiedergleiche,* an eternal replication of the Same. By a kind of Brechtian *Umfunktionierung,* citation thus ceases to be an appeal to precedent or a strategy whereby the past is invoked to legitimize the present, but instead becomes a means of subverting authority altogether—not only the authority of tradition, but in the case of Benjamin's Arcade, the very authority of author over text. By reducing himself to a "modest recording device" (Breton's characterization of the Surrealist poet), Benjamin in effect gives up any authorial claim to his work: the words he copies are, after all, not *his,* but belong to other voices, other eras and, for the most, adopt a language (French) that is not his own. Preferring to let the documents he has collected speak for themselves, Benjamin vanishes into the intertextual murmur of the Archive, present only as the invisible hand that attaches quotation marks to the past or sites its passages into new constellations.

Benjamin's Arcade is both the book of a dream (like *Finnegan's Wake*) and the dream of a book (like Mallarmé's *Livre*). In its most Utopian conception—a text without author, speaking entirely by quotation—it approaches that "pure language" ("which no longer means or expresses anything, but is") evoked in "The Task of the Translator" and which Benjamin associates with the divine *logos* of Holy Scripture, for only the Bible is "unconditionally translatable," just as "only for a redeemed mankind does its past become citable in all its moments."[40] Total translatability, total citability: Benjamin's Messianic perspective, as Giorgio Agamben has shown, telescopes historical and linguistic categories into a single prophetic vision of universal history as (or in) universal language, all of time gathered into a single Arcade, all the tongues of Babel stilled in the passage of the Word:

The Messianic world is the world of total and integral actuality. Only in this world can a universal history exist. What is termed universal history today can only be a kind of Esperanto. Nothing can correspond to it as long as the confusion that proceeds from the Tower of Babel still persists. Universal history presupposes a language into which every text of a living or dead tongue can be translated intact. Or better yet, it is itself this language. But not as a written language but rather as a celebrated language. This celebration is pure of all ceremony and knows no songs of celebration. Its language is the idea of prose itself, understandable to all men, just as the language of birds is understandable to all of Sunday's children.[41]

The *Passagenarbeit,* however, is not quite (or not yet) this transparent Messianic language—the anonymous speech of the prose of the world. Indeed, what makes its manuscript such a philological enigma is that its pages are not simply a collective of quotations but also include, dispersed here and there, Benjamin's own personal commentaries and meditations. This has led Tiedemann to compare the entire project to a blue-print for an eventual edifice whose building blocks would be provided by the documentary quotations and whose mortar would in turn be supplied by the theoretical reflections (12). In his edition he has accordingly printed those portions of the manuscript that feature commentary on Benjamin's part in larger type than the unannotated citations. Although apparently a neutral editorial procedure designed to facilitate the reading of the text, Tiedemann's decision in fact typographically *privileges* commentary over quotation, theoretical reflection over scholarly research, while strongly suggesting that the project would have eventually taken a discursive form not unlike Benjamin's essays on Baudelaire (i.e. with all the excess quotation pared away and somehow integrated into or subordinated to the large-type commentary). Benjamin's letters show that he was perfectly aware of this antinomy between materialist scholarship and metaphysical (or theological) speculation. But his manuscripts would seem to indicate that he meant this divorce to stand, or more precisely, that he wanted to inscribe citation and commentary, the text and its interpretation on the *same plane* of the page (with the uncanny result that even his own authorial intrusions, many of which can be found in his other published works, themselves begin to sound like quotations).

By situating its "primary" sources and "secondary" reflections on the same textual (or graphological) level, Benjamin's manuscript places into radical question the very possibility of *metalanguage,* that is, of a discourse that might somehow stand above, outside, or beyond that of which it speaks. Composed in the Utopian image of the classless society, the Arcade's handwritten pages institute a communism of discourse that not only assembles the voices of high and mass culture on an equal footing but, more crucially, democratizes the traditional hierarchies separating author from reader, original from copy, citation from commentary, philology from theory[42]—like the *passage* itself, the text that thus emerges has no *outsides.* In this it resembles that polyphonic play of language which Bakhtin terms heteroglossia—different voices, different discourses refracting each other in dialogue.[43] Rather than move beyond contradiction into some monologic synthesis, Benjamin's hybrid text pointedly displays the heterogeneity of its component parts in order to maintain precisely those aporias (*aporos,* without passage) that, according to Schlegel, define dialogue as "a crown of fragments."

"Many of the works of the Ancients have become fragments. Many works of the Moderns are fragments the moment they come into being" (Schlegel again).[44] Or as Benjamin observes in his study of the *Trauerspiel:* "That which lies here in ruins, the highly significant fragment, the remnant, is in fact the finest material of baroque creation. For it is a common practice of the literature of the baroque to pile up fragments ceaselessly, without any strict idea of a goal, and to take the repetition of stereotypes for a process of intensification, in the unremitting expectation of a miracle."[45] But if Benjamin's Arcade piles up fragments like some baroque apotheosis, it does so under an empty sky and only in the most tenuous hope of the miracle that might ultimately put an end to its years of exile. Like the celebrated angel of the late "Theses on the Concept of History," the composition of the *Passagen* reverses the traditional figure of progress: backing its way into the future of its eventual completion, Benjamin's Arcade turns its face toward the past—where, page after tiny page, its writing gradually takes on the shape of a permanent catastrophe and assumes the eloquence of a giant ruin. The melancholy conclusion of Benjamin's *Trauerspiel* book provides, even before the project has begun, its prophetic epitaph:

In the ruins of great buildings the idea of their plan speaks more impressively than in lesser buildings, however well preserved these might be; and for this reason the (Arcade) merits interpretation. In the spirit of allegory it is conceived from the outset as a ruin, a fragment. Others may shine resplendently as on the first day; this form preserves the image of beauty to the very last.[46]

NOTES

1 *Reflections,* ed. Peter Demetz, trans. Edmund Jephcott (New York: Harcourt Brace, 1978), p. 64.
2 *Gesammelte Schriften,* vol. 5, ed. Rolf Tiedemann (Frankfurt: Suhrkamp, 1982), p. 1094. Hereafter all page numbers in the text refer to this volume. Most of the background material to the *Arcades Project* is drawn from Tiedemann's introduction to the volume, as well as from the "Editorischer Bericht" and the "Zeugnisse zur Entstehungsgeschichte" on pp. 1068-1205. Among useful studies of the *Arcades Project* in English are Susan Buck-Morss's two essays, "Benjamin's *Passagen-Werk:* Redeeming Mass

Culture for the Revolution," *New German Critique,* no. 29 (Spring-Summer, 1983), and "The *Passagen-Werk:* Walter Benjamin's Theory of Mass Culture," *New German Critique* (1984); and Richard Wolin's "Experience and Materialism in Benjamin's *Passagen-Werk,*" this volume, pp. 210-27. Readers of French will find some 46 essays on the project in the recently published proceedings of the 1983 international colloquium on Benjamin and Paris: *Walter Benjamin et Paris,* ed. Heinz Wisman (Paris: Cerf, 1986).

3 Hannah Arendt, "Introduction," in *Illuminations,* ed. Hannah Arendt, trans. Harry Zohn (New York: Schocken, 1969), p. 12.

4 *The Origin of German Tragic Drama,* trans. John Osborne (London: New Left Books, 1977), p. 182.

5 "Theses on the Philosophy of History," in *Illuminations,* p. 264.

6 Benjamin's early drafts of the *Arcades Project* have been gathered by Tiedemann under the titles "Erste Notizen" and "Frühe Entwürfe" on pp. 991-1059 of his edition. They include "Pariser Passagen I" (a series of fragments that Tiedemann places somewhere between 1927 and 1929); "Passagen" (the draft of an essay apparently related to the newspaper article on the Paris arcades that Benjamin had planned to write with Franz Hessel in 1927); "Pariser Passagen II" (a more "finished" series of fragments that Benjamin apparently showed to Adorno and Horkheimer in 1929); "Der Saturnring oder Etwas vom Eisenbau" (a short essay of 1928 or 1929). If I emphasize these early drafts in my discussion, it is because they constitute the blueprint beneath the palimpsest, the Ur-Arcade onto which later extensions of the text will be annexed. Like some Goethean *Urphänomen,* they reveal a process of (or at) origin, a beginning that Benjamin's project will continue to repeat.

7 See also "On Language as Such and on the Language of Man" and "On the Mimetic Faculty" in *Reflections,* pp. 314-336, as well as "Doctrine of the Similar" in *New German Critique,* no. 17 (Spring, 1979). Irving Wohlfarth, "Sur quelques motifs juifs chez Benjamin," *Revue d'Esthétique,* no. 1 (1981), contains an important analysis of the notion of name in Benjamin's work.

8 Cf. Benjamin's remarks on Breton in his 1929 "Surrealism" essay: "He was the first to perceive the revolutionary energies that appear in the 'outmoded,' in the first iron constructions, the first factory buildings, the earliest photos, the objects that have begun to be extinct, grand pianos, the dresses of five years ago, fashionable restaurants when the vogue has begun to ebb from them." *Reflections* p. 181. See also Jacques Leenhardt, "Le passage comme forme d'expérience: Benjamin face à Aragon," in *Walter Benjamin et Paris,* pp. 163-172.

9 The standard architectural and social history of the *passages* is Johann Friederich Geist, *Arcades: The History of a Building Type* (Cambridge: MIT, 1983).

10 *The Origin of German Tragic Drama,* p. 178.

11 See Richard Wolin, *Walter Benjamin: An Aesthetic of Redemption* (New York: Columbia, 1982), pp. 129 and 174.

12 The implications of *passages* for modern French poetry are explored by Mary Ann Caws, *A Metapoetics of the Passage: Architextures in Surrealism and After* (Hanover: University Press of New England, 1981).

13 See Winfried Menninghaus, "Science des seuils," in *Walter Benjamin et Paris,* pp. 529-558.

14 Benjamin uses the term several times in the *Arcades Project* (e.g. p. 617), which would seem to indicate an acquaintance with Van Gennep's work.

15 Benjamin's *Trauerspiel* study reaches its visionary apex with a similar prophecy of

redemption or resurrection via *Umschlag:* "Ultimately in the death-signs of the baroque the direction of allegorical reflection is reversed; on the second part of its wide arc it returns, to redeem. . . . All this vanishes with this *one* about-turn, in which the immersion of allegory has to clear away the final phantasmagoria of the objective and, left entirely to its own devices, re-discovers itself, not playfully in the earthly world of things, but seriously under the eyes of heaven. And this is the essence of melancholy immersion: that its ultimate objects, in which it believes it can most fully secure for itself that which is vile, turn into allegories, and that these allegories fill out and deny the void in which they are represented, just as, ultimately, the intention does not faithfully rest in the contemplation of bones, but faithlessly leaps forward to the idea of resurrection." (pp. 232-233)

16 *Gesammelte Schriften,* vol. 4, p. 284. See also the comments on this passage by Henri Meschonnic, "L'allégorie chez Walter Benjamin, une aventure juive," in *Walter Benjamin et Paris,* p. 735. Meschonnic sees in Benjaminian dialectics the "structure renversive" (or *vav*) of Biblical Hebrew.
17 *Reflections,* p. 69. See also "Lob der Puppe," *Gesammelte Schriften,* vol. 3, p. 213.
18 Irving Wohlfarth, "Et Cetera? De l'historien comme chiffonnier," in *Walter Benjamin et Paris,* pp. 559-609. Here and throughout this essay I am most indebted to Wohlfarth's path-breaking study.
19 See "Walter Benjamin's 'City Portraits'" in Peter Szondi, *On Textual Understanding and Other Essays,* trans. Harvey Mendelsohn (Minneapolis: University of Minnesota Press, 1986), pp. 133-144.
20 *Moscow Diary,* ed. Gary Smith, trans. Richard Sieburth, *October* 35 (Winter 1985), p. 132.
21 Theodor Adorno, *Prisms,* trans. Samuel and Shierry Weber (London: Neville Spearman, 1967), p. 231.
22 See Hugh Kenner, *The Pound Era* (Berkeley: University of California, 1971), p. 162, and Marjorie Perloff, *The Poetics of Indeterminacy: Rimbaud to Cage* (Princeton: Princeton University Press, 1981).
23 *Illuminations,* p. 152.
24 Maurice Blanchot, *Le Livre à venir* (Paris: Gallimard, 1959), p. 351.
25 Michel Espagne and Michael Werner, "Les manuscrits parisiens de Walter Benjamin et le *Passagen-Werk,*" in *Walter Benjamin et Paris,* pp. 849-882. These "Paris manuscripts" were discovered by Giorgio Agamben in 1981 among Georges Bataille's papers at the Bibliothéque Nationale.
26 See Wolin, *Walter Benjamin,* p. 25, and Fredric Jameson, *Marxism and Form* (Princeton: Princeton University Press, 1971), pp. 145-159.
27 *The Origin of German Tragic Drama,* p. 140.
28 "Fantasia of the Library," in Michel Foucault, *Language, Counter-Memory, Practice,* ed. Donald Bouchard (Ithaca: Cornell University Press, 1977), p. 91. In his "Konvolut K" ("Dream-City, Dream-House"), Benjamin quotes Pierre Mabille's Borgesian vision of "a library where all the books have blended into each other and where all the titles have been erased" (490).
29 *Reflections,* p. 66; further comments on copying may be found on pp. 68, 77-81.
30 See "On the Mimetic Faculty" in *Reflections,* pp. 335-336, and "Zur Graphologie" in vol. 6 of the *Gesammelte Schriften,* p. 185. Benjamin, it might be added, occasionally worked as a professional graphologist.
31 *Illuminations,* p. 79. Derrida's reading of "The Task of the Translator" is the centerpiece

of *Difference in Translation,* ed. Joseph Graham (Ithaca: Cornell University Press, 1985), pp. 209-248.

32 "Fantasia of the Library," p. 109.

33 *Reflections,* pp. 252-253.

34 "Eduard Fuchs: Collector and Historian," in *The Essential Frankfurt School Reader,* ed. Andrew Arato and Eike Gebhardt (New York: Urizen Books, 1978), p. 243.

35 Quoted in Hannah Arendt, "Introduction," *Illuminations,* pp. 8 and 49-50. On Benjamin and citation see also Dietrich Thierkopf, "Nähe und Ferne," *Text + Kritik,* nos. 31/32 (October 1971), pp. 3-18, and Dolf Oehler, "Science et poésie de la citation dans le *Passagen-Werk,*" in *Walter Benjamin et Paris,* pp. 839-847.

36 *Reflections,* p. 269.

37 Antoine Compagnon, *La seconde main, ou le travail de la citation* (Paris: Seuil, 1979) develops a semiotic analysis of citation, in Peircean terms. Benjamin's quotations may be said to resemble *iconic* signs, that is, signs that *exhibit* their object.

38 *Reflections,* p. 234.

39 *Illuminations,* p. 151.

40 Illuminations, pp. 80 and 254.

41 *Gesammelte Schriften,* vol. 1, p. 1238. See Giorgio Agamben, "Langue et histoire, Catégories historiques et catégories linguistiques dans la pensée de Benjamin," *Walter Benjamin et Paris,* pp. 793-807. Agamben relates the idea of universal "prose" in the above passage to an observation of Valéry's that Benjamin noted down: "The essence of prose is to perish, that is, to be understood, that is, to be dissolved, completely destroyed, entirely replaced by image or impulse." Prose, in other words, is language as pure passage. Cf. Benjamin's comments in his "Theologico-Political Fragment:" "For nature is Messianic by reason of its eternal and total passing away (*Vergängnis*)." *Reflections,* p. 313.

42 Cf. Paul de Man, "The Return to Philology," in *The Resistance to Theory* (Minneapolis: University of Minnesota, 1986), pp. 21-26.

43 See M. M. Bakhtin, *The Dialogic Imagination,* ed. Michael Holquist (Austin: University of Texas, 1981). Benjamin's vision of universal history/language as celebration or *Fest* can be linked to the "carnivalization" of which Bakhtin speaks in his study of Rabelais. A useful comparison of Benjamin and Bakhtin (mediated by Adorno) is provided by Pierre Zima, "L'ambivalence dialectique: entre Benjamin et Bakhtine," *Revue d'Esthétique,* no. 1 (1981), pp. 131-140.

44 Friedrich Schlegel, *Schriften zur Literatur,* ed. Wolfdietrich Rasch (Munich: DTV, 1972), pp. 27 and 32.

45 *The Origin of German Tragic Drama,* p. 178.

46 Ibid., p. 235 (translation slightly modified).

TRANSLATORS' INTRODUCTION TO "N"

The "Notes and Materials" of Benjamin's *Arcades Project* are composed of hundreds of 22×28 centimeter sheets of yellowish paper that have been folded in half to create 14×22 folios, the first and third sides of which contain Benjamin's miniscule notes in blue or black ink.[1] Each group of these folios is in turn gathered into a *Konvolut* or sheaf according to its central paradigm or theme. The manuscript is divided into 36 such sheafs, their titles keyed to the letters of the alphabet. In addition to Benjamin's occasional crossreferences to the rubrics of other sheafs (indicated between asterisks in the following translation), 32 mysterious symbols (squares, triangles, circles, vertical and horizontal crosses, etc. in various inks and colors) also punctuate the manuscript, apparently privately coded to those portions of the *Arcades* that Benjamin intended to incorporate into the Baudelaire book he was planning in 1937-1938.[2] Rolf Tiedemann, the editor of the text, reproduces a table of contents at the outset of the "Notes and Materials" which may or may not correspond to the "provisional division into chapters" of which Benjamin speaks in a 1934 letter (1103). Its rubrics, at any rate, allow an overview of the 900 pages of "Aufzeichnungen und Materialien" that make up the bulk of the *Passagen:*

A   arcades, magasins de nouveauté, calicots
B   fashion
C   ancient Paris, catacombs, demolitions, decline of Paris
D   boredom, eternal return
E   Haussmannization, barricade combat
F   iron construction
G   aspects of exhibition, advertisements, Grandville
H   the collector
I   the intérieur, the trace
J   Baudelaire

K   dream-city and dream-house, dreams of the future, anthropological nihilism
L   dream-house, museum, indoor springs
M   the flâneur
N   re the theory of knowledge, theory of progress
O   prostitution, gambling
P   streets of Paris
Q   panorama
R   mirror
S   painting, Jugendstil, novelty
T   types of lighting
U   Saint-Simon, railroads
V   conspiracies, compagnonnage
W   Fourier
X   Marx
Y   photography
Z   the doll, the automaton
a   social movements
b   Daumier
c   . . . .
d   literary history, Hugo
e   . . . .
f   . . . .
g   the stock exchange, history of commerce
h   . . . .
i   techniques of reproduction, lithography
k   the Commune
l   the Seine, ancient Paris
m   idleness
n   . . . .
o   . . . .
p   anthropological materialism, history of sects
q   Ecole polytechnique

Konvolut "N," as the above table indicates, is (together with "K") something of an anomaly within the *Arcades,* given the fact that it is far more explicitly theoretical in thrust than the remainder of the rubrics and contains an unusually high proportion of methodological reflections and philosophical meditations on Benjamin's part. Tiedemann accordingly recommends that readers choose "N" as their entry-point into the work since it in a sense functions as a meta-Arcade, a series of passages on the epistemological and historico-philosophical foundations of the *Passagen.*

Like most of the other sheafs of the *Arcades,* "N" is a layering of textual strata that range from late 1928 to mid-1940. The dating of these strata is facilitated by the fact that Benjamin had his manuscript photographically copied at the Bibliothèque Nationale in June, 1935 and December, 1937. The first three folios of "N"—namely, N1 through N3a (the "a" indicating the third side of a folio)—were composed before mid-1935 and transcribe many of the methodological observations collected in Benjamin's 1927-29 notebook of the "Pariser Passagen." N4 through N7a, more explicitly Marxist in orientation, were largely written between 1935 and late 1937. N8 through N20, which deal with Jungian archetypes, the question of "rescue" (*Rettung*), and the theory of progress, date from late 1937 through May, 1940. The evolution of Benjamin's concerns over the course of "N" thus provides a miniature model of his larger work-in-progress.

In a 1930 letter to Scholem, Benjamin observes that his "Pariser Passagen," like his earlier *Trauerspiel* book, will need "an introduction dealing with the theory of knowledge, and this time, especially with the theory of the knowledge of history. It is here that I will find Heidegger on my path and I am waiting for a few sparks to fly from the collision of our two, very different ways of envisaging history". (1094) Heidegger's notion of "historicity" (*Geschichtlichkeit*) is fleetingly attacked in N3,1, but Benjamin doesn't seem to have pursued the head-on confrontation with Heidegger announced in the letter to Scholem[3]—just as he never fully develops the critique he had intended to undertake of the Fascist implications of the archetypes of Jung (mentioned in N8, N11, N18).[4] Instead, the major philosophical interlocutors of "N" are Adorno (N5), Marx (N4-N6), Horkheimer (N8), Turgot (N11-N12), Lotze (N13-N14), and Korsch (N16-N18).

A preface that falls in Sternean fashion at the alphabetical middle of his manuscript, "N" is to the *Arcades Project* what the "Epistemo-Critical Prologue" ("Erkenntniskritische Vorrede") is to the *Origin of German Tragic Drama* (1927) or what the "Task of the Translator" is to Benjamin's versions of Baudelaire (1923). All of these texts seek to establish a theoretical ground for praxis, the praxis of commentary in the case of the *Trauerspiel* study, the praxis of translation in the case of Benjamin's Baudelaire: the *Arcades Project* conflates both, since it is at once a philological commentary on, and translation of, the *passages* of 19th-century Paris. While the prologue to the *Trauerspiel* study probes the relation of epistemology to aesthetics from a neo-Kantian perspective, the *erkennt-*

nistheoretische portions of "N" address themselves more specifically to the knowledge of history, proposing a "materialist" epistemology based not on concepts but on images that dialectically relate historical subject and historical object, present and past, into what Benjamin terms the *Jetzt der Erkennbarkeit* (the "Now of recognizability"). Determined as he is to reorient historiography toward a revolutionary re-cognition in (and of) the Now, Benjamin accordingly devotes the latter portions of "N" to a radical critique of the bourgeois (and Marxist) theory of progress whose teleology has deluded the Left while providing an intellectual justification for the technological fantasies of Fascism.

At once the most speculative and the most political *Konvolut* of the *Arcades,* "N" has many (verbatim) features in common with Benjamin's late fragment on Baudelaire ("Central Park") as well as with the visionary "Theses on the Concept of History" of 1940. The paratactic, apodictic tone that it shares with these two other late compositions would seem to suggest that Benjamin was definitively moving beyond the essay form into the fragmentary tractatus à la Schlegel, Novalis, Nietzsche or Wittgenstein.

The polyphony of "N" is inevitably lost in translation. The interplay of quotations in French and German—from the initial epigraphs taken from Balzac and Marx to the passages from Turgot, Michelet, Proust, Aragon, on the one hand, and Engels, Lotze, Adorno, Korsch, on the other—has been necessarily sacrificed to a monolingual English text. Where appropriate, however, the German originals of a number of crucial terms are given in brackets after their English translations. An earlier version of this translation appeared in *The Philosophical Forum* (Fall-Winter, 1983-84). Most of its glaring errors have, thanks to Gary Smith, now been rectified.

—R.S.

NOTES

1 *Gesammelte Schriften,* vol. 5, ed. Rolf Tiedemann (Frankfurt: Suhrkamp, 1982), pp. 1260-1261. All page numbers in parentheses refer to this edition.

2 See Michel Espagne/Michael Werner, "Les manuscrits parisiens de Walter Benjamin et le *Passagen-Werk,*" in *Walter Benjamin et Paris,* ed. Heinz Wisman (Paris: Cerf, 1986), pp. 852-856, 864-867.

3 Indeed, Julian Roberts, *Walter Benjamin* (Atlantic Highlands: Humanities Press, 1983) rather persuasively *parallels* Benjamin's and Heidegger's theories of history, linking both back to Klages.

4 Benjamin's 1937 letters to Adorno and Horkheimer mention his desire to undertake a

critique of the notion of the "archaic image" in the work of Klages and Jung in order to distinguish it from his own concept of the "collective unconscious and its image-fantasy" (1157). Though Adorno encourages Benjamin to pursue his anti-Jungian reformulation of "archaic images" (1160), Horkheimer instead suggests Benjamin write a "materialist article on Baudelaire" and warns him away from investigating "the importance of psychoanalysis for the subject of materialist dialectics". (1158) Bowing to Horkheimer's suggestion, Benjamin as a result never fully explores one of the richest (and most prophetic) directions of the *Arcades Project,* namely, a psychoanalysis of capitalism in which Marx's concept of commodity fetishism would be conjoined with Freud's *Interpretation of Dreams.*

N
[RE THE THEORY OF KNOWLEDGE, THEORY OF PROGRESS]

WALTER BENJAMIN

"*Times* are more interesting than men."
  Honoré de Balzac, critique littéraire, Introduction de Louis Lumet 1912 p. 103 [Guy de La Ponneraye: Histoire de l'Amiral Coligny]

"The reformation of consciousness lies *solely* in the awakening of the world . . . from its dreams about itself."
  Karl Marx: Der historische Materialismus Die Frühschriften Leipzig, [1932], I p. 226 (Marx an Ruge Kreuzenach September 1843)

In the fields with which we are concerned, knowledge (*Erkenntnis*) exists only in lightning flashes. The text is the thunder rolling long afterward.
[N 1, 1]

Comparison of others' attempts to setting off on a sea voyage in which the ships are drawn off course by the magnetic north pole. Discover *that* North Pole. What for others are deviations, for me are data by which to set my course. I base my reckoning on the differentia of time that disturb the "main lines" of the investigation for others.
[N 1, 2]

Say something about the method of composition itself: how everything that comes to mind has at all costs to be incorporated into the project one is working on at the time. Be it that its intensity is thereby disclosed, or that, from the very outset, the ideas bear this project within them as a telos. So it is with the present method, which should characterize and maintain the intervals of reflection, the distances between the most intensively exoteric, essential parts of the work.
[N 1, 3]

43

To clear fields, where until now only delusion (*Wahnsinn*) ran rampant. Forge ahead with the whetted axe of reason, looking neither left nor right, in order not to fall victim to the horror beckoning from the depths of the primeval forest. At a certain point, reason must clear the entire ground and rid it of the underbrush of delusion and myth. Such is the goal here for the nineteenth century.

[N 1, 4]

These notes, which deal with the Paris arcades, were begun under the open sky—a cloudless blue which arced over the foliage—and yet are covered with centuries of dust from millions of leaves through which have blown the fresh breeze of diligence, the measured breath of the researcher, the squalls of youthful zeal, and the idle gusts of curiosity. For the painted summer sky that peers down from arcades in the reading room of the Paris National Library has stretched its dreamy, unlit ceiling over them.

[N 1, 5]

The pathos of this project: there are no periods of decline (*Verfallszeiten*). Attempt to consider the nineteenth century as positively as I attempted to find my way through the seventeenth in my *Trauerspiel* study. No belief in periods of decline. In the same way (limits aside), I find every city beautiful and the argument over the greater or lesser value of languages unacceptable.

[N 1, 6]

And later the glassed-in spot in front of my seat at the [Prussian] State Library; a space never violated, terrain vierge for the soles of figures I conjured up.

[N 1, 7]

Pedagogic side of this undertaking: "To train our image-making faculty to look stereoscopically and dimensionally into the depths of the shadows of history." The phrase is Rudolf Borchardt's: Epilegomena zu Dante, I, Berlin, 1923, pp. 56-57.

[N 1, 8]

Setting off the slant of this work against Aragon: whereas Aragon persistently remains in the realm of dreams, here it is a question of finding the constellation of awakening. While an impressionistic element lingers on in Aragon ("mythology")—and this impressionism should be held responsible for the many nebulous philosophemes of his book—what matters here is the dissolution of "mythology" into the space of history. Of course, that can only happen through the awakening of a knowledge not yet conscious of what has gone before.

[N 1, 9]

This project must raise the art of quoting without quotation marks to the very highest level. Its theory is intimately linked to that of montage.

[N 1, 10]

"Apart from a certain *haut-goût* charm, the artistic trappings of the last century have gone musty," says Giedion. Giedion, Bauen in Frankreich, Lpz Berlin, 1928, p. 3. By contrast, we believe the charm they exert on us reveals that they still contain materials of vital importance to us—not, of course, for our architecture, the way iron truss-work anticipates our design; but they are vital for our perception, if you will, for the illumination of the situation of the middle class at the moment it shows its first signs of decline. Materials of politically vital importance, at any rate; the Surrealists' fixation on these things proves it, as does their exploitation in contemporary fashion. In other words: just as Giedion teaches us we can read the basic features of today's architecture out of buildings of the 1850s, so would we read today's life, today's forms out of the life and the apparently secondary, forgotten forms of that era.

[N 1, 11]

"In the windswept stairwells of the Eiffel Tower, and even more in the steel supports of a pont transbordeur, one encounters the fundamental aesthetic experience of today's building: things flow through the thin net of iron spanning the air—ships, sea, houses, masts, landscape, harbor. Lose their definition: swirl into one another as we climb downward, simultaneously commingling." Sigfried Giedion, Bauen in Frankreich, Lpz Berlin, p. 7. So today, the historian has only to erect a narrow but sturdy scaffolding—a philosophic one—in order to draw the most contemporary aspects of the past into his net. But just as the glorious views of the cities the new iron structures afforded—see Giedion illustrations 61/63—were initially the exclusive privilege of the workers and engineers, so here the philosopher who wants to gain the first vistas must be an independent, sure-footed, and—if necessary—solitary worker.

[N 1a, 1]

Much as the Baroque book illuminates the seventeenth century through the present, so the nineteenth century should be treated here in analogous but more distinct fashion.

[N 1a, 2]

Minor methodological recommendation re the cultural-historical dialectic. It is very easy, given a specific perspective, to establish binary divisions for the various "fields" of any given epoch, so that the "fruitful," "forward-looking," "vital," "positive" lies on one side, and the fruitless, backward, extinct part of the epoch on the other. The contours of this positive part will only emerge clearly when profiled against the negative. Every negation, in return, only has value as the backdrop for the outlines of the vital, the positive. So it is of decisive importance to subject this tentatively isolated, negative part to another division so that, with a shift of point of view (but not of criteria!), it too will reveal a new positive element, different from the one previously described. And so on *in infinitum,* until all of the past has been brought into the present in a historic apocatastasis.

[N 1a, 3]

The foregoing, rephrased: the indestructibility of the highest life in all things. As against the prophets of decline. And of course: isn't it profaning Goethe to make a film of "Faust"; and isn't there a world of difference between Faust as text and Faust as film? True. But isn't there also a whole world of difference between a bad and a good film of "Faust"? It is never a matter of the "major," but only of the dialectic contrasts, which often seem nothing more than nuances. But it is from them that the life always springs anew.

[N 1a, 4]

To encompass both Breton and Le Corbusier—that would mean drawing the spirit of present-day France like a bow and shooting knowledge to the heart of the moment.

[N 1a, 5]

Marx describes the causal connection between economic system and culture. The expressive relationship is what matters here. The expression of an economic system in its culture will be described, not the economic origins of culture. In other words, the point is to attempt to grasp an economic process as a concrete primal phenomenon (*Urphänomen*), from which proceed all the vital manifestations of the arcades (and—to that extent—of the nineteenth century).

[N 1a, 6]

This investigation, which deals, basically, with the expressive character of the earliest industrial products, the earliest industrial structures, the earliest machines, as well as the earliest department stores, advertisements etc., thus becomes important for Marxism in two ways. First, it will explore the way the environment from which Marx's teachings arose influenced the latter through its expressive character, and not just through its causal relationships; and secondly, it will show those features that Marxism shares with the expressive character of the material products that are contemporary with it.

[N 1a, 7]

Method of this project: literary montage. I need say nothing. Only exhibit (*zeigen*). I won't filch anything of value or appropriate any ingenious turns of phrase. Only the trivia, the trash—which I don't want to inventory, but simply allow it to come into its own in the only way possible: by putting it to use.

[N 1a, 8]

Keep reminding oneself that the commentary on reality (since here it is a question of commentary, a construing of detail) calls for a method completely different from that required for a text. In the one case theology is the basic science, in the other philology.

[N 2, 1]

One of the methodological objectives of this project can be considered the demonstration of historical materialism which has cancelled out the idea of progress in itself. Historical materialism has good cause, here, to set itself off sharply from the bourgeois cast of mind; its basic principle is not progress, but actualization.

[N 2, 2]

Historical "understanding" (*Verstehen*) is to be viewed primarily as an afterlife (*Nachleben*) of that which has been understood; and so what came to be recognized about works through the analysis of their "afterlife," their "fame," should be considered the foundation of history itself.

[N 2, 3]

47

How this project was written: rung by rung, as chance offered a narrow foothold; and always like someone climbing dangerous heights, not looking around for a second, in order not to get dizzy (but also to save the full power of the panorama stretched before him for the very end).

[N 2, 4]

Overcoming the concept of "progress" and the concept of "period of decline" are two sides of one and the same thing.

[N 2, 5]

A central problem of historical materialism, which ought finally to be seen: must the Marxist understanding of history necessarily come at the cost of graphicness (*Anschaulichkeit*)? Or: by what route is it possible to attain a heightened graphicness combined with a realization of the Marxist method. The first stop along this path will be to carry the montage principle over into history. That is, to build up the large constructions out of the smallest, precisely fashioned structural elements. Indeed, to detect the crystal of the total event in the analysis of the small, individual moment. To break, then, with the vulgar naturalism of historicism. To grasp the construction of history as such. In the structure of commentary. *Trash of history*

[N 2, 6]

A Kierkegaard quotation in Wiesengrund, followed by commentary: " 'One can arrive at the same view of the mythic, working from the imagistic. That is, if in a reflective era and a reflective representation one sees the imagistic emerge so slightly as to be easily missed, reminding one like some antediluvian fossil of another life form which washed away all doubt—when one sees this, one may wonder how the imagistic ever played such a major role.' Kierkegaard wards off 'wonder' with what follows. And yet it indicates the most profound insight into the relation of dialectic, myth, and image. For nature doesn't prevail as eternally alive and present in the dialectic. The dialectic comes to a halt in the image and in the historically new it cites myth as that which is long gone: nature as prehistory (*Urgeschichte*). That is why the images, which like that of the Intérieur, neutralizing dialectic and myth, really are 'antediluvian fossils.' They can be called dialectical images, in a phrase of Walter Benjamin, whose striking definition of allegory also applies to Kierkegaard's allegoric intention taken as a figure of historical dialectic and mythical nature. According to this definition, 'in allegory the facies hippocratica of history lies before the viewer's eyes like a frozen, primordial landscape.' " Theodor Wiesengrund-Adorno, Kierkegaard, Tübingen, 1933, p. 60. *Trash of History*

[N 2, 7]

Only a thoughtless observer would deny that there are correspondences between the world of modern technology and the archaic symbol-world of mythology. Initially, the new technology appears no more than that. But in the next childhood memory, it has already changed its features. Every childhood achieves something great, irreplaceable for mankind. Through its interest in technical phenomena, its curiosity about all kinds of discoveries and machinery, every childhood ties technological achievement to the old symbol-worlds. There is nothing in the realm of nature that would by definition be exempt from such a tie. But it takes form in the aura of habit, not in the aura of novelty. In memory (*Erinnerung*), childhood, and dreaming. *Waking*

[N 2a, 1]

The prehistoric impulse to the past—this, too, at once a consequence and a condition of technology—is no longer hidden, as it once was, by the tradition of church and family. The old prehistoric dread already envelops the world of our parents, because we are no longer bound to it by tradition. The remembered world (*Merkwelt*) breaks up more quickly, the mythic in it surfaces more quickly and crudely, a completely remembered world must be set up even faster to oppose it. That is how the accelerated pace of technology looks in the light of today's prehistory. *Waking*

[N 2a, 2]

It isn't that the past casts its light on the present or the present casts its light on the past: rather, an image is that in which the Then (*das Gewesene*) and the Now (*das Jetzt*) come into a constellation like a flash of lightning. In other words: image is dialectics at a standstill. For while the relation of the present to the past is a purely temporal, continuous one, the relation of the Then to the Now is dialectical—not development but image [,] leaping forth (*sprunghaft*).—Only dialectical images are genuine (i.e., not archaic) images; and the place one happens upon them is language. *Waking*

[N 2a, 3]

In studying Simmel's presentation of Goethe's concept of truth, I realized quite clearly that my concept of origin (*Ursprung*) in the *Trauerspiel* book is a strict and compelling transfer of this fundamental principle of Goethe's from the realm of nature to that of history. Origins—the concept of the primal phenomenon, carried over from the pagan context of nature into the Jewish contexts of history. In the Arcades Project I am also involved in fathoming origin. That is to say, I am pursuing the origin of the construction and transformation of the Paris arcades from their rise to their fall, and laying hold of this origin through economic facts. These facts, seen from the point of view of causality, that is, construed as causes, do not however constitute originary phenomena; they become this only insofar as in their own development (*Entwicklung*)—unfolding (*Auswicklung*) might be a better word—they allow the whole series of the arcade's concrete historical forms to emerge, like a leaf unfolding forth from itself the entire wealth of the empirical plant kingdom.

[N 2a, 4]

"In studying this period, so close and yet so distant, I see myself as a surgeon operating with a local anesthetic; I work in areas which are numb, dead, and yet the patient is alive and can still talk." Paul Morand, 1900, Paris, 1931, pp. 6-7.

[N 2a, 5]

What differentiates images from the "essences" of phenomenology is their historic index. (Heidegger seeks in vain to rescue history for phenomenology abstractly, through "historicity.") These images must be thoroughly marked off from "humanistic" categories, such as so-called habitus, style, etc. For the historical index of the images doesn't simply say that they belong to a specific time, it says above all that they only enter into legibility at a specific time. And indeed, this "entering into legibility" constitutes a specific critical point of the movement inside them. Every Now is determined by those images that are synchronic with it: every Now is the Now of a specific recognizability (*das Jetzt einer bestimmten Erkennbarkeit*). In it, truth is loaded to the bursting point with time. (This bursting point is nothing other than the death of the intentio, which accordingly coincides with the birth of authentic historical time, the time of truth.) It isn't that the past casts its light on what is present or that what is present casts its light on what is past; rather, an image is that in which the Then and the Now come together into a constellation like a flash of lightening. In other words: an image is dialectics at a standstill. For while the relation of the present to the past is a purely temporal, continuous one, the relation of the Then to the Now is dialectical: not of a temporal, but of an imagistic nature. Only dialectical images are genuinely historical, i.e., not archaic images. The image that is read, that is, the image at the Now of recognizability, bears to the highest degree the stamp of that critical, dangerous impetus that lies at the source of all reading.

[N 3, 1]

An emphatic refusal of the concept of "timeless truth" is in order. Yet truth is not—as Marxism maintains—just a temporal function of knowledge; it is bound to a time-kernel (*Zeitkern*) that is planted in both the knower and the known. This is so very true, that the eternal is far more the frill on a dress than an idea.

[N 3, 2]

Sketch the history of the Arcades Project as it has developed. Its truly problematic component: to give up claim to nothing, to demonstrate that the materialistic presentation of history is imagistic in a higher sense than traditional historiography.

[N 3, 3]

Ernst Bloch's comment on the Arcades Project: "History flashes its Scotland Yard badge.["] It was in the context of a conversation in which I set forth how this project—whose method may be compared to the splitting of the atom—releases the enormous energy of history that lies bonded in the "Once upon a time" of classical historical narrative. The history that showed things "as they really were" was the strongest narcotic of the century.

[N 3, 4]

"The truth won't run off and leave us," reads one of Keller's epigrams. This defines the concept of truth with which these presentations break.

[N 3a, 1]

"Prehistory (*Urgeschichte*) of the nineteenth century"—this would have no interest, if we understood it to mean that prehistoric forms are to be rediscovered among the inventory of the nineteenth century. The concept of a prehistory of the nineteenth century has meaning only where this century is to be presented as the original form of prehistory, that is, as a form in which all of prehistory groups itself anew in images peculiar to the last century.

[N 3a, 2]

Can it be that awakening is the synthesis whose thesis is dream consciousness and whose antithesis is consciousness? Then the moment of awak-

51

ening would be identical with the "Now of recognizability," in which things put on their true—surrealistic—face. Thus, in Proust, the importance of staking the whole of life on its ultimate dialectical breaking point—the moment of awakening. Proust starts out with the presentation of the space of someone waking up.

[N 3a, 3]

"If I insist on this mechanism of contradiction in a writer's biography . . . , it is because the course of his thought cannot overlook facts which have a logic other than that of his thought taken in isolation. It is because there isn't an idea he holds to that really holds up . . . in the face of primordial and very simple facts: that the police are facing the workers with cannon, that war is threatening and fascism already reigns. . . Man's dignity requires that he submit his concepts to those facts, not that he fit those facts into his concepts by sleight of hand, no matter how ingenious the latter may be." Aragon, D'Alfred de Vigny à Avdeenko (Commune II, 20 avril 1935 pp. 808-09). But it is quite possible that, contradicting my past, I establish a continuity with someone else's which he, for his part as a communist, may simply dismiss. In this case, it is Aragon's past, when he rejects his *Paysan de Paris* in the same essay: "And like most of my friends, I liked the failed, the freakish, what can't survive, what can't succeed . . . I was like them, I preferred error to its opposite." p. 807.

[N 3a, 4]

In the dialectical image, the pastness of a particular epoch is always also "things as they always have been." As such, though, at times it comes into view only at a very specific epoch: that is, the epoch in which humanity, rubbing its eyes, suddenly recognizes the dream image as such. It is at that point that the historian takes on the task of dream interpretation.

[N 4, 1]

The phrase "the book of nature" indicates that we can read reality like a text. That will be the approach here to the reality of the nineteenth century. We open the book of past events.

[N 4, 2]

Just as Proust begins his life story with the moment of awakening, so every presentation is history must begin with awakening; in fact, it should deal with nothing else. This one deals with awakening from the nineteenth century.

[N 4, 3]

The utilization of dream elements upon awakening is the canon of dialectics. It is an example for the thinker and an exigency for the historian.

[N 4, 4]

Raphael seeks to correct the Marxist perception of the normative character of Greek art: "If the normative character of Greek art is . . . an explicable fact . . . we will have to determine . . . what special conditions brought on each renascence and consequently . . . what special factors of . . . Greek art these renascences adopted as models; renascences . . . have their own history . . . Only historical analysis can indicate the period in which the abstract notion of a 'norm' . . . attributed to Antiquity was born . . . The notion was created by the Renaissance, that is by primitive capitalism, and was then adopted by a classicism that began to assign it its place among historical sequences. Marx didn't follow this line to the full extent of the possibilities of historical materialism." Max Raphael, Proudhon Marx Picasso, Paris, [1933], pp. 178-79.

[N 4, 5]

It is the peculiar property of *technical* forms of creation (as opposed to artistic forms), that their progress and their success are proportionate to the *transparency* of their social content. (Whence glass architecture.)

[N 4, 6]

An important passage in Marx: "It is accepted that, where . . . the epic, for example . . . is concerned, some significant forms of artistic expression are only possible at a relatively early stage of artistic development. If this is true of relations among the various art forms, within the realm of the arts, it will hardly seem surprising that the same holds true for relations between the whole of the artistic realm and the general development of the society." cit without reference (possibly Theory of Surplus Value I?) in Max Raphael, Proudhon Marx Picasso, Paris [1933], p. 169.

[N 4a, 1]

The Marxist theory of art: now swaggering, now scholastic.

[N 4a, 2]

Proposal for a gradation of the superstructure in A. Asturaro: Il materialismo storico e la sociologia generale, Genua, 1904 (discussed in Die Neue Zeit, Stuttgart, XXIII, I p. 62, by Erwin Szabó): "Economy. Family and Kinship. Law. War. Politics. Morals. Religion. Art. Science."

[N 4a, 3]

53

Curious comment of Engels' on "social forces": "Once their nature has been understood, they can be turned from daemonic rulers into willing servants in the associated producers' hands." (!) Engels, Die Entwicklung des Sozialismus von der Utopie zur Wissenschaft, 1882.

[N 4a, 4]

Marx, in the afterword to the second edition of *Kapital:* "Research must appropriate the material in detail, analyze its various forms of development, and work out their inner connection. Only when this work is done can the true movement be presented accordingly. If this succeeds and the life of the material is reflected back as ideal, it may seem as though one is dealing with an a priori design." Karl Marx: Das Kapital, I, Berlin, [1932], ed. Korsch, p. 45.

[N 4a, 5]

The particular difficulty of doing historical work on the period after the close of the eighteenth century must be set forth. Since the rise of the mass press, an overview of the sources has become impossible.

[N 4a, 6]

Michelet is quite willing to see the common people labelled "barbarians"—"Barbarians. I like the word, I accept it"—and he says of their writers: "They love without reservation, without measure, giving themselves with the saintly awkwardness of Albrecht Dürer or the excessive polish of Jean-Jacques to a detail that doesn't really hide the artifice; they compromise the whole with that scrupulous detail. One mustn't criticize them too harshly: it is . . . the abundance of sap; a sap . . . that wants to produce everything simultaneously, leaves, fruits, and flowers; it bends and twists the branches. These defects of hard workers often appear in my books, which however lack their qualities. No matter!" J. Michelet, Le peuple, Paris, 1846, pp. xxxvi-xxxvii.

[N 5, 1]

Wiesengrund's letter of 5 August 1935: "My attempt to reconcile your 'dream' impetus—as the subjective element in the dialectical image—with the concept of the latter as a model, has led me to several formulations. . .: As things lose their use value, they are hollowed out in their alienation and, as ciphers, draw meanings in. Subjectivity takes control of them by investing them with intention of desire and dread. Because dead things stand in as images of subjective intentions, these latter present themselves as originary and eternal. Dialectical images are constellations of alienated things and thorough-going meaning, pausing a moment in the undifferentiation of death and meaning. While things are in appearance awakened to what is newest, death changes meanings into the most ancient." In the context of these reflections, one must keep in mind that, in the nineteenth century, the number of "hollowed out" things increases on a scale and at a rate hitherto unimaginable, because technical progress is constantly removing more utensils from circulation.

[N 5, 2]

"The critic can . . . connect with any form of theoretical and practical consciousness and, from *his own* forms of existing reality, elaborate true reality as the obligation and end purpose of the present." Karl Marx, Der historische Materialismus, Die Frühschriften. hg von Landshut und Mayer, Leipzig, [1932], I, p. 225 (Marx an Ruge Kreuzenach September 1843). The linkage of which Marx speaks here needn't necessarily follow the most recent stage of development at all. It can be undertaken for epochs long gone, the obligation and final purpose of which then must be presented not with reference to the next stage of development, but in its own right and as a preformation of the final purpose of history.

[N 5, 3]

Engels says (Marx und Engels über Feuerbach. Aus dem Nachlass Marx-Engels-Archiv, hg von Rjazanov, I, Frankfurt a/Main, [1928], p. 300): "One must not forget that Law has as little of its own history as does Religion." What is true of both these only begins to apply in a decisive way to culture. It would be absurd to conceive modes of existence for a classless society on the model of humanistic culture.

[N 5, 4]

"Our electoral slogan must . . . be: reform of consciousness, not by dogma, but by an analysis of the mystical, self-obfuscating consciousness, whether it manifests itself in religious or in political terms. It will then become evident that the world has long possessed the dream of a thing that, made conscious, it would possess in reality." Karl Marx, Der historische Materialismus, Die Frühschriften. Hg von Landshut und Mayer, Leipzig, [1932], I, pp. 226-227 (Marx an Ruge Kreuzenach September 1843).

[N 5a, 1]

Mankind must reconcile itself to parting with its past—and one form of reconciliation is gaiety. "The present German regime . . . the nullity of

55

the ancien régime on view to the world . . . is now merely the *comic actor* of a world order in which the *real heroes* have died. History is thorough and goes through many phases as it carries an old figure to the grave. The last phase of a world historical figure is the *comic*. The Greek gods were tragically wounded in Aeschylus' Prometheus Bound; but they had to die again comically, in the dialogues of Lucian. Why this pattern in history? So that humanity can part from its past *gaily*." Karl Marx, Der historische Materialismus, Die Frühschriften, ed Landshut und Mayer, Leipzig, I, p. 268 (Zur Kritik der Hegelschen Rechtsphilosophie). Surrealism is the death of the last century via comedy.

[N 5a, 2]

Marx (Marx und Engels über Feuerbach. Aus dem Nachlass Marx-Engels Archiv, I, Frankfurt a/Main, [1928], p. 301): "There is no history of politics, law, science, etc., of art, religion etc."

[N 5a, 3]

"The Holy Family," on Bacon's materialism: "In a poetic-sensual glow, matter smiles on the whole man."

[N 5a, 4]

"I am sorry I could only discuss in a very incomplete fashion those facts of daily life—food, clothing, shelter, family habits, civil law, entertainment, social relations—that have always been the essential concern of the vast majority of individuals." Charles Seignobos, Histoire sincère de la nation française, Paris, 1933, p. xi.

[N 5a, 5]

ad notam a phrase of Valéry's: "That which is truly general ought, properly, to be fertile."

[N 5a, 6]

Barbarism inheres in the very concept of culture: taken as the concept of a hoard of values that is independent, not of the production process from which those values emerged, but of the process in which they survive. In this way, they serve the apotheosis of the latter, no matter how barbaric it may be.

[N 5a, 7]

To discover how the concept of culture arose, what meaning it had in various epochs, and what needs it corresponded to when it was articulated. It could turn out that, insofar as the concept represents the sum total of our "cultural heritage," it is of recent origin; the clergy certainly didn't have it when they mounted their war of destruction against the legacy of Antiquity in the early Middle Ages.

[N 6, 1]

Michelet—an author who, no matter where he is quoted, makes the reader forget the book in which the quotation appears.

[N 6, 2]

The particularly careful scene-setting in early writings on social problems and charity should be emphasized; Naville, for example: De la charité légale, Frégier: Des classes dangereuses etc.

[N 6, 3]

"I can't stress enough that, for an enlightened materialist like Lafargue, economic determinism is not the 'absolutely perfect instrument' that 'might become the key to all the problems of history'." André Breton, Position politique du surréalisme, Paris, (1935), pp. 8-9.

[N 6, 4]

Every historical perception can be visualized by substituting the image of a pair of scales, one pan of which is weighted with what was, the other with a recognition of what now is. While the facts collected on the first pan can never be too trivial or too numerous, only a few heavy, massive weights need lie on the other.

[N 6, 5]

"The sole dignified posture for philosophy . . . in the industrial age is . . . restraint. The 'scientificity' of a Marx doesn't mean that philosophy has surrendered . . . , but rather that philosophy is restraining itself until the dominance of a lowly reality is broken." Hugo Fischer, Karl Marx und sein Verhältnis zu Staat und Wirtschaft, Jena, 1932, p. 59.

[N 6, 6]

The stress Engels places on the "classical ideal" in relation to the materialist notion of history is not insignificant. He bases his demonstration of dialectics in development on the laws "that real historical trends themselves supply, since each impulse can be considered at the point of ripeness, of the classical ideal." Cit Gustav Mayer, Friedrich Engels, Zweiter

Band, Engels und der Aufstieg der Arbeiterbewegung in Europa, Berlin, [1933], pp. 434-35.

[N 6, 7]

Engels to Mehring in his letter of 14 July 1893: "It is primarily this appearance of an independent history of state constitutions, legal systems, ideological notions in every specialized field that dazzles most people. When Luther and Calvin 'move beyond' the official Catholic Church, when Hegel moves beyond Fichte and Kant, when Rousseau indirectly moves beyond the constitutionalist Montesquieu with his Contrat Social, they all engage in a process which remains within the domain of theology, philosophy, political science; it represents a phase in the history of these disciplines and never escapes them. And since the bourgeois illusion of the permanence and final authority of capitalist production has been added on, even the Physiocrats and Adam Smith moving beyond the Mercantilists is considered a triumph of the intellect— not an intellectual reflex in response to altered economic facts, but rather an accurate insight finally wrested from constant and generally valid factual limitations." Cit Gustav Mayer, Friedrich Engels, Zweiter Band, Friedrich Engels und der Aufstieg der Arbeiterbewegung in Europa, Berlin, pp. 450-51.

[N 6a, 1]

"What Schlosser could and would say in response to those reproaches [peevish moral rigor] is this: that, no matter how cheerfully disposed one is in body and spirit, one doesn't learn a superficial *joie de vivre* from life at large, from history as opposed to the novel and the novella; that one may not absorb a contempt for humanity by studying it, but certainly a harsh sense of the world and sober principles for living; that the way of the world has always made an impression encouraging seriousness and rigor at least on the greatest judges of the world and men, those who were capable of measuring the outer against their own, inner life—a Shakespeare, a Dante, a Machiavelli." G. G. Gervinus, Friedrich Christoph Schlosser, Lpz, 1861 [Deutsche Denkreden besorgt von Rudolf Borchardt [München 1925] p. 312].

[N 6a, 2]

The relationship of transmission (*Überlieferung*) to techniques of reproduction must be investigated. "Transmission . . . relates to written communication the way reproduction of the latter by pen relates to those by the press, the way serial copies relate to simultaneous printings of a book." [Carl Gustav Jochmann:] Über die Sprache, Heidelberg, 1828, pp. 259-60 (Die Rückschritte der Poesie).

[N 6a, 3]

Roger Caillois: Paris, mythe moderne (Nouvelle Revue Française XXV, 284 1 mai 1937, p. 699) gives a list of the investigations that need to be undertaken in order to illuminate the subject further. 1) Descriptions of Paris that antedate the 19th century (Marivaux, Rétif de la Bretonne); 2) the struggle between the Girondists and the Jacobins over the relationship of Paris to the provinces; the legend of the days of revolution in Paris; 3) the secret police during the Empire and under the Restoration; 4) peinture morale of Paris in Hugo, Balzac, Baudelaire; 5) objective descriptions of the city: Dulaure, Du Camp; 6) Vigny, Hugo (Paris incendié in the Année terrible) [,] Rimbaud.

[N 7, 1]

The connection between presence of mind and the "method" of dialectical materialism needs to be established. Not simply that one can always reveal a dialectical process in presence of mind as one of the highest forms of relevant behavior. What is decisive is that the dialectician can't see history as anything other than a constellation of dangers that he is always ready to ward off as he follows its development in his thinking.

[N 7, 2]

"Revolution is perhaps more a drama than a history, and its pathos is a condition as imperious as its authenticity." Blanqui (Cit Geffroy, L'enfermé, Paris, 1926, I, p. 232.)

[N 7, 3]

Necessity of listening for every accidental quotation, every fleeting mention of a book, over many years.

[N 7, 4]

To contrast the theory of history with Grillparzer's comment, translated by Edmond Jaloux in "Journaux intimes" (Le Temps, 23 mai 1937): "To read into the future is difficult, but to see *purely* into the past is even more so: I say *purely,* meaning without clouding that retrospective gaze with everything that has happened in the meantime." The "purity" of the gaze is not so much difficult as impossible to attain.

[N 7, 5]

For the materialist historian, it is important to distinguish the construction of a historical state of affairs very rigorously from what one generally calls its "reconstruction." "Reconstruction" by means of empathy is one-sided. "Construction" presupposes "destruction."

[N 7, 6]

In order for a part of the past to be touched by actuality, there must be no continuity between them.

[N 7, 7]

The fore- and after-history of historical evidence is made manifest in it by dialectical presentation. Further: every historical state of affairs presented dialectically polarizes and becomes a force field in which the conflict between fore- and after-history plays itself out. It becomes that field as it is penetrated by actuality. And thus historical evidence always polarizes into fore- and after-history in a new way, never in the same way. And it does so beyond itself, within actuality per se; as a length divided according to the Apollinian measure experiences its division beyond itself.

[N 7a, 1]

Historical materialism strives neither for a homogeneous nor for a continuous presentation of history. As the superstructure works back on the base, it turns out that a homogeneous history, say, of economics, exists as little as does one of literature or jurisprudence. On the other hand, since the various epochs of the past are touched in varying degrees by the present of the historian (and often the most recent past is not touched at all; the present doesn't "do it justice"), a continuity of historical presentation is unattainable.

[N 7a, 2]

Telescoping of the past through the present.

[N 7a, 3]

The reception of great, much-admired works of art is an ad plures ire.

[N 7a, 4]

The materialist presentation of history leads the past to place the present in a critical condition.

[N 7a, 5]

It is my intention to resist what Valéry calls "a reading slowed by and bristling with the defenses of a demanding and refined reader." Charles Baudelaire, Les fleurs du mal, Introduction de Paul Valéry, Paris, 1928, p. xiii.

[N 7a, 6]

My thinking relates to theology the way a blotter does to ink. It is soaked through with it. If one were to go by the blotter, though, nothing of what has been written would remain.

[N 7a, 7]

It is the present which polarizes the event into fore- and after-history.

[N 7a, 8]

On the question of the incompleteness of history, Horkheimer's letter dated 16 March 1937: "The assertion of incompleteness is idealistic, if completeness isn't included in it. Past injustice has occurred and is done with. The murdered are really murdered. . . If one takes incompleteness completely seriously, one has to believe in the Last Judgment. . . Perhaps there's a difference with regard to incompleteness between the positive and the negative, such that only injustice, terror, and the pain of the past are irreparable. Application of justice, joy, works, all related differently to time, because their positive character is largely negated by transience. This is primarily true of individual existence, in which sadness rather than happiness is sealed by death." The corrective to this line of thought lies in the reflection that history is not just a science but also a form of memoration (eine Form des Eingedenkens). What science has "established," memoration can modify. Memoration can make the incomplete (happiness) into something complete, and the complete (suffering) into something incomplete. That is theology; but in memoration we discover the experience (Erfahrung) that forbids us to conceive of history as thoroughly a-theological, even though we barely dare not attempt to write it according to literally theological concepts.

[N 8, 1]

The clearly reactionary function that the doctrine of archaic images serves for Jung comes out in the following passage from the essay "On the Relationship of Analytical Psychology to the Poetic Work of Art": "The creative process . . . consists of an unconscious animation of the archetype and of its . . . elaboration into a complete work. The shaping of the original image is to some extent a translation of it into the language of the present. . . Therein lies the social significance of art: . . . it brings those forms to the surface, that the spirit of the age most lacked. The nostalgia of the artist retreats from dissatisfaction with the present until it reaches that primal image in the unconscious that serves . . . to compensate for . . . the one-sidedness of the spirit of the age. His nostalgia seizes upon the image, and as he brings it . . . into consciousness, the image changes its shape until it can be adapted by contemporary man to his own context." C. G. Jung, Seelenprobleme der Gegenwart, Zürich Leipzig und Stuttgart, 1932, p. 71. Thus, the esoteric theory of art amounts to an attempt to make archetypes "accessible" to the "spirit of the age."

[N 8, 2]

We can now see that one of the elements that Expressionism initially and explosively brought to light subsequently comes to particularly emphatic fruition in Jung's work. This element is a peculiarly medical nihilism, such as may be encountered in Benn's work and that finds its camp-follower in Céline. Jung himself ascribes the increased interest in the spiritual to Expressionism, and writes: "Expressionist art prophetically anticipated this turn of events, just as art always intuitively foresees coming trends of the general consciousness." (Seelenprobleme der Gegenwart, Zürich Lpz u Stuttgart, 1932, p. 415—Das Seelenproblem des modernen Menschen). In this context, one shouldn't lose sight of the connections Lukács makes between Expressionism and Fascism. (see K7a, 4)

[N 8a, 1]

"Tradition, wandering tale we inherit,
Fitful as the wind in the leaves that bear it."
Victor Hugo, La fin de Satan, Paris, 1886, p. 235.

[N 8a, 2]

Julien Benda, in "Un régulier dans le siècle," cites Fustel de Coulanges' phrase: "If you want to relive an epoch, forget that you know what has happened since." That is the secret magna charta for the presentation of history according to the historicist school, and it has slight conclusive value when Benda adds: "Fustel never said that such practices were valid for understanding the role of an epoch in history."

[N 8a, 3]

Pursue the question of whether a link exists between the secularization of time into space and the allegorical perspective. The former, in any case, is hidden in the "world view of the natural sciences" of the second half of the century, as becomes apparent in Blanqui's last composition. (Secularization of history in Heidegger.)

[N 8a, 4]

Goethe saw the crisis in bourgeois education approaching. He confronts it in "Wilhelm Meister." He characterizes it in his correspondence with Zelter.

[N 8a, 5]

Wilhelm von Humboldt places the emphasis on languages, Marx and Engels on the natural sciences. The study of languages also has economic functions. It responds to cosmopolitan commerce, while the study of the natural sciences responds to the production process.

[N 9, 1]

Scientific method distinguishes itself by developing new methods as it moves into new subjects. Just as artistic form distinguishes itself by developing new forms as it moves into new contents. Only from the outside does the work of art have one and *only* one form; only from the outside does the treatise have one and *only* one method.

[N 9, 2]

Re the concept of "rescue" (*Rettung*): the wind of the absolute in the sails of the concept. (The principle of the wind is the cyclical.) The trim of the sail is the relative.

[N 9, 3]

From what are phenomena rescued? Not just or not so much from the ill-repute and contempt into which they've fallen, but from the catastrophe when a certain form of transmission often presents them in terms of their "value as heritage."—They are rescued by exhibiting the discontinuity that exists within them. There is a kind of transmission that is a catastrophe.

[N 9, 4]

It is the unique property of dialectical experience to dissipate the appearance of things always being the same (*das Schein des Immer-Gleichen*). Real political experience is absolutely free from this appearance.

[N 9, 5]

What matters for the dialectician is having the wind of world history in his sails. Thinking for him means: to set the sails. It is the way they are set that matters. Words are his sails. The way they are set turns them into concepts.

[N 9, 6]

The dialectical image is a lightning flash. The Then must be held fast as it flashes its lightning image in the Now of recognizability. The rescue that is thus—and only thus—effected, can only take place for that which, in the next moment, is already irretrievably lost. Cf., the metaphoric passage from the introduction to Jochmann on the prophet's gaze, which catches fire from the summits of the past.

[N 9, 7]

To be a dialectician means to have the wind of history in one's sails. The sails are the concepts. It isn't enough, though, to have sails at one's disposal. The art of setting them is the decisive factor.

[N 9, 8]

The concept of progress should be grounded in the idea of catastrophe. That things "just keep on going" *is* the catastrophe. Not something that is impending at any particular time ahead, but something that is always given. Thus Strindberg—in "To Damascus"?—: Hell is not something that lies ahead of us, but this very life, here and now.

[N 9a, 1]

It is good to put a truncated end to materialist investigations.

[N 9a, 2]

Salvation includes the firm, apparently brutal grasp.

[N 9a, 3]

The dialectical image is that form of the historical object that meets Goethe's demands on the object of analysis: it exhibits a true synthesis. It is the primal phenomenon of history.

[N 9a, 4]

An appreciation or apologia seeks to cover up the revolutionary moments in the course of history. The establishment of continuity is dear to its heart. It only gives importance to those elements of a work that have already generated an after-effect. It misses those points at which the transmission breaks down and thus misses those jags and crags that offer a handhold to someone who wishes to move beyond them.

[N 9a, 5]

Historical materialism has to abandon the epic element in history. It blasts the epoch out of the reified "continuity of history." But it also blasts open the homogeneity of the epoch. It saturates it with *ecrasite,* i.e., the present.

[N 9a, 6]

In every true work of art, there is a place where anybody who positions himself within it encounters the cool wind of a coming dawn. Which therefore demonstrates that art, which has often been considered as resisting any connection to progress, can serve to give the latter its true definition. Progress does not reside in the continuity of temporal succession, but rather in its moments of interference: where the truly new first makes itself felt, as sober as the dawn.

[N 9a, 7]

For the materialist historian, every epoch with which he occupies himself is only a fore-history of the one that really concerns him. And that is precisely why the appearance of repetition doesn't exist for him in history, because given their index as "fore-history," those moments in the course of history that matter most to him become moments of the present and change their character according to whether this present is defined as a catastrophe or a triumph.

[N 9a, 8]

Scientific progress—like historical progress—is never more than the first step, never the second, third, or n + 1; that is, assuming that these latter belonged not just to the operations of science, but to its corpus. But that isn't in truth the case, because every stage of the dialectical process (just like every one in the historical process itself), no matter how determined by every preceding stage, realizes a completely new trend, which demands a completely new treatment. The dialectical method distinguishes itself, therefore, by developing new methods as it moves into new contents. Only from the outside does the work of art have one and *only* one form; only from the outside does a dialectical treatise have one and *only* one method.

[N 10, 1]

65

Definitions of fundamental historical concepts: catastrophe—to have missed the opportunity; the critical moment—the status quo threatens to hold firm; progress—the first revolutionary measures taken.

[N 10, 2]

If the historical object is to be blasted out of the continuum of the historical process, it is because the monadological structure of the object demands it. This structure only becomes evident once the object has been blasted free. And it becomes evident precisely in the form of the historical argument which makes up the inside (and, as it were, the bowels) of the historical object, and into which all the forces and interests of history enter on a reduced scale. The historical object, by virtue of its monadological structure, discovers within itself its own fore-history and after-history. (Thus, for example, the fore-history of Baudelaire, according to current scholarship, lies in allegory, while his after-history is found in the Jugendstil.)

[N 10, 3]

The argument against conventional historiography and "appreciation" is based on the polemic against empathy (Grillparzer, Fustel de Coulanges).

[N 10, 4]

The Saintsimonian Barrault distinguishes between "époques organiques" and "époques critiques." The defamation of the critical spirit begins immediately in the wake of the July Revolution victory by the bourgeoisie.

[N 10, 5]

The destructive or critical impetus in materialist historiography comes into play in that blasting apart of historical continuity which allows the historical object to constitute itself. It is in fact impossible to target a historical object in the ongoing process of history. All along, historiography has simply plucked its object out of this ongoing process. But this was done without foundation, as an expedient; and the first impulse was always to reinsert the object into a continuum that would be reinvented by means of empathy. Materialist historiography does not choose its objects casually. It does not pluck them from the process of history, but rather blasts them out of it. Its precautions are more extensive, its occurrences more essential.

[N 10a, 1]

The destructive impetus in materialist historiography is to be understood as a reaction to a constellation of dangers that threatens both that which is being transmitted and those to whom it is transmitted. The materialist presentation of history sets itself up in opposition to this constellation of dangers; in this lies its actuality and the proof of its presence of mind. Such a presentation of history must, to borrow a phrase from Engels, move "beyond the field of thought."

[N 10a, 2]

Thinking involves both thoughts in motion and thoughts at rest. When thinking reaches a standstill in a constellation saturated with tensions, the dialectical image appears. This image is the caesura in the movement of thought. Its locus is of course not arbitrary. In short, it is to be found wherever the tension between dialectical oppositions is greatest. The dialectical image is, accordingly, the very object constructed in the materialist presentation of history. It is identical with the historical object; it justifies its being blasted out of the continuum of the historical process.

[N 10a, 3]

The archaic form of prehistory, which has been summoned up in every era and most recently by Jung, is the one which makes appearance in history all the more delusive by assigning it a home in nature.

[N 11, 1]

To write history means giving dates their physiognomy.

[N 11, 2]

The events surrounding the historian and in which he takes part will underlie his presentation like a text written in invisible ink. The history that he lays before the reader will, as it were, shape the quotations in the text, and these quotations alone are put forward in a fashion readable to anybody and everybody. To write history therefore means to *quote* history. But the concept of quotation implies that any given historical object must be ripped out of its context.

[N 11, 3]

Re the basic doctrine of historical materialism. 1) A historical object is whatever is redeemed by knowledge. 2) History breaks down into images, not into stories. 3) Wherever a dialectical process takes place, we are dealing with a monad. 4) The materialist presentation of history goes hand in hand with an immanent critique of the concept of progress. 5) The procedures of historical materialism are founded on experience, on common sense, on presence of mind, and on dialectics. (Re the monad, N 10a, 3).

[N 11, 4]

The present defines where the fore-history and after-history of the object of the past diverge in order to circumscribe its nucleus.

[N 11, 5]

To demonstrate through example that only Marxism can apply high philology to the texts of the past century.

[N 11, 6]

"The areas which were the first to be enlightened are not the ones in which they [the sciences] have made the most progress." Turgot, Oeuvres II, Paris, 1844, pp. 601-602 (Second discours sur les progrès successifs de l'esprit humain) (1750). This idea plays a role in later writers, and in Marx.

[N 11, 7]

When the bourgeoisie conquered its position of power in the 19th century, the concept of progress may increasingly have forfeited those critical functions that originally characterized it. (The doctrine of natural selection played a decisive part in this process, for it popularized the notion that progress was automatic. Furthermore, it promoted the extension of the concept of progress to the entire realm of human activity.) In Turgot, the concept of progress still served a critical function. Above all, it made it possible to direct people's attention toward retrogressive tendencies in history. Significantly enough, Turgot saw progress as guaranteed above all in the realm of mathematical research.

[N 11a, 1]

"What a spectacle the succession of mankind's opinions offers: I look for the progress of the human spirit in them, and find little but the history of its errors. Why is its advance, so steady in the initial steps of the study of mathematics, so wavering, so easily misled when it comes to the rest? . . . In this slow progression of opinion and errors . . . I seem to see those first leaves, those sheaths which nature gives to the nascent stems of plants, emerging from the ground and successively withering as other sheaths arise, until finally the stem itself appears, crowned with flowers and fruits, image of the belated truth." Turgot, Oeuvres II, Paris, 1844 (Second discours sur les progrès successifs de l'esprit humain), pp. 600-01.

[N 11a, 2]

A *limes* to progress still exists in Turgot: "In later times . . . it was necessary to return, through perfection, to the stage at which earlier men had arrived through blind instinct; and who is not aware that this is the supreme effort of reason?" Turgot, loc. cit., p. 610. This *limes* still exists in Marx; later it is lost.

[N 11a, 3]

It is already evident in Turgot that the concept of progress aligns itself with science, but that it has its corrective in art (but art cannot be exclusively seen in terms of retrogression; Jochmann's essay does not pursue this notion without reservations). Obviously Turgot defines art differently than we would today: "The knowledge of nature and of truth is as infinite as they are. The arts, whose purpose is to please us, are as limited as we are. Time constantly brings about new discoveries in the sciences; but poetry, painting, music have a fixed point which is determined by the genius of language, the imitation of nature, and the limited sensibility of our organs. . . The great men of the century of Augustus reached this point and remain our models." Turgot, Oeuvres II, Paris, 1844 (Second discours sur les progrès successifs de l'esprit humain), pp. 605-6. Hence, a programmatic refusal of originality in art!

[N 12, 1]

"There are certain aspects of the fine arts which have been perfected over the course of time, for example perspective, which derives from optics. But local color, imitation of nature, the very expression of passions, all are constants." Turgot, Oeuvres II, Paris, 1844 (Plan du second discours sur l'histoire universelle), p. 658.

[N 12, 2]

A militant conception of progress: "It is not error which blocks the progress of truth. Rather, it is laxity, stubbornness, habit, everything that leads to inaction.—Among the ancient people of Greece and their republics, the progress of even the most peaceful arts was punctuated by continual wars. They were like the Jews, building the walls of Jerusalem with one hand, and waging battle with the other. Their minds were always active, their courage always stimulated, and the light of reason grew

69

brighter every day." Turgot, Oeuvres II, Paris, 1844 (Pensées et fragments), p. 672.

[N 12, 3]

Presence of mind as a political category is beautifully brought out in these
words of Turgot. "By the time we come to discover that things are at a
given juncture, they have already changed several times. Hence we always perceive events too late and politics must always foresee, as it were,
the present." Turgot, Oeuvres II, Paris, 1844 (Pensées et fragments), p.
673.

[N 12a, 1]

"The thoroughly transformed landscape of the 19th century remains visible to this day, at least in traces. It was shaped by the railroad. . .
Wherever mountain and tunnel, ravine and viaduct, torrent and funicular,
river and iron bridge . . . are intimately related, we find the focal points
of this historical landscape. . . Curiously, they testify that nature did not
sink into namelessness or imagelessness under the triumph of technological civilization, and that the construction of a bridge or a tunnel did not
become the exclusive feature of the landscape; rather, the river or mountain immediately rallied to their side, not as victim to victor, but as a
friendly power. . . The iron train entering the walled portals of the moun-
tains . . . seems . . . to be returning to its homeland, where the raw
materials lie out of which it was made." Dolf Sternberger, Panorama oder
Ansichten vom 19. Jahrhundert, Hamburg, 1938, pp. 34-35.

[N 12a, 2]

It was inevitable that the concept of progress should run up against the
critical theory of history the moment that progress was no longer presented as a measure of specific historical changes, but rather as a measure
of the span separating a legendary beginning from a legendary end of
history. In other words: as soon as it becomes the signature for the course
of history *in its totality,* the concept of progress is associated with an
uncritical hypostatization rather than with a critical placing into question.
This latter questioning can be recognized in the concrete view of history
by the fact that it throws retrogression in as sharp a perspective as it does
any progression. (Thus Turgot, Jochmann).

[N 13, 1]

Lotze as a critic of the concept of progress: "Contrary to those who
fondly asserted mankind's linear progress . . . those of a more considered

opinion had long found themselves pressed to the discovery that history winds its way in spirals; others favored epicycloids. In short, there was no lack of profound disguises for the admission that the overall impression of history is not only far from exhilarating, but for the most part depressing. An unprejudiced observer will always at first be amazed at and to lament the fact that so many achievements of culture, so many beautiful ways of life . . . have fallen into ruin, never to return." Hermann Lotze, Mikrokosmos III, Leipzig, 1864, p. 21.

[N 13, 2]

Lotze as a critic of the concept of progress: "It is muddled thinking . . . to conceive of education as something distributed among successive human generations, and to allow the most recent of these to enjoy the fruits that have grown out of the unrewarded effort and often out of the misery of earlier generations. Though it may be an enthusiasm inspired by noble sentiments, it is nonetheless thoughtless to dismiss the claims of individual eras or individual men and to ignore all their misfortune, provided that mankind as a whole has made progress. . . There can be no . . . progress which does not add to the happiness and perfection of those individuals who previously suffered an imperfect lot." Hermann Lotze, Mikrokosmos III, Leipzig, 1864, p. 23. If the idea that progress runs through the entire course of history is peculiar to the satiated bourgeoisie, then Lotze's work registers the reinforcements of an attitude that is on the defensive. Cf. by contrast Hölderlin: "I love the race of centuries to come."

[N 13, 3]

A thought-provoking comment. "One of the most noteworthy peculiarities of the human heart is . . . that so much individual selfishness should coexist with the general lack of envy which every present feels toward its future." This lack of envy indicates that our idea of happiness is deeply colored by the times in which we live our life. We can only conceive of happiness in terms of the air that we have breathed, or among those people with whom we have lived. In other words, the idea of happiness— and here is what the evidence teaches us—resonates with the idea of redemption. This happiness is founded precisely upon the despair and the forsakenness which were ours. Our life is, as it were, a muscle strong enough to contract the whole of historical time. Or, to put it differently, the true conception of historical time is wholly based on the image of redemption. (The passage is from Lotze, Mikrokosmos III, Leipzig, 1864, p. 49).

[N 13a, 1]

The notion of progress is rejected by the religious view of history: "Whatever its various movements, history cannot reach a destination that does not lie within its own plane, and we will save ourselves the trouble of searching for progress in the duration of history, since history is not fated to make such progress longitudinally, but rather in an upward direction at every single one of its points." Lotze, Mikrokosmos III, Leipzig, 1864, p. 49.

[N 13a, 2]

The notion of progress connected with the notion of redemption in Lotze: "Because the coherence of the world would thereby be rendered incoherent, we reject the idea that in the end the work of earlier generations will only be of benefit to those that follow, while they themselves irrevocably lose the products of their toil." (p. 50) This cannot be so, "otherwise the world and all the travails of its historical development will appear as an absurd and futile commotion. . . The belief that the progress of history also takes place (in however mysterious a fashion) for mankind's own sake allows us to speak of humanity as we do." (p. 51) Lotze calls this "the notion of . . . a preservation and a restoration." (p. 52)

[N 13a, 3]

Cultural history, according to Bernheim, emerged out of the positivism of Comte; Beloch's Greek History (vol. I, 2nd ed., 1912) is, according to him, a textbook example of the influence of Comte. Positivistic historiography "ignored the State and political events, but conceived the collective intellectual development of society as the sole content of history. . . The elevation . . . of cultural history into the only subject worthy of historical research!" Ernst Bernheim, Mittelalterliche Zeitanschauungen in ihrem Einfluss auf Politik und Geschichtsschreibung, Tübingen, 1918, p. 8.

[N 14, 1]

" 'The logical category of time does not dominate the verb as much as one might believe.' As strange as it may seem, the expression of the future does not appear to be situated on the same level of the human mind as the expression of the present and the past. '. . . The future often does not have its own tense, or if it does have one, it is a very complicated expression which is not parallel to that of the present and the past.' '. . . There is no reason to believe that prehistoric Indo-European ever possessed a true future tense. . .' (Meillet)." Jean-Richard Bloch, Langage d'utilité, langage poétique (Encyclopédie française XVI, 16-50, 10).

[N 14, 2]

Simmel touches on a very important discovery when he deals with the
antinomy between the concept of culture and the domains of autonomy in
classical Idealism. The distinctions between these three autonomous
spheres kept classical Idealism from a concept of culture that has been of
much assistance to barbarism. Simmel says of the ideal of culture: "The
crucial thing . . . is . . . that it abolishes the autonomous status of aesthetic, scientific, ethical . . . and even religious endeavors, in order to
locate them as elements or building blocks within humanity's development beyond the state of nature." George Simmel, Philosophie des
Geldes, Leipzig, 1900, pp. 476-77.

[N 14, 3]

"There has never been a period in history when the level of culture
unique to it permeated the whole of mankind or even the entirety of the
nation that was its principal bearer. All degrees and shades of moral
coarseness, spiritual obtuseness, and corporeal misery have always co-
existed with the cultivated refinement of life and the free enjoyment of
advantages characteristic of bourgeois order." Hermann Lotze, Mikrokosmos III, Leipzig, 1864, pp. 23-24.

[N 14a, 1]

Lotze counters the opinion that "enough progress has taken place when
. . . in the general context of an ongoing level of ignorance, the education
of a small minority strives ever higher" with the question: "How can one
speak of a history of mankind given these assumptions?" Lotze, Mikrokosmos III, p. 25.

[N 14a, 2]

"The fashion in which the culture of antiquity is almost exclusively transmitted" leads, as Lotze says, "straight back to the very thing which
historical study aims to oppose; I mean to the development of an instinct
of culture that seizes on an ever increasing number of elements of good
breeding and divorces them from spontaneity as so much dead property."
(p. 28) Similarly: "The progress of science . . . is not inevitably progress
for mankind; this would only be the case if, as the volume of truth accumulated, so did mankind's commitment to it . . . and the clarity of its
perspective on it." Lotze, loc. cit., p. 29.

[N 14a, 3]

Lotze on mankind: "One cannot say that it becomes what it is with a consciousness of its becoming and a memory of its earlier states." Lotze, loc. cit., p. 31.

[N 14a, 4]

Lotze's vision of history could be related to Stifter's: "That the fulfill-ment of the unruly will of individuals is limited by general conditions, which are independent of volition and inhere in the laws of the mind and in the fixed order of nature." Lotze, loc. cit., p. 34.

[N 14a, 5]

To be compared with Stifter's preface to "Bunte Steine": "Let us first of all take it for granted that a major effect is always the result of a major cause, never of a minor one." Histoire de Jules César, I, Paris, 1865 (Napoléon III).

[N 14a, 6]

A phrase which Baudelaire coins to describe the temporal consciousness of someone intoxicated by hashish can also be applied to the definition of revolutionary historical consciousness; he speaks of an evening during which he was absorbed by the effects of hashish: "However long it ap-peared to me . . . it nevertheless seemed that it had only lasted several seconds, or in fact that it had not taken place in eternity." Baudelaire, Oeuvres, ed. Le Dantec, Paris, 1831, I, pp. 298-99.

[N 15, 1]

Those who are alive at any given time see themselves in the midday of history. They are obliged to prepare a banquet for the past. The historian is the herald who invites those who are departed to the table.

[N 15, 2]

Re the dietetics of historical writing. The contemporary who reads a work of history and recognizes just how long his own overwhelming misery has been in preparation—and the demonstration of this must lie close to the historian's heart—thereby acquires a high opinion of his own powers. A history which teaches him this kind of lesson does not inspire resignation, but instead provides him with weapons. Nor does such a history stem from sadness, in contrast to the history Flaubert had in mind when he confessed: "Few people will guess just how sad one had to be to embark on the resuscitation of Carthage." Pure curiosity stems from sadness and heightens it.

[N 15, 3]

An example of a "cultural historical" approach in the worst sense of the term. Huizinga speaks of the depiction of the life of common people in the pastorales of the late Middle Ages. "Here also belongs the fascination with rags and tatters . . . which is already beginning to make itself felt. The calendar miniatures register with pleasure the threadbare knees of reapers in the field, or paintings show beggars in their rags . . . Here begins a line which leads to Rembrandt's etchings. Murillo's beggar boys, and the street types of Steinlein." J. Huizinga, Herbst des Mittelalters, München, 1928, p. 488. Of course what is really at issue is a far more specific phenomenon.

[N 15, 4]

"The past has left behind in literary texts images of itself that are comparable to the images which light imprints on a photosensitive plate. Only the future possesses developers active enough to bring these plates out perfectly. Numerous pages of Marivaux or Rousseau possess a mysterious meaning which their first readers were unable to decipher fully." André Monglod, Le préromantisme français I, Le héros préromantique, Grenoble, 1930, p. XII.

[N 15a, 1]

A revealing vision of progress in Hugo's "Paris incendié" (L'année terrible):
    What! sacrifice everything! even the granary of bread!
    What! the Library, this ark where the dawn gleams,
    This unfathomable ABC of ideals, where Progress,
    Eternal reader, leans on its elbows and dreams . . .

[N 15a, 2]

As to the style for which one should aim: "It is by means of everyday words that style bites and penetrates the reader. It is by means of them that great thoughts circulate and are accepted as genuine, like gold or silver stamped with a known seal. They inspire confidence in the person who uses them to render his thoughts more sensible; for one recognizes by this use of common language a man who knows about life and about things, and who remains close to them. In addition, these words make for a frank style. They show that the author has long nourished himself on the thought or opinion expressed, and that he has so taken possession of them and rendered them so habitual that the most common expressions allow him to express ideas which have become commonplace to him in the course of prolonged conception. Finally, whatever one says will thereby seem more true; for there are no words so clear as those which are called commonplace, and clarity is so much a characteristic of truth that it is often confused with it.'' Nothing more subtle than the advice to be clear in order at least to appear true. The advice to write simply, usually imparted with resentment, acquires the highest authority when delivered in this fashion. J. Joubert, Oeuvres, Paris, 1883, II, p. 293, du style, XCIX.

[N 15a, 3]

Whoever managed to develop the dialectics of Joubert's precepts would discover a stylistics worth mentioning. Joubert advises the use of everyday words, but warns against colloquial language ''which expresses things relevant only to our present customs.'' du style, LXVII, loc. cit. p. 286.

[N 16, 1]

''All well-turned phrases are susceptible of more than one meaning. If a well-turned phrase offers a meaning more attractive than its author's, one should appropriate it.'' J. Joubert, Oeuvres, Paris 1883, II, p. 276 (du style XVIII).

[N 16, 2]

With regard to political economy, Marx characterizes its ''vulgar element'' as above all ''that element in it that confuses the mere reproduction of appearance with its conceptualization.'' Cit. Korsch: Karl Marx Manuskript, II, p. 22. This vulgar element should also be denounced in other sciences.

[N 16, 3]

Marx's concept of nature: ''If for Hegel . . . 'physical nature also intervenes in world history,' Marx, by contrast, conceives nature from the beginning in terms of social categories. Physical nature does not intervene directly in world history, but rather indirectly, as a process of material production which takes place from its very outset not only between man and nature, but between man and man. Or, in order to be clear to philosophers as well: in Marx's strictly social science, pure *nature,* the prerequisite for all human activity (the economic *natura naturans*), is replaced as 'matter' by nature as *material production* (the economic natura naturata), mediated and transformed by human social activity, and thus at once modifiable and transformable in the present and the future.'' Korsch, loc. cit. III, p. 3.

[N 16, 4]

Korsch proposes the following reformulation of the Hegelian triad via Marx: Hegelian 'contradiction' is replaced by class struggle, dialectical 'negation' by the proletariat, and dialectical 'synthesis' by the proletarian revolution." Korsch, loc. cit. III, p. 45.

[N 16, 5]

Korsch's restriction of the materialist notion of history: "As the material code of production changes, so does the system of mediations that exists between the material base and its political and juridical superstructure and its corresponding social forms of consciousness. Therefore the general assertions of materialist social theory concerning the interrelations of *economics and politics* or *economics and ideology* or such general concepts as *class and class struggle* . . . have different meanings for different epochs and apply in the specific form that Marx articulated for contemporary bourgeois society—strictly speaking—only in this context . . . Only for contemporary bourgeois society, where the spheres of *economics and politics* are totally separated from each other on a formal level and where workers as citizens are free and equal, does the scientific demonstration of their actual ongoing lack of freedom in the economic sphere acquire the character of a theoretical discovery." Korsch III, pp. 21-22.

[N 16a, 1]

Korsch makes the "apparently paradoxical observation, which is nonetheless valid for the final and most mature form of Marx's science . . . that in Marx's materialist social theory the totality of social relations, which bourgeois sociologists treat as an autonomous domain . . . is instead investigated according to its objective . . . content by the historical and social science of economics. *Marx's materialist social science is in this sense not sociology but economics.*" Korsch loc. cit. III, p. 103.

[N 16a, 2]

A quote from Marx on the mutability of nature (in Korsch loc. cit. III, p. 9): "Even such organic differences among species as, for example, racial differences . . . can and must be overcome historically."

[N 16a, 3]

Theory of superstructure according to Korsch: "To determine the specific kind of relationships and connections between the economic 'base' and the juridical and political 'superstructure' and the 'corresponding' forms of consciousness . . . neither the philosophical concept of 'dialectical' causality, nor 'causality' as conceived by the natural sciences and

77

supplemented by the notion of 'reciprocal effects' can suffice. The natural sciences of the 20th century have learned that the 'causal' relations a researcher in a given field has to establish for that field should not be defined in terms of a general concept or law of causality, but rather must be 'specific' to every particular field. [See Philipp Frank, The Law of Causality and its Limits, Vienna, 1932] . . . The most significant results . . . achieved by Marx and Engels do not lie in theoretical formulations of the new principle, but in its specific application to a series of questions . . . some of fundamental practical importance, some of extreme theoretical difficulty. [To these belong, for example, questions touched upon at the end of the 1857 Introduction pp. 779ff and which deal with the 'unequal development' of different fields of social life: the unequal development of material production vis-à-vis artistic production (and of the various arts among themselves), the level of education in the United States vis-à-vis that of Europe, the unequal development of conditions of production as legal conditions, etc.] A more precise definition of the aforementioned connections still remains a task for the future . . . its crucial point should not be theoretical formulation but the continued application and testing of those principles implicit in the work of Marx. One should not cling too anxiously to the phraseology, often intended only metaphorically, that Marx used to describe specific existing connections as a relation between 'base' and 'superstructure,' as 'correspondences,' etc. . . In all these cases, Marx's concepts, as Sorel and Lenin among the later Marxists understood best, are not intended as new dogmatic fetters: not a priori conditions that a line of investigation proclaiming itself materialist must absolve in a specific sequence, but rather totally undogmatic guidelines for investigation and praxis." Korsch: Karl Marx Ms III, pp. 93-96.

[N 17]

Materialist notion of history and materialist philosophy: "The formulas of materialist history which Marx and Engels applied solely to the investigation of bourgeois society and which were then transferred to other historical epochs only with suitable elaboration . . . these formulas have been severed from this context, or for that matter from any kind of historical application, by the epigones of Marx who have transformed so-called 'historical materialism' . . . into a universal sociological theory. From this . . . reduction . . . of materialist social theory, it was then only a step to the notion that still today—or especially today—imposes the grounding of Marx's historical and economic science not only in a general social philosophy, but even in a total materialist worldview encompassing nature and society. That is, in Marx's terms . . . it entails leading the scientific forms into which the . . . actual content of 18th-century philosophical materialism had meanwhile evolved, back toward the 'philosophical phrases of the materialists regarding matter.' Materialist social science . . . does not need . . . any such philosophical foundation. This most important advance . . . of Marx has subsequently . . . gone unrecognized even by 'orthodox' interpreters of Marx . . . They have thus imposed their own philosophical backwardness on the Marxian theory which had consciously progressed from philosophy to science. This historical fate of Marx-orthodoxy appears in almost grotesque fashion when, in warding off revisionist attacks, it ends up coinciding in all its main points with the position of its opponents—for example, when the leading exponent of this tendency, Plekhanov . . . in his assiduous search for the 'philosophy' at the basis of Marxism, is in the end reduced to describing Marxism as 'a Spinozism (freed from its theological component by Feuerbach).' " Korsch, loc. cit. III, pp. 29-31.

[N 17a]

Korsch cites Bacon from the Novum Organum: " 'For in fact the daughter of Time is rightly called Truth and not Authority.' On this authority of all authorities, *Time,* he had founded the superiority of the new bourgeois empirical sciences over the dogmatic sciences of the Middle Ages." Korsch, loc. cit. I, p. 72.

[N 18, 1]

"For *positive* use, Marx replaces Hegel's extravagant postulate that the truth must be concrete with the rational principle of *specification* . . . The actual interest lies . . . in those specific traits through which each particular historical society *distinguishes* itself from the shared characteristics of society in general and which therefore constitute its *development.* A rigorous social science therefore . . . cannot erect its general concepts by simply abstracting some and holding on to other more or less arbitrarily selected characteristics of the given historical form of bourgeois society. It can arrive at the knowledge of the universals contained in this specific form of society only through a precise investigation of all the historical conditions of its emergence out of a previous social condition and out of the change in its present form brought about under specific and firmly determined conditions . . . The only genuine laws in social science are therefore the laws of development." Korsch, loc. cit., pp. 49-52.

[N 18, 2]

The authentic concept of universal history is a messianic one. Universal history, as it is understood today, is the business of obscurantists.

[N 18, 3]

The Now of recognizability is the moment of awakening. (Jung wants to keep awakening at a distance from dream).

[N 18, 4]

In his characterization of Leopardi, Sainte-Beuve declares himself "convinced . . . that literary criticism only achieves its full validity and originality when it is applied to subjects whose background, environment, and various circumstances have long been familiar to us." C.-A. Sainte-Beuve, Portraits contemporains, IV, Paris, 1882, p. 365. On the other hand, one should emphasize how valuable the omission of certain of these criteria can be. An inadequate feeling for the smallest nuances of the text itself can lead the observer to investigate all the more attentively the subtle traces of those social conditions which underlie all art work. Furthermore, an insensitivity toward its most delicate shadings can lead the critic to establish the contours of a poem more sharply, and can result in a certain superiority over other critics, since a feeling for nuances is not always associated with analytical talent.

[N 18a, 1]

Critical statements about technological progress turn up quite early. The author of the treatise *On Art* (Hippocrates?): "I believe that intelligence . . . ever desires to discover some of those things which are still unknown, *if it is better to have discovered them than not to have done so at all.*" Leonardo da Vinci: "How and why I have not written about my technique of going under water and remaining there for as long as I can go without food. If I have not published or divulged this, it is because of the wickedness of men who would put it to use to commit murder at the bottom of the sea by staving in ships and sinking them with their crews." Bacon: "In . . . the *New Atlantis* . . . . he entrusts to a specially chosen commission the responsibility of deciding which new inventions will be made public and which ones will be kept secret." Pierre-Maxime Schuhl, Machinisme et philosophie, Paris, 1938, pp. 7 and 35. "Bombers remind us of what Leonardo da Vinci had expected of the flight of man; he was to have risen into the air 'in order to seek snow on mountain peaks and then return to scatter it over city streets shimmering with the heat of summer.' " Loc. cit., p. 95.

[N 18a, 2]

It could be that the continuity of tradition is only an appearance. But if this is the case, then it is precisely the persistence of this appearance of permanence that establishes continuity.

[N 19, 1]

Proust apropos of a quote (from a letter of Balzac's to M. de Forgues) which he probably borrowed from Montesquiou, to whom he writes as follows. (The passage may contain a slip of the pen or a printer's error.) "I had already eliminated it [i.e., the quotation] from my proof sheet a fortnight ago . . . Since in all likelihood my book will have few readers, there was little risk that your quotation would be robbed of its freshness. Also, I have removed the quotation less for your sake than for the sake of the sentence itself. I believe, in effect, that all fine sentences are endowed with an inalienable right which renders them untransferable to any ac-quisitor other than the one whom they have been awaiting and for whom they are destined by fate." Correspondance générale de Marcel Proust I, Lettres à Robert de Montesquiou, Paris, 1930, pp. 73-74.

[N 19, 2]

The pathological aspect of the notion of "Culture" comes to light most emphatically in the scene where Raphael, the hero of La Peau de chagrin, ventures into the overwhelming warehouse of the four-story *magasin d'antiquités:* The young stranger first compared . . . three rooms stuffed with civilization, with sects, with divinities, with masterpieces, with roy-alites, with debaucheries, with reason and with madness to a mirror of many facets, each one representing a world . . . The sight of so many national or individual existences, attested by these human tokens which had survived them, in the end altogether numbed the young man's senses . . . The ocean of furniture, of inventions, of fashions, of works, of ruins, composed an endless poem for him . . . He clung to every joy, seized on every pain, took hold of every formula of existence and generously scat-tered his life and his emotions among the simulacra of this plastic and empty world . . . He was suffocating under the debris of fifty vanished centuries, he was sick with all these human thoughts, done in by all the luxury and art . . . If modern chemistry boils creation down to a gas, does not the soul just as capriciously concoct terrible poisons by the rapid concentration of its pleasures . . . or its ideas? Do not men perish under the devastating effect of some moral acid which has suddenly spread throughout their inner being?" Balzac, La Peau de chagrin, ed. Flammar-ion, Paris, pp. 19, 21-22, 24.

[N 19, 3]

A few theses of Focillon that appearances seem to support. The materialist theory of art is clearly interested in destroying this appearance. "The state of the life of forms can not be legitimately confused with the state of social life. A work of art's location in time does not define its principles nor the particularity of its form." (p. 93) "The combined action of the Capet monarchy, the episcopacy, and the urban centers on the development of gothic cathedrals shows what influence a conjunction of social forces can exert. But this powerful action is incapable of solving a problem involving statics, or of establishing proportions. The mason who strung two nervures of stone at right angles under the north belfry of Bayeux . . ., the author of the chancel of Saint-Denis were calculators working with solids, and not historians interpreting their times. [!!] The most attentive study of the most harmonious milieu, the most closely-bound bundle of circumstances, will not give us the design of the towers of Laon." (p. 89) One should elaborate on these reflections, in order to demonstrate once and for all the difference between the theory of milieu and the theory of the forces of production on the one hand, and the difference between a "reconstruction" and a historical interpretation of works on the other. (Henri Focillon, Vie des formes, paris, 1934).

[N 19a, 1]

Focillon on technology: "Technology was for us like an observatory from which to see and to study within the sweep of a single perspective the greatest number of objects in all their diversity. This is because technology can be construed in several different ways: one can consider it as a living force, or as mechanics, or as sheer amusement. For us, it involved neither a "professional" reflex nor . . . a "school" of cooking, but a poetry all action and . . . the vehicle of metamorphoses. It has always seemed to us that . . . the observations of technological phenomena not only guaranteed us a certain verifiable objectivity, but that it led us into the heart of problems, *in that it posed them to us in the same terms and from the same point of view that it does for the artist."* The phrase underlined by the author points out the essential error. Henri Focillon, Vie des formes, Paris, 1934, pp. 53-54.

[N 19a, 2]

The "activity of a style in the process of defining itself . . . is generally presented as an 'evolution,' this term being taken in the most general and vague sense. Whereas the notion of evolution was carefully examined and verified by the biological sciences, archaeology took it up . . . as a classificatory device. I have elsewhere shown that the notion of evolution is dangerous because of its falsely harmonious character, because of its unilinear course, because the expedient of 'transitions' . . . is applied to dubious cases out of an incapacity to make way for the revolutionary energy of inventors." Henri Focillon, Vie des formes, Paris, 1934, pp. 11-12.

[N 20]

Translated by Leigh Hafrey and Richard Sieburth

PROGRESS[1]

THEODOR W. ADORNO

For Josef König

A theoretical account of progress requires that this category be examined so closely that it loses the appearance of obviousness from both its positive and negative usages. But at the same time, such closeness makes this account more difficult. More than other concepts, progress vanishes upon specification of what is really meant by it, that is, what progresses and what does not. Whoever wants to make the concept more precise easily destroys what he aims for. The subaltern cleverness which refuses to speak of progress before being able to decide: progress in what, on what, and in relation to what, shifts the unity of the moments within the concept which work exhaustively upon each other into mere contiguity. By insisting on exactitude when the impossibility of the clear-cut belongs to the matter itself (*Sache selbst*), incorrigible theory of knowledge misses the matter, sabotages insight, and serves the preservation of the bad by assiduously prohibiting meditation upon that which, in this age of both utopian and absolutely destructive possibilities, the consciousness of those entangled would like to learn: whether there is any progress. Like every philosophical term, progress has its equivocations; and every such term's equivocations also register a commonality. At the present moment, one knows what is supposed to be thought with the term progress vaguely yet accurately; therefore, one cannot employ the concept roughly enough. Pedantry in its use merely cheats out of what it promises: an answer to the doubt and the hope that things will finally get better, that one day human beings will be allowed to breathe easily. What progress should mean to them cannot be said accurately; for the distress of the situation is that, while everyone feels distressed, the salving word is missing. Only those reflections on progress partake of truth which immerse themselves in progress and yet maintain distance—stepping back from paralyzing facts and special meanings. Today such reflections come to a head in contemplation of whether humankind is able to prevent catastrophe. The forms of humankind's own overall social constitution endanger its life insofar as no self-conscious overall subject develops and intervenes. The possibility of progress—of averting utmost, total disaster—has devolved to this overall subject alone. All else involving progress must crystallize about it. The physical want, which long seemed to mock progress, has potentially been eliminated: with the present state of technical forces of production, no one on earth needs to suffer poverty. As to whether there continues to be want and suppression—both are one—this will be decided solely by warding off catastrophe through a rational establishment of overall society as humankind. Kant's project of a doctrine of progress was also fastened to an "idea of the human:"[2] "The highest design of nature, which is the development of all its capacities, can be achieved by humankind only in society, and more specifically in the society with the greatest freedom. Hence, such a society is one in which there is pervasive antagonism among its members, yet also the most exact determination of freedom and securing of freedom's limits so that it may be consistent with the freedom of other societies. Nature wills that society should attain this end, like all other ends of nature's determination, for itself. Thus, a society in which freedom under external laws is found bound up to the greatest possible degree with irresistible power, i.e. a perfectly just civic constitution, is the highest of nature's tasks for the human species; for nature can achieve her other designs for our species only by means of the discharge and completion of this task."[3] The concept of history in which progress would have its place is emphatically the Kantian universal or cosmopolitan concept, not that of particular spheres of life. But the dependence of progress on totality is a thorn in its side. Consciousness of this dependence inspires Benjamin's polemic against the coupling of progress and humankind in his theses on the concept of history, likely the weightiest thinking toward a critique of the idea of progress from the ranks of those accounted for crudely as political progressives: "Progress as pictured in the heads of the Social Democrats was, first of all, a progress of humankind itself (not just of its skills and knowledge)."[4] However little humankind *tel quel* progresses according to the advertising recipe of the new-and-improved, there is still no idea of progress without the idea of humankind. The meaning of this Benjaminian passage must be more a reproach against the Social Democrats for confusing the progress of skills and knowledge with humankind's progress, than a wish to expurgate progress from philosophical reflection. Progress procures justification in Benjamin's doctrine that the notion of the happiness of unborn generations, without which one cannot speak of progress, indefeasibly carries with it the notion of redemption.[5] The concentration of progress on the survival of the species is thereby confirmed: no progress should be supposed in such a way as to imply that there already is a humankind which could therefore progress. Rather, progress would be humankind's very establishment, a perspective for which opens in the face of extinction. It follows from this, as Benjamin further teaches, that the concept of universal history cannot be saved; the concept is plausible only as long as the illusion of an already existing humankind, thoroughly harmonious and ascending in unity, remains credible. If humankind remains entrapped by the totality which it itself fashions, then, as Kafka wrote, progress has not yet taken place at all, while totality alone is nevertheless what permits progress to be thought. The simplest way to elucidate this is through the determination of humankind as that which excludes nothing whatsoever. If humankind were to become a totality which no longer contained within itself a limiting principle, it would also be rid of the duress which subjects all its members to such a principle; it would no longer be a totality: no forced unity. The passage from Schiller's "Ode to Joy": "Who has failed, let him with weeping / From our fellowship steal away!",[6] banishes in the name of all-encompassing love one who never shared in it; the passage thus unintentionally confesses the truth about the bourgeois concept of humankind, which is at once totalitarian and particular. In this verse, what he who is unloved or unable to love meets with in the name of the idea (of humankind) unmasks this idea, as does the affirmative violence with which Beethoven's music hammers the idea home. It is hardly accidental that, with the word 'steal' in humiliating the one who is joyless and to whom joy will therefore again be denied, the poem calls forth associations from the spheres of property and criminology. Continuing antagonism is inherent in the concept of totality, as it is in politically totalitarian systems; thus, the evil mythical festivals in fairy-tales are defined by those festivals not charged with evil. Only where the limit-setting principle of totality vanished—even if the principle were the commandment to simulate totality—would there finally be humankind and not its illusory image.

Historically, the conception of humankind was already implicit in the middle Stoic's theorem of the universal state; objectively at least, this theorem ended up as progress, regardless of how foreign the idea of progress might otherwise have been to pre-Christian antiquity. That this Stoic theorem also lent itself to the grounding of Rome's imperial claims betrays something of what befell the concept of progress through its identification with growing "skills and knowledge." Existing humankind is substituted for humankind yet unborn; history immediately becomes salvation history. This was the prototype for the notion of progress up until

Hegel and Marx. In Augustine's *civitas dei,* it is bound to redemption through Christ: the historically successful redemption; only an already redeemed humankind can be viewed as if, after the judgment fell and by dint of the grace imparted it, it were moving in the continuum of time toward the kingdom of heaven. Perhaps it was the ill fate of later thinking on progress that it took over from Augustine this immanent teleology and the conception of humankind as the subject of all progress, while Christian soteriology faded into speculations by the philosophy of history. In this way, the idea of progress was absorbed in the *civitas terrena,* its Augustinian counterpart. As with the dualist Kant, the *civitas terrena* is supposed to progress according to its own principle, its "nature." In such enlightenment, however, which puts progress toward humankind in its own hands for the first time and thus concretizes the idea of progress as realizable, there lurks the conformist confirmation of what merely is. What is received the aura of redemption when redemption did not come and evil continued undiminished. This immeasurably far-reaching modification of the concept of progress was unavoidable. Just as the emphatic claim of successful redemption came to protestation in the face of post-Christian history, so, conversely, in Augustine's *theologoumenon* of an immanent movement of the species toward the blessed state lay already the motif of irresistible secularization. The temporality of progress itself, progress' very concept, connects it with the empirical world; yet without such temporality, the wickedness of the way of the world would become utterly eternalized in thought, and the Creation itself the work of some Gnostic demon. The intimate constellation of the ideas of progress, redemption and on immanent course of history can be read in Augustine; yet these ideas may not be absorbed into each other if they are not to reciprocally annihilate each other. If progress is equated with redemption as sheer transcendent intervention, it forfeits any graspable meaning along with the dimension of time, and evaporates into ahistorical theology. But when mediatized into history, idolization of history threatens, as does the absurdity, both in the reflection of the concept and in reality, that what inhibits progress is itself already progress. Auxiliary constructions of an immanent-transcendent concept of progress condemn themselves through their very nomenclature.

The greatness of Augustine's doctrine was that of the for-the-first-time. This doctrine has all the abysses of the idea of progress in it, and aspired to conquer them theoretically. The structure of his doctrine brings the antinomous character of progress into unmitigated expression. Already in Augustine, and again at the level of secular philosophy of history since Kant, antagonism is in the center of that historical movement which would be progress since it is directed toward the kingdom of heaven; for Augustine, this movement is the battle between the earthly and the heavenly. All thoughts on progress since then have received their depth from the burden of historically mounting calamity. While for Augustine, redemption constitutes the *telos* of history, the latter neither leads directly to the former, nor is the former entirely unmediated to the latter. Redemption was planted in history by the divine world plan, though set against history after the Fall. Augustine recognized that redemption and history are not without each other, nor within each other, but rather in tension, the stored up energy of which ultimately wishes nothing less than sublation of the historical world itself. In the age of catastrophe, however, the thought of progress can only be thought with this sublation and nothing less. Progress should no more be ontologized or unreflectively attributed with being than should decline, though the latter admittedly pleases recent philosophers more. Too little of what is good has power in the world for progress to be ascribed to the world in a predicative judgment; yet no good, not even its trace, is without progress. If, as according to a mystical doctrine, innerworldly events down to the most trivial dealings are supposed to have consequences for the life of the absolute itself, then something similar must be true for progress. Every single aspect of the coherent context of deception is certainly relevant to its possible end. Good is what wrests itself away, finds language and opens the eye. As that which wrests itself away, the good is woven into history which, without clearly orienting itself toward reconciliation, allows the possibility of reconciliation to flash in the progression of its movement.

According to established custom, the moments from which the concept of progress live are part philosophical, part social. Without society, the notion of progress would be entirely empty; all its elements are drawn from society. Had society not passed from a gathering or hunting horde to agriculture, from slavery to the formal freedom of subjects, from fear of demons to reason, from want to parrying pestilence and hunger and to the improvement of overall living conditions; if one sought, *more philosophico,* to keep pure the idea of progress, to spin it out of the essence of time, for instance, then it would have no content at all. But once the meaning of a concept makes necessary a transition to facticity, this transition cannot be halted arbitrarily. The idea of reconciliation itself—by finite measurement the transcendent *telos* of all progress—cannot be broken out of the immanent process of enlightenment; for enlightenment removes fear, and by putting forward the human being as an answer to human beings' questions, it wins the concept of humanity which alone raises itself above the immanence of the world. All the same, progress is not absorbed into society, and is not identical to society; as society is, it is at times the opposite of progress. Philosophy in general, whenever it was worthwhile, was at the same time a doctrine of society; yet ever since philosophy delivered itself over without demur to societal power, it must assertively separate itself from society; the purity it fell back upon is the bad conscience of its impurity—its complicity with the world. The concept of progress is philosophical in that it articulates social movement while simultaneously contradicting it. Social in origin, the concept of progress requires critical confrontation with real society. The moment of redemption, however secularized, cannot be erased from the concept. Its irreducibility to either its facticity or its idea suggests its own contradiction. For the enlightened moment in it, which terminates in reconciliation with nature by calming nature's terror, is sibling to the enlightened moment of nature domination. The model of progress is the control of outer and inner—or human—nature, even if progress is relocated into the deity. The oppression practiced in such control, and which has its highest spiritual form of reflection in the identity principle of reason, reproduces antagonism. The more identity is postulated by the dominating spirit, the more injustice the non-identical meets with. Injustice is passed on by the resistance of the non-identical. Resistance, then again, strengthens the oppressing principle, while the oppressed, though poisoned, simultaneously trudges on. All that is within the whole progresses; only the whole, so far, does not. Goethe's "And all urgency, all struggling / Is eternal rest in God the Master"[7] codifies this experience; and Hegel's doctrine of the process of world-spirit, of absolute dynamic, as a turning back within itself or even its game with itself, comes exceedingly close to Goethe's epigram. Only one *nota bene* should be added to the sum of its intuition: that this whole stands still in its movement, that because it knows nothing outside of itself, it is not the divine absolute but rather its opposite made unrecognizable by thought. Kant neither bowed to this deceit nor absolutized the break. When at the most sublime place in his philosophy of history he teaches that antagonism, the entanglement of progress in myth, in captivation by nature through domination of nature, in short, in the realm of unfreedom, tends toward the realm of freedom by force of its own law—Hegel's cunning of reason later came out of this— this says no less than that the condition of the possibility of reconciliation is its contradiction, and that of freedom, unfreedom. Kant's doctrine stands at a watershed. It conceives the idea of this reconciliation as immanent in antagonistic "development" by deriving it from a design which nature harbors for human beings. The dogmatic-rationalistic rigidity, on the other hand, with which such a design is supposed in nature—as if nature itself were not comprehended in development and its own concept altered thereby—is a reprint of the violence which identity-fixing spirit does to nature. The statics of the concept of nature is a function of the dynamic concept of reason; the more the latter usurps from the non-identical, the more nature becomes a residual *caput mortuum*, and precisely this makes it easy to outfit nature with the qualities of eternity which sanctify and justify its ends. The "design" can only be thought insofar as reason is attributed to nature itself. Even in the metaphysical use Kant makes in the above passage of the concept of nature—a usage which brings it close to the transcendant thing-in-itself—nature remains a product of spirit just as in the *Critique of Pure Reason*. While spirit subdued nature, according to Bacon's program, by making itself at all its stages equal to nature, at the Kantian stage spirit projected itself back upon nature—insofar as nature is supposed to be an absolute and not merely constituted—for the sake of a possibility of reconciliation in which nonetheless the primacy of the subject does not diminish. At the place where Kant comes closest to the concept of reconciliation—in the thought that antagonism terminates in its abolition—the catchword occurs of a society in which freedom is "bound up . . . with irresistible power." But even talk of power recalls attention to the dialectic of progress itself. While the continuing oppression which set progress loose has always simultaneously arrested it, this oppression—as emancipation of consciousness—also first made the antagonism and the whole of deception recognizable at all, the prerequisite for settling the antagonism. The progress which the ever-same brought forth is that finally progress can begin, of any instant. While the image of humankind progressing may remind one of a giant who slowly gets moving after immemorial sleep, but then storms forth and tramples down all that gets in his way, still, his ungainly awakening is the sole potential for a coming of age (*Mündigkeit*); the potential that captivation by nature, in which progress itself plays a part, will not have the last word. For eons, the question of progress made no sense. It only posed itself when the dynamic became free from which the idea of freedom could be extrapolated. While progress—which since Augustine has been the transferal of the individual's natural course of life, suspended between birth and death, to the species—may be as mythical as the notion of the course which fate's command prescribes for the stars, the idea of progress is just as much the anti-mythological idea as such which explodes the circulation to which it belongs. Progress means: a coming out of the spell, even out of the spell of progress which is itself nature, when humankind becomes aware of its own indigenousness to nature and halts the mastery which it exerts over nature through which mastery by nature continues. In this respect it could be said that progress only properly occurs where it ends.

This *imago* of progress is encoded in a concept which all camps today univocally defame, that of decadence. The *Jugendstil* artists professed it. This is certainly not merely because they wanted to express their own historical state, which in many cases seemed to them biological morbidity. In the urgent desire to eternalize their state in images lived this sentiment (and here they agreed deeply with the philosophers of life): whatever it was about themselves which seemed to prophecy both their own and the world's downfall, in this alone is the true rescued. Hardly anyone has expressed this more succinctly than Peter Altenberg: "Mistreatment of horses. This will cease when passers-by will be so irritable and decadent that they become raving mad in such cases and, losing control of themselves, commit a desperate crime, shooting down the vile, cowardly coachman—. Inability to tolerate mistreatment of horses is the deed of the decadent, weak-nerved human being of the future! So far, human beings have just had the miserable strength to steer clear of such troubling affairs and mind their own business."[8] Just so, Nietzsche, who condemned pity, collapsed in Turin when he saw how a coachman beat his horse. Decadence was the *fata morgana* of the progress which has not yet begun. The ideal of complete, life-renouncing heedlessness to purpose, even if narrow-minded and willfully obstinate, was the reverse image of the false purposiveness of industry, in which everything is for something else. The irrationalism of *décadence* denounced the unreason of the reigning reason. To irrationalism, a split off, arbitrary, privileged happiness is holy because it alone stands up for being an escapee, whereas every immediate notion of the happiness of the whole—the greatest possible happiness for the greatest number according to the current liberal formula—barters happiness away to the self-preserving apparatus, the sworn enemy of happiness, even where happiness is proclaimed as an aim. In just such a spirit, the notion dawns in Altenberg that extreme individuation is the place-holder of humankind: "For inasmuch as an individuality tending in any direction has a justification . . ., it must be none other than a first, a forerunner in some organic development of the human in general which, however, lies along the naturally determined route of possible development for all human beings! To be the "one-and-only" is worthless, fate's miserable playing-around with an individual. To be the "first" is everything! . . . he knows, the whole of humankind comes behind him! He is merely sent out in advance by God! . . . All human beings will one day be quite fine, quite delicate, quite loving. . . . True individuality is to be— alone and in advance—what later everyone but everyone must become."[9]

91

THEODOR W. ADORNO

Humankind can be thought only through this extreme of thorough differentiation, individuation, not as a comprehensive master concept.

The forbiddance issued by Hegel's and Marx's dialectical theories against depicting utopia smells the betrayal of utopia. Decadence is the nerve center at which the dialectic of progress becomes, as it were, bodily appropriated by consciousness. Whoever inveighs against decadence inevitably sides with the standpoint of sexual taboos, the violation of which makes up the antinomian ritual of decadence. In the insistence upon these taboos for the benefit of the unity of the nature-dominating I drones the voice of deceived, unreflective progress. But progress can therefore be convicted of its own irrationality because it always magically transmutes the means it employs into the ends it isolates. Of course, the counterposition of decadence remains abstract, and this helped bring the curse of ridiculousness upon it. It mistakes the particularity of happiness upon which it necessarily becomes bent for immediate utopia, for realized humankind, while itself being disfigured by unfreedom, privilege and class mastery; it admits to these, yet also glorifies them. The unleashed erotic disposition of its wishful thinking would also be perpetuated slavery, like in Wilde's "Salomé."

The explosive tendency of progress is not merely the Other to the movement of progressing domination of nature, the abstract negation of this movement; rather, it exacts the unfolding of reason precisely through domination of nature. Only reason, the principle of social mastery turned inside the subject, would be able to abolish this mastery. The possibility of that which wrests itself away is made actual by the pressure of negativity. On the other hand, reason—which wants out of nature—molds nature in the first place into what it must fear. The concept of progress is dialectical in a strict, unmetaphorical sense in that its organon, reason, is unitary; rather than a nature-dominating level and a reconciling level being contiguous in reason, both share in all its determinations. The one moment changes into its other only by literally reflecting itself, by reason turning reason upon itself and emancipating itself, in its self-confinement, from the demon of identity. Kant's incomparable greatness proved itself not least in that he held firmly and incorruptibly to the unity of reason, even in its contradictory usage: the nature-dominating usage as causal-mechanical—according to his language, theoretical—reason, and the conciliatively nature-conforming usage as judgment; he displaced reason's difference strictly into the self-limitation of nature-dominating reason. A metaphysical interpretation of Kant should impute no latent ontology to him, but instead should read the structure of his entire thinking as a dialectic of enlightenment; Hegel, the dialectician par excellence, fails to notice this dialectic because, in consciousness of Unitary Reason, he erases its limits and thereby gets caught in the mythical totality which he considers "reconciled" in the absolute idea. Progress does not merely circumscribe, as in Hegel's philosophy of history, the range of what belongs to dialectic; rather, it is dialectical in its own concept like the categories of the *Science of Logic*. Absolute domination of nature is absolute subjugation by nature (*Naturverfallenheit*) and yet goes beyond this in meditation on itself, myth which demythologizes myth. The protest of the subject, however, would no longer be theoretical and also not contemplative. The notion of the mastery of pure reason as a being-in-itself, separate from the praxis, subdues even the subject and disciplines it to be an instrument toward ends. Reasons's helpful self-reflection however, would be its transition to praxis: reason would see through itself as a moment of praxis; instead of mistaking itself for the absolute, it would know that it is a mode of compartment. The anti-mythological aspect of progress cannot be thought without the practical act which seizes by the bridle the delusion of the autarchy of spirit. Thus, progress is not at all ascertainable through disinterested consideration.

Those who, since antiquity and with ever new words, make the same wish: that there be no progress, have the most dangerous pretense of all. This pretense lives from the false inference that since no progress has taken place until now, there will never be any. It presents the disconsolate return of the same as the message of Being which must be heard and respected, whereas Being itself, to whose voice this message is imputed, is a cryptogram of the very myth, liberation from which would be a moment of freedom. The translation of historical despair into the norm which must be followed resounds of that horrid construction—the theological doctrine of original sin—according to which the corruptness of human nature legitimates domination, and radical evil, evil. This sentiment has a catchword with which it obscurantistically proscribes the idea of progress in modern times: belief in progress. The habitus of those who chide the concept of progress as trite and positivistic is usually positivistic itself. They declare the way of the world, which repeatedly cashed in progress and which always indeed was progress, to be evidence that the world plan does not tolerate progress, so that whoever does not give it up commits sacrilege. The side of the terrible is taken with self-righteous profundity, and the idea of progress is slandered according to the scheme: whatever miscarries for human beings is ontologically refused them; in the name of their finitude and mortality, it is their duty to fully appropriate both of these. Sobriety would reply to this false reverence that progress from the slingshot to the megaton bomb may indeed be satanic laughter;

yet in the age of the bomb, it would also envisage for the first time a situation in which all violence might disappear. All the same, a theory of progress must absorb what is sound in the invectives against belief in progress as an antidote against the mythology from which this theory suffers. The last thing that would suit a doctrine of progress conscious of itself would be to contest that a shallow doctrine exists simply because derision of the latter belongs in the treasure house of ideology. In spite of Condorcet, the much-chided idea of progress of the eighteenth century is certainly not as shallow as is that of the nineteenth century; in Rousseau, the doctrine of radical perfectibility is brought together with that of the radical corruptness of human nature. As long as the bourgeois class was oppressed, at least as regards political forms, it opposed the dominant stationary situation with progress as its slogan; the slogan's pathos was the echo of this. Not until this class had moved into the decisive positions of power did the concept of progress degenerate into the ideology of which ideological profundity accused the eighteenth century. The nineteenth century ran into the limit of bourgeois society; this society could not realize its own reason, its own ideals of freedom, justice and humane immediacy, without its order being sublated. This compelled society to untruthfully ascribe to itself what had been neglected as if achieved. The lying, for which educated bourgeois then reproached the belief in progress of the uneducated or of reformist labor leaders, was an expression of bourgeois apologetics. Of course, as the shadow of imperialism fell, the bourgeoisie quickly dispensed with this ideology and latched onto the desperate one of falsifying negativity—which belief in progress disputed away—into something metaphysically substantial.

Whoever smugly rubs their hands in remembrance of the sinking of the Titanic because the iceberg supposedly dealt the first blow to the thought of progress, forgets or surpresses that this unfortunate accident, otherwise in no way fateful, prompted measures which guarded against unplanned natural catastrophes in shipping during the following half-century. It is a part of the dialectic of progress that the historical setbacks which are themselves instigated by the principle of progress—what would be more progressive than the race for the blue ribbon?—also provide the condition for humankind to find means to avoid them in the future. The coherent deception of progress pushes beyond itself. It is mediated to that order in which the category of progress would first win its justification in that the devastation which progress brings about can only be made good again, if at all, by its own powers, never through reestablishment of the older situation which was its victim. The progress of domination of nature which, according to Benjamin's parable, proceeds in contradiction to that

94

true progress which would have its *telos* in redemption, is still not without all hope. The two concepts of progress communicate with each other not just in the averting of final calamity, but rather in each actual form of the easing of persistent suffering.

The belief in internality feels itself to be a corrective of belief in progress. But internality does not guarantee progress, nor does the improvability of human beings. Already in Augustine, the notion of progress—he was not yet allowed to use this word—is as ambivalent as is required by the dogma of succeeded redemption in the face of an unredeemed world. On the one hand, progress is historical, in accord with the six ages of the world which correspond to the periodization of human life; on the other hand, it is not of this world but internal, or according to Augustine's own language, mystical. Supposedly, *civitas terrena* and *civitas dei* are invisible empires, and no one can say which of the living belong to which; the secret election to grace decides on that, the same divine will which moves history according to plan. Already in Augustine, however—according to Karl Heinz Haag's insight—the internalization of progress permits the world to be assigned to the powers that be, and thus Christianity to be commended—as later by Luther—for preserving the state. The Platonic transcendence which becomes fused in Augustine with the Christian idea of salvation history makes it possible to cede *this* world to the principle against which progress is thought and, in spite of all philosophy of history, to allow not until judgment day abrupt reestablishment of undisturbed creation. This ideological mark has remained engraved in the internalization of progress to this day. As opposed to this mark, internality itself, as historically produced, is a function of progress or of its opposite. The constitution of human beings makes up only one moment in innerworldly progress; and today, this is certainly not the primary moment. The argument that there is no progress because none occurs within the inward is false because it fabricates society in its historical process as an unmediatedly human society, having as its law what human beings themselves are. But it is the essence of historical objectivity that the human-made, institutions in the broadest sense, render themselves independent from human beings and become second nature. This fallacy then allows the thesis of the constancy of human nature, whether this constancy be transfigured or deplored. Innerworldly progress has its mythical moment in that, as Hegel and Marx recognized, it transpires above the heads of subjects and forms them in its own image; yet it would be foolish to dispute progress simply because it does not completely have done with its objects, the subjects. To halt what Schopenhauer calls the self-unrolling wheel would certainly require that human potential which is not entirely

95

absorbed by the necessity of historical movement. The idea of a progress which leads out and away is presently blocked, this because the subjective moments of spontaneity are beginning to wither in the historical process. To desperately set an isolated, allegedly ontological concept of the subjectively spontaneous against societal omnipotence, like the French existentialists, is too optimistic even as an expression of despair; ever-turning spontaneity cannot be conceived of outside of societal entwinement. The hope that such spontaneity would be sufficient here and now would be illusionary and idealistic. One fosters this hope only in an historical hour in which no support for hope is visible. Existentialist decisionism is merely the reflex reaction to the seamless totality of world-spirit. Yet this totality is itself an appearance. Indurated institutions, the relations of production, are not being plain and simple but something human-made and revocable, even though omnipotent. In their relationship to subjects, from whom they stem and whom they enclose, they remain antagonistic through and through. Not only does the whole demand its own alteration to avoid ruin; because of its antagonistic essence, it is also impossible for it to force that complete identity with human beings which is relished by negative utopias. Therefore, innerworldly progress, adversary of the other progress, is simultaneously also open to the possibility of this other, no matter how little it is able to tie this possibility to its own law.

It will be plausibly asserted, on the other hand, that all does not proceed quite as robustly in the spiritual spheres, art, and especially law, politics and anthropology, as it does with regard to the material forces of production. Hegel himself articulated this about art, as did Jochmann to an extreme; Marx then formulated in principle the non-simultaneity in the movement of superstructure and substructure in the proposition that the superstructure transforms itself more slowly than the substructure. Evidently, no one was astonished that spirit, fleeting and mobile, should be considered stationary, as opposed to the *rudis indigestaque moles* of that which, even in the context of society, is not named 'material' gratuitously. Analogously, psychoanalysis teaches that the unconscious—from which consciousness and the objective forms of spirit are fed—is ahistorical. To be sure, even what is subsumed in brutal classification under the concept of culture and which subjective consciousness also contains within itself raises a perennial objection to the every-sameness of the merely existing (*des bloss Seienden*). But it perennially finds its objection futile. The ever-sameness of the whole, human beings' dependence upon vital necessity, upon the material conditions of their self-preservation, all this hides, as it were, behind its own dynamic, that of the growth and accumulation of alleged societal riches; this benefits ideology. Spirit, however, the authentically dynamic principle which would like to get above and beyond this, can easily be shown that it has not succeeded; that pleases ideology no less. Reality produces the appearance of developing upwards, while it remains *au fond* what it was. Spirit, which aspires to the New so far as it is not itself a mere piece of apparatus, smashes its head in its hopelessly repeated attempts, like an insect flying toward the light into a pane of glass. Spirit is not what it enthrones itself as, the Other, the transcendent in its purity, but itself a part of natural history. Because natural history appears in society as a dynamic, spirit since the Eleatics and Plato fancies that it has found the Other, that which is removed from *civitas terrena,* in the unchangeable self-same; spirit's forms—logic above all, which is latently inherent to all that is spiritual—are tailored accordingly. In these forms, spirit is seized by something stationary, precisely that against which it strives and of which it nevertheless remains a part. Reality's spell over spirit debars it from doing what spirit's own concept wants to do vis-à-vis the merely existing: to fly. As the more delicate and fleeting, spirit is all the more susceptible to oppression and mutilation. The place-holder of what progress would be above and beyond all progress stands askew to progress which actually occurs, and this, in turn, also does honor to the place-holder: by lacking complicity with progress, it reveals what progress is up to. Yet wherever it can be judged with reason that spirit as a being-for-itself progresses, there spirit itself participates in domination of nature simply because it is not, as it imagines, *choris,* but rather entwined into the same life process from which it divorced itself in keeping with this process' own law. All progress in cultural spheres is that of domination of material, of technique. The truth content of spirit is not indifferent to this. A Mozart quartet is not simply better made than a symphony of the Mannheim School; it also ranks higher as better made and more thoroughly consistent in an emphatic sense. On the other hand, it is problematic whether High Renaissance painting really outdid so-called primitive painting through the development of perspectivist technique; whether the best in works of art is not the for-the-first-time, an abrupt emergence achieved when domination of material is incomplete and which vanishes as soon as it becomes technically mastered. Progress in domination of material in art is in no way immediately one and the same with progress in art itself. In the Early Renaissance, however, had one defended the gold background against perspective, this would not only have been reactionary but also objectively untrue by being counter to what the Early Renaissance's own logic demanded; only historically does the complexity of progress unfold itself

97

as well. In the afterlife of spiritual creations, what may prevail or find acceptance *à la longue* above and beyond their level of advance is their quality, at bottom their truth content, though here again, only by dint of a process of progressing consciousness. The notion of the canonical essence of Hellenism which survived still in the dialecticians Hegel and Marx is not merely an undissolved rudiment of the educational tradition but also, in all its questionableness, a precipitate of a dialectical insight. Art—and in the spiritual sphere, art is hardly alone—must unavoidably absorb the increasing domination of nature in order to express its content. However, it thereby also secretly works against what it wants to say; it distances itself from that which, without word or concept, it sets in opposition to the increasing domination of nature. This might help explain why the seeming continuity of so-called spiritual development often breaks off, and does so with an appeal—albeit guided by great misunderstanding—for a return to nature. Social moments, among others, are especially to blame for spirit's terror at the contradiction in its own development and for spirit's attempt, futile of course, to rectify this contradiction by resorting to that from which it estranged itself and which it therefore mistakes as invariant.

The paradox that there is some progress and yet is none is perhaps nowhere so drastic as in philosophy, where the idea of progress itself is at home. As compelling as the transitions from one authentic philosophy to an other, mediated by criticism, might be, the assertion that there was progress between them—Plato and Aristotle, Kant and Hegel—or indeed in a philosophical universal history as a whole would remain dubious all the same. Neither is the invariance of the alleged philosophical object, true Being—whose concept dissolved irrevocably in the history of philosophy—to be blamed for this, nor would a merely aesthetic view of philosophy be defensible which placed imposing thought architecture or even the ominous great thinkers higher than the truth, which in no way coincides with the immanent closure and stringency of philosophies. The verdict would be completely pharisaical and false that progress in philosophy would lead it away from what the jargon of bad philosophy dubs philosophy's concern: for in this way need would become the guarantor of truth content. On the contrary, the inevitable and questionable progress of that which receives its limit from its theme—the limit—is established by the principle of reason, without which philosophy would be unthinkable because without this principle, thinking cannot be. One concept after the other tumbles into the Orcus of the mythical. Philosophy lives in symbiosis with science; it cannot dissociate itself from science without dogmatism, and ultimately, without a relapse into mythology. Yet its content would be to express what is neglected or cut away by science, by division of labor, by the forms of reflection of the industry of self-preservation. Philosophy's progress therefore moves away from that toward which philosophy would simultaneously have to progress; the force of experience which it registers is weakened the more it polishes and sharpens scientific apparatus. The movement which philosophy as a whole carries out is the pure self-someness of its principle. The price for philosophy is always also paid by what it would have to grasp and can only grasp by dint of the self-reflection through which it leaves behind the standpoint of stubborn immediacy also called, in Hegelian terms, the philosophy of reflection. Philosophical progress dupes because the tighter it joins its foundational connections and the more airtight and unassailable its statements become, the more it becomes identity-thinking. Philosophical progress covers over objects with a net which presumptuously thrusts itself in place of the matter at hand (*Sache selbst*) by stopping up the gaps of that which it itself is not. In harmony with society's real retrogressive tendencies, the progress of philosophy seems in the end indeed to have revenge taken on it for hardly having been progress. To assume progress from Hegel to the logical positivists who reject Hegel as unclear or senseless is simply comical. Whether in narrow minded scientification or in denial of reason, even philosophy is not immune to lapsing into the sort of regression which certainly is no better than the maliciously ridiculed belief in progress.

In bourgeois society which created the concept of total progress, the convergence of such progress with the negation of progress arises from this society's principle: exchange. Exchange is the rational form of mythical ever-sameness. In the equal-for-equal of all exchange proceedings, one act cancels the other; the balance remains the same. If the exchange were just, nothing should have happened; all remains as it was. But at the same time, the assertion of progress, which conflicts with this principle, is as true as the doctrine of equal-for-equal is a lie. From time immemorial, not just since the capitalist appropriation of surplus value in the exchange of labor power as commodity for the cost of its reproduction, the one, socially more powerful opponent receives more than the other. Through this injustice, something New occurs in the exchange; the process, which proclaims its own stasis, becomes dynamic. The truth of expansion lives off of the lie of equality. Social acts must reciprocally sublate each other in the overall system, and yet they do not. Where bourgeois society satisfies the concept which it harbors for itself, it knows no progress; where it knows progress it violates its own law in which this delict already lies, and eternalizes, along with the inequality, the injustice above which progress is supposed to raise itself. Yet this injustice is simultaneously the condition for possible justice. The fulfillment of the incessantly broken exchange contract would converge with its abolition; exchange would disappear if true equals were exchanged; true progress would not merely be an Other vis-à-vis exchange but also exchange become conscious of itself. So thought the antipodes Marx and Nietzsche; Zarathustra postulates that the human being will be redeemed from revenge. For revenge is the mythical prototype of exchange; as long as domination occurs through exchange, myth will dominate as well. The intersection of ever-sameness and the New in the exchange relationship manifests itself in the *imagines* of progress under bourgeois industrialism. It strikes one as paradoxical about these *imagines* that anything Other at all still comes into being, that the *imagines* grow old, because the ever-sameness of the exchange principle intensifies by dint of technology into domination by repetition in the sphere of production. The life process itself rigidifies in the expression of the ever-same; hence the shock of photographs from the nineteenth century and now already from the early twentieth. The absurdity explodes that something happens where the phenomenon says that nothing more could happen; the habitus of the phenomenon becomes horrifying. In the shudder of horror, the habitus of the system congeals into appearance; the more the system expands, the more it hardens into what it has been since time immemorial. What Benjamin called dialectic at a standstill is certainly less a Platonizing remnant than an attempt to philosophically bring about consciousness of such paradox. Dialectical images: these are the historical-objective archetypes of that antagonistic unity of standstill and movement which defines the most general bourgeois concept of progress.

Both Hegel and Marx bore witness that even the dialectical view of progress needed correction. The dynamic which they taught is thought not as a dynamic plain and simple but as united with its opposite: something firm from which alone dynamic can be read in the first place. Marx, who criticized all notions of society's genuine naturalness as fetishistic, also rejected just as much—counter to the Lassallean Gotha Program— the absolutization of dynamic in the doctrine of labor as the sole source of societal wealth; and he conceded the possibility of relapse into barbarism. It may be more than mere accident that Hegel, in spite of his famous definition of history, includes no detailed theory of progress, and that Marx himself seems to have avoided the word, even in the repetitiously cited programmatic section of the "Preface" to *A Contribution to the Critique of Political Economy*.[10] The dialectical taboo on concept fetishes, on inheritance from the old anti-mythological Enlightenment in its self-reflective phase, also extends to the category which formerly molli-fied reification: progress, a category which deceives as soon as it—as a single moment—usurps the whole. Fetishization of progress confirms its particularity, its limitation to techniques. Were progress to truly assume power over the whole, the concept of which bears the marks of the vio-lence it does, then progress would no longer be totalitarian. Progress is not a conclusive category. It wants to disrupt the triumph of radical evil, not to triumph in itself. A situation is thinkable in which this category loses its meaning and yet which is not that of the universal regression which today allies itself with progress. Then, progress would become transformed into resistance against the perpetual danger of relapse. Prog-ress is precisely this resistance at all stages, not capitulation to the main-stream which courses through them.

Translated by Eric Krakauer

NOTES

1 The German original, "Fortschritt," was a lecture given by Adorno at the *Münsteraner Philosophenkongress* on October 22, 1962, published first in Harold Delius and Günther Patzig (eds.), *Argumentationen, Festschrift für Josef König* (Göttingen, 1964); and re-printed in Theodor W. Adorno, *Stichworte* (Frankfurt: Suhrkamp, 1978), and in Peter Bulthaup (ed.), *Materialien zu Benjamins Thesen "Über den Begriff der Geschichte"* (Frankfurt: Suhrkamp, 1975). Translator's Note (TN)

2 Cf. Immanuel Kant, "Idea for a Universal History From a Cosmopolitan Point of View" in *On History*, trans. Lewis White Beck (New York: Bobbs-Merrill, 1963), p. 14.

3 Cf. Kant, p. 16.

4 Walter Benjamin, "Theses on the Philosophy of History" in *Illuminations,* trans. Harry Zohn (New York: Schocken, 1977), p. 260.

5 Benjamin, p. 254.

6 "Und wer's nie gekonnt, der stehle / Weinend sich aus diesem Bund." (TN)

7 "Und alles Drängen, alles Ringen / Ist ewige Ruh in Gott dem Herrn." From "Zahme Xenien VI", translated in *Goethe: Selected Verse,* ed. David Luke (New York: Penguin, 1981), p. 280. (TN)

8 Peter Altenberg, *Auswahl von Karl Kraus* (Zürich: Atlantis Verlag, 1963), p. 122.

9 Altenberg, pp. 133-134.

10 The German text of the "Preface" mentions "progressive Epochen der ökonomischen Gesellschaftsformation" ("progressive epochs in the economic formation of society"). (TN)

PRODUCTION, RECEPTION, CRITICISM: WALTER BENJAMIN AND THE PROBLEM OF MEANING IN ART

JENNIFER TODD

Walter Benjamin's work speaks directly to the contemporary debates in aesthetics between the conventionalists and deconstructionists, who hold that we may legitimately invent an indefinite multiplicity of meanings for any artwork, and the objectivists who argue that we can discover the real meaning of an artwork.[1] I argue that Benjamin's work offers a qualified critique of both relativism and objectivism. By focusing on the processes of production and reproduction of artworks we can "rub history against the grain" (I,257) and rescue the real meaning of a work from a traditional interpretation which bolsters ruling class power.

The structure of my argument is as follows. In the first section of the paper I explore Benjamin's view that relativist theories accurately describe the contemporary mode of perception in which the public takes artworks as suits its immediate purpose. While Benjamin does not himself adopt this stance he does argue that public reception of artworks conditions their meaning. This argument against objectivist theories is the topic of the second section of the paper. In the third section I argue that the radical critic, by attending to the processes of production and reproduction of artworks, may re-discover the real meaning of the works. In the final section of some internal tensions in Benjamin's thought are noted.

THE DECLINE OF THE AURA AND THE DISINTEGRATION OF MEANING

"Beauty has nothing for the uninitiated." (*OGTD*, 181). Benjamin argues that in the twentieth century languages of art have lost their traditional contexts of meaning. Artistic reference has become arbitrary; works can be interpreted in any manner. He distinguishes allegorical and symbolic modes of reference and sees the modern trend as descendent of allegory.

Benjamin writes that in allegory "any person, any object, any relationship can mean absolutely anything else" (*OGTD*, 175), while "word, syllable and sound are emancipated from any context of traditional meaning and are flaunted as objects which can be exploited for allegorical purposes" (*OGTD*, 207). The conventional nature of that artistic reference Benjamin here sees as specific to allegory/has recently been argued to be an essential feature of all artistic symbol systems.[2] Benjamin's distinction between allegory and symbol can be clarified from this modern perspective. The audience is spontaneously stirred by symbolism and understands the meaning of the symbol as if immediately; it responds to this meaning without question. The audience is absorbed in the symbol and in the work, following what appears to be its objective meaning albeit unable to state it.[3] To say that there is an "indivisible unity of form and content" (*OGTD*, 160) in the symbol is, in part, to say that the artist is able to form a "language of art" which appears transparent because it uses the tacit perceptions and reactions of the audience without calling attention to itself or to them; as if naturally the symbol calls attention to what it represents and expresses.

In allegory, on the other hand, the conventional nature of artistic reference is apparent; we need an explicit key or code to unlock the artistic language. As Gadamer points out, allegory "rests on firm traditions and has always a fixed statable meaning which does not resist rational comprehension through the concept—on the contrary, the concept and concern of allegory is closely bound up with dogmatics."[4] Explicit rules of artistic reference are needed because in allegory anything can be used to represent anything else. Benjamin writes that "with this possibility a destructive, but just verdict is passed on the profane world: it is characterized as a world in which the detail is of not great importance" (*OGTD*, 175).

In contemporary literature, on Benjamin's view, just such a destructive verdict is passed on the profane world but without a tradition of dogmatic theology which might anchor one particular interpretation of a work or a sign.[5] In the contemporary world anything can represent anything else, artworks are detached from their traditional meanings and opened to use for any purpose by any audience (*I*, 221). The objectivity of the work's meaning is lost in the subjectively experienced needs of the audience. "A man who concentrates before a work of art is absorbed by it. . . . In contrast, the distracted man absorbs the work of art" (*I*, 239).

Benjamin has identified as a contemporary phenomenon that lack of

103

attachment between signifier and signified, that conventional, open, and contestable nature of the rules of artistic reference, which philosophers of such different persuasions as Nelson Goodman and Jacques Derrida argue is central to all artistic symbolism.[6] I would argue that it follows from Derrida's position (and despite contrary tendencies in his thought from Goodman's also) that we cannot say that any socially accepted interpretation of a work is wrong; we can merely invent a newer interpretation which is more exciting; an artwork means whatever we (any of us) happen to say it means. For Benjamin, in the contemporary world we take the artwork to mean whatever we say it means: in fact consumers increasingly project their interpretations and interests on artworks without concern for the authority of the works. But in identifying this social tendency Benjamin does not unambiguously affirm it.

Consider Benjamin's diagnosis of the contemporary arts and his claim that the "aura" of the artwork is now lost. The aura is a "semblance of distance" (*OWS*, 250) which gives an object a human presence as though it would look back at us (*I*, 188). The auratic artwork has such a unique presence; its very history of production and reception contribute to this presence, just as the continuous repetition of a story by different storytellers who respect past retelling gradually forms the uniqueness of the story itself, as a pearl is formed (*I*, 93). The auratic artwork imposes itself on the audience, forcing it to subdue its own concerns and to respond appropriately to the work. "The uniqueness of a work of art is inseparable from its being imbedded in the fabric of tradition" (*I*, 233). Such a work possesses an authority which demands that the audience respond to the work in the light of tradition. (Benjamin uses the term "tradition" in a double sense—as the "dominant tradition" and the "tradition of the oppressed." In this article I use the term to refer to the dominant tradition.)

The existence of the aura is conditional on the social context. Storytelling is only possible where experiences are communicable and can be assimilated in a relaxed manner; it flourishes in a society of peasants, seamen, and journeymen (*I*, 83ff). Benjamin argues that capitalism has destroyed the audience's ability to recognize an auratic artwork at the same time as it promotes forms of artistic production which do not lead to auratic works.

Marx showed that capitalist commodity production, where exchange value dominates use value, leads to the universal equality of all things.[7] Benjamin traces the parallel reifying effects of capitalist production on the consciousness and experience of the public. In factory work, in city life with its ever increasing crowds and traffic, in mass societies where the individual is anonymous, isolated, socialized only by impersonal institutions and rules, life has become ruled by "mechanisms" so that integrated experience and praxis become impossible. In the twentieth century, Benjamin says, experience comes as a series of shocks. Time no longer integrates experience but splits it up. The entertainment industry, from the world exhibitions of the nineteenth century to the twentieth century cinema, offers distractions and stimulants, additional commodities to be inspected. Thus "technology has subjected the human sensorium to a complex kind of training" (*I*, 175) whereby the aura can no longer be appreciated. "To pry an object from its shell, to destroy its aura, is the mark of perception whose 'sense of the universal equality of things' has increased to such a degree that it extracts it even from a unique object by means of reproduction" (*I*, 223). This, the least rewarding audience for an artist, is already in existence in the nineteenth century; for such audiences "will power and the ability to concentrate are not their strong point; what they prefer is sensual pleasures" (*I*, 155).

At the same time, Benjamin argues, the new artistic techniques of photography and film have allowed for a vast expansion of the commodity market in art. Photography has provided surrogate holidays in its images of strange lands and excitement in its pictures of rich, poor, and freak.[8] Even the older forms of art—painting and theater—are affected. "The technique of reproduction detaches the reproduced object from the domain of tradition" (*I*, 221) and "enables the original to meet the beholder half-way" in "situations which would be out of reach for the original itself" (*I*, 220). Thus, the audience, which can use reproductions as it will, need no longer be so impressed by the authority of the original work.

In this coincidence of audience reactions and artistic developments Benjamin detects the shattering of tradition, the destruction of the aura and a change in the entire function of art. Since artworks can be used for the immediate needs and interests of the public, art—of the past and of the present—should be used to further the political interests of the working class. Art "begins to be based on another practice—politics" (*I*, 224). The critic's task of interpreting works correctly is outmoded. Not interpretation but polemics in "the battle of minds" is needed since "the critic is the strategist in the literary battle" (*OWS*, 67).

Benjamin accepts as inevitable that the aura of the artwork, and with it all sense of the objectivity of artistic meaning, will be lost in advancing capitalism.[9] Sometimes he seems to affirm this trend. He comments on the politically progressive attitude of the mass public towards films (*I*, 234); he is impressed by a Moscow gallery where the worker-viewer has overturned the traditional criteria of artistic masterpieces, concentrating on "minor" genre paintings which "have for him a very transitory but solid meaning" (*OWS,* 184); he notes that mechanical reproduction "emancipates the work of art from its parasitical dependence on ritual" (*I,* 224). Benjamin's temptation to accept the reduction of the meaning of an artwork to its immediate effect on the audience (a view he scornfully rejected in *OGTD,* 51-52) is shown in "The Author as Producer" (R, 220-38) when, in an argument against contemporary attempts to insert socialist content into bourgeois art forms, he accepts Brech't dictum that we should not ask for the meaning of a work but for its usefulness (*UB,* 110). In this article he focuses so exclusively on the technology of artistic production that he seems to lose sight of the referential functions of the works produced.

Benjamin would face serious political and philosophical difficulties if he adopted the relativist trend outlined above. It might be possible to blast works out of the continuum of history on these grounds, but only to replace them in the continuum of everyday politics. The suggestion that there is revolutionary potential in the utilitarian attitude of the mass public is surely wrong. It is, after all, a commonplace of Marxist theory that the working class is not immediately aware of its real interests and of what is politically most useful for it. As Adorno has pointed out, when the relationship between audience and art-object is reversed so that the audience sees what it pleases in the work, the audience simply projects its own psychology, needs, and obsessions onto the work and sees a standardized echo of itself; thereby it learns nothing.[10]

Susan Buck-Morss argues convincingly that Benjamin did not adopt the historicist view that we interpret works of the past in the light of our everyday concerns; rather we should interpret works of the past in the light of the revolutionary potential of the present.[11] To the extent that the sole criteria of interpretation are the uncriticized needs of revolutionaries, this position is also open to serious criticism. Benjamin's tendancy to concentrate on the needs of the "revolutionary present" is underpinned by his tendency to view revolution as a total rupture with all past cultures as well as with past social relations. Habermas sees this "anarchist" view as based on the theological concept of the "Jetztzeit" which emphasizes the radical discontinuity of history and of redemption.[12] The effects of Benjamin's "anarchism" are shown in his praise of the Surrealists' "revolutionary nihilism" (*OWS,* 229), their "radical concept of freedom" (*OWS,* 236), their gay disdain for all traditions and their situationist view of art and politics where all that matters is the effect of their work on the audience. Here again the view that the revolutionary present might *learn* from the past is rejected; it can simply *use* the past. The goals of the revolutionary present are not articulated and criticized in the light of past struggles and experiences; rather past struggles are interpreted in terms of present revolutionary goals.

Philosophically, the reduction of the meaning of a work to its effectiveness on an audience allows that all responses to a work (however absurd) are equally appropriate. It prevents the development of an adequate concept of politically progressive art. When Benjamin tends towards this position in "The Author as Producer" he measures political progress in the arts in terms of the use of new artistic techniques. This purely quantitative, and therefore inadequate, criterion of progress is inevitable inasmuch as Benjamin does not consider how the new techniques open new imaginative possibilities, i.e., inasmuch as he abstracts from questions of meaning.

Finally, the view that artworks of the past can and should be read in whatever ways contemporary observers wish to read them is tantamount, as Lukacs notes in another context, to seeing history as "a great jumble sale." It is to regard the culture of the past as "a heap of lifeless objects in which one can rummage around at will."[13] This "rag-bag" approach to history prevents the fulfilment of Benjamin's own aim of redeeming the "oppressed past" (*I*, 263) not by forgetting about it or inventing arbitrary stories about it, but by re-appropriating it "from a conformism that is about to overpower it" (*I*, 255). Benjamin's view that "every image of the past that is not recognized by the present as one of its own concerns threatens to disappear irretrievably" (*I*, 255) is not an invitation to anachronism or historical invention. Rather I think it is an assertation that there is an objective, albeit concealed, meaning to past events and works and further that this meaning can only be recovered when we see its relations to our contemporary concerns. In subsequent sections I will explore this objectivist strand of Benjamin's thought.

My argument in this section has been that the value of Benjamin's analysis does not lie in his espousal of a relativist approach like Goodman's where anything can represent almost anything else and realism is simply a matter of convention; no more does it lie in an anticipation of Derrida's view that absurd interpretations of works are no less central, and probably more fun, than "standard" interpretations.[14] Benjamin did not adopt a relativism of either Goodman's or Derrida's variety. Benjamin did not adopt a relativism of either Goodman's or Derrida's variety. Rather Benjamin's importance lies in his identification of the social and artistic conditions which have destroyed the authority of the art object, opened it to multiple subjective interpretations, and thereby make the relativist position accurate as a description of our contemporary responses toward art.

OBJECTIVISM AND IDEOLOGY

If the concept of culture is a problematical one for historical materialism, the disintegration of culture into commodities to be possessed by mankind is unthinkable for it. . . The concept of culture as the embodiment of entities that are considered independently, if not of the production process in which they arose, then of that in which they continue to survive, is fetishistic (*OWS,* 360).

Benjamin vigorously opposed all attempts to consider artworks in isolation from their social context. The concept of an artwork as a particular thing which holds its meaning in itself, essentially independent of its genesis and reception, is alien to him. To think of works as isolated masterpieces is precisely to treat cultural history as a jumble sale. Indeed the dialectical approach has "no use for such rigid isolated things as work, novel, book" (*R,* 222). Instead, we must see the works in the historical context of their production, reproduction, and reception (*OWS,* 262-3; *R,* 222).

Contemporary objectivists accept that artworks are not meaningful as isolated physical objects but only when they are seen in their appropriate artistic context. They also maintain that an artwork has real meaning independent of its reception. An investigation of this approach will show more clearly the value of Benjamin's alternative.

Eva Schaper holds that an artwork is meaningful only inasmuch as it belongs to a given symbol system with given rules of reference, i.e., only inasmuch as it uses a shareable language of art. She argues, following E. D. Hirsch, that the real meaning of an artwork is given by the artist's intention.[15] The artist consciously chooses to use certain colors, patterns, or words which have a definite meaning in the language of art within which he/she works. Through these choices and other deliberate omissions and combinations, the artists places the work within a given language of art. Whether or not the artist is conscious of the full consequences of his/her choices, he/she has placed the work in a language which is public, in principle open to others, and which has an objective set of rules of reference independent of any particular artist or viewer. Schaper argues that we can "ground" our interpretation of a work by showing that it captures the objective import of the artist's choices. Of course, the audience may misunderstand or misapprehend the appropriate language. This does not challenge the epistemological basis of the objectivist view, since artists can work within an esoteric tradition, as if hermetically sealed from the general public.

Benjamin, however, would have found this approach politically dubious. In assuming that the meaning of an artwork is constituted by a given language of art we assume that the rules of this language are fixed and univocal, not essentially contestable, not a matter of social or political debate. We rely on the dominant traditional interpretations of particular styles and works modifying these interpretations only through the historical research of scholars, which itself relies on tradition. In this we may unconsciously accept the interpretation of the artworld authorities— church dignitaries, princes, collectors, artists, publishers, gallery owners, critics, university lecturers, museum curators, or arts council directors, depending on the social and political context. This would be to equate the authentic meaning of a work with what is institutionalized in social life as the socially dominant meaning. Inasmuch as the objectivists do not allow for radical reinterpretations and criticisms of traditional readings of works and styles, their theory may serve as an ideology concealing the interests of those in authority in the artworld. Benjamin commented: "The danger affects both the content of the tradition and its receivers. The same threat hangs over both: that of becoming a tool of the ruling classes. In every era the attempt must be made anew to wrest tradition away from a conformism that is about to overpower it" (*I*, 255).

There is an important philosophical issue hidden in this political criticism, since the objectivist approach overemphasizes the settled nature of language. Perhaps even scientific languages use open-textured concepts but languages of art are open to a degree far surpassing scientific and natural languages. Artists do not, typically, put down a series of figures or words whose meaning is pre-determined. Rather they change the given language and create a new construal of the world by using signs in slightly (or radically) new ways and in new combinations. I shall argue that this fact crucially undermines the view of Hirsch and Schaper that the ultimate criterion of artistic meaning is the artist's intention.

Whether the artist's innovations re-form a langugage of art and thus achieve meaningfulness, or whether they fail to create a new, shareable language, depends on the audience's ability to "read" the innovations. If communication fails the artist has failed to change the language at all; his/her work has simply not achieved meaningfulness. Consider two examples. Cézanne's innovations in painting constituted a new language for future artists to work within or re-form. It is said, however, that at the first showings the audience failed to see bathers in Cézanne's series of that name. Now we have learned to see the bathers. Cézanne's experiments in stretching the limits of human representation and perception have worked. Yet if we had not been able to "see" bathers in these pictures, whatever their title, we could not say that Cézanne invented a new way of representing bathers. We could not define Cézanne's intentions with any precision as his intentions are fully articulated only through his successful works. That it is now possible to define Cézanne's intention as being able to create this particular new language and that Cézanne fulfilled this intention is dependent on circumstances beyond Cézanne's control, namely on the structure and malleability of human perception in the nineteenth and twentieth centuries.

In contrast, when Picasso painted "Guernica" he used new forms of imagery in order to make a picture which expressed some form of strong political protest. But, at least if we accept Max Raphael's interpretation, Picasso not only failed to realize his intentions but also failed to voice them clearly.[16] The imagery is too private to communicate even to an initiated audience. Because he did not create a new public language Picasso's precise artistic and political intentions remain unclear. Note that Picasso's failure was not due to his invention of new forms of symbolism but to the failure of this symbolism to form and inform the perceptions of his audience as Cézanne's work did.

These examples illustrate, against Hirsch's intentionalist position, that we cannot point to a clear and unambiguous artistic intention in many central cases of artistic production. For such a clear intention to exist, the relevant language of art would have to exist before the artwork was produced. The openness of languages of art to creative re-formation and the fact that successful creative achievement depends on the *subsequent* response of audiences means that we cannot speak of an objective or essential artistic meaning which comes into existence at the time the artwork is produced.

Benjamin adds a further argument against objectivism, emphasizing again the crucial role of the audience's perception in constituting meaning. He points out that the very nature of a natural language is to change historically: so too the place and meaning of a literary work within the language changes. A fresh metaphor becomes hackneyed, a current form of speech becomes quaint. " . . . in its afterlife . . . the original (work) undergoes a change. Even words with fixed meaning can undergo a maturing process. The obvious tendency of a writer's style may in time wither away, only to give rise to immanent tendencies in the literary creation" (*I*, 223). While in an early article Benjamin sees the essence of this phenomenon in the nature of language, he says that the root cause lies in the way posterity receives the work (*I*, 73). In other writings Benjamin notes the importance of studying the changing modes of reception of artworks (*I*, 155; 222-23). He speaks of "the decisive importance of reception" which "allows the correction, within limits, of the process of reification undergone by the work of art" (*OWS*, 362-63). Only by seeing the changing work within the context of a language which changes in response to the interests and perceptions of the public and which in turn changes the language and the public's interests and perceptions, can we overcome the fetishistic view of cultural artifacts as self-contained, independent commodities.

Benjamin's strategy here may seem to lead to the relativism which I criticised in the previous section. For to say that the meaning of an artwork is constituted or changed by the reaction of any audience to it is to espouse the anarchist semiotics of Derrida. For Benjamin, however, the meaning of a work is not changed by the arbitrary responses of just any audience. It is rather the historically conditioned changes in modes of perception, common throughout a society or an historical period and provoked by wide-ranging social and technological developments, that are crucial in constituting and changing a work's meaning (*OWS*, 363). Benjamin himself focuses on the contemporary change in our mode of perception which has brought about the decline of the aura and the potentiality for overcoming the distinction between artist and audience, writer and reader (*R*, 225). If Benjamin is a relativist he holds to a broad historical relativism, not a narrow individualist relativism. It follows from this position that Cézanne's experiment was successful and Picasso's a failure, not because of the accidental responses of particular audiences but because the former and not the latter accurately sensed the direction of development of human perception in the twentieth century and the limits to which it might be stretched by art.[17]

I think that even this account overstates Benjamin's relativism although we must be wary here. The Marxist alternative to relativism is a belief in historical progress and Benjamin's scorn for any comforting belief in progress is especially clear in his later works, written under the shadow of fascism (*I*, 257-61). His position raises questions. Does he, for example, suggest that it is impossible for those sharing the dominant mode of perception of a period to misunderstand a work of the past? He argues that past generations have crucially misunderstood the *Trauerspiel* (*OGTD*, 48-53) and suggests that the contemporary mass public misunderstood the import of Picasso's work (*I*, 234). Does he suggest that each historically conditioned mode of perception is "equally valid" so that, for example, our contemporary mode of interpreting works as it suits our present purposes is as good a way to understand them as any other? He is certainly critical of a historicism which believes that each age is equally close to God (*I*, 255, 261-63). Is he saying that if our generation fails to understand the aura of a work then the work has lost its aura irretrievably? Habermas has argued that Benjamin intends that the aura be transcended, not destroyed, but freed from its "parasitic dependence on ritual" (*I*, 244) and opened for the profane illumination of the mass public.[18]

Consider Benjamin's attitude towards historical relativism in more detail. Benjamin holds that the mode of perception developed in a later age may enable us to see previously unappreciated values in the art of an earlier period (*OGTD*, 54-56; *OWS*, 184; *I*, 87, 210). Such a historical development opens for us the possibilities of a fuller understanding of certain works of the past. Benjamin does not think that this fuller understanding is in any sense a "re-creation" of the past (*OWS*, 353: *I*, 255). Past ages may themselves have misunderstood the import of their own works; the interrelations of artistic and religious practices is a clear example of how in the past art was appreciated in a mystified, ideological manner. The fuller understanding which we can gain is one where we divest past modes of understanding of their mystification and see what the works show us about human life and the possibility of freedom and happiness.

While particular historical developments may lead us to a mode of perception which illuminates some past art, it does not lead to the accumulation of multiple modes of perception. Past modes of perception are lost and thus historical development closes to us the possibility of understanding some works of the past. This possibility is not lost irretrievably. In Benjamin's Utopian vision of communism the fully developed individual, in harmony with his/her fellows and with nature, will re-appropriate the modes of perception of the past and will have the capacity to see the meaning and value of all past works. Thus no mode of understanding or perception should be regarded as lost for history although "only a redeemed mankind receives the fullness of its past" (*I*, 254).

We may then see Benjamin as giving a qualified critique of relativism and as holding a qualified Marxist belief in "progress." Modes of perception do not change arbitrarily but in response to real socio-economic developments. While some possibilities of understanding may be closed through these developments, in the communist future (which is only possible because of the historical development of the economy) full understanding will become possible. It follows that even if our present mode of perception closes to us any understanding of Kafka's works, this does not mean that the works have become meaningless. Rather we are unable to see the real meaning of his works or the real lessons they might teach us.

It is a valid response to objectivist and intentionalist theories to argue that the public reception of works is partly constitutive of their meaning. By itself, however, the focus on reception does not lead to a fully historical, let alone materialist, analysis of art. This approach only avoids relativism by over-intellectualizing the appropriate criteria of interpretation of artworks. I wrote of the "full understanding" possible in communist society and came close to suggesting that those modes of perception were best which allowed us to gain most insight from works of the past. If this is true we will be tempted to find insight even in the most trite works and to overinterpret art. If we make cognitive coherence the criterion of appropriate interpretation we are, in effect, holding that critical and theoretical practice is more important than artistic production and reception. This is against the whole tenor of Benjamin's work. We must look beyond artistic reception and criticism to artistic production while retaining Benjamin's insight that the conditions and limits of artistic meaning lie in the historical development of human perceptual structure.

ARTISTIC PRODUCTION AND RADICAL CRITICISM

Rather than ask "What is the *attitude* of a work to the relations of production of its time?" I should like to ask "What is its *position* in them?" This question directly concerns the function the work has within the literary relations of production of its time. (*R*, 222).

In "The Author as Producer" Benjamin shows how the artist can be political. He cites Tretjakov and Brecht as examples of authors who, by changing the artist's role in artistic production, produce successful revolutionary art. Benjamin argues that Brecht's works combine revolutionary potential and artistic quality because Brecht has changed the traditional social relations of playwright/director/character/actor/audience. In contrast, the traditional theater with its separation of stage and audience expresses the ritualistic value of art and the heroic nature of the dramatic characters. The illusionism, extravagant spectacles, and surprises of the bourgeois theater encourage a passive watching of the play—obliquely they express the view that the audience should "receive" the completed play rather than discuss, criticize, or even participate in it (*UB*, 1-4). It is futile, according to Benjamin and Brecht, to try to express socialist values or to criticize a dehumanized bourgeois society within this form. Brecht says that it is "a means against the producers . . . for a sated class for

113

which everything it touches becomes a stimulant" (*R*, 233). The progressive author must rather change the artistic production relations. He/she must "induce other producers to produce . . . and . . . put an improved apparatus at their disposal. And this apparatus is better the more consumers it is able to turn into producers—that is, readers or spectators into collaborators" (*R*, 233).

Methodologically Benjamin's essay has implications beyond the question of political art. He states that the artist's position in the social relations of production in the art world conditions the aesthetic quality, the artistic tendency, and the political tendency of the work produced. He does not start from an analysis of class society to see how artists may function in the class struggle. This, he says, is to consider the artist as external to society. Artists, however, are producers. Benjamin says that the type of product they make can best be explained in terms of the social relations of production within which they work. On his view the motive force of artistic development is the conflict between the entrenched, artistic production relations and the forces of production—the technological advances which open new areas for the artist's creativity but which cannot be used to the full within the old relations of production. Here Benjamin anticipates Raymond William's demand that Marxists treat artistic and literary production as forms of material production.[19]

In this section I extrapolate from Benjamin's suggestions and argue that a focus on the conflicts within the social relations of artistic production provides the key to the radical critique of traditional interpretations of artworks which Benjamin thought to be a central critical task. The danger of "rubbing history against the grain" and giving a reading of a work radically different from traditional interpretations is that we may be anachronistic, arbitrarily reading our own concerns into the work. The danger is avoided by grounding our reinterpretation in the conflicts which artists faced in their daily practice. This approach shows that works which seem of no contemporary relevance, perhaps because of their religious themes, are indeed relevant to us when we recognize that the struggles, conflicts, and problems of artists in the past share important common features with our contemporary struggles. Fredric Jameson has recently argued that literature is a "socially symbolic act";[20] even works which seem empty of social context have a "political unconscious." His arguments, based on textual readings and analyses of ideologies, could only be strengthened by showing the material origins of the "socially symbolic acts" in the problems and conflicts embodied in the artists' actual practice, which are transformed in art.

I am not suggesting that a focus on the artistic production relations solves all problems of interpretation or that it provides a full-blown alternative to standard methods of interpreting works based on textual analysis in the light of the intellectual and social context of the time. The task of following and modifying traditional interpretations may be carried out by normal hermeneutic methods. I am arguing that analysis of the artistic production relations is important when we question the whole basis of traditional readings and disrupt the continuity of the tradition by our innovative reading. Even here, detailed textual analysis in the light of the social context is necessary: this Benjamin's own method in his critical studies of Baudelaire, Kafka, and Proust. My point is that these new readings may be suggested, tested, and grounded by considering the ways in which the actual artistic practices of the time condition the meaning of the works.

Consider the relationship between artistic production and the rules of artistic reference. We may distinquish two sets of rules of reference which may or may not coincide: the rules of reference from the point of view of the audience ($Rules_c$), i.e., the rules the audience uses to interpret the work, on the one hand; and the rules of reference from the point of view of the artist ($Rules_p$), on the other hand. My initial concern is with the rules of reference from the point of view of the artist. Actual artistic production, as Hirsch and Schaper note, involves the artist making conscious choices in light of given rules of reference. These rules guide the artist's practice, suggesting the words, forms, or patterns which should be used to describe, represent, or express a particular content; the rules also disallow certain combinations of contents (for example, in religious works or commissioned portraits, satirical and critical content is excluded). Artists' work is guided rather than fully determined by these rules. As I noted in the previous section, artists may also create new sets of rules in their practice. The guiding rules of reference are handed down to the artist by other artists and by participants in the artworld who have authority, for example, critics, gallery owners, directors of arts councils. Works made according to these rules are comprehensible to the artists and to the authoritative participants in the artworld. They may not be comprehensible to a mass audience. In this case where $Rules_p$ and $Rules_c$ diverge, to say that $Rules_p$ are correct is to accept the authority of the select artworld participants. If, however, artists agree with the artworld authorities without qualm or conflict there may be some merit to this acceptance.

The rules of reference which guide artists are not simply abstract "thought-entities"; nor is it wholly up to the artist which rules he/she will choose. As Benjamin has argued, the actual institutional setting within which the artist works determines some of the rules which he/she must follow. For example, the playwright who writes for the traditional theater must follow certain guiding norms, while the photographer who works for a glossy magazine must make an attractive or stimulating image out of any subject. The institutional setting also determines the persons whose advice must be accepted as authoritative. This is obviously true of commissioned portraits and of works commissioned by state agencies. It is more subtly true when the artists must win the approval of critics, publishers, gallery owners, museum curators, or directors of arts councils before his/her work reaches the public. There are institutionally-vested interests built into these social roles. Publishers must sell books, producers must fill theaters, gallery owners must build their reputations, directors of arts councils must be politically non-contentious while protecting aesthetic "quality" from populist "excesses." Also it is for the most part true that those in authority in the artworld hold certain general values and world views in virtue of their class position. The germs of conflict between artist and artworld are thus clear. One possible form of conflict which Benjamin discussed is when the full technical means at the artist's control cannot be used without disrupting the artworld institutions; thus we see photographers destroying their negatives so that "original" signed prints may be sold in galleries.

When a conflict threatens to occur in the artworld artists typically do not follow Benjamin's revolutionary prescription to change the forms of artistic production. It is much more common that latent conflict is neither expressed, fought out, nor resolved. Rather the conflict is prevented from reaching an explicit level of formulation by what Steven Lukes call "the second and third dimensions of power."[21] Through the "mobilization of bias," manipulation (perhaps barely conscious), agenda-setting, and the exercise of influence and authority through appeal to shared norms, seeming compromises are reached. Such compromises often lead to systematic confusions about the appropriate rules of reference ($Rules_p$). In these cases artworks of the past and the present require Benjamin's radical "redeeming" criticism.

Consider a sketch of how such referential confusions arise. Assume that the aesthetic aims of creative artists (who do not simply follow the given rules of artistic reference) are incompatible with the institutions within which they work. We may distinquish two types of imcompatibility. On the one hand, the artists' aims may be unrealistic given their working conditions. On the other hand, the artists may succeed in making work which poses a challenge to the existing structures. Take the first case where the artists' aims cannot be fulfilled. I would argue, for example, that the Abstract Expressionists in the late 1940s and early 1950s could not sustain original and creative vision into "tragic and timeless" human themes, given the pressure of their working conditions which Clement Greenberg describes: "What we have . . . is the ferocious struggle to be a genius, which involves the artists downtown even more than the others . . . Their isolation is inconceivable, crushing, unbroken, damning."[22] Similarly I would argue that Minor White's aim in photography, to create sacred images, could not succeed without a ritual setting which he lacked in his successful and energetic career at M.I.T. in the 1960s and 1970s. In such cases artists are bound to fail in their central creative goals. Yet the artworks produced may well be instructive failures. I have argued elsewhere that while some works do not reach the norms to which they explicitly aspire, in this failure they may yet give us important insights into human and social life.[23] Minor White's failure to show the mystical resolution of conflicts makes all the more poignant and powerful his portrayal of contemporary psychic conflicts and individual isolation.

Artists in the situation sketched above will not be fully aware of their failure or even of their precise intentions since the success or failure of a creative work is partly constituted by its ability to communicate a new way of seeing to the audience. It is at this point that the artworld authorities, as the primary and privileged audience of the work, may systematically distort the work's meaning.

It is in the interests of the artworld authorities that successful works be created. It is in their interests to prevent artists realizing that the artistic production relations prevent the creation of such works. The authorities are unlikely to be attuned to the implicit socially critical meanings of the works produced. Thus they say that the works successfully achieve that artists' stated aims. If this interpretation cannot be sustained in a fully convincing manner on the textual evidence alone, the norms to which the artist originally aspired must be redefined to justify the works. The problems which artists experienced in their practice—crushing isolation—may be expressed and generalized in the works they produce, however, they are given a false halo of "sacredness" or "tragic and timeless" vision. Typically neither artists nor authorities consciously perpetrate such distortions. Yet the distorted reading of the works is communicated to the wider audience as the authoritative reading through reviews, criticism, and the modes of presentation of the works.

Consider the distortions which may arise when the artists successfully fulfill their intentions and create works which cannot easily be accepted by the artworld insitutions. Artists may make strong documents of social protest as did James Agee and Walker Evans;[24] they may express through their works their interest and concern "only for people . . . only in human destiny" as did Aaron Siskind, the Abstract Expressionist photographer;[25] they may produce works which challenge settled audience responses just as Manet's "Olympia" prevents the (male) viewer from looking comfortably at the naked woman; they may even voice what Adorno called "the last cry of despair of the shipwrecked."[26] These works challenge the interests of the artworld authorities both because of their critical stance and because such "negative" works will not attract the requisite audience. While the artist was successful in his/her aims, the works cannot be used within the existing production relations. Overt conflict is avoided when the artworld authorities reinterpret the meaning of the works and the aesthetic norms guiding the works.

Recall that creative artists are not fully conscious of their intensions or of the meanings of their works until the works have been communicated to the audience. Artists' own understanding of their work-in-progress is often inarticulate or inconsistent. The Abstract Expressionists, for example, saw their work at once as tragic and timeless, concerned with people and human destiny, personal, and of essentially formal interest in its move away from representation. The artworld authorities are the artists' primary audience. They can pick the least socially challenging of the artists' self-interpretations and plausibly present this as the definitive meaning of the work. So the Abstract Expressionists' works were said to be of formal interest, not of social interest.[27] Such an authoritative interpretation by the primary audience can plausibly be accepted by the artists and is relayed to the wider audience. By such subtle superimpositions of not-quite-appropriate rules of reference onto artworks, meanings which might otherwise have been sensed are lost, perhaps even to the artists themselves.

Even more radical pasteurizing of "dangerous" works takes place. As John Berger has argued, Franz Hals' portrait of the Poor House is made safe when it is interpreted as expressing deference towards these dignified persons.[28] This "laundered" interpretation may be more plausible to later generations than it would have been to Hals and his contemporaries.

The authoritative distortions of meaning have severe consequences for subsequent artistic work. To the extent that the artists accept the inappropriate rule of reference they lose the force and inspiration of the original works. Thus good art turns into bad.

The result, for successful works as much as unsuccessful works, is a systematic confusion of two sets of norms—those embodied in the artists' practices, and those to which artists and authorities refer to justify the practices. The norms embodied in the practices of artists are expressed in the works produced. They are not reflected in the artworks but worked upon, generalised, and transformed in the socially symbolic act that is art. Yet the actual conflicts and problems of the practices remain as the recognizable material of the finished products which can guide us in interpretation. The presence of these "material causes" in the finished artworks is not recognized by the authoritative interpretations. If the works were read in the light of more appropriate rules of reference, the hidden meanings would emerge and more illuminating readings would be possible. Without this the authoritative readings are taken to define the appropriate rules of references ($Rules_P$); they enter the traditional corpus of readings and are confirmed by the readings of subsequent generations. Thus are formed the "cultural treasures" which Benjamin said were carried in triumphal processions by succeeding generations of rulers (*I*, 256). The authoritative interpretations are ideological inasmuch as (i) they are plausible but not fully adequate to the details of the texts, distorting or ignoring important features; (ii) they serve the interests of the artworld authorities by furthering the smooth running of the institutions of the artworld.

The public becomes more alienated from the "cultural treasures." The concerns expressed in the works which might have moved the public are lost under the dominant interpretation. Why then should the public feel any responsibility to accept $Rules_P$ as authoritatively defined? When the social context allows the audience to reinterpret the works for its immediate purposes it does so and $Rules_C$ increasingly diverge from $Rules_P$. Benjamin noted the progressive aspect of this development in the public cynicism about the ideologies of the artworld.

In these cases Benjamin's radical criticism becomes necessary. We must "rub history against the grain" and "wrest tradition away from a conformism that is about to overpower it." For when these works are interpreted solely in terms of the authoritative reading, they seem to lack power, force, and relevance in our lives. Of course the authoritative reading is relevant to a more appropriate interpretation; the norms expressed in it are those that the artists themselves used to justify their practices or that the artists aspired to but failed to achieve. Yet the works tell us most when we recover the unarticulated norms embodied in the artists' practices. The works should be interpreted in the light of both sets of norms, as expressing those embodied in the practices and as failing to express the authoritative norms. In this task the radical critic redeems the damage and distortions caused by the primary authoritative audience. He/she articulates a new set of $Rules_P$ which were implicit in the artist's practice and which speak more directly to the public than does the authoritative interpretation. If the criticism rekindles the interest of the audience it also recreates the possibility of a coincidence of Rules$_C$ and Rules$_P$.

Radical criticism, of course, involves a close reading of the text, identifying its omissions and absences and the omissions, absurdities, and difficulties in the authoritative reading.[29] To claim that the new reading is more appropriate than the old *tout court* (not simply more appropriate to the interests of the working class or the interests of women) requires that we show that the new reading is more appropriate to the artist's interests and practices. We must ground the reading in an analysis of the artistic production relations, showing the range of implicit conflicts between artists and authorities, and tracing the authoritative mis-readings of the works to their origins in the exercise of all dimensions of power on artists and audience by the artworld authorities.[10] Thus we reveal the hidden social content of the works. Those works which not only express conflicts akin to our contemporary ones but also suggest new ways of seeing and dealing with these conflicts will be of direct relevance and use to the contemporary audience.

Benjamin did not refer to the artistic production relations in his studies of Baudelaire, Kafka, and Proust. Only in the case of Baudelaire did he connect his re-reading with a detailed discussion of the social context. This is not solely a matter of Benjamin's mistrust of systematic argument. It follows from my argument that Benjamin's reinterpretations are not fully justified in the absence of an analysis of the artistic production relations. Yet Benjamin's critical practice also points to the schematic nature of my argument. "Private" artists like Proust or Kafka had only minimal contact with the artworld authorities. This is significant on my account since their literary innovations are not directly related to the contemporary artistic production relations nor to any contemporary audience. Rather they are much mediated responses to contemporary artistic and social practices, the meaning of which becomes defined only for subsequent generations. Their work must be interpreted in the light of the wider social context with a resulting lack of precise evidence based on the artist's social practice. Subsequent authoritative misinterpretations may of course be traced to their social bases.

In this section I have argued for a modified objectivist view in which we can recover the real meaning of an artwork from authoritative misinterpretations by identifying the conflicts within the artistic production relations. The political criticism that objectivist theories sustain ruling class dominance does not apply to this view which shows the radical, even revolutionary, import of works of the past. Benjamin has written that "every image of the past that is not recognized by the present as one of its own concerns threatens to disappear irretrievably" (*I*, 255). This statement is particularly true of the critical approach outlined above. For our imaginative ability to project a radical reinterpretation of a text, against all the weight of tradition, depends on our grasp of the hidden struggles, conflicts, and defeats of the past. Their import will escape us unless our motivation comes from the experience of similar struggles and analogous defeats.

WALTER BENJAMIN AND CONTEMPORARY CAPITALISM

. . . the tasks which face the human apparatus of perception at the turning points of history cannot be solved by optical means, that is, by contemplation, alone. They are mastered gradually by habit, under the guidance of tactile appropriation (*I*, 240).

In contemporary capitalism the political right are objectivists. Left and center tend to an easy relativism, whether from despair of any alternative or from a romantic attachment to the immediacy of political action. Contemporary theorists have projected the relativism of the modern left onto Benjamin's thought, overemphasizing his attraction to "revolutionary nihilism."[31] Benjamin's own writing was situated in a very different political and intellectual context. Benjamin at once stood against the objectivism of mainstream academic criticism, fascist tendencies to ritualize and aestheticize politics, social democratic concepts of historical continuity and progress, the Stalinist orthodoxy of socialist realism and Lukács' systematicity, his respect for tradition and his blindness to the meanings of modernism. Benjamin's mistrust of systematic thinking and his belief that "all the decisive blows are struck left-handed" (OWS, 49) are intelligible as an attempt to steer the narrow straits between the given intellectual options. His apparent relativism is, at least in part, a reaction against the dominant objectivist current of thought of East and West.

The plausibility of contemporary readings of Benjamin as a relativist lies in the lack of coherence of his own thought. His utopian theological concept of the redemption of the past and his concept of the revolutionary *Jetztzeit* sit unhappily beside his view that profane illuminations and the coincidence of artistic and political progress are brought about by the development of technology which allows the audience to use artworks as it will. I think that one root of this lack of coherence lies in Benjamin's characterization of the modern mode of perception. Benjamin argued that the twentieth century public was incapable of sustained concentration or disinterested appreciation; the result is the inevitable disintegration of the aura of artworks. Benjamin's own radical criticism is incapable of restoring public interest in works of the past. Only a limited number of progressive possibilities remain. The increasing fragmentation and distraction of perception may itself provoke a qualitative transcendence of reification. New artistic techniques allow for public and profane illuminations which open "our taverns and our metropolitan streets, our offices and our furnished rooms, our railroad stations and our factories" (*I*, 236) which previously imprisoned us. Adorno has rightly criticized this over-optimistic view of the potential of artistic technology in capitalism.[32]

Alternatively the answer lies in a total revolutionary rupture with the past, in the immediacy of working class political *praxis* to which all other "values"—aesthetic, cognitive, traditional—must be subordinated. It remains unclear how the reified public will be motivated towards such *praxis*. This revolutionary relativism has already been criticized. Finally, one may hold that the possibility of transcendence of reification lies only in a future communism where primeval correspondences will be restored and all past sufferings will be redeemed. Habermas has shown the theological and mystical elements of this aspect of Benjamin's thought.[33] The only alternative is the deep pessimism typical of Adorno's later work.

I suggest that the perceptual tendencies which Benjamin identifies are not the only ones at work in the modern world. We can also find signs of a reemergence of integrated experience and "auratic" works in seemingly marginal areas of contemporary social practice, a re-emergence which is not essentially bound up with ritual or mystification. I am thinking of the growing popularity of folk and traditional music, the newly documented emergence of storytelling in urban centers, the integration of art and political practice in the songs of protest movements and the art of the feminist and gay communities, the festivals common to the West Indian population of Britain and increasingly frequent in other urban centers, and the grass-roots enthusiasm for community arts programs. The political and artistic implications of each of these forms deserves detailed attention beyond the scope of this paper. None of these developments remains untouched by capitalism. Western social democratic governments have, for example, funded community arts programs (and often killed their most progressive aspects) in order to defuse protests in the inner cities and to give the appearance of a caring welfare state. Nonetheless, an undercurrent may be detected which runs counter to the reification and disintegration which Benjamin described. These practices, in their recreation of communities and the correlative (although uneven) emergence of intersubjective agreement on appropriate standards of interpretation and judgment, are as distinct from contemporary relativism as they are from the authoritative powers of the artworld. They may provide a perceptual and ideological basis on which radical artistic and critical practice can build. If this is so we do not have to choose between technology and utopia, relativism and theology, but can work to further the immanent tendencies developing within public consciousness which point beyond capitalism to a humane socialism and communism. I have argued that the theoretical need is for a properly historical aesthetics which takes neither a utilitarian nor a deferential attitude to the art of the past or to traditional interpretations. Rather, through critique of traditional interpretations in the light of the social context of production and reception of art, the real lessons expressed in the art of the past may be opened to contemporary audiences.

University College, Dublin

NOTES

1 Walter Benjamin, *Illuminations* (New York: Schocken, 1969), hereafter cited as *I; Charles Baudelaire: A Lyric Poet in the Era of High Capitalism* (London: New Left Books, 1973), hereafter cited as *CB; Understanding Brecht* (London: New Left Books, 1977), hereafter cited as *UB; The Origin of German Tragic Drama* (London: New Left Books, 1977), hereafter cited as *OGTD; Reflections* (New York: Harcourt Brace Jovanovich, 1978), hereafter cited as *R; One-Way Street* (London: New Left Books, 1979), hereafter cited as *OWS*.
2 See Nelson Goodman, *Languages of Art* (Indianapolis: Hackett, 1976), Ch. 1; *Ways of Worldmaking* (Sussex: Harvester, 1978), Ch. 1.
3 *OGTD*, p. 164; *I*, pp. 187–239. See also H. G. Gadamer, *Truth and Method* (London: Sheed and Ward, 1975), pp. 111-14, where he argues that the properly aesthetic attitude is one where the spectator is lost in the objectivity of the play.
4 Gadamer, p. 71.
5 *I*, pp. 122, 144: *R*, p. 156. Compare Georg Lukács' parallel discussion of the allegorical nature of modernist literature in *The Meaning of Contemporary Realism* (London: Merlin, 1963), pp. 40-46.
6 Goodman, *Languages of Art*, Ch. 1; *Ways of Worldmaking*, Ch. 1. For an accessible introduction to Derrida's writing see Jacques Derrida, "Limited Inc." in *Glyph 2: Johns Hopkins Textual Studies*, ed. S. Weber & Sussman (Baltimore: Johns Hopkins University Press, 1977), pp. 194-95, 201.
7 Karl Marx, *Capital*, Vol. I, Part I, Ch. 1, Section 4.
8 *R*, p. 232. Susan Sontag expands on Benjamin's suggestions in *On Photography* (New York: Farrar Straus & Giroux, 1978).
9 See, for example, *OWS*, p. 89 where he suggests that only "fools lament the decay of criticism."
10 Theodor W. Adorno, *Gesammelte Schriften*, Bd. 7, *Ästhetische Theorie* (Frankfurt: Suhrkamp, 1970), p. 33.
11 Susan Buck-Morss, "Walter Benjamin—Revolutionary Writer (1)," *New Left Review*,

123

No. 128 (July-Aug. 1981); "Walter Benjamin—Revolutionary Writer (II)" *New Left Review*, No. 129 (Sept.-Oct. 1981). Especially "Walter Benjamin (I)," pp. 59-61.

12. Jürgen Habermas, "Bewusstmachende oder rettende Kritik—die Aktualität Walter Benjamins," in *Zur Aktualität Walter Benjamins,* ed. Siegfried Unseld (Frankfurt: Suhrkamp, 1972), p. 207.

13. Georg Lukács, "Realism in the Balance," in Ernst Bloch et al., *Aesthetics and Politics,* (London: New Left Books, 1977), p. 54.

14 Goodman, *Languages of Art,* p. 38; Derrida, pp. 180, 206, 212, 231-34.

15 Eva Schaper, "Interpreting Art," *Proceedings of the Aristotelian Society,* Supplementary Volume LV (1981); E. D. Hirsch, Jr., *The Aims of Interpretation* (Chicago: University of Chicago Press, 1976), Part 1.

16 Max Raphael, *The Demands of Art* (Princeton: Princeton University Press, 1968).

17 The question of the historical nature of human perception and the role of art in informing perceptual structure is much debated. I follow the view of Marx W. Wartofsky in his "Perception, Representation and the Forms of Action," *Ajatus,* 36 (1976), and his "Pictures, Representation and the Understanding," *Logic and Art: Essays in Honor of Nelson Goodman,* ed. R. Rudner and I. Scheffler, (New York: Bobbs Merrill, 1972).

18 Habermas, pp. 196-201.

19 Raymond Williams, *Marxism and Literature* (Oxford: Oxford University Press, 1977), pp. 19, 210-12: *Problems in Materialism and Culture* (London: Verso, 1980), pp. 31-63.

20 Fredric Jameson, *The Political Unconscious: Narrative as a Socially Symbolic Act* (Ithaca: Cornell University Press, 1981), p. 20.

21 Steven Lukes, *Power: A Radical View* (London: Macmillan, 1974).

22 Clement Greenberg, "The Present Prospect of American Painting and Sculpture," *Horizon,* 93-94 (Oct. 1947).

23 Jennifer Todd, "Insight and Ideology in the Visual Arts," *British Journal of Aesthetics,* 21, No. 4 (Autumn 1981).

24 James Agee and Walker Evans, *Let Us Now Praise Famous Men* (New York: Houghton Mifflin, 1960). This work was commissioned by *Fortune* but later rejected by the magazine.

25 Aaron Siskind, *Aaron Siskind, Photographer,* ed. Nathan Lyons (Rochester: Eastman House, 1965), p. 21.

26 T. W. Adorno, *The Philosophy of Modern Music* (London: Sheed and Ward, 1973), p. 133.

27 See Peter Fuller's discussion in his *Beyond the Crisis in Art* (London: Writers and Readers Publishing Cooperative, 1980), pp. 70-103.

28 John Berger, *Ways of Seeing* (New York: Viking, 1973), pp. 12-16.

29 This approach has become general among Marxist critics. See Pierre Macherey, *A Theory of Literary Production* (London: Routledge & Kegan Paul, 1978); Terry Eagleton, *Criticism and Ideology* (London: New Left Books, 1976); Fredric Jameson, *Political Unconscious.* While these writers acknowledge the need to go beyond such a purely textual analysis, their own critical writings tend to stay on the level of text ideology.

30 T. J. Clark's work incorporates the type of analysis which I am suggesting. See his *Image of the People: Gustave Courbet and the Second French Republic, 1848-51* (Greenwich, CT: New York Graphic Society, 1973).

31 Susan Sontag takes the relativist aspects of Benjamin's thought to an extreme. In *On Photography* she suggests that photographs mean whatever the majority says they mean. See my "Roots of Pictorial Reference," *Journal of Aesthetics and Art Criticism,* XXXIX, No. I (Fall 1980). Terry Eagleton, in *Walter Benjamin or Towards a Revolu-*

tionary Criticism (London: Verso, 1981), pp. 51-52, criticizes Colin McCabe's relativist reading of Benjamin as "left idealist." While Eagleton poses the problem and explicitly rejects relativism, his own reading of Benjamin implicitly retains it. Ultimately he takes history and texts as political constructs (pp. 32, 34, 57). Susan Buck-Morss, in her two essays in *New Left Review,* distinguishes Benjamin's position from historicism (I, pp. 59-61) and from propaganda (II, p. 83). Yet she fails to show how either his "revolutionary gesture" (II, p. 95) or the concept of "mimetic correspondences" (II, p. 89) provide a non-relativist ground for interpretation. While I do not question the accuracy of Buck-Morss' interpretation, in this respect it reproduces the problems and lack of coherence of Benjamin's own work.

32 T. W. Adorno, "Letters to Walter Benjamin" in *Aesthetics and Politics,* pp. 120-26.
33 Habermas, p. 206ff.

BENJAMIN'S DIALECTIC OF ART AND SOCIETY

SÁNDOR RADNÓTI

> *Honored public, go on, find your own ending!*
> Bert Brecht

1

The life work of the reception-theorist Walter Benjamin is certainly more strongly marked by fundamentally conflicting receptions and views than that of all of his associates. This reception-complex is a noteworthy contribution to the intellectual life of the sixties. For here, competing with one another are the theologian of the revolution intended for the streets of Paris, the classical exponent of Frankfurt School ideology critique, the Moscow-visitor who was drawing closer to the officially sanctioned forms of revolution, the surrealist philosopher traveling the Paris-Berlin circuit, the tragic cultural critique in a Marxist mask, the Jewish messianist, and the aesthete deeply rooted in German tradition. Benjamin's works resist the restful continuity of historical and sociological studies of their influence; his fate compels us to apply to him his own doctrine of the difference between reception and influence. A decisive aspect of this fate is the very belated, but all the more sensational, acceptance of this author. Overnight his life work fell under a penetrating light—a light which in a Benjaminian spirit might be called a redeeming light—taken up as enumerated above, by the most varied schools of thought; and not merely as a result of errors or misreading.

What is the difference between effect and reception? Nowhere does Benjamin openly relate the two concepts, nor does he contrast them. His anti-systematic attitude and cast of mind, as it were, determined the limited presence of lacunae in this theory. Therefore, his theory needs and depends on reconstruction. To this end, it seems appropriate to compare Benjamin's standpoint with that of Hans-Georg Gadamer—the philosopher who extricated the concept of influence from its subaltern position and interpreted "historical effective consciousness" as a basic ontological concept. This comparative analysis will clarify and sharpen the differences between the two, despite their basic affinities (hardly noticed by Gadamer).

We can easily discern common goals in both Gadamer's and Benjamin's philosophies of art. What Gadamer defined as the critique of the "pure" work of art—the abstraction of aesthetic consciousness—can be regarded as Benjamin's driving force for two decades. Gadamer, too, was suspicious of the abstraction of purpose, function and meaning of the work of art, of the independence of beautiful form, standing outside the real world and ultimately capable of reintegration—an autonomy which, in the tradition of German classicism, is called "beautiful illusion," and a reintegration in which the work of art either becomes a prototype or a copy.[1]

Instead of trying to reintegrate the two thinkers, we will present an apparently old-fashioned program: the understanding of the work of art's truth content, and the concept of the work of art not as a separate world but as a world-view. The rehabilitation of allegory and Benjamin's book on *Trauerspiel* are fruits of this program; and this same rehabilitation is a very powerful motif of Gadamer's *Truth and Method*. The obverse of giving such free rein to justice is breaking with aesthetics, whose paradigm is the masterpiece. This is the openly avowed point of Benjamin's philosophy of art; but the same thing necessarily follows from Gadamer's thought, which in principle distances itself from normative considerations. The reason why I called such a philosophy "old-fashioned" is not because its program (and its rejection of the masterpiece paradigm) entails the study of objects which grow older; that is the very reason why it can also be very modern and illuminate a will-to-art which has not yet crystallized. Rather, the quest for the truth-content of art leads both thinkers *back* behind the legitimation crisis of art, to the world of consensus of taste. The emancipation of aesthetic consciousness, which here becomes the object of critique, was the answer to this crisis: insofar as it must be confirmed, taste will either be relativized or become an arbitrary dictatorship. Gadamer rightly counters unitary taste, which includes lifestyle, with the simultaneous and contentually indeterminate sense of quality. "As aesthetic consciousness, it is reflected out of all determinant and determinate taste and itself represents a zero-degree of determinancy."[2] The strikingly romantic origin of the alienated condition of aesthetic consciousness is secondary compared with art's immediate claim to reality, or, in Benjamin's case, the origin of the critique of modern auratic art:

they are based on the experience of the chasm between art and life. And yet that is not Romanticism, neither for Benjamin nor for Gadamer, for the regression behind the legitimation crisis does not mean the replacement of the question of legitimation by a reconstructed unity of taste, world-view, and lifestyle. On the contrary, both philosophers turn emphatically toward given reality: toward the *sensus communis,* which really exists—insofar as there is one—and not toward the one that ought to be. That is another reason why the radical difference of these two solutions leads consistently in Gadamer to a certain disengagement as regards *description,* while Benjamin's self-contradictions result in lacunae and strained formulations. Furthermore, if the question of the truth-content of the work is raised, this is as much a sign of the need for legitimation as a way of satisfying the need to ban art from the sphere of the true. For Benjamin, as well as for Gadamer, truth-content is conceivable only in a hermeneutic situation, in the dialogue of understanding in which the creator, the work, every person the work reaches, and the whole historical world participate.

According to Gadamer, the truth is what emerges in the context of historical effect. The polemical point of this idea is directed against certainty and demonstrability, against a philosophical view patterned after the scientific model of truth—but we are interested in something else. If, however, Gadamer's concept of truth is excluded from the background of this significant and justified critique, then one realizes that within the universal truth or the historical specificity, the specific question of the truth of falsehood of the various effects approaches the "zero-degree of determinacy." Actually, effect does not address consideration of truth and falsehood; rather it forms a historical continuum which cannot possibly be made conscious or legitimated in its entirety. Effect is value-free and descriptive according to its very concept. But since its universal truth stands in contrast to all methodologies which abstract from it (that is also how Gadamer understood the methodology of aesthetic consciousness), then Gadamer's historical concept of truth can be interpreted within the ontological framework of the effective historical context in such a way that it comes into being wherever it becomes determinate, wherever reflection wants to make conscious and legitimate the effective context. Gadamer deduces the fact that it cannot want this everywhere from another basic ontological fact: the existential finitude of the reflecting person and the corresponding particularity of reflection. But where the concrete consciousness of the effective historical context is made explicit, it will disrupt the continuum and conflate past and present, always privileging the present as the organizing center: the horizon of the present merges with the horizon of the past. Thus history is rewritten again and again from the particular vantage point of the present. This idea guarantees the historicity of truth and at the same time excludes the possibility of its cumulative historical value: one can understand only differently, but not better.

Even on this point, the structural affinity with Benjamin's concept of understanding is very striking; but at the same time the underlying material differences appear more strongly. By distinguishing, in his essay on elective affinities, between the material content and the truth-content of the work of art, Benjamin presupposes a qualitative difference between the two. But this is precisely the opposite of Gadamer's assertion, and stands, strangely, closer to the hermeneutic tradition: Benjamin would like to understand better, with greater universal significance, than any contemporary understanding. Each work is a web of common material contents for its community or public, and precisely this fact makes possible its effect on its circle of contemporaries. This effective context is shattered by time; it must be reconstructed. Only after this work of reconstruction can the question be raised about the truth-content of the work: namely, whether the truth confirmed by effect is appearance and attributable merely to the vitality of the material content, or whether the survival of the material content in the work is ascribable to the truth of the work. Thus, the task is twofold. First, reconstruction—Benjamin calls it commentary—a historical task, but one which can be interpreted as the prelude to the genuinely philosophical task. For the reconstruction the effective influences do not construct what once existed: this cannot in principle be reproduced, for it is open, with fluid borders. Reconstruction changes the mobile and open effective context into a static and closed monadic structure, which, in radical contrast to that which is to be reconstructed, contains exclusively the effect that has become conscious. But that means a conscious, active *attitude,* in contrast to the unconscious-conscious conglomerate that allowed the material content to exert its effect. Commentary is past-directed; it makes conscious the effective content of the past, brings it to the surface. Only the second step, namely critique, can make conscious the principles of selection at work in the activity of the commentary, for it is not anchored in the past, but in the present. *This* bringing-to-consciousness accords with the question of legitimation. The latter is represented by the primary question of the normative basis for reception that emerges in the dialectics of selection and illumination of the effective-context and changes the reconstruction into construction. How far the norm confirms artistic values and how far it transcends them in favor of historico-philosophical or historico-theological values still remains to be considered.

Let it be noted that the structure of better understanding just described is by no means followed by continuous progress in understanding the truth-content. The image of the present is just as static and closed as the image of the past after reconstruction. Paraphrasing Benjamin, one could say, the respective—slight—messianic chance of reception consists in the fact that the present is not understood as the unfolding of a causal series, but as time arrested, to whose question something of the past offers an answer precisely *now*. This does, of course, presuppose a very strong discontinuity. The various monadic constructions which Benjamin used throughout his career and its philosophical implications are appropriate to discontinuity: they contradict the method of historicism as emphatically as they do the form of the philosophical system. The discontinuity which a selected portion of the past—a work, a consensus, a genre—concentrates in itself (with the help of the category of the monad discussed in the book on the *Trauerspiel*) is also developed by Benjamin from the material of the historical continuum. He, too, sees history as a continuum, but not as development of progress, as does Gadamer. But what a difference there is in their judgment and their conception of the discontinuities that provide the basis for understanding! Even their differences in terminology are quite revealing: Gadamer speaks of a fusion of the horizons of past and present, Benjamin of an explosion of the continuum. In Gadamer the containment of the continuum's extension by the existential finitude of being is made impossible. In part what extends beyond it will necessarily always be a bit blurred; in part, however, it can only and must extend beyond this continuum. For Benjamin the continuum of history is a homogeneous scandal from which one must be redeemed, and therefore the efforts to break out are always cast in perhaps too glaring a light. For him, redemption promises reception as well as revolution, and this common denominator of the philosophy of culture and history emerges—symbolically—in Benjamin's last work, in the theses "On the Concept of History." There one reads in the third thesis that only a redeemed mankind can cite the whole past with all its moments. Gadamer's history changes under the Heideggerian sky of care; the Blochian star of hope shines its friendly light on Benjamin's concept of history. Only a redeemed mankind can cite its entire history, but the collecting of quotations and their combination into a monad, together with their little critical redemptions, is the asylum of truth in the interstices of the universe. This is the deeper basis of Benjamin's *furor citatologicus,* of his nature as a collector. But since critique is the model of reception, it wants to represent a reason shared in common; therefore hope and asylum have a practical aspect in the philosophy of history.

The mutual relation of effect and reception can thus be formulated as follows: reception is effect which has become conscious and been confirmed, an *active* relation to the object. Effect is tradition-embedded; reception brings about new tradition: even in Jürgen Habermas's interpretation of Benjamin,[3] in which he called him a conservative-revolutionary force (conservative here referring to the tradition-reorientedness of Benjamin's theory), and also in a strictly conservative, traditional reading, reception recreates its object, it becomes a co-constituent. The presupposition of this new creation is, for Benjamin, as was mentioned, reconstruction. In regard to effect, the work, genre, or epoch is thereby closed; so much so that the discovery of effect becomes a commentary on contemporary material contents, allegories, arcades, etc. It is not as if Benjamin had no knowledge of the developing effective-contexts; he considers this to be merely a part of the empty continuum of history. This is precisely why permanency and obsolescence mean so little to him; for he does not understand *this history* as a legitimate critical authority. In relation to reception, however, reconstruction renews the work. It asks it what its contents are, and what its specific form is; for with the help of these answers, the recipient can participate in construction. As a self-contained commentary, reconstruction necessarily builds on an unconfirmed judgment (or one treated as evidence), at any rate, on a prejudice: namely, that the work deserves commentary. This prejudice must be based on the object of commentary, i.e., must fit into a coherent structure of tradition, such as, for instance, classicism. Now Benjamin breaks the seal of commentary, and this is his inherent prejudice: the objects which he comments on or reconstructs are not fitted into any tradition which would make reconstruction self-evident as affirmation of tradition. The act of selecting objects is the harbinger of a new tradition; thus, reconstruction itself contains the question that opens up its hereticism and awaits confirmation.

This process of reception can also be applied to Benjamin's life work, especially since it had little effect and was less embedded in the culture. Rather it was received as the tradition of one or several new cultures. And because it must be clear to everyone familiar with his writings—e.g., the book on the *Trauerspiel* and the essay on technical reproducibility, together with the essay on Kafka which was written at the same time (!) and the lecture "The Author as Producer"—that to describe his career in terms of "development" explains very little; one must employ reconstruction. Not trends and movements, but rather thinkers and artists, prescribe his course. A great many possibilities present themselves as models for this field of force. To me the boundaries seem to be four works which are lumped together as if by chance in a far-reaching review by Benjamin, "Books Which Have Remained Alive" (1929): Alois Riegl's *Late Roman Art Industry,* Alfred Gotthold Meyer's *Ironworks,* Franz Rosenzweig's *The Star of Redemption,* and Georg Lukács' *History and Class Consciousness.* These four books, on art history, architecture, theology, and the philosophy of history, can, as regards their topics or aims, be considered as points of reference, so-to-speak, for Benjamin's principal themes and research. These are, successively 1) the second tradition, artistic will, and the open form; 2) the crisis of experience and collective reception; 3) thought on language and redemption; 4) the secularization of redemption in the theory of social activism and revolution.

p.229 -

2

Benjamin's *The Origin of German Trauerspiel* is based on two insights. First, that the genre of the baroque *Trauerspiel* stands in contrast to ancient tragedy; that the essence of the contrast consists in the fact that ancient tragedy integrated the public while baroque *Trauerspiel* is integrated by the public. The active presence of the audience is incorporated into the form of classical tragedy, while baroque *Trauerspiel* can be understood only if it is followed from the audience's vantage-point. This is Benjamin's aesthetic insight. The second insight transcends the bounds of aesthetics. For according to an aesthetic conception the form that comes about in this way is lacking precisely in form. It is fragmentary, crude; formlessness is its form: that is a paradox. Only *reintegration* in a sphere with universal validity can eliminate the contradictions.[4] In *The Origin of German Trauerspiel* this higher sphere is theology. Both statements are aimed against the classical tradition, i.e., against aesthetic reception raised to a norm; a reception whose ideal is the rounded, well-formed work, and whose world is profane beauty. The wholeness of form and the specific value of the work of art—of art itself—are thus the two pillars which Benjamin is shaking in order to pull down the temple of aesthetics. Apparently he restricts himself to developing a historically based counterpart to the classical ideal. It would be a mistake, however, to think that the radical consequences that result for the philosophy of art are a late development in Benjamin's writings. For two stages of investigation can be distinguished: historical reconstruction and critical reception.

Historical reconstruction means the elaboration of the *second traditon.*

A particular genre of dramatic literature must, compared with the neo-Aristotelian standards of classical tragedy—in *The Origin of German Trauerspiel* it is the German lamentation play, whose relation to certain dramatic genres of other epochs is clearly visible—simply be accused of crudeness, imbalance, or decadent disintegration. Compared with the accusation of a loss of moderation, of intemperance and the corresponding bad taste, Benjamin raises the obvious question of historicism: it must be asked whether what is expected of this epoch was actually a norm of the epoch, whether *that art* with whose standards it is being confronted *was called for* at that time. The results of investigation are a new reference system: the genre *Trauerspiel,* the untragic drama, is so detached from tragedy that the latter is relegated to the quarantine of antiquity, while the *Trauerspiel* turns out to be closely related to epic genres, to the reading of allegorical signs, the mystery plays, ballet, etc. A forceful, hidden course of cultural history is developed here, which was repressed by the victorious cultural ideals, but whose relevance was demonstrated by expressionist drama, by Hofmannsthal's and later Brecht's similar attempts at stylization. And this tradition transcends the genre of drama as well as its relevance: even if it is separated from untragic drama, one can discover its nodal points, e.g., allegory, which will play a leading role in the understanding of Baudelaire's lyric poetry. The combination of a third nodal point of the second tradition with the other two came only later, after Benjamin's emancipatory turn to social criticism. What is meant are the epic, narrative genres. The epic material of *Trauerspiel,* the affinity of chronicles and fables with allegory, offers a sufficient foundation for this connection: for him the obstacle here was actually of an ideological nature. In the book on the *Trauerspiel* the second tradition is treated as a document of the suffering of human nature, of the arbitrariness of historical fate, and it is contrasted with the practice of the symbolic-classical tradition, which lifts the work out of this continuum and marks it off from these factors. The history of decline which this tradition presents bears a relation to salvation, but the relation is a transcendent one, which is therefore understandable only from a theological perspective.

Benjamin's aforementioned turn means the secularization of the history of salvation. Only after this turn could a bifurcated possibility of the second tradition arise; for it can express not only the eternal decline similar to that which occurs in natural history—the empty continuum of history—but also the this-worldly, Chiliastic cessation of this process. In the first variant, the hero of the untragic drama is not tragic, because his fate is not determined by his character, because he is exposed to external determinations. Martyr and tyrant, loyal servant and intriguer, are not far apart in this scenario. In the second variant, the hero is not tragic, because he goes beyond tragedy, because he reflects cleverly and intelligently on the contradictions of society. This was precisely the possibility which Benjamin saw in Brecht's dramas: the dramatic hero as the wise man who is not impotently subjected to fate, because he sees through it. This character, in Benjamin's view, combines the story-telling genre with the second tradition, for only he can tell the story intercalcated with generalizable experiences and the wisdom of life. Like untragic drama, this genre too is bifurcated, although with a different content: in one instance—for example, in the essay on Leskov—it is a lost possibility (the younger sibling of the concept of the epic in Lukács' *The Theory of the Novel*), as an updated version of the older epos-concept and in the other—when it deals with Kafka or Brecht—a renewed possibility. The circular return is, according to Benjamin, characteristic of the empty continuum of history. Its model is fashion, which reaches back to the old as something new. And yet—it is a matter of the same ambivalence as before—he sought the impetus for salvation in this eternal circularity. In his theses "On the Concept of History" he even used the model of the "leap of fashion" to illustrate the dialectical leap of revolution. Actually, in Benjamin, the possibility of salvation is based on a dialectical principle: on the overcoming of difficulty by an accumulation of difficulty. He returned to commentary in order to escape from its inherent prejudice and reverentialness. He set his hope on untragic dramatic forms to save himself from creatureliness by illuminating the creaturely human life inherent in them; he relied on storytelling to cause the transparent circumstances of life and the simple morality inherent in this genre to collide with the opposite experiences in a hopeless world (Kafka), or to take root in the same world (Brecht) in a manner that satisfies untragic form. The most important among the specific elective affinities which exist between the theories of the young Lukács and Benjamin is the correspondence of Lukács' untragic aesthetics of drama with Benjamin's. *Die Ästhetik der Romance* has been discussed by Ferenc Feher in the essay, "Die Geschichtsphilosophie des Dramas: die Metaphysik der Tragödie und die Utopie des untragischen Dramas."[5]

The relation between old and new, conceived in eternal leaps, raises great difficulties for historical generalizations. But that is not the only obstacle to what Benjamin insisted on in the first stage and viewed as his program in the historical elaboration of the second tradition. Mikhail Bakhtin, for instance, perceived just as broad a second tradition, which he labeled "the popular humorous culture." But this second tradition has a well-recognizable, to some extent complementary relation to the first tradition. It possesses an appropriate and a clearly recognizable value-hierarchy, recognized by historical research: namely, a theory of realism enriched with new points of view. In contrast with this sound expansion of the concepts "culture" and "art," Benjamin propagated a new concept of culture and art, but one matched by an adventurous historical method. The latter, though it incorporates the precise reconstruction of the context of effect, cannot be integrated into a conception of history that in principle interprets every phenomenon. For we know that according to Benjamin only redeemed mankind will be able to perform the complete reconstruction, and relevance brings about a connection between past and present only at certain points. The second tradition does not (yet) have any continuum; process there means at most a secret path visible here and there, or rather a constellation. The continuity of the other tradition is hollow and false. Thus, huge gaps are formed in the history of art. Tragedy is actually in quarantine: its present-day reception is ruled out, since it no longer has the public which once integrated it. Or let us take Shakespeare. In Benjamin's understanding of the second tradition, only a few scenes, or at most a few works, out of his entire opus could survive. German classicism, however, is just as much the dark background of the form of allegory, since allegory served as the contrasting background to the concept of the symbol in Goethe's age. But this is only logical, since Benjamin does not question the existence of value; rather he criticizes the concept of artistic value in the name of relevance. He recognized very early that the historical life of the work of art can be preserved and raised to a new level not be extensive art history but only by intensive interpretation. Defects of interpretation do not reveal defects of the work, but of its historical actualization. The critique of value, so understood, does not halt before the critique of certain eternal artistic values; instead, this critique, also functions within the new concept of art. As a whole, German *Trauerspiel* in its imperfection expresses the artistic will of its time much better, Benjamin believes, than do the isolated masterpieces of the same genre, e.g., Calderon's plays. For the latter, by virtue of their formal perfection, entail a playful reduction of the problems, which by virtue of their closed nature produce their own limitation and pseudo-redemption.

This critique of value is linked with that methodological indifference to artistic values which Alois Riegl introduced into art history. Riegel turned away from the conception of artistic periods of decline and thereby brought into relief a new tradition where prior critics had seen only eccentricity and decay. A precondition for this was that his interest was directed not at the individual work of art, but at the comprehensive phenomenon of art and its public, which he called artistic will. He understood the history of various artistic wills primarily as the history of perception, out of whose possibilities developed a system of concepts which made it possible to understand the individual works. One might also then construct a historical typology based on changes and modifications of these concepts. Riegel drew the material from the collectively received circle of the graphic arts—architecture, carpetweaving, ornamentation, group portraits, etc.—which retain the possibility of repetition. The extremely narrow correspondence of the selected material and the theoretical preconditions allowed Riegl to understand his activity with a strict historiographical framework; his scientistic self-misunderstanding went so far that he believed that, in relation to the above-mentioned indifference to value, he stood close to positivist historicism. In reality, aesthetic values are replaced by historico-philosophical dilemmas of value, which Riegl, however, brackets. Benjamin found one of the possible ways to remove the brackets. For there is no answer to the question one repeatedly runs up against in the first stage in the course of describing the reconstruction. Historical science is determined from the outside by pre-scientific evidences and historico-philosophical value-choices, but its immanent methodology does not answer the question of the relevance of the object.

In the second stage of the investigation in the *The Origin of German Trauerspiel,* we find reception: relevance or making relevant. When dealing with the art of older periods, the duration, the validity of the individual work, is called aesthetic relevance. Benjamin, however, does not accept this as an unalterable fact. Thus he follows two courses which he never separated systematically from one another; two courses which, by virtue of their related nature—sometimes mutually refuting and sometimes corroborating one another—bring out the ambivalence that characterizes his thinking. The transformation of aesthetics (art) is the first way; the transcendence of aesthetics (the end of the epoch of art) is the second. For Benjamin this is true only in broad terms; but the twofold tendency stemming from the book on the *Trauerspiel* is interpreted in the first way in the case of the Brecht, Kafka, and Baudelaire exegeses, and according to the second way in the case of the essay on "technical reproducibility." Habermas writes that Benjamin's stance was ambivalent on the loss of aura. The term "aura" summarizes the uniqueness, the individual atmosphere of a work of art, an object, or a person. The ambivalence of the relation to it results because (in accordance with Benjamin's well-known dialectic) the aura is lost but then returned in the unique act of redemption. If one compares the idea of happiness—whose generalization was for Benjamin the secular meaning of redemption—with the description of the aura of natural objects (i.e., compare the second thesis on the philosophy of history with the third chapter of the essay on technical reproducibility), one encounters very similar phenomena. The contradiction between the loss and the affirmation of the return of aura could be resolved via the beaten track which so many have walked—from Schiller, through the young Lukács, to Bloch—i.e., those who understood the auratic work of art as the utopian homeland of mankind, as the means of the emancipatory education of man. Benjamin has also been reinterpreted in this sense by Wilhelm Höck.[6]

In reality, Benjamin is far from holding this view. His own contrasting standpoint shows very well the slight difference between the two aforementioned descriptions of aura. In the aftermath of Riegl, the bearers of this difference seemed to be the categories of spatio-temporal perception: the uniqueness of the aura of a work of art, or of a natural object, resulted from the fact that it brings something distant near for a moment, although the distance remains, however near the object may be. The uniqueness of happiness results from the instantaneous nature of redemption; and it never again revokes the nearness which it brings about—the nearness of intersubjectivity and not of objectivation or of the object. The world of works of art and of nature reveals in this difference its demonic fateful countenance: it offers the unfulfillable promise, the false appearance of redemption.

This idea was also known to the young Lukács, although in his early aesthetics he always headed in the opposite direction, toward validating the being of works of art. A document of Lukács' reservations—which he shares with Max Weber—is a passage from Max Weber's "Science as a Vocation" which quotes and is aimed at Lukács: "The fact that there are works of art is a given for aesthetics. It tries to establish under what conditions this situation exists. But it does not raise the question whether the realm of art may not perhaps be a realm of diabolical splendor, a realm of this world, therefore against God in its deepest core and unbrotherly in its utterly aristocratic spirit. Accordingly, it does not ask whether there *should be* works of art."[7] Benjamin, on the other hand, asks just that, and gives two kinds of answers: first, negative, with art's radical change of function; and second, affirmative, in connection with the condition of the radical change of function of the principle of artistic style.

In both answers, the critique of aesthetic value is correlated with the reintegration of art. Everything really depends on whether the universal, with which art must be reintegrated if it wants to avoid demonic pseudo-fulfillment, stands before art (*universalis ante rem*) or despite reintegration, stands *after* it (*universalis post rem*) in a being which must be immediately determined. Benjamin never answers this question.[8] In the first case, the work of art is derived from the idea, and the task of theory is to trace it back to its metaphysical or theological idea. The work of art does not prove to be a Platonic shadow-image; on the contrary, its being, meaning, and content are more immediate and more specific than any formed work of art; but its being is determined immediately by the universal, from which it receives its meaning. Thus *Trauerspiel* or allegory is not a formal ideal, not a mode of stylization, but a metaphysically transcendent ideal. Or, more precisely, it is the direct identificaton of being and ideal; *Trauerspiel* is a play of mourning, determined by its allegorical meaning, the universal grief of nature which must succumb to death. This fact would not necessarily annihilate aesthetics, for transcendence is just as determinant for the formal principle of allegory as it is for the stylistics of *Trauerspiel*. But that is a question of the effective context, and Benjamin goes further, to the actual reception of the *Trauerspiel,* and allegorizes the allegory: the precision corresponds to the history of decline of a creatureliness subject to fate. The world-view of *universalis ante rem* may, on the other hand, produce an art (naive arts, the art of belief without doubt, allegory, etc.), but no aesthetics, or at most a universal aesthetics and artistic canon. Benjamin, too, must decide against aesthetics, even against the works of art as works of art, in order to carry out the reintegration of art in metaphysics. But since the content of this metaphysics represents the state of the unredeemed creature, a universal aesthetics—the aesthetics of creation—is, for him, not possible. But that means the radical refunctioning of art as a direct expression of life.

Only later, after the turning-point, did Benjamin sketch the historico-philosophical scheme of the universals before the work of art. The autonomy of art, its independent value, becomes, in this sketch, the outmoded, illusory peculiarity of a transitional period, a value which stands between cult-value and an exhibition-value which has lost every remnant of culture and is thoroughly politicized. Benjamin relegates the uniqueness, the authority of past art to a cultic origin, and sees its value in its creation of means: at first means of magic, then of ritual. The hope of the new art, however, consists in its becoming a political instrument due to its exhibition value. In the cultic works of a community of believers the aesthetic has little inherent value, since it is not a component of the utilitarian exhibition-values intended for political masses. In the latter conception, art is reintegrated into the universal monolith of political society, and in "The Author as Producer" Benjamin enunciates the canonical conclusion that follows from this: he criticizes not only existing works and schools of art, but he prescribes from the start, in the name of universals, which arts can be revolutionary and which ones must necessarily be counterrevolutionary. That a theology was, no doubt, behind such a line of thinking was stated by Benjamin himself in late years—with a candor unparalleled in those days: in his first thesis on the philosophy of history. But neither did the artistic-political conclusions from this theology coincide with existing tendencies, nor did the prophecy on the quality of controlled and organized art prove to be true. The leftist *avant-garde* did not become the accepted art of the state-backed Communist mass-movement, and the rightist *avant-garde* did not become the appropriate art of the fascist mass-movement. Both promoted an art *ante rem*—though one suited for the primacy of politics: a crude amalgamation of an intimately human, primitive bucolics and a monumental classicism of man in the public sphere.

Now we will go back to *The Origin of the German Trauerspiel* in order to consider the second path that leads from this work. The first transcends art toward God; the second toward the public. God is the universal who stands before the work, the public the universal that stands after the work—and the two cannot share peacefully in the work. For the former, the transcendental solution, there are two models. First there is tragedy, which is the closed form of the cultic work of art that integrates the public, but is "not quotable," and due to a lack of contemporary relevance cannot come up with its own inherent aesthetic theory. Secondly, the currently relevant model, on the other hand, means the end of art, of the epoch of art. The first model is the closed work which, according to Benjamin, does not open itself up to the contemporary recipient (or at least to the recipient collective), which can be an individual experience, but never a collective one; the second is not a work but the expression of lament and pain, or a later political means. The former has for the—abolished—historical premise the prior *consensus omnium* on the universal; the latter posits the consensus at the end of the historical era—or if you wish, at the end of pre-history—i.e., in the era of redemption; but it can see things only in this light, in the glory of salvation and in the reflection of the Fall. The other approximation, which can also be gleaned from Benjamin's book, contains a *question* concerning the presence and the possibility of the consensus of universals. Obviously the system of the prior consensus, or the instances of meaning and content therein, are the preconditions for any effect and reception. But it is no longer obvious that this consensus—for example, that of a common language—refers not just to names which are oblivious to questions of value, but also to the valuable and evaluable reality of the universals. Through the open form of the work of art that is integrated in the community, one obtains relevant answers to this question. Since every society can be described as possessing a basic consensus on universal values, the question can be reformulated as to what extent the common-ness, which is revealed in the determinant reception of works of art, lies in the valuative function of a community oriented by a single value (in the case of the German baroque *Trauerspiel*, truth in emphatic contrast to beauty). The *universalis post rem* is the public, as was said above. But the public that potentially receives the work of art entails two comprehensive, interrelated concepts: those of art and community. The category of artistic will connotes their mutual interrelation, which, as consensus of the unconscious acceptance and the conscious legitimation, includes the entire realm of creation and reception. And yet it can be determined only *post rem,* from the things themselves, from the works; and this fact accounts for the problematic nature of the consensus as well as the new situation of art: its becoming autonomous is simply correlated with the growing significance of generalization *post rem.*[9]

Benjamin's generalizations, however, must not lead to inductive conclusions but to directly perceived realities. This does not at all presuppose the annihilation of aesthetics, but rather its transformation: a broader, though in one respect narrower, concept of artistic stylization than usual. The concept is broader since the immanent interpretation of the closed work is not one of the criteria. In a copiousness comparable only to that of Simmel, Benjamin recognizes in fragmentary forms and problematic objectivations—which hardly differ from the everyday—great problems of artistic intent. He sought the task with greater passion, not the answer; for his purpose consisted in integrating the work into the greater sphere which assigns tasks: the present community and the new concept of art— second tradition—which binds the former privileged community of the arts with the current community of the now. The essence of the transformation still consists in the fact that—as Benjamin claimed—it is not an alterable or growing quantity of selected individual works—ideally, masterpieces—that comprises the realm of art. Such a selection is to a certain extent embedded in the ongoing history of culture. But Benjamin is not seeking to save the objectivations themselves, but their context, their origin, their medium, and their community. For that very reason, his view is more broadly aimed: he considers not just the work to be substantial, but also the concepts of classification; not just the concrete work, but the ideal of form as well. In this sense, *Trauerspiel* and the allegory are a form, bound to the world-view of a particular community; they are the form of a particular content. *Trauerspiel* is the form of contemplative necessity; and in relation to allegory Benjamin finds it important to stress that the allegory of the seventeenth century is not convention of expression, but the expression of convention. These definitions contain the narrower element of the broader convention: since he understands art to be the will and product of a community, its content appears to be univocally defined. The work is open toward the community, but only toward a particular community: that community together with which it is always conceptually associated. Multiple meaning, the rich substantive reconstruction of artistic structures (at the price that this world-view at work in them is understood as a formless principle of order and as such substitutable) must be lost in this aesthetics so that one can take into account a far greater *praxis* of art that strives toward the same substantive center and artistic will: the perfected totality of the individual works of art that go all the way—and must pay the price of isolation—must perish so that the community of those who are following the same route may be sublated; the symbolic truth of the artistically beautiful must be replaced by the truth-content of the work of art; the work must cease to be world in order to be able to become expression of the world. All this is, however, an alternative and not the abolition of aesthetics.

The theoretical plans to sublate or transform aesthetics are closely interwoven in the book on the *Trauerspiel,* but their contradictoriness does not create tension. The reason is that the *same* contradiction, the contradiction of *ante rem* and *post rem,* the indissoluble dualism in the historical material of the book itself, is closely related in baroque culture. The authority of Christianity as *universalis ante rem,* unshaken internally, and the atomized experience of life, can be traced back—*post rem*—to the *same* universals only by the arbitrariness of fate and the dismemberment of character. Thus a profanization results, which has as a precondition that it must be experienced in a religious framework as creatureliness; thus the unshakable (religious, princely, etc.) representation practiced by melancholy private citizens arises, citizens who dissolve irrationality into an atmosphere of melancholy.

The tension latent in Benjamin's dual conclusion finds release in a thorough analysis of the indissoluble tension between life-contents and artistic forms, for quite differennt conclusions result if the transcendent factor of the work of art leads to God or to community. But precisely the interweaving of the two transcendentals characterizes the German baroque *Trauerspiel.* That is, as Benjamin already suggested in his book, the limit of its contemporary relevance, in the internally acknowledged symbiosis of the church (absolutism) with unredeemed creatureliness. In all Benjamin's later works the dual perspective of the reintegration of aesthetics emerges without a decision ever being made for this or that perspective. At best, an inconsistent unification ever being made for this or that perspective. At best, an inconsistent unification can be observed. Therefore, *The Origin of the German Trauerspiel* is the classical work of his youth, never to be repeated; as are *The System of Transcendental Idealism,* the *Phenomenology of Spirit, Either/Or* and *Spirit of Utopia,* the youthful works of their respective authors.

3

Every transformation, every reform of aesthetics is accompanied by a paradigm shift. Not just value, but also works and genres can be paradigmatic. Even more than drama, Benjamin regards architecture as the paradigmatic art, because its greater usefulness and practicalness links it more closely with the social mission and effect of collective art than all other arts. Even the collective, social possibilities which find expression in a technical culture are manifested with striking transparency in the technical foundations of architecture. The few pages which Benjamin devotes to iron construction in his work demonstrate tersely the two possibilities in which collective experience is summed up: unveiling, the uncamouflaged display of the structure (the constructivism of the Bauhaus artists is an example of this), and the providing of form for a utopian dream-world: the reconquest of the structural elements with the help of ornamentation, of natural forms, etc. (for which *art nouveau* provides the historical documentation).

The last two lines of Brecht's untragic drama, *The Good Person of Sezuan,* could serve as a motto for aesthetic transformation. After the gods have returned to heaven leaving all problems unsolved, a player addresses the audience with the following words: "Honored public, go on, seek your own ending." The fact that the unknown key to the work is left to the audience, this *post rem* (in Schiller's terminology: sentimental) structure of reception characterized every philosophy of art. For the philosophy of art which has become independent, that of Schiller and the Jena Romantics is the expression of that new need, which the artistic world of homogenous taste and the homogenous idea did not know: the need to *understand.* The explanation of meaning which satisfies a different need—practically identifying the words with the homogenous idea and homogenous taste—does not produce aesthetics but a canon, poetics, commentaries, and glosses. The divergence of explanation and understanding was explained in opposite but somewhat complementary ways by the classical and Romantic philosophies of art. Classicism froze this situation by extricating the work from life and barring explanation from the philosophy of art. Thus it solidified the work of art's independence as a value, which from then on can be incorporated as such into every value-whole. Romanticism had a sharper eye for the dilemma between life and the work of art, but its program was that life had to be made into a work of art and poeticized. Therefore the understanding of works of art could merge with the explanation that led to the understanding of the Platonic universe. It thus laid the foundation for the infinite reflection upon works of art as *fragments of value*. The classical reception model was symbolic understanding, the Romantic one was allegorical explanation, which however did not resort to a given, known factor, as the old allegories had done, but to the wish of intuitive reason. Benjamin linked up with Romantic tradition.[10]

Benjamin wrote his doctoral dissertation on the concept of art criticism in German romanticism. The journal *Angelus Novus,* which he planned in his early twenties, was even supposed to be a parody of the *Athenaeum.* But Benjamin's secularized theory is, despite a strongly Romantic vein, not romantic. With the help of methodology of commentary and critique, it creates a peculiar balance between explanation and understanding—in the book on the *Trauerspiel,* the ideas, in the essays on Paris and Baudelaire, the dialectical images—receives a symbolic aspect. This artistic structure of philosophy could still be very typical of romanticism, but it is by no means what explanation and understanding seek in common. For it is not a moral imperative, but a reality, a given: the audience whom the actor addresses.

The audience is not a postulate, also not an empirical fact, but a structure whose given traits Benjamin articulates and makes hierarchical on the basis of a postulate—there must be a good ending. The basis of this articulation is the new concept of experience. Benjamin expands Riegl's experience of perception—the way of seeing as the foundation of the artistic will, of collective reception—into social experience, into the world-view; and he always considers it tradition-oriented and communal. In contrast, he calls individual, atomized reception *Erlebnis* (personal experience). This direct personal experience is non-communicable, but it is complemented by communicable information which, however, cannot become one's own experience. Where commentary becomes information and critique becomes personal experience, the result is the empty, mortally rigid continuum of history. The communal experience of a non-atomized but integrated public[11] is directed against continuity, against "things continuing in this way." And yet it is a depraved experience, a sign of chance, of shock, of the dream and the blurred memory-image which link the entire public (essentially discontinuous) with a second tradition. Two of Benjamin's books, *The Origin of German Trauerspiel* and *Paris of the Second Empire in Baudelaire* are dedicated to the investigation of the depraved experience of community and the quest for the origin of our experience in unnoticed traditions, i.e., traditions which are unnoticed insofar as they are not recognized as such. The loose relation that links Baudelaire's allegories with the baroque and both with the present age, seems to serve as an example of the correspondences of involuntary memory, the way of discovering the second tradition. Collective experience is concentrated in the idea of the *The Origin of German Trauerspiel* and in the dialectical image of the arcade. Unlike the individual work of art, material content is not discarded but kept by the spectator-public of the first tradition and the peripatetic public of the second one.

At any rate, the method of collecting the given experience shows two aspects which coalesce. The dialectic of the dialectical image actually signifies this duality. The distinction between personal and collective experience is already ambiguous, assuming that the former has some *common* element, i.e., that it is an experience that is received individually; and though it may be incommunicable, it must have a generalizable content. Mass experience, which for Benjamin is one of the most important experiences, is precisely of this kind; so is "interior" experience—a form of immediate individual private experience—when it becomes a common style. A second ambiguity is the linkage of collective experience with new and old content and its corresponding revolutionary or restorative function. A third ambiguity is the utopian experience which finds expression in objectified wish-dreams [*Wunschträume*] and hopes, and their conversion into a commodity. This uninterrupted transfiguration of matter does not favor theoretical clarity; phenomenology sometimes leans toward empiricism. The ambiguity—without the dialectical mediation of dialectics what remains is a mystical dialectics—overlaps, however, with Benjamin's ideas and is an ambivalence typical of his thought as a whole. For he regards unredeemed history as a continuum of catastrophes, and in it he called the possibility of redemption (using a term from the tradition of Jewish mysticism) *sparks* of hope in the *past*. The future as past, the future in memory, find their secularized meaning in the second tradition, which acts as the will of communal forms even in the midst of an unfavorable milieu, or respectively reworks the material of the first tradition, the prevailing culture. It fragments the latter, robbing it of unity, thereby ascribing a second meaning to it and preserving it in this new context. Let me stress again: in its rare, involuntary revelations the public is depraved, although it is so much deeper and universal than the culture that is foisted upon it that Benjamin resorts to ideological parallels and the relation between the Freudian consciousness and subconscious to describe the relationship between the two. Arcades and avenues, iron buildings and panoramas, photo and film (to name just a few of the collectively received ambiguous objects), and the great shared experiences behind them (masses, commodity-fetishes, spleen, neurosis, etc.), all of which Benjamin combined into dialectical images, all oscillate between atomistic and integrated social structure.

Benjamin considers the shared nature of experience to be a transcendental, *a priori* given. Redemption, which is simutaneously revolution and *restitution in integrum,* means liberation, because both forms of the bourgeois world—atomistic socialization as well as the irreducible communal life in symbiosis with it—are diseases of communal experience. The dialectic at a standstill betrays this two-fold image: perverted culture as a commodity, and impotent culture as a wish-image. After his turn to social criticism, Benjamin was convinced that only people of the latter culture could find the key to a "good ending," to emancipation: neither transcendental nor economic necessity could provide it. The "dialectic" at a standstill would have to be replaced by a genuine dialectic. He had two ideas of how this could take place. Typical of both is that the accent is on the dialectical leap and not on mediation; but the first idea has contact with the social, the second with the communal sense of the ambiguous dialectical images. I call the first a dialectic of destruction, the second a dialectic of awakening, in order thus to characterize also the two aspects of the Benjamin path to liberation.

Destructive dialectics—in its encounter with the culture of personal experience, and the atomization and languishing of experience—chooses annihiliation, the great reduction, the depravation of experience. One must destroy in order to be able to build; it is a matter of overcoming difficulties by accumulating them. Karl Kraus's critique of language, his bitter struggle against journalism and feuilletonism, is the monumental reminder of this dialectic. The dialectic of awakening—of social awakening—abolishes the communal elements and references (wishful thinking) of the bourgeois world as elements of a dream-world. This, too, is the overcoming of difficulties by the accumulation of difficulties; but while in the first case withdrawal represents the accumulated difficulty, in the second it is characterized by elevation to a higher level. This, too, is in a certain sense destruction, for what is raised to a higher level is torn from a context and eternalized in fragmentary form. Elevation to a higher level and destruction are the two poles in the modern artistic undertakings which Werner Hofmann, after Kandinsky, called "the great realistics" or "the great abstraction,"[12] and which constitutes the real theory of two tendencies of the *avant-garde*, surrealism and constructivism. These are the schools which Benjamin supports stylistically; but in expressionism and *Neue Sachlichkeit* (which Benjamin sharply rejected, despite being very strongly influenced by the first), one likewise sees the same parting of ways. But here—and this is the real foundation of his critique—the great realism and the great abstraction separate *within* the social atomization of culture: expressionism expresses subjectivistic experiences; *Neue Sachlichkeit,* which responds to it, conveys objective *information.* These are the four main points of Benjamin's theory of style. Thanks to his theoretical-critical guardian angel, he saw the crossroads not where art produced the material of its own form out of the material of bourgeois reality (on the basis of two opposing principles of selection), but where art, in this or that direction, accepted the antinomy of bourgeois thought (not identical with being), the subject-object division—in order later to protest against it even extremely sharply. Precisely for that reason, expressionism and *Neue Sachlichkeit,* according to Benjamin, could not produce any artistic result, but at most a pathological insight or a dry abstraction; but these are, in contrast to *Trauerspiel,* the object of critique because they cannot be integrated into the public qua community. How much less the man of expressionism is suited to this purpose than the *creature* of the baroque *Trauerspiel!* The artistic genres of destructive dialectics and dream-dialectics, on the contrary, carry out the reintegration, and in such a way that in their forms the strategy of reception corresponds to communal needs. Benjamin sums up these needs in the former case with the concept of "dispersion," in the second as function or usefulness; and he regards both as necessary for emancipation. He studies how the strategy of reception becomes a form-creating principle by the examples of the great aesthetic problems such as distracted reception, shock, the familiarity of the story, etc. With their help he interprets the art of Baudelaire and Brecht, of Kafka and Proust.

With the concepts "usefulness" and "distraction" and, less than Benjamin thought, with "technical reproducibility," one has of course again reached the crossroads between the transformation and sublation of aesthetics. For these happen to be the concepts in whose name art is still contested even today, if mostly only in the form of a family quarrel between art for the elite and art for the masses. But the disputes in which Benjamin had taken a standpoint are a thing of the past: constructivism and surrealism proved to be renewers and not fragmentors of artistic forms, and the direct political engagement of art did not promote the emancipation of man. As for the individual artists whom Benjamin interpreted, artistic quality was always decisive for the great critic. And if this seems understandable in the cases of Baudelaire or Leskov, whom Benjamin clearly understands as theorists of the end of art because of the *arrière-garde* aspect of their writing, this explanation is no longer tenable in the case of the great figures of the artistic *avant-garde*. But the old disputes over the material content and the *ad hominem* arguments practiced by critics are not decisive. The questions to what extent Benjamin's theory prophesies the end of art and to what extent it recommends the transformation of thinking about art—do not even have to be asked.

Benjamin's cultural philosophy is based on a value choice: on the choice of communal culture instead of an individual culture. At first he pictured the community as a religious community, later as a communal society emancipated by political revolution. If redemption is—in contrast to the deviation from the *a priori* given communality of experiences as original sin—nothing else but the return, then the universals of the community can only be religious: givenness is not transcendental, but transcendent. That was the goal of Benjamin's early critique of Kant when he wanted to replace the formal *a priori* nature of experience with substantive religious *a priori*. This metaphysical solution, related to mysticism, was merely secularized by Benjamin, but never given up completely. But he also worked at a different solution in which he did not want to establish the nature of his conception of community. In this case the transcendental communality of experience and the communal values and forms of a *society* replace the possibility of creating a communal *culture*. The reception of the artistic movements of destructive withdrawal or of the elevation to a new context are the communal practice and elaboration of a new culture. The public is made into a community by the creation and appropriation of a culture: that would have to be the final conclusion. But once again the contrast between the *universalis ante* or *post rem* is thereby established. In the community of the first type, the religious or quasi-religious policy establishes from the outset the communal values according to which art must orient itself; in the second type, values such as community, collective reception, and communal culture develop.

But this second way also touches upon the following question: *out of what* does this new culture develop, and who is its subject? Of course, many answers are possible to this question. Thus one could distinguish between the subject of the emancipatory movement and the subject of culture. The leftist intelligentsia of the twenties often did this. It saw the former in the revolutionary class, the latter in the individual heirs of cultural tradition, and eventually embraced the latter for the sake of the former. But to do this the philosophy of history and the philosophy of culture had to be transferred to two different levels (their unification was to be effected in the distant future) which Benjamin could not accept. The isolated, private individual as the recipient of culture seems to Benjamin unacceptable for two reasons: either because in his view it cannot be the recipient of *culture,* or because its isolation, its atomization in the phenomenality of culture-reception turns out to be an ideological fiction (thus with the ambivalence so typical of Benjamin, the "traces" of "interior" experience are first considered something that must be destroyed, then as something to be raised to a higher level). But what follows from this second possibility—namely, that it is culture itself that generates its own community and (carrying this topic one step further) leads to emancipation—is likewise unacceptable to him, for the concept of culture, homogenized in such a way, would lose its specific contents. In both solutions, the first, the classical tradition, is the envoy of culture; but Benjamin on the other hand understands the diaspora of the second tradition to be the bearer of communal culture. One could thus say that the concept of universal communal culture as *universalis post rem* could have run precisely contrary to knowledge; for that from which it develops is also a type of community, and its subject is also not the individual but a community.

Several possibilities thus present themselves: e.g., to study the communities from which the new relevant culture emerged; to study the communities which receive the new culture. Such scientific studies appreciate Benjamin's ideas, but the philosophical problems that occupy him do not lie in this field. From this point of view, the beautiful pages in Benjamin's study of Paris on the *flaneur,* the conspirator, the waves of masses, the Boheme, or the ragcollector, are actually mere materials—as Adorno writes in a clever yet uncomprehending letter. The very title *Paris of the Second Empire in Baudelaire* shows that the materials do not so much interpret the work but the work interprets them, i.e., the elements of community in the work.

And this applies, of course, not just to Baudelaire's *Oeuvre,* but also to the most varied objectivations of artistic will; to the arcade, the panorama, etc. This is the real relevance to the philosophy of art: he derives artistic will from the works. Of course, there is no question of primacy of the works over will, over the communities, the given and real associations manifested in the artistic intention. But this means that as a result of their heterogeneity they are comprehensible only insofar as their determinacy is revealed in the nature as form—however fragmentary or formless it may be.

Instead of an art of universal culture capable of being interpreted in many ways, there would be several particular arts which do not transcend their own context. Instead of being the product of individual achievement, art is shown to be a communal form of being. The utility of works of art vouches for their self-interpretation in the contexts and in the cultures of their reception; the dissemination they acquire through reception is the guarantee of their self-interpretation. The principle of utility, like the pleasure principle, becomes anti-artistic only when it is torn from its context and counterposed to the work of art as an extraneous demand. But the contexts can be seen only starting from the objectivations. From this follows Benjamin's deep solidarity with every school that introduces a new calendar, and at the same time his deep distrust of every artistic achievement, however great, that is based on continuous cultural traditions. For the former is creative only culturally, it is not incorporated into the existing culture, and it satisfies a real need; while the cultural universe of the latter is only appearance, and receivable only individually. It is one of Benjamin's most characteristic convictions that the new calendar is a very old calendar; but the second tradition is hidden: its scientific discovery and its collective reception do not compete with one another.

All this is the culture of an unredeemed world; for it already seems to Benjamin intrinsically apocalyptic that one can reason back to the real communities only from their objects. The antinomic principle of Benjamin's theory is not only unresolved, but is even shown in an unsettled contradiction. For the fact that the communities are determined only by their objectivations, that they are heterogeneous and numerous, but we ourselves can be recipients of and participate in several of them, points clearly to the universality of culture. Benjamin knows and appreciates this fact. But at the same time, due to fear of the idea of the endless progress of universal cultural history, his theory lacks the element that would universalize these communities in their plurality. The monadic asceticism of his procedure follows from this fact, but also his contradictoriness: a critical interpreter of many associations, communities, artistic intentions, he focuses in each work on just one of them. He creates an inner tension, since each one wants to universalize its own consensus without reflecting on the others. Therefore, the theological element in Benjamin's thinking had to be present to the end: ultimately this tension can be overcome only when its universals stand prior to the culture, the art of a community, as its ordering principle. Where Benjamin *wanted* to overcome the tensions of his theory is a different question—apparently where it touched his historico-philosophical perspective most directly.

A different way to release the tension is to reflect the contradiction. For opposite the universal, pluralistic community of culture stand the relatively homogeneous communities of the individual subcultures, and the origin of each work of art, leads to some kind of subculture. More precisely, the origins of the old arts, for which the decision is not meaningful, leads to some kind of closed culture. This closed culture considers every other culture to be a scandal and madness; that of the art of the bourgeois world epoch, on the contrary, leads to a subculture or to a complex of subcultures. But not every culture can cross its own boundaries, not every culture is capable of being understood and experienced by other communities too. But if culture intends to take this step, then it can, by sublating aesthetics, reach beyond its own community as religious or quasi-religious consciousness, or—what is the same thing—it can hypostasize its own community as universal. But that is by no means necessary. Arts, building on the consensus of given or chosen communities, can persist within their own culture and yet reflect the universal culture without demanding initially what they can receive only afterwards. Although the first half of the twentieth century was characterized by the avantegarde movements, and the exchange economy of the national and class cultures was characterized by the radical intolerance which wanted to strengthen and hermeticize the individual factor so much that it was identified with the universals, thus excluding all other cultures; such striving stands on the same universal basis as a possible theoretical and practical radical tolerance (the expression comes from Agnes Heller): namely, that the communities are not organic, natural, closed communities, and accordingly are not monolithic, since we are all integrated into numerous communities and are bound by numerous cohesions of varying strength, depth, and breadth.

It is the task of aesthetics to integrate works of art and arts within the artistic will and thus within a sub-culture: Baudelaire in Paris of the Second Empire, together with its street scenes, its buildings, its industrial art, its panoramas and arcades. But it is just as much the task of aesthetics to lift Baudelaire out of this setting and to understand him within universal culture. Benjamin's concept of relevance (the raising of contents to a new level, for which it is, in his view, not too high a price to pay that significant areas of culture will remain hidden as irrelevant until the Last Judgment of redemption) does not do justice absolutely to this second requirement. This historico-philosophical process whereby the Idea of the work of art

150

is made relevant with the help of reconstruction is just one possibility. The irrelevant (*das Nichtaktuelle*), which contradicts our world-view, and in which we can not recognize our own origin, may still have relevance (*Aktualität*); and the dialectic of construction and reconstruction has a legitimate, often victorious competitor in the dialectic that consciously rejects reconstruction or, with reason, considers it impossible. On the basis of form, a reception constitutive of a new world-view results. For as soon as the work of art moves out of its own culture—the cathedral out of the Christian city, jazz out of the sub-culture of the North American blacks—it loses some of its substantive intensity—indeed its contents may even be completely destroyed. All that it loses and all that is lost must become an element of form, must be taken over by form. Form must be the central concept of aesthetics, which integrates the work of art into universal culture.

Two aesthetics stand in opposition: the aesthetics of art and the aesthetics of artistic intention. Their opposition must not be derived from the opposition between the first and the second cultural traditions, for even the canonized concept of art—the first tradition—has its subculture; the culture of the educated bourgeois, of Lubeck as a spiritual form of life; and it also has an art (epigonism) which does not become a component of universal culture. The aesthetics of artistic intention discloses the particular form of life, the particular valuation of life and world-view in the forms of the works of art. This is certainly the primary point of view, for the work stems from the particular valuation of life, and it can also be received only with the help of a particular valuation of life. But even the "abstraction" of aesthetic consciousness, (aesthetic formatism) receives, through a radically completed *general fraternity* of various forms, an existing norm of form of life, which is less specific, but of more general validity than any subculture; universal culture as the radically tolerant form of life. Thus, just as the aesthetics of artistic intention must reflect the aesthetics of form in order to be able to change its episodic nature as critique, or not be forced to universalize any particular artistic intention, so also the aesthetics of form must reflect the aesthetics of artistic intention in order not to be enjoyment of beautiful illusions, not auratic, *ersatz* for life in a world deprived once and for all of aura,[13] so that there be no refinements which barbarity—as universal culture of the owners of power—*presupposes*. Benjamin was aware of this danger, so that he looked with reserve upon the universal cultural goods which were inherited due to their form. The Benjaminian transformation of aesthetics is a foundation of the philosophy of artistic intention. This pole of bipolar

151

aesthetics can perhaps not be separated otherwise than through global attacks on the other pole—and yet the contradictions and hiatuses of the theory result precisely from this.

4

The emancipatory turn to a critique of society, the choice in values favoring communal culture, the turning away from the purely theoretical sphere, and the insight into the necessity of social activism led Benjamin to Marx; but in such a way that his position is sometimes called a deficient Marx-reception (this was the aim of Adorno's critique), and sometimes a Marx-critique. The decisive point where Benjamin's philosophy of history deviates from the Marxian one is the problem of communities. In Benjamin's view, the bourgeois world is not a society without communities, but a world of the open, plural communities embedded in many different traditions; a world which is not transcended but depraved by the tendency of commodity production to universalize the market, to atomize the individual and to destroy tradition. Since he sees real and not illusory communities, and he regards the formations as being rather than as consciousness, the path of *critique of ideology,* of the disclosure of false consciousness does not stand open to him—the great methodological models are the unmasking of the fetish character of the commodity in *Capital* and the analysis of the antinomies of bourgeois through in *History and Class Consciousness.* Furthermore, since he does not trace every repression back to economic exploitation, the concept of emancipation receives new dimensions and cannot be reduced to economics and politics. In the aforementioned essay by Habermas, one reads: "Now in the tradition that goes back to Marx, Benjamin was one of the first to stress an additional factor in the concepts of exploitation and progress: besides famine and represession—renunciation, besides prosperity and freedom—happiness."[14] Consequently, the subject of emancipation is the repressed, humiliated, and offended masses, but in an even more general sense, the whole human race awaits redemption. Certainly, by the insertion of these additional factors in our life different from those mentioned above—renunciation and happiness—the universally valid social and economic determinacy of the subject of liberation is eliminated; there is no individual community whose liberation, even as a tendency, would be *identical* with universal liberation.

As is known, Benjamin transferred liberation to messianic perspectives. That is, because he regarded every community of the bourgeois era as depraved and in a state of *rigor mortis*—just as, on the other hand, because of messianic hope which holds every existing thing in existential insecurity, he considered everything to be provisional—these communities are only evidence derivable from the truth content of cultural products, of works of art. From the point of view of aesthetics this meant the transcendence of the strict distance between art and life, but it could also mean the complete elimination of distances and thus the abolition of art. When he examined his own memories, he came back to art. However, in contrast to an esthete, in a direct form: his *A Berlin Childhood around Nineteenhundred* is a work of art. When in a different manner he wanted to investigate his own experiences, his own collective experiences— namely in the hashish experiments—he anticipated the form of life of a leftist subculture in the soft-drug intoxication that would come in vogue three or four decades later; but this was especially because of external circumstances—of medical controls, record-keeping, etc.—far more an experiment at understanding than an experiment in life.

Benjamin's messianism is fostered especially by traditions of Jewish messianism. This is shown not only by the future drawn from the past and the taboo against depicting the future. The principle characteristics of Jewish messianism can be summed up according to Gershom Scholem[15] as follows: it is mainly a theory of catastrophe, which, within the duality of apocalyptical existence and of utopian hope, stresses the destructive and revolutionary aspect of redemption. There is no mediation between history and redemption; the element of progress or development leading to redemption is missing. Redemption is essentially unexpected, unless, in a reversed sense, it is sunk in the deepest catastrophe. Since the theory is not oriented to mere interiority, the possibility of messianic activism is nonetheless not lost; from lack of a mediation by the future, the destructive, anarchistic element is predominant. Those are the birth-pangs which prepare for the Messiah. Of course, there was within Judaism—from Maimonides to Buber—also a current counter to this apocalyptic messianism. From the eighteenth century on, the progressively secularized idea of redemption absorbed the idea of progress, thereby abolishing the past-oriented, restorative factor, but Benjamin's reliance on ancient tradition is simply a very modern critique of the depravation of precisely this idea of progress.

The other element in Benjamin's theory based on Jewish tradition is his thinking on language, whose revivers were theorists who stood close to Benjamin: Rosenzweig, Martin Buber, and even Florens Christian Rang. The model of this thinking is not the isolated individual oriented by the object, but the speech situation between I and Thou. The great tradition of the I-Thou experience, of language as the bearer of thought, is the

SÁNDOR RADNÓTI

Bible—the dialogue between God and man; the preservation of this tradition holds together the community of linguistic consciousness. Though it may sound archaic, the connection between the language theorists and the modern philosophical endeavors, such as existential hermeneutics and Heidegger, was pointed out from the most various directions—by Else Freund, Karl Löwith, Karl-Otto Apel. At any rate, the stand taken against the transcendental philosophy of the isolated private individual and against the resulting antinomy of subject and object actually has similarities with the great problems of philosophy which have been on the agenda since the crisis of Kantianism at the beginning of this century. Dialogic thinking and life both place their objects in the relation of intersubjectivity. Because of the above remarks, there is no need for a separate proof that Benjamin's philosophy centering on the questions of reception, the community, and collective reception, aims to restore intersubjectivity. To show that this is correlated with the traditions of linguistic theory, two factors of his theory can be pointed out: first, his philosophy of language, in which speaking becomes creative naming and communication of essence, while communication and mediation are pushed completely into the background compared with the direct, expressive and even onomatopoetic nature of language: the I-it relation is replaced by the I-Thou relation. And secondly, the secret main theme in his work, the fable, which is a genre turned directly toward "the Other," directly toward the community. The subterranean tradition of the Hasidic legend is an important example of this.

Neither messianism nor the hermeneutics of particular form could find their ways back to the tradition from which they were taken. This would have required a series of practical decisions which Benjamin pondered for more than a decade: emigration to Palestine, immersion in study of the Hebrew language, etc. Benjamin was never associated with the Jewish community, a community which he finally sought out only in the thinking of his friend Gershom Scholem. Through Benjamin's typical hesitation these ties dwindled at the beginning of the thirties; he could not decide on a complete break. But he had been thinking since 1924 of the possibility of becoming politically active, and for a long time he considered joining the Communist Party. It is questionable to what extent a modern political party can be considered a community. The leftist intelligentsia of the twenties, however, considered the revolutionary workers' party not as one party among many, but as the organization in which every single member is absorbed with his whole personality and his whole being in the life of the party.[16] This could be based on the idea of progress and necessity, but then precisely the factor which represented internal cohesion

154

is weakened if not lost. One could demonstrate it through minimalizing of necessity, while retaining it on an essential point. This was Lukács' opinion and he retained the theory of the necessary collapse of capitalism, which made the seizing or missing of the *moment* (and thus the relapse into barbarism) dependent on the activity of the proletariat. In the section "Fire Alarm" in the *One-Way Street,* Benjamin repeats this idea. But while in Lukács the party is considered the custodian of correct consciousness, of the "maturity" of the class, and becomes the subject of the mythologically assigned class-consciousness, Benjamin directed his gaze rigidly at the catastrophe of progress. He could regard as preserver and redeemer of the more general consciousness of servitude, disappropriation, and dissatisfaction only an organization whose being was also directed at the aforementioned moment and exhausted in it: thus his early sympathies for the direct activism of anarcho-syndicalism and the anti-parliamentary communist factions, and his later interest in Blanqui. He considered as his party only a party of action, destruction, or salvation, and the action had to be of a momentary nature: he could find a home in the idea of the redeeming leap of revolution, but in the long run no party. This momentariness, however, also contradicts the possibility of a community. More precisely, a sect oriented to a messianic expectation is possible, but a messianic party is impossible. But Benjamin did not go so far as to make political organization into a sect by stylizing it into a community—the prospect with which the generation of the twenties was faced. For as a result of the historical example of the October events, they equated the political party with the emancipatory social movement or its *avant-garde.* Yet, more typical of his attitude is what he predicted in a letter from the year 1926—it deals with his considering joining the party: "The task is here not to decide once and for all, but to decide at every moment."[17] This idea was certainly helpful for the openness of his *Oeuvre,* but did little to aid its unity.

But unity consists only insofar as everything awaits a decision; for the moment (every moment in the catastrophe-laden continuum) is a moment of danger, and Benjamin is deeply convinced that even the past, even the dead, are exposed to this danger. A correspondingly direct interrelation between destruction and salvation, the antinomic world-view of catastrophe and redemption could, of course, not do without theological confirmation—naturally, that of an innerworldly theology. And this extends from the insertion of materialist-metaphysical elements into his theory, to the numerous motifs expressing his idea of happiness. For he can, "as a theologian, save the revolutionary opportunity at every moment, but as a social theorist, not depict it politically."[18] Culture is the *corrective* of the hidden theodicy. Liberation theology and liberating cultural philosophy: they constitute the final ambiguity of Benjamin's thinking. For if cultural philosophy harnesses theology into its service, it makes culture into the means of liberation; but this culture which has become a means is depraved. And that is completely in accord with Benjamin: to him every moment of existing reality is depraved. Liberation, when it comes, or redemption, can on the other hand, mean only the auratic idea of happiness in a communal and thus already universal culture. This hope permits the other interpretation of the Benjamin texts: cultural philosophy can translate the wishes, hopes, and needs which have assumed a theological form into its language and thus completely secularize them, and grasp communal culture and its movements as the goal of liberation.

Budapest, Hungary

Translated by David Parent and Richard Wolin

NOTES

1 Benjamin's early work on *Elective Affinities* shows the genesis of his standpoint. There, form can still evoke a magic world, freezing life into a harmony and making act momentaneous; art is beauty and what is true in it is the expressionless. And yet the whole essay is a dispute with these ideas: with beautiful illusion and its mythological relation to life. Even later he considers these two phenomena to be the arch-enemy (cf. his critique of the fascist aesthetization of politics). Just as remarkable, however, is the fact that he never tried his hand in the opposite direction with a theory of reflection.
2 H. G. Gadamer, *Wahrheit und Methode* (Tübingen: Mohr, 1975), p. 80.
3 J. Habermas, "Bewußtmachende oder rettende Kritik: die Aktualität Benjamins," in *Zur Aktualität Walter Benjamins,* ed. S. Unseld (Frankfurt: Suhrkamp, 1972).
4 The expression is borrowed from Heinz Paetzold's Benjamin interpretation: *Neomarxistische Ästhetik* (Düsseldorf: Schwann, 1974).
5 Heller, et al., *Die Seele und das Leben* (Frankfurt: Suhrkamp, 1977), pp. 41ff.
6 *Kunst als Suche nach Freiheit* (Köln: DuMont-Schauberg, 1973).
7 Max Weber, "Science as a Vocation," In *From Max Weber,* ed. H. H. Gerth and C. W. Mills (New York: Oxford, 1949).
8 The quarrel over universals, which is taken up again in *The Origin of German Trauerspiel,* was analyzed from an epistemological point of view by Rolf Tiedemann in his *Studien zur Philosophie Walter Benjamins* (Frankfurt: Suhrkamp, 1965), pp. 18ff.
9 "The science of art is . . . far more necessary in our time than in the times when art granted full satisfaction for itself as art" (Hegel, *Ästhetik I* (Berlin & Weimar: Akademie, 1965), p. 23).—For application of the *ante rem* or *post rem* concepts in aesthetics cf. G. Lukács, *Heidelberger Philosophie der Kunst 1912-1914* (Darmstadt & Neuwied: Luchterhand, 1974), p. 216. However, Lukács considers only the third possibility, the classically auratic stylization *in re* as the genuine solution of art, in which "the possibility

of a distancing is posited as a possibility; its overcoming, however, is done without a struggle, by the mere homesickness of things for order." *Ibid.*, p. 230.

10 And this is just a small leap, and not—as one might think—very far removed from Hermann Cohen, the contemporary philosopher most important for Benjamin in his youth, who abolished all givenness, understood axioms as a moral imperative and believed that determination of origin—the fundamental concept of his thinking—is brought about by the judgment via the detour of nothingness.

11 Cf. Martin Jay, *The Dialectical Imagination* (Boston: Little, Brown & Co., 1973), pp. 208ff.

12 Werner Hofmann, *Grundlagen der modernen Kunst* (Stuttgart: Kröner, 1963).

13 Malraux's "museum without walls" is an example of how the recipient attitude determined by aesthetics of form fluctuates between the liberated and liberating cultural man and the gourmet.

14 Jürgen Habermas, pp. 216f.

15 Gershom Scholem, "Zum Verständnis der messianischen Idee im Judentum," in *Über einige Grundbegriffe des Judentums* (Frankfurt: Suhrkamp, 1970), pp. 121ff.

16 G. Lukács, "Methodisches zur Organizationsfrage," *Geschichte und Klassenbewuβtsein.*

17 Walter Benjamin, *Briefe* (Frankfurt: Suhrkamp, 1966), p. 425.

18 Hartmut Engelhardt, "Der historische Gegenstand als Monade," in *Materialien zu Benjamins Thesen "Über den Begriff der Geschichte"*, ed. Peter Bulthaup (Frankfurt: Suhrkamp, 1975), p. 302.

BENJAMIN ON REPRODUCIBILITY AND AURA: A READING OF "THE WORK OF ART IN THE AGE OF ITS TECHNICAL REPRODUCIBILITY"

JOEL SNYDER

If men and their circumstances appear upside down in all ideology as in a camera obscura, then this phenomenon is caused by their historical life process, just as the inversion of objects on the retina is caused by their immediate physical life.

Marx and Engels, *The German Ideology*

Walter Benjamin's essay "The Work of Art in the Age of its Technical Reproducibility,"[1] is a linked series of theses concerning the redefinition of art in a pre-revolutionary period. It is a fragile and frustrating set of observations about the developmental tendencies of art in a period in which the technological conditions of production are in the process of accelerated evolution. Under these conditions, art is pulled in opposing directions at once by antagonistic perceptions of reality. Benjamin's theses are dialectical and their terms in dynamic opposition. It is the dialectical character of the essay that accounts both for its fragility and power of frustration. It would therefore be wrong and ultimately distorting to the sense of the essay to demand stable and univocal definition for any of Benjamin's terms. For him terms like "art," "nature," "perception," and "reality" are inherently universal in application and indeterminate in sense. They achieve meaning and application only in specific contexts, governed by specific use.

Benjamin's essay is devoted in great part to a discussion of standards—exemplars we employ in determining the kinds of things and sorts of relations that we have a legitimate claim to call "real." The standards we use for judging what is real and the "medium"in which we construct our perceptions of reality are, according to Benjamin, in an ongoing state of evolution. In a typically dense and difficult statement, Benjamin says:

With [sound motion pictures] technical reproduction achieved a standard that not only made the totality of traditional works of art its object and brought about the most profound change in their effect, but also won its own place among the artistic processes. For the study of this standard, nothing is more revealing than the way in which the twin functions of photography—the reproduction of the work of art and the art of the film—permeate one another.[2]

The sense of the essay pivots on an understanding of the expression, "achieved a standard," and in order to gain some insight into what Benjamin means by this opaque locution, it will be necessary to examine it in conjunction with his notion of the inter-relationship of depiction and perception. By "achieved a standard," Benjamin does not mean that technical reproduction (photography and sound motion pictures) merely reached a better or higher level of representation than had formerly been attained, because this way of putting it presupposes that we are already in possession of an existing standard of representation by means of which we are able to grade hierarchies of depiction. That we often speak as if this is the case is beyond question. Much of the recent work in this country in the philosophy of representation—I have in mind, in particular, the work of Nelson Goodman[3] and the work inspired by it—can be understood as a broad attack on the notion that we are equipped with a "natural" standard by means of which we are able to grade pictures as more or less realistic. Benjamin insists that the very possibility of accepting certain kinds of photographs as being accurate pictures of the world implies that a new standard has been achieved for making such determinations and that this implies further that the old standard has been, or is in the process of being supplanted. He sees an ongoing adjustment between human perception and works of visual art—one that finds a reciprocal relation between an evolving mode of perceiving and the new mode of depiction. Photography and film represent a new vision of reality, but only a revolutionary consciousness can appreciate this vision as both accurate and unprecedented. Benjamin's argument in support of this observation is spread throughout the text, indeed, much of the essay is devoted to establishing just this conclusion. I shall outline in a few sentences what I take to be the backbone of the argument and then fill-in the sketch. Benjamin wants to assert this: new methods of production engender new means of depiction because they bring about specifiable changes in the perception of the world. Art itself is intimately involved with the expression of perception. In a period of technical, industrial production in which the work of the hand is given over to the machine, the character of human perception—at least the perception of those who maintain and run the machines—the workers—changes in accord with the manner of production. Technical production brings about technically informed perception that, in turn, engenders technical depiction or reproduction. The standard for judging technically manufactured art cannot be the same standard used to judge manually produced art since the latter is derived from non-technically informed perception. This means that a film or a still photograph cannot be properly understood and evaluated by falling back onto the sense perception that characterized the pre-technical period. It demands a new standard and finds it in the revolutionary masses whose "sense of reality" is in the process of being adjusted to the new means of technical production.

This way of speaking about "standards" and the relation of perception to depiction has a vague and unspecific ring and Benjamin typically fails to give specific, concrete examples of just what he has in mind when he speaks this way. It will be useful to find an example of the sort of problem he must have in mind and to pursue the implications of the example. Let us say that a photographer at the Olympics takes an instantaneous exposure of a single runner in a hundred-meter run. The photograph is made at 1/1,000th of a second and shows the runner with both feet off the ground, each leg "frozen" and sharply delineated. What Benjamin is asking is this: in virtue of what standard (or principle) are we to accept this photograph as an accurate depiction of our world? This a difficult question. Numerous recent writers on photography[4] have suggested that *the* photograph displays for us "what we would have seen if we had been there ourselves"—i.e., if we had seen the depicted event. But it should be clear that this explanation cannot work because the very interest that the photography of the runner has for us is grounded in our *inability* to see this sort of thing at all. The standard of representational accuracy here cannot be "natural" vision, for if it were, we would have to say that the picture is inaccurate—we never could have seen anything at all like what is depicted here. What possible standard then, do we invoke when we judge the picture to represent the world with accuracy? The only available means of checking the photograph would be by producing another photograph of the same runner under the same conditions, or by devising some other technical machinery that would analyze the runner's stride. But what that means is that what we might have seen at the Olympics cannot serve as the standard of accurate representation for the photograph. Vision that is somehow not technically informed cannot come to terms with this kind of picture. It must reject the photograph. And of course, various critics and artists of the nineteenth century did reject this kind of photograph as being "untrue to our experience of the world." But, it is just this way of thinking about pictures and the world that Benjamin is in the process of being undermined by photography. The standard invoked by such critics by instantaneous photographs seems to be universal and stable—"our experience of the world," but Benjamin wants to show that perceptual standards are neither stable nor fixed for all time. The "natural" or traditional standard for pictures cannot endorse these photographs. But then, what can it possibly mean to say that a picture that shows us something unseeable—something that can only be shown by means of a technical process—is, nonetheless, accurate? If the photograph fails to show us "the way things look," does it achieve accuracy by showing us "the way things *are?*" How shall we characterize the relation of photographs to the world? In Benjamin's view, the photograph destroys the traditional relationship of the picture to the world as perceived. It might be said that the traditional mode of representation assured the world—in it, depiction and the perception it expressed were mutually reinforcing. But, photography calls such mutual reassurance into question. It raises a doubt about "natural" perception. With the old mode of representation, the world as perceived provides the constraint as well as the standard for depiction. It is the "original" in Clement Greenberg's sense of the word—it is the object of imitation.[5] Photography calls into question the ontological primacy, the authority of the original. With photography, the world as perceived—at least as perceived by non-proletarian eyes—is threatened. The photograph can reveal, unmask, discover the real world and "natural" or "unaided" vision cannot overcome the threat.

Benjamin's point here is not a trivial one. If photographs are about "the visible world" and most writers on photography maintain at least this, then in what sense is a picture that shows us something unseeable still to be thought of as about "the visible world?" We are left in the unusual predicament of maintaining at one and the same time photographs show us facts about "the visible world" that have no counterparts in our world outside their occurrence in photographs. Thus, photography challenges our traditional notions of what constitutes our world, our reality. And by so doing, it disturbs the delicate balance between traditional modes of depiction and perception. If the photograph becomes the arbiter of what is real—and Benjamin believes that it is in the process of so doing—the older conception of reality that found its expression in the tradition of painting, is called into question. And what happens in the process of raising questions about the way in which the world has traditionally been perceived is this—the authority of non-technical perception and of the objects of this perception is overthrown.

This last point is difficult to make with clarity and it will be useful to turn to Benjamin's discussion of the reproduction of traditional works of art to gain some measure of insight into his claims. Benjamin makes two major claims about the photographic reproduction of "received" works of art. The first is rather easy to understand: by making a full color reproduction of a masterpiece and by disseminating copies of it throughout the world, the original painting loses some of its authority. By this he means that for nearly any *use* a viewer might have, the copy can be substituted for the original. Thus, non-specialists can view and enjoy the painting without having to visit it. University students can view transparencies of the work in classrooms and learn much of what they might learn if the original were immediately before them. Even experts, though they might claim the contrary, can use good reproductions as the basis of their specialized research. Prior to the period of technical reproducibility, the work itself possessed a special authority. Handmade reproductions could and most often did fail to reproduce works of art with the kind of accuracy necessary to study and contemplation. Here, of course, the standard of accuracy is the way the work looks under reasonably standard lighting conditions. Thus, the original had the power to "pull" art lovers to the museum or collection in which it was housed. Technical reproduction ends this kind of power—at least insofar as nearly all uses that might be made of the original. But Benjamin makes a second and even more important claim on behalf of photographic reproducibility. A technical reproduction cannot reproduce all the properties of the original—it can only show the way it "looks" to the camera. It may reproduce the appearance of the original with great accuracy, but it cannot reproduce the basis of its originality—its materiality, its *Hier und Jetzt,* its presence. A reproduction of a masterwork, no matter how good, cannot acquire the provenance or the "autogenic" character of the original. So, it would seem that a central element of the authority of the original is left untouched by technical reproduction, but Benjamin's second claim is that even the materiality, the presence of the original, is disturbed by technical reproduction and in an important and interesting way. While it is obvious that in order to examine an original painting, the work itself must be present, the odd fact is that photographic examination of the work can be and often is used to *reveal* aspects of the work that "natural" vision cannot detect. Thus, photomicrographic or photofluoroscoic investigation may reveal hidden information about the way in which the picture was made, about changes that were brought about during the process of painting or after, and so on. But this means that the painting itself, meaning here what the viewer sees when standing in front of the work, is no longer autonomous. Technical reproduction can represent it in an entirely new way, in a way that unaided vision cannot see it, in a way that is available only to technical means of reproduction. And Benjamin claims that the original surrenders an important part of its authority to the new means of reproduction. The work of art is no longer independent; it has grown dependent upon technical reproduction to reveal its mysteries. Benjamin claims further that the work of art cannot withstand the dual assault of mass reproduction (and distribution) together with the possibility of the kind of revelation brought off by technical means. The *Hier und Jetzt,* the "presence," the "aura" of the work is damaged. The "aura" of an artwork cannot be reproduced because it is an immaterial mist, or, to use Benjamin's metaphor, a "pod" that encapsulates the work of art. Photography "shucks" the seed from its pod because the pod is not a real thing—because it has no material substantiality. In destroying the aura, in removing the work of art from the tradition in which it is embedded, photography corroborates an evolving class perception of "the sense of the similar in the world."[6]

Thus far, in speaking of Benjamin's views about the way in which photography challenges traditional notions of reality and the reigning standard of depiction, I have touched upon, but have not given an account of his belief that there is an intimate linkage between perception and depiction. Benjamin's description of the evolution of art is grounded in his belief that perception is historically and socially conditioned, and that the material basis of society somehow gives structure to the perception of "collectives"—classes within it. In a sweeping statement, he says:

> *During long periods of history, the perception by the historical collectives changes with the changes in their historical mode of being.* The way in which human perception organizes itself—the medium in which it takes place—is conditioned not only naturally, but also historically. The period of migration in which the late Roman art industry and the *Vienna Genesis* came into being, had not only a different art, but also a different perception from classical times. The great scholars of the Viennese School, Riegl and Wickhoff . . . were the first . . . [to] draw conclusions from this art about the way in which perception was organized in the period of its production. [They] were content to point out the formal characteristics that were peculiar to perception in late Roman times. They did not try—and perhaps they could not even

hope—to show the social revolutions that found their expression in these changes in perception. The conditions for such an insight are more favorable at present.[7]

In Benjamin's view, a biological account of vision, one that gives the structure of the eye and the nervous system together with a biochemical analysis of the chemistry of the visual processes as well as an account of the necessary forms of immediate stimulation, would, even if exhaustive and accurate, fail to explain both how and what we see. A truly exhaustive account of perception can only be provided within an historical context that provides a description and explanation of the means and manner of economic production in a given society. The way in which we perceive the world, Benjamin contends, is certainly conditioned biologically, but it is socially conditioned as well. From this it follows that since the society itself is an expression of a given mode of economic production, the manner in which perception is organized is also conditioned upon the mode of production. Benjamin is surely borrowing here from the well-known section in the first volume of *Capital* dealing with the "fetishism of commodities."[8] In that discussion, Marx notes that visual perception requires a "physical relation between physical things"—the passage of light from one thing to another. However, certain perceived qualities of commodities have no immediate physical basis—they are fantastic— productions of the human brain that are not reproductions of any immediate material qualities of the world. Such qualities of objects have a physical basis but the qualities are misplaced in the object at hand. There is no doubt that such qualities are genuinely perceived, but they have as their cause a variety of factors that cannot be established by biological investigation. Marx likens the perception of fantastic qualities of commodities to the perception of similar qualities by religious believers: "In [the religious world] the productions of the human brain appear as independent beings endowed with life and entering into relation both with one another and the human world." The perception of fantastic qualities is explained by the notion of misplaced attribution of qualities to objects and the mechanism of such excitement must be sought in the economic conditions of society. An account of perception that fails to deal with ideology—with the stimulative capacity of ideas—will necessarily fail to explain why various qualities are attributed to objects and perceived as properly belonging to them, i.e., perceived as real properties of objects. Thus, for example, the perceived aura of objects has no immediate physical counterpart outside the human brain and cannot be explained biologically. If I am correct in pointing to Marx's explanation of perception as fundamental to Benjamin's account, then it is reasonably clear what he has in mind when he suggests that the way in which "human perception organizes itself" changes from one historical period to the next. Still, this account of perception cannot explain why works of art change stylistically, or, more in keeping with Benjamin's primary interest, how the very definition—of art can change. Some step is missing from the account—a step that can bridge the gap between perception and artistic practice.

What Benjamin needs to show is that changes in perception are expressed in some evident fashion in the formal character of artworks. Here, he cites the work of Alois Riegl and Franz Wickhoff, the Austrian art historians who devoted considerable attention to Imperial Roman art and to the *Vienna Genesis*.[9] According to Benjamin, Riegl and Wickhoff analyzed late Roman art, noted the differences between it and the Greek art that preceded it, and explained the changes in terms of differences in perception in the respective periods of production. On this view, formal, stylistic changes in art are explained by changes in perception and art is seen as an "expression" of perception. Benjamin is committed to the belief that the depiction of the world is always guided by the artist's perception and that "perception" here means more than just "attitude toward the world," but something like "sensuous experience of the world." This is the basis for his linkage of perception with depiction, though it is odd that he relies upon the authority of Riegl and Wickhoff in this regard. Neither of those historians draws conclusions about perceptual changes in relation to stylistic developments in Roman art. Indeed, Riegl denies that visual perception is subject to change; for him it is a constant through history. Art, for Riegl, may clarify perception or express an attitude toward the world. Similarly, Wickhoff never addresses the issue of changes in perception, suggesting rather that the change from Greek "naturalism" to Roman "illusionism" finds its roots in national differences that are perceptual in nature. Benjamin would have done better to have allied himself with Wölfflin's *Principles of Art History*,[10] published twenty-one years prior to the essay on reproducibility. Wölfflin's argument is, in part, a psychological one in which works of art are formally analyzed in keeping with categories of "the forms of representation" that are themselves "forms of artistic apprehension, or beholding," or forms of artistic perception. He notes:

Nobody is going to maintain that the "eye" passes through developments of its own account. Conditioned and conditioning, it always impinges on other spiritual spheres. There is certainly no visual schema which, arising from its own premises, could be imposed on the world as stereotyped pattern. But, although men have at all times seen what they wanted to see, that does not exclude the possibility that a law remains operative throughout all change. To determine this law would be a central problem, the central problem of art."

Wölfflin's interest lies in describing stylistic changes in art and in finding the source or origin of such change. While he is concerned with maintaining the autonomy of art, i.e., in showing that these changes are somehow internal to artistic practice, the changing forms of beholding or perceiving ultimately play an important role in his explanation of stylistic change. Changes in style are systematically and intimately linked by him to changes in perception. Such developments in style are an expression of changes in the forms of beholding that are not entirely reducible to the progressive working out of a dominant style. Whether or not Benjamin relies upon Wölfflin's principles, it is clear that he reads Riegl and Wickhoff as if they were giving Wölfflin-like accounts of artistic development. He shares with Wölfflin a common belief in the perceptual/expressive character of visual art. Nonetheless, it is just this principle that Benjamin needs to flesh-out his account, not merely of stylistic change in art, but of a basic definitional change as well.

This doctrine of the relation of art to perception forms the theoretical backbone of Benjamin's essay and without a thorough appreciation of the reliance he places upon it, it is impossible to understand why he believes that technical reproduction challenges tradition modes of depiction and perception. All these elements come together in a single line embedded deep within an early thesis of the essay (which, in the first draft, carries the title, "Technical Reproducibility"). "For the first time in the process of pictorial reproduction, photography freed the hand of the most important obligation in the process of pictorial reproduction which now fell upon the eye alone."[12] Until the advent of technical reproduction, pictures had to be made by hand and Benjamin suggests that there is a parallel here to the way that manufactured goods had to be made prior to the development of industrial machinery. The new methods of manufacture—technical production—are in the process of changing the environment and of changing the way that people "organize their perception." Technical reproduction will express this change and assist in its completion. A manual artist must be educated in his art, must learn the tradition of exemplary works and the traditional way of laying down lines and applying ink or paint. Education within the tradition is a molding of the hand and the eye as well. To depict the world from within the tradition, one must have the means (the education and the materials). An artist must see the world in the form in which it is to be depicted and also see it as worthy of being depicted. Thus, it is a precondition of the traditional arts that its objects, motifs, and theses be seen as "enveloped in a mist," as having an aura, as dictating the terms of their own reproduction. Technical reproduction dispenses with the education of the hand and in so doing, with the education of the eye as well. An eye that is "armed" with a camera can "test" the world. It can reveal unsuspected aspects of reality. It can cut through the apparent and reveal the world. Thus, when used by an eye informed by a sensibility that perceives the similarity of all things, photography becomes anti-auratic, opposed to tradition—in a word, "revolutionary." This is not to say that photography and film are inherently revolutionary, since a sensibility that is wedded to "eternal mystery" and to "genius" can use photography for conservative purposes, but even when so used, e.g., in typical Hollywood films of the thirties, photography still displays features that distinguish it from older art forms. Benjamin maintains that this can be seen in the "distracted" attitude of all audiences towards films (an attitude quite similar to the one that characterizes workers on a production line). Auratic art requires "quiet contemplation" while film, with its quick cuts and jumps, can viewed only with distraction. Moreover, Benjamin contends that the relation between the mass audience and the film producer is one that cannot arise in the context of auratic art. The producer is forced to produce what the mass audience will pay for and is constantly concerned by the need to meet its demands.

Before discussing Benjamin's contention that photography and mass reproducibility have resulted in a definitional change of art, I think it would be useful in light of my reading thus far, to reconsider his thoughts about "natural" and what I have called "technically informed" vision. I have tried to mirror Benjamin's use of the expressions "normal vision" and "unaided vision." It should be obvious that he cannot mean that vision is to be understood as fixed and universal. He does mean that in any given period, a certain kind of visual perception will be accepted as "normal"—as being in balance with "the way things are." Under present conditions of production, this harmony has been disturbed by a new perception that is coming into being and that is not in balance with the world as "given." In other words, a revolutionary sensibility takes a negatively critical stance towards the world as "given"—it tests the world and accepts or rejects it in conformity with an evolving perception of reality. Such a sensibility anticipates certain relations in the world and tests the world in search of them. Technically informed perception can perceive these relations with the aid of the camera—it can find confirmation of its anticipations in films and photographs. It can also find in these media revelations of the world that it will come to anticipate in the future. Thus, photography and film have an enormous didactic potential, because they can confirm and inform the evolving perception of reality. This does not mean, however, that the revolutionary masses will come to see the world as just so many photographs or strips of film, but that it will seek clarification and confirmation of its perception in photographs and film. This is the new role of art.

Benjamin finds the origin of art in magic and its original use as a ritual one in service of magic. Throughout its history until around 1900,[13] art was suffused with ritual—it was in service first to magic and then to religion. Art, for Benjamin, is defined in relation to two distinct values— cult and exhibition (display) values. The first artworks had pure use values that served cult. This means that they were defined solely by their function within ritual. Primitive art evolves within a society in which the existing technology is "in a total fusion with ritual."[14] It is only as conditions of production move beyond primitive forms of agriculture that the exhibition of art takes on a special significance and the definition of art changes accordingly to accommodate both values, although the ritual value remains dominant. When the perception expressed by this art is no longer tolerable, owing to the rise of capitalism, a "negative theology of art" is devised (*l'art pour l'art*) that maintains the ritual, authoritative character of art while giving up the vestigial "positive theology." At the extreme of this accomodation between cult and exhibition values, art is defined as useless, as having a value in and of itself, devoid of any functional possibilities. The theory of autonomous art—of art that gives itself its own formative principles—*apparently* releases art from ritual and does so by establishing its own, independent domain, with its own, critical vocabulary—the lexicon that includes "creativity, genius, external value and style, form and content."[15] The older theology demanded veneration for the objects of art by assigning their value to a higher realm. The new theology derives eternal value from independence of any other realm. The categories of artistic criticism and evaluation become internal to art itself and ultimately find their justification in the theory of the *Kunstwollen*.[16] The apparent release of art from function allows its evaluation to proceed in a "pure" fashion, relieved of any concern with nonartistic matters. But, for Benjamin, this art has a hidden social/political dimension—it serves the power interests of the class for which it is produced. The autonomy of art is itself a phantasm, as illusory as the aura that surrounds objects of autonomous art.

It may seem, at first sight, that Benjamin is describing the "self-

liquidation"[17] of art, but this is, at best, a misleading way of characterizing his interest. Art is itself no more capable of self-liquidation than it is
of self-establishment. What Benjamin is describing is the redefinition of
art under present conditions of economic production. Art is not in the
process of disappearing, it is in the process of reconstruction. The new art
will be defined solely in terms of a pure use—of exhibition in service of
politics; meaning by "politics" those ways by which power over the
machinery of production is acquired or maintained. Art is coming to be
defined in the only way that it ever achieves definition—by expressing the
perceptions, interests, and values of the class for which it is produced.
The present process of the redefinition of art is, however, quite different
from any that has occurred in the past because the new art will be established in reality and not in illusory perceptions of the real. Under the old
conditions of production, art objects were worshipped for their possession of qualities that inhered in or adhered to unique objects housed in
museums—temples to the muses—or in private collections. Through their
singularity, these works expressed and maintained a perception of the
world that sought out the unique and individual. The genius of the artist
resided in his individual, often idiosyncratic perception or style. Matched
to this was the singularity of the work itself. Thus, a society that emphasized individual merit and initiative expressed this value in highly indi-
viduated works of art that were themselves one-of-a-kind. In Benjamin's
terms, the authority of such works rests on the uniqueness of the artist's
vision (which is the "original" that is given expression in the work of art)
and on the original, non-reproducible character of the work. Benjamin
aims his attack, ultimately, at these twin sources of authority—this pair of
originals. He takes it as a fact that the evolving mass perception is one
that is fundamentally opposed to the individual and irreproducible. Symp-
tomatic of this is the increasing importance of statistics in the contemporary world. Statistics is concerned with the similarity of all things—of the
objects and events that it analyzes; i.e., it drains each of any individuality
and comprehends the world in terms of graphs or columns of numbers in
which individual cases count, but not as individuals. Photography and
film reproduce the world in much the same way. The personal vision of
the photographer or cinematographer is of no more importance, insofar as
use value is concerned, that is the vision of the statistician. But more than
just this is at stake in photography. By revealing more than can be seen by
the unaided eye, a photographer can "penetrate reality"—can show
things that are unseeable without the machinery.[18] For Benjamin, nothing
can count as individual and independent vision in film and photography,
because what can be shown cannot be seen without dependence upon the

camera. The authority of individual vision disappears in photography not because it is unwanted (though it should be unwanted), but because it is unachievable. Benjamin takes great care to demonstrate that what can be shown in film cannot be seen on the film set—that what can be shown requires a total dependence upon large crews running the highly technical means of production. What is seen on the screen has no independent existence, it cannot be understood as the record of an original. In film, nothing answers to the role of the original. Even the cinematographer cannot see on the set what is shown on the screen, without total dependence on the camera. Beyond this, Benjamin suggests that the film as an entirety answers to no pre-existent unit that enforces its authority in its production. The film becomes a work of art only after all its individual pieces (that are not themselves works of art) are constructed, accepted or rejected (i.e., "tested"), spliced together, and so on. The resulting work does not reproduce the world so much as it makes a world. Thus, the authority of a pre-existing world that is imitated in a work of art is demolished. There simply is nothing in the world that answers to, say, *Potemkin* except the film itself. Moreover, the film does not have a "life of its own" in the way that a painting does. It is not only the obvious fact that there is no such things as *the* original Potemkin, meaning one print that has primacy over all others, but the film exists as a work of art only when projected, i.e., when used. It is on the screen and then off. The screen goes blank. There is no material residuum left over that might hang on a wall and exercise authority. Its life as a work of art and its use coalesce. The dual loci of traditional art's authority, the originality of the artist's vision, and the originality or singularity of the work of art properly have no counterparts in film and photography.

The redefinition of art proceeds, then, by way of demolition of the authority of traditional forms of art. According to Benjamin, the question of the art status of film and photography is misconceived because it asks if these media measure up to a fixed standard of art. He recasts the question by showing that the standard is not fixed and that it is, in fact, in the process of change. For him, the question is more general—it concerns the way in which art achieved definition in any period.

Throughout the essay and especially in its first draft form, Benjamin characterizes the new perception as coming into being—as only partially formed. He speaks of the new technical machinery of production as being at once a "second nature" to the workers and yet, beyond control. The role of art is to bring about an adjustment between the evolving perception and the changing environment. On speaking of this function, Benjamin says:

The film serves as a way of preparing man for those new apperceptions and reactions that are conditioned by contact with mechanical devices whose role in his life increases almost daily. To make this immense technical apparatus of our time into the object of human excitation— that is the historical task in the service of which the film finds its true meaning.[19]

The social functions of film become its artistic functions. In evolving into a pure function, art will exhibit—reproduce—man in his environment. In its revolutionary use, films will be made by workers, of workers, and for them. Film will show man in an environment re-made (re-produced) and managed by himself. In a thesis that comes near the end of the essay, Benjamin discusses the most important function of the film:

Among the social functions of film, the most important is the achievement of a balance between the individual and the mechanical device. This problem is not only solved in the film by the way in which each person perceives the recording device, but by the way in which the individual perceives his environment. On the other hand, as he increases the insight into the necessities that govern our existence, by using close-ups from the environment, by emphasizing hidden details in the "state properties" that are well known to us, by investigating banal milieus while directing his lens in an inspired manner, he manages on the other hand to ensure for us a massive and undreamed of latitude. We seemed to be hopelessly encircled by our pubs, our city streets, our offices and furnished rooms, our railroad stations and factories. Then came the film and blew-up our prison world with the dynamite of tenths of a second, so that we now casually undertake adventurous journeys among its widely scattered ruins. It thus becomes obvious that it is a different nature that speaks to the camera from the one that speaks to the eye."[20]

Benjamin concludes the essay with a call for the "politicization of art." He does not, cannot mean that art should be put into the service of sloganeering, of the packaging or beautifying of political statements. To politicize art is to put the machinery of art production into the hands of the workers and allow them to show themselves the world they are in the process of making. Art in its new definition is the sole means by which the members of the revolutionary class can come to see themselves as shown by themselves. Through this art they can test the world, accept the real,

171

reject the illusory. They can reproduce the world in their own image—in the image that they themselves produce.

University of Chicago

NOTES

1 The title of this essay in German is "Das Kunstwerk im Zeitalter seiner technischen Reproduzierbarkeit." The essay has a strange history. It was originally published in the *Zeitschrift für Sozialforschung* [5, no. 1 (1936)] in French translation as "L'oeuvre d'art à l'époque de sa reproduction mécanisée." There are significant differences between the manuscript Benjamin hoped to publish and the French translation. The nature and background of these changes is discussed by Susan Buck-Morss, *The Origin of Negative Dialectics* (New York: Free Press, 1977), p. 286, fn. 98. Benjamin wrote a second, revised version of the essay that was not published until long after his death in 1940; Benjamin, *Schriften,* ed. Gretel & Theodor Adorno (Frankfurt: Suhrkamp, 1955). It is a translation of the second draft that appears in *Illuminations,* ed. Hannah Arendt, trans. Harry Zohn (New York: Schocken Books, 1969). I have relied upon both the first and second drafts of the essay as they appear in Walter Benjamin, *Gesammelte Schriften*, I, pp. 431-508, ed. Rolf Tiedemann & Hermann Schweppenhäuser (Frankfurt: Suhrkamp, 1974). Dr. Gary Smith, co-editor of this volume, has informed me that he has located, among Max Horkheimer's papers, the first finished version of the essay from which the French translation was made and which reflects Benjamin's intentions more faithfully than the edited version of the essay which first appeared in the *Zeitschrift*. This version was thought lost by the editors of Benjamin's works: *Gesammelte Schriften*, I, p. 985.
2 Benjamin, *ibid.,* I, p. 437.
3 Nelson Goodman, *Languages of Art* (Indianapolis: Hackett, 1968).
4 See, e.g., Susan Sontag, *On Photography* (New York: Farrar, Straus & Giroux, 1976); Rudolf Arnheim, "On the Nature of Photography," *Critical Inquiry* 1, no. 1 (Fall 1974), 149-63; and Rosalind Krauss, "The Photographic Conditions of Surrealism," *October,* no. 19 (Winter 1981). Krauss, who calls Benjamin's essay "The most important yet made about the vocation of photography," (p. 17) appears to argue against Benjamin's fundamental belief about photography. She notes, "The photograph carries on one continuous surface the trace or imprint of all that vision captures in one glance" (p. 23). I should also add that these authors also argue that "the photograph" enjoys a special relation to reality irrespective of what any particular photograph may look like. In brief, they argue for an against the position I shall suggest is exclusively advanced by Benjamin.
5 Greenberg provides a good discussion of his notion of the "original" in "Avant Garde and Kitsch," Clement Greenberg, *Art and Culture* (Boston: Beacon Press, 1961), pp. 3-21.
6 Benjamin, *Gesammelte Schriften,* I, p. 440.
7 *Ibid.,* p 439.
8 Karl Marx, *Capital,* Vol. I, Part I, Ch. I, Section 4, "The Fetishism of Commodities and the Secret Thereof." The two quotations from Marx that follow in my text are from this section and may be found in *The Marx-Engels Reader,* ed. Robert C. Tucker (New York:

W. W. Norton, 1972), p. 321. I am indebted to Marx Wartofsky for clarification of Marx's thought on commodities and perception.

9 The *Vienna Genesis* is a celebrated fifth century illustrated manuscript of the Book of Genesis that was in the collection of the Imperial Library in Vienna. The paintings that illustrate the manuscript (as well as Greek and Roman art) are discussed in *Die Wiener Genesis*, ed. Wilhelm Ritter von Hartel & Franz Wickhoff (Vienna: F. Tempsky, 1895) and in Alois Riegl, *Spatrömische Kunstindustrie* (Vienna: K. K. Hof-und Staatsdruck-erei, 1901-23).

10 Heinrich Wölfflin, *Principles of Art History*, trans. M. D. Hottinger (New York: Dover, 1950).

11 *Ibid.*, p. 17. To a reader well acquainted with the Wölfflin text, it will quite rightly appear that I am emphasizing the psychological/perceptual aspects of the text while eliminating the great emphasis he places upon the internality to artistic practice of stylistic development. In the concluding chapter of the *Principles*, Wölfflin asks, "Is the change in the forms of apprehension the result of an inward development, of a development of the apparatus of apprehension fulfilling itself to a certain extent of itself, or is it an impulse from the outside, the other interest, the other attitude to the world, which determines the change?" (pp. 299-330). He answers that the motive for change is both internal and external and adds, "It is true, we can only see what we look for, but we only look for what we can see. Doubtless certain forms of beholding pre-exist as possibilities; whether and how they come to development depends on outward circumstances" (p. 230). My sole point as regards the Benjamin text is that neither Riegl nor Wickhoff claim that the way we see changes and that such changes influence artistic practice, while quite clearly, Wölfflin does argue in this way. Finally, it might be maintained that Wölfflin is only addressing the issue of "artistic" beholding, which may or may not be the case. Again, the point is that he does explicitly connect depiction to perception in the way that Benjamin is also required to bring them together.

12 Benjamin, *Gesammelte Schriften*, I, p. 436.

13 Benjamin singles out the period "around 1900" twice in the essay. By 1900, the technology of photomechanical reproduction had been perfected and the principles of sound motion pictures had been established. These are technological developments that constitute the standard achieved by technical reproduction; *Gesammelte Schriften*, I, p. 445 & p. 475.

14 *Ibid.*, p. 444.

15 *Ibid.*, p. 435. In the second draft, the list is slightly altered and reads, ". . . creativity, genius, external value and mystery" (p. 474).

16 The *Kunstwollen* is the formative principle that lies "beneath" the surface appearance of a work of art. It is determined a *priori* through the deduction of categories essential to the "being of the work." See Erwin Panofsky, "Der Begriffe des Kunstwollens," reprinted in *Aufsätze zu Grundfragen der Kunstwissenschaft* (Berlin: B. Hessling, 1964).

17 Susan Buck-Morss, *The Origin of Negative Dialectics*, (New York: Free Press, 1977), p. 147. "[Benjamin] argued that the new technologies of audio-visual production—photography, sound recording and film—had on their own accomplished the dialectical transformations of art, in a way which led to its self-liquidation." According to Benjamin, the technologies of photography and film could not, "on their own" transform art. These technologies are themselves part of a broader process that accomplishes the transformation of art.

18 Stanley Cavell supports this way of thinking about photography (without making refer-

ences to Benjamin) in *The World Viewed,* enlarged ed., (Cambridge: Harvard University Press, 1979). Cavell makes the following point about photography: "What is revealed to and by (the camera) can only be known by what appears upon the print or screen . . . You cannot know what you have made the camera do, what is revealed to it, until the results have appeared . . . The mysteriousness of the photograph lies not in the machinery which produces it, but in the unfathomable abyss between what it captures (its subject) and what is captured for us (*this* fixing of the subject), the metaphysical wait between exposure and exhibition, the absolute authority or finality of the fixed image," pp. 184-85. Clearly, Benjamin would not endorse the elements of "mystery" in Cavell's remarks.

19 Benjamin, *Gesammelte Schriften,* I, p. 445.

20 *Ibid.,* I, pp. 460-61.

HISTORICAL MATERIALISM OR POLITICAL MESSIANISM? AN INTERPRETATION OF THE THESES "ON THE CONCEPT OF HISTORY"

ROLF TIEDEMANN

. . . until late into Stalinism, and even without full installation, Marxism was at home only in the Soviet Union, which hardly seemed to possess the economic and democratic prerequisites for its realization. Until finally the czarification of Soviet Marxism became more and more obvious and even began to affect the image of Marxism itself. Right up until the problematic issue that had become almost too wide-spread although it properly only concerned true Marxists: Had Marxism changed beyond all recognition under Stalinism, or had it in the process changed to such an extent that it had also become recognizable as well? This question should finally be addressed to the proper party, namely, to the Russian state religion . . .

Ernst Bloch, *Politische Messungen, Pestzeit, Vormärz*

1

When Brecht read the theses "On the Concept of History" a year after Benjamin's death, he made the following note in his journal: "The short piece is clear and dispels confusion."[1] The entry does credit to the diarist, who in 1938 had still dismissed the essay "The Work of Art in the Age of Its Mechanical Reproduction" as a "rather frightful adaptation of the materialistic view of history."[2] But Brecht's remark does not hold water. Benjamin was more prescient about the reception of his theses: he rejected the "thought of publication," which "would leave the door wide open to enthused misinterpretations" (1227).[3] Not the least among those susceptible to this form of misunderstanding are such interpretations as would claim Benjamin's later work totally and unconditionally for Marxism. One first has to canonize certain of Benjamin's texts, especially

175

"The Author as Producer" and the treatise on Eduard Fuchs, if one is to transform them into the chief witness for the kind of Marxism that sees a seamless continuity between the critique of political economy as Marx left it 100 years ago and the policies of communist parties as well as those of the Soviet Union under Stalin. Other works from the same period, such as the essay on Kafka and "The Storyteller" are treated as being of negligible importance. In the theses "On the Concept of History," where Benjamin unflinchingly maintains that—"if it were left to me"—historical materialism "would win" (1247), he also makes obvious use of the theological terminology of his earlier writings: he sees "redemption" as the Other of history, cites the true believers' "Judgment Day," and speaks of both the Antichrist and the Messiah.

Interpreters have fought off their irritation at encountering such terminology by resorting to subterfuges such as the one that the Messianism of the text can "be adopted by secular liberation movements only after pruning it of its ideological ingredients."[4] Although in the *Arcades Project* as well as in drafts of the Theses, Benjamin himself wrote of an experience that "prevents us from fundamentally understanding history without theology" (V, 589; 1235), others denounce the theology which is coyly resident in the Theses as something "shockingly imposed" on them.[5] Like his later work as a whole, the Theses have, along with the fame that has come to them, been subject for some time to that "deceptive animosity" which, in Rilke's words, threatens to render an author's works harmless by disseminating them. Only a critique directed at their material and truth-contents—and not primarily at political applications—can further an interpretation of the Theses.[6]

2

The title[7] of Benjamin's last work promises a discussion of the *concept* of history. Little could be more characteristic of the author and less typical of the time, however, than the fact that there is no discursive explication at the center of the text, but an *image* instead. History itself seems to do away with philosophy's old conceptual games, and transform concepts into images which spoil the promise of security offered by logic: identity and the absence of contradiction. Materialists, even those of a historico-dialectical nature were no less inclined than the foremost Idealist thinkers to impute forceful concepts to the course of history. For Kant it was a plan of Nature that for all time has worked toward the peaceful unification of the species. For Hegel it was the autonomy of reason under the domination of which freedom supposedly has already been realized. According to Marxism, it is "true human beings" who always "make their own history," in order to consummate it in the foreseeable future as a "Realm of Freedom"[8] . . . "according to a collective will to a collective plan" and "in full consciousness."[9] But that which had been constituted by traditional concepts of history evaporated for Benjamin as he wrote the Theses. He could no longer be convinced that every historical event derives from another by necessity and that all events together constitute a progressive motion. In the ninth of his theses this appears as "a complete catastrophe which keeps piling wreckage upon wreckage" (697), the "pile of debris" so incredibly vast that it even "grows ever higher up into the skies" (698). This image is reminiscent of the Baroque and is Benjamin's own at the same time. In the allegories of the 17th Century—according to Benjamin—everything about history that from the very beginning has been untimely, sorrowful, unsuccessful confronts ". . . the observer . . . with the *facies hippocratica* of history as a petrified, primordial landscape" (343). In like manner, in the 1940 theses Benjamin views the real constitution of the world as a "pile of debris" into which history is collapsing; a "complete catastrophe" in which the history of mankind—all its efforts and toils—is shown to be a failure. The basis for Benjamin's image of the pile of debris growing up into the skies and the basis for the catastrophic concept of history in the Theses goes beyond its linguistic conceptualization. It is in essence an image, one that the observer can only stare at, condemned to silence, unable to differentiate or to identify details. All that remains is this sheer horror to which Benjamin referred in a note, probably written before 1920. With this horror, "language in the broadest sense" would "cease to apply" and mankind would find itself dependent on "imitation," or mimesis.[10] The stigma of philosophical language, which since Aristotle has almost always been a language of concepts, is that it does not extend to mimesis.[11] Images, on the other hand, to the extent they were admitted into philosophy at all, attempt to make direct use of mimesis. Naturally they thus take on the concomitant risk of ambiguity. Benjamin's image of history, as projected in the ninth thesis, is a mimesis of the dead and the smashed: a sign of solidarity with the oppressed, in spite of being—at least at first glance it seems—just as helpless as they have been in history thus far and just as unable to control the future.

There can be little doubt that the image of the ninth thesis presents history as Benjamin himself understood it at that moment; still, he hides behind the *interpretation* of another image, a painting: "There is a painting by Klee called *Angelus Novus*. It depicts an angel looking as though he is about to move away from something he is contemplating fixedly. His eyes are staring, his mouth is open, his wings are spread. This is what the angel of history must look like. *Angelus Novus* is an oil drawing colored with aquarelle by Paul Klee dating from the year 1920—one year after Klee had begun to experiment with the dating technique. Benjamin purchased the drawing in 1921 and kept it until his death. To use Gershom Scholem's phrase, it served as his "meditative focal point": Benjamin repeatedly cloaked his own speculations—including some of the most precarious—in the form of interpretations of Klee's angel,[12] which in a final metamorphosis becomes the "angel of history" in the Theses. Scholem seems to have interpreted it as the Biblical *Mal'ach,* one of the "messengers from the world of Paradise."[13] It was their duty to "stand before the Lord" (Tobias 12:15) and sing his praise. But as God's messengers to mankind, too, they were to "interpret his face, that they might understand it" (Daniel 8:16). The angel described by Benjamin fails in his mission to mankind. Perhaps this is because he has tried to usurp the *tikkun,* the messianic restoration and perfection of history. This task is reserved for the Messiah himself, according to the view of history in the Kabbalah.[14] "The angel would like to . . . awaken the dead, and make whole what was smashed" (697). Scholem points out that "this angel no longer sings any hymns."[15] But is he still a messenger at all? "His mouth is open," but he is speechless; clearly he has nothing more to communicate to mankind. What he is probably seeing appears to have robbed him of speech. "His face is turned toward the past"—i.e. humanity's past— and there "*he* sees a complete catastrophe which keeps piling wreckage upon wreckage and hurls it at his feet" (697). This angel doesn't understand what he himself sees; how should he be able to interpret it? Although Benjamin's image is both plaintive and accusatory, there is no hint that the angel bears these traits. Benjamin does indeed make use of the words "the angel" and also speaks of his "wings," but only in order to enter the sphere of Klee's painting, which *he* is interpreting. One might take the word "paradise" as an indication of a religious or theological meaning for Benjamin's angel: "But a storm is blowing from Paradise; it has got caught in his wings with such violence that the angel can no longer close them" (697f.). But this does not mean that the angel himself comes from Paradise and was sent by God. "This storm irresistibly propels him into the future" (698): What this future will be—the Kingdom of God or whatever else may come—is left open. In the same sentence it is said that the earthly pile of debris "grows ever higher up into the skies." There is at least a suggestion here that it also cries out to heaven—accusingly. And is this heaven to be the heaven of prophesy, of redemption, as well? Completely human himself, Benjamin's angel seems to express superhuman despair in the face of the inhumanity of history. Although unable to help, he is also unable to avert his gaze from what is hurled in front of his feet. But this is how mankind experiences the horror of its own history. If anything still propels humanity onward, it is the memory of the lost Paradise. This utopian strength is an *impulse* which has not yet expired. Clearly religion has done much to preserve it, especially Judaism. This impulse has found its way into philosophy in general and even lives on in the Marxian hope of an empire of freedom. It *can* only live on as an impulse, as a promise which does not fetishize what it promises. Benjamin speaks of "paradise" in the ninth thesis almost exactly as Jewish Messianism does. For Jewish Messianism the "very ancient" is also "not at all the real past, but something transformed and exalted by a dream: the radiance of utopia has been cast upon it."[16] Similarly, even the young Marx spoke of it in the famous formulation "that the world has long possessed a dream of something which it need only possess consciousness of in order to possess it truly."[17]

In a seemingly abrupt twist, the storm that blows from "paradise" also becomes "what we call progress"—which is trenchantly criticized in other theses. Here Benjamin is simply referring to the dialectic of history; what was good has become bad; any concept of progress which makes "dogmatic claims" is doomed to failure. Benjamin's angel's "back is turned" on the "future" (698); he sees nothing of what is to come. This represents both the theological prohibition of images and their profane adaptation: Marx's refusal to describe communist society in detail. For Hermann Schweppenhäuser the *Angelus Novus* symbolizes one who, "in constant retreat, with a gaze kept open, takes leave of the horror."[18] For Gerhard Kaiser this view is flawed for the simple reason that the angel does not retreat, but is propelled.[19] But the more serious flaw is the philologist's fixation on an isolated word, to such an extent that he misses its meaning and immediate context. Perhaps there is no alternative for someone propelled by a force over which he has no control but to give in to it and retreat. But beyond this, Benjamin has made it clear enough that *his* angel, for all his passivity, also transcends this force. He sees more than others do, and sees more correctly. He penetrates appearances which imprison common ideas of history: "Where *we* perceive a chain of events, *he* sees a complete catastrophe" (697). But he does look "as though he is about to move away from something"—the catastrophe. Even if catastrophe is not to be averted, at least this is a first step, precarious as always. The future into which Benjamin's angel retreats— by being propelled into it—may prove to be either an "endlessly renewed horror" or the ultimate achievement of the empire of freedom. The ninth thesis does not say which. But Kaiser's interpretation attempts an answer all the same. He perceives in this Thesis a three-fold "non-identity of perception": i.e. those perceptions "which we have, those which the angel has, and those which the image actually conveys."[20] The perceptions "we" have, Kaiser correctly holds to be "false pronouncements about the chain of events and progress."[21] But he mistakenly ascribes them to "the" historian who is not present in Benjamin's thesis. The Theses provide a clear enough contrast between the criticized representative of historicism and the historical materialist "who is schooled in Marx' and who "always has the class struggle . . . in view" (694). The critique of "false" concepts of continuity and progress applies only to the former. For Benjamin, the angel obviously sees more "correctly" than *historicism:* because his view is that of the historical *materialist,* as Benjamin understands it. But after all this, what is the image "really meant to say"? And which image? Klee's? Or its interpretation in Benjamin's words? According to Kaiser, it is meant to be "the historian," "from whose perspective the image of the angel is developed."[23] This opinion becomes untenable simply for lack of a basis in the text, but it also virtually ignores Benjamin's interpretation of Klee's angel. At the same time, a third image is put in its place, which Kaiser himself has created: "The angel has no message, he *is* the message."[24] He quickly becomes a "universal consciousness of salvation" or an "objective redeeming presence." He appears as "a messianic power and hope" and is elevated to the level of guarantor of the "Kingdom of God."[25] An initial argument against such an interpretation would be the fact that none of these words appears in the ninth thesis; most of them aren't even found elsewhere in the "Theses on the Philosophy of History" or anywhere in Benjamin's work. The angel Benjamin refers to metaphorically is taken out of context and literally transported into religious history (one is tempted to say "transported bodily," but that would contradict all the principles of Angelology). But this also means that Kaiser has imposed a sacred stylization onto a secular text by a secular author. The image in the ninth thesis is an allegory of history as natural history; but the angel is a part of this image. He stands for the "true" historian, the historical "materialist" who has stripped himself of all illusions about human history. In order to *use* the "*weak* messianic power" bestowed on us "like every generation that preceded us" (694), we must perceive history as historical materialists—not in Marx's sense but in the sense of Benjamin's ninth thesis: History as the catastrophic pile of debris that continually "grows up ever higher into the skies." Historical materialism understands—according to that previous thesis—the "claim" (694) implicit in accepting this power.

It may well appear in the angel-thesis that this claim cannnot be honored. But to magically transform it into an "objective redeeming presence" almost amounts to mockery of the dead who make this claim. The angel in the ninth thesis by no means represents the Messiah. This is unmistakably audible in the sentence, "The angel *would like to stay,* awaken the dead, and make whole what has been smashed" (697) [author's italics]. Especially in Theses II and XVII, Benjamin cedes this motif—the truly messianic aspect of the *tikkun*—to the historian for whom he means to pave the way in the "Theses on the Philosophy of History" as a whole. This supports the conclusion that Benjamin indeed intended the angel to stand for the historical materialist.

3

The messianic motifs encountered in the Theses undoubtedly arise from the young Benjamin's interest in Jewish—and especially mystical—theology.[26] Its renewed relevance for the late Benjamin has, however, a rather accidental basis—a discussion in the correspondence with Max Horkheimer of March, 1937. Benjamin had written the essay "Eduard Fuchs, Collector and Historian" for the *Zeitschrift für Sozialforschung,* edited by Horkheimer. The essay contains the sentences, "Historical materialism may find the concept of culture itself problematic, but it could never accept the idea of culture's degeneration into commodities, as an object of human ownership. For historical materialism the work of the past is incomplete. Not even a part of the work of any epoch is seen as an object which falls conveniently into one's lap" (II, 477). Regarding this, Horkheimer wrote to Benjamin:

> I have long been thinking about the question of whether the work of the past is complete. Your formulation can certainly stand as is. I have but one personal reservation: that I think this a relationship only to be perceived dialectically. The pronouncement of incompleteness is idealistic if it does not incorporate completeness as well. Past injustice is done and finished. Those who have been beaten to death are truly dead. Ultimately you are making a theological statement. If one takes incompleteness absolutely seriously, then one must believe in the Last Judgment. My thinking is too contaminated with materialism for that. Perhaps there is a distinction between positive and negative incompleteness, so that the injustice, the terror, the pain of the past are irreparable. Justice in practice, pleasures and works behave differently in relation to time, since their positive character is largely negated by their transitoriness. This is indeed true for individual life, for which

death validates its unhappiness, but not its happiness. Good and bad do not relate to time in the same way. Thus discursive logic is inadequate to these categories as well (II, 1332).[27]

Immediately upon receipt of this letter, Benjamin answered Horkheimer:

> I find your excursus on the completeness or openness of the work of the past very significant. I think I understand it thoroughly, and if I am not mistaken, your idea corresponds to a theme that has often concerned me. To me, an important question has always been how to understand the odd figure of speech, "*to lose* a war or a court case." The war or the trial are not the entry into a dispute, but rather the decision concerning it. Finally I explained it to myself thus: the events involved for a person who has lost a war or a court case are truly concluded and thus for that person *any avenue of praxis has been lost.* This is not the case for the counterpart, who is the winner. Victory bears its fruit in a way much different from the manner in which consequences follow defeat. This leads to the exact opposite of Ibsen's phrase: "Happiness is born of loss,/ only what is lost is eternal" (II, 1338).

Since it mentions neither Horkheimer's reservations about Idealism nor the issue of theology, this answer may seem evasive, dilatory. Benjamin would hardly have accepted the charge of Idealism, and this could have been refuted stringently. But he may have had nothing to say against the second charge. This is supported by the manuscript of the *Arcades Project,* which includes the cited section of Horkheimer's letter, with the following commentary by Benjamin: "The corrective of this line of thought lies in the reflection that history is not only a science, but equally a form of remembrance. What has been "established" by science can be modified in remembrance. Remembrance can make the incomplete (happiness) complete, and render the complete (suffering) incomplete. That is theology; but remembrance gives us an experience which forbids us to regard history completely without theology, any more than we should record it directly in the form of theological concepts" (V, 589). The fact that the theorum of the incompleteness of the work of the past is theological is thus, for Benjamin, no basis for criticism. On the contrary, it is an element which, in a sense, historical understanding cannot do without. What Benjamin did not mention in his immediate answer to Horkheimer in 1937 became a theme of the "Theses on the Philosophy of History" three years later. Here the author incorporated several formulations from the essay on Fuchs, but not the ones which had set off the debate with Horkheimer. It is conceivable that in this exchange Benjamin had for the first time become aware of the explosiveness for historical materialism which lay in the concept of incompleteness of the past.[28] In the theses there is no more talk of the "work of the past" as ominous "cultural treasures," as in the Fuchs essay. Rather, Benjamin mostly refers to the "past" or "what has been" in general, and in the most involved passages, to "past generations" (694) the "tradition of the oppressed" (697), and finally, to the dead (cf. 695, 697). In the Theses, Benjamin is not "writing" history, but is developing a "concept" of history which in no way excludes "immanently theological concepts." Thus the theses "On the Concept of History" have at times the quality of a continuation of the correspondence with Horkheimer. They are an attempt to justify the theological moments of Benjamin's thinking in the face of Horkheimer's pronounced materialism.

4

No one more emphatically integrated the incompleteness of history into its completeness than Marx. In the *Eighteenth Brumaire*—one of the few works of Marx that Benjamin was familiar with—he saw "the tradition of all dead generations" weigh "on the brains of the living like a nightmare."[29] For past revolutions, there may have been some sense in "waking the dead," as in the Roman masquerades of the French revolution. "The revolutions of the nineteenth century:—Marx meant the proletarian revolutions he thought were imminent—"must let the dead bury their dead, in order to arrive at their own identity."[30] Benjamin inveighs against this in the Theses. Succeeding generations cannot simply ratify the fact that what has been lost (the loser's *own praxis*) has been lost for all time, and that the dead have no more access to any praxis, for another *praxis* is within reach, even if it is primarily that of historiography. The history written by historical materialists takes up a certain "idea of the past . . . as its cause" (693). Benjamin does not establish this conceptually in Thesis II, nor by way of metaphor in the ninth thesis, but rather by means of analogy. "The idea of salvation is inherent" in the "idea of happiness"—for the individual and for the history of each individual life. The same should hold true for the idea of the past in the history of the group: "The past carries with it a temporal index by which it is referred to redemption" (693). With the theological concept of redemption, Benjamin is indeed going back beyond Marx, who referred only to its secular form—liberation; but this does not destroy the parallel to Marx. He does not assign the task of redemption to a redeemer who is to intervene in history from the outside. Instead, it is "our" task: as Marx maintained, "humanity makes its own history."[31] Benjamin seems to want to add to this that humanity thereby, first of all, renders the past's history complete. "There is a secret agreement beween past generations and the present one. Our coming was expected on earth" (694). Although this may sound mystical, it has a materialistic intent. It is historical materialists who are "aware" that "the past has a claim" on us, and they will not "settle" this claim "cheaply" (cf. 694) as other historians do. Benjamin does not depend on the Messiah promised by religions: according to Thesis II, "like every generation that preceded us, we have been endowed with a *weak* messianic power" (694).—*How* this power with which humanity is endowed is to be put to work is not treated in Thesis II. But Benjamin has no doubts about *who* is to put it to work: namely the historical materialist. It is only for the historical materialist that writing history is inextricably linked to "making" history. He should possess a theory of history that itself becomes historical praxis, a part of the class struggle.

There is a correspondence between the second and the next-to-the-last of the historico-philosophical theses. In the former, Benjamin outlines the task of the historical materialist, whereas in the latter, he describes his procedure. In both cases he does not hesitate to use the concept of the Messianic. In a letter to a friend, Benjamin referred "especially" to thesis XVII: "It is this one which should reveal the hidden but logical connection between these ruminations and my previous work, by offering a conclusive commentary on its method" (1226). Benjamin first provides a convincing summary of "materialistic historiography," under which he subsumes his works: it "is based on a constructive principle. Thinking involves not only the flow of thoughts, but their arrest as well" (702). That indeed does describe Benjamin's specific form of philosophizing, which uses "thought images" (*Denkbilder*) in the attempt to decipher profane existence as the enigmatic form of something beyond existence. In the seventeenth thesis, the "flow of thoughts" seems to stand to stand beside "their immobilization"; Benjamin also combined these ideas in the paradoxical formulation "dialectics at a standstill." His insistence on the immobilization of the flow of thoughts opposes the traditional dialectical concept of universal transmission, especially Hegel's identification of subject with object. In the conception of dialectical imagery, Benjamin retained to the end certain motifs of his earlier, allegorical methods of thinking. Elements which Benjamin discovered in art were essential to the theory of dialectics at a standstill. Benjamin found in epic theater's alienation of social conditions and the politically didactic *gestus* a prototype for the approach he himself took which does not seek to assimilate itself into the temporal course of history via empathy or understanding. Instead, it seeks precisely to gain its meaning physiognomically from the separated, from the particular. Cognition—as released by the freezing of movement—is something that "flashes up":

> Where thinking suddenly stops in a configuration pregnant with tensions, it gives that configuration a shock, by which it crystallizes into a monad. A historical materialist approaches a historical subject only where he encounters it as a monad (702ff.).

To this extent, Thesis XVII contains a methodological discussion of materialistic historiography[33] which may relate somewhat eccentrically to the more familiar Marxist debates, but which is by no means incompatible with the method of Marx himself. One might refer only to the difficulty which any reader has with the beginning of *Capital*. In the afterword to the second edition, Marx himself unhappily described this as the distinction between the "method of presentation" and the "method of research." The first chapter's discussions of use value, value, and the form of value gave only an "ideal" representation of "the life of the material." Therefore it gave the impression "that what was at issue was *a priori* a construction."[34] What Marx points out rather apologetically here, Benjamin has merely taken literally: he demonstrates that there is nothing to apologize for. What seems in this representation to be *a priori* construction, would be a legitimate construction according to the seventeenth thesis. It immediately distills the "rational shape"[35] out of the tensions of history, out of the given historical configuration. While Marx seeks to grasp "each form that has evolved within the course of movement,"[36] Benjamin's method seems to involve merely an optical change: the lens in the historical camera has been replaced. In order to grasp the movement of history at all, in order to recognize communication in what is communicated, the flow must come to a halt. It must crystallize into a shape and be constructed as something immediately present.[37] Concerning the subject of history which is in this way crystallized into a monad, Benjamin goes on: "In this structure he (the historical materialist) recognizes the sign of a messianic cessation of happening" (703). The surprising introduction of this theological concept in the context of Thesis XVII cannot disguise the fact that there is still no thought here of a Messiah in the religious sense. It is again the historical materialist who brings about the "cessation of happening." By virtue of his "constructive principle," by means of this "shock" which he gives to history, the historical materialist causes it to crystallize into a monad. Just as Marx's dialectics are "revolutionary . . . by nature,"[38] so is their "messianic" arrest by Benjamin: in this, the historical materialist also recognizes, "but differently," the sign of "a revolutionary chance in the fight for the oppressed past." No Messiah, but rather "he," the historical materialist, "takes cognizance of it" (703).

In Theses II and XVII, the Messianic appears in adjectival form, as in "messianic power" and "messianic Cessation." But in Thesis VI, the text confronts us with the noun form, "Messiah."[39] Like Thesis XVII, it deals with historical materialism's "chance" to make use of history as object. The latter Thesis, based on Thesis VI, is content with a general reference to a "cessation" in which the object crystallizes itself into a monad. In Thesis VI, this cessation has been described more precisely as "a moment of danger": historical materialism wishes to retain that image of the past which unexpectedly appears to man singled out by history at a moment of danger" (695), namely the political danger "of becoming a tool of the ruling classes" (695). Thus historical understanding as well is integrated into class struggles, the history of which is also the history of all previous society, according to Marxism. Without reservation Benjamin accepts the cause of the oppressed, the class position of the proletariat, as his own. "In every era the attempt must be made anew to wrest tradition from a conformism that is about to overpower it" (695). The term "tradition," which furthermore corresponds to the aforegoing "content of the tradition," seems to indicate that Benjamin was thinking here mainly of what bourgeois historiography treats under the heading of cultural history. Its subjects are coolly apostrophized in Thesis VII as "cultural treasures" (696). There is also reference to them in the essay on Fuchs. There Benjamin connects the theological idea of the incompleteness of the work of the past with the "decline" of culture into "treasures," its character as property.[40] Since Marx this has been discussed as reification and fetishism. Scholem is undoubtedly correct in his tracing of the motif of making whole what has been smashed, as found in Thesis IX. It derives from baroque ideas, which concerned Benjamin in *The Origin of German Tragic Drama,* but more significantly for Scholem, from the Kabbalah. But it must be added that Benjamin had a third thing in mind as well: the authentically Marxist recognition that the "smashed," the corruption of the "Being of things," is based on what seems to be its counterpart, namely universal reification, the fetish character of commodities. "The concept of the tradition" becomes the "tool of the ruling classes," is abandoned to "conformism," because under

186

capitalist conditions of production "the particular social relations of humanity itself," which in a narrow sense determines cultural commodities in the same way it does commodities, "takes on the phantasmagorical form of a relationship among things."[42] It is the task of the historical materialist to dispel the phantasmagoria, to wrest tradition from the ruling classes. As an explanation of *this* task, Thesis VI continues with this sentence: "The Messiah comes not only as the redeemer, he comes as the subduer of the Antichrist" (695). Nowhere in the historico-philosophical theses does Benjamin use language that is more directly theological than this: nowhere does he mean it more materialistically. The sentence regarding the Messiah interprets the previous sentence, and also requires the previous one for its own interpretation. The Antichrist is an image for the "ruling classes," their "conformism." But the Messiah who overcomes him is their opponent in the class struggle: the proletariat and its science, historical materialism. Otherwise it makes no sense. "Even the dead will not be safe from the enemy if he wins" (695). This anticipates an idea in the ninth thesis, the wish to be able to "awaken the dead" (697). In both cases, it represents an answer to Horkheimer's assertion that those who have been beaten to death are truly dead, and that history is therefore always complete.[43] Granted, it was only a wish that one could wake the dead. But the motivation behind Benjamin's argument is the idea that without the preservation of this wish as a wish they would die a second time. In the New Testament conception of the Antichrist, which adopted older Jewish beliefs as well, the "enemy" is "subdued" in the end (Revelation 12:11). But in Benjamin's Theses, the victory remains uncertain: "And this enemy has not ceased to be victorious" (695). As the Theses were being written, the news was full of reports of victories by the fascist armies. Still, "fanning the spark of hope" is reserved for *him* who, in solidarity with the victims, the dead of past and present class struggles, is aware of both the "danger" and the "chance" offered by his undertaking, and that person is—"if it were left to Benjamin" (cf. 1247)—the historical materialist.

5

"In the concept of the classless society, Marx secularized the concept of the messianic age. And that was as it should be" (1231), thus the formulation in a preliminary study to the Theses. The theorem of secularization is not to be discredited, although in the discussion of Marxism after 1945 it came back into favor in evangelical and other academies and fulfilled certain anti-communist functions. Aside from that of the critique of political economy in the narrow sense, the principle theories of Marx, hence especially the doctrines of historical materialism, can—in terms of a history of ideas—indeed be seen as secularizations of originally religious ideas. This is not to say that Marx consciously appropriated and modified certain *theologumena:* instead he was relieved of this task by the historical fate of theology itself. It had long before relinquished its contents to the great philosophy, where they then found their way into Marxism, however modified and in part unrecognizable. Whenever Benjamin's language in the historico-philosophical theses invokes anew the theological origin of Marxian concepts, the secularized content of these ideas is always maintained.[45] The Messiah, redemption, the angel and the Antichrist are all to be found in the Theses only as images, analogies, and parables, and not in their real form. Benjamin does not for a moment contemplate a representation of what Marx had at long last achieved in terms of theory and what the working class movement preserved in practice.

In spite of this, an interpretation of the Theses would stop halfway if it did not ask *why* Benjamin proceeds in this manner: at certain points he translates back into the language of theology that which Marx "had secularized"—which Benjamin thought was "as it should be." The emphasis on a metaphorical manner of speaking in Benjamin's thought in general is enough to prevent one's being content with mere explications of his metaphors, similies, and analogies. If Benjamin is playing a game here, then there must be rules. If this is more than mere arbitrariness—and the deadly seriousness of the subject of the Theses suggests that it is—then it can be assumed that there are objective, historical justifications for these rules. In the notation for the *Arcades Project* already cited, which was integrated in part into the preparations for the Theses, Benjamin clearly says of the form of historiography he has in mind, "That *is* theology" (V, 589; author's italics). A notation made about the same time and directly related to this says, "My thinking is to theology as the blotter is to the ink. It is soaked through with it. If it were up to the blotting paper, nothing of what is written would remain" (V, 588; 1235). The historico-philosophical theses demonstrate that it is not up to the blotter. Apparently there are reasons beyond thought's control that force the latter to leave some of theology intact, to make it legible again.

Aside from the first, none of the theses contains any reference to theology or the theologian, instead only referring to the historian schooled in Marx, materialistic historiography and historical materialism. The *relationship* between the two, which Benjamin either posits or attempts to bring about, remains unclear. One would expect that it could be explained by the first thesis, which has this relationship as its theme and is programmatic for all subsequent theses.

6

Like the ninth thesis, the first consists of an image (drawn this time from literature rather than art) and its interpretation. It is the automatic chess player with which a certain Johann Nepomuk Maelzel toured the carnivals and fairs of America in the 1820s and 1830s. Its riddle was solved by Edgar Allan Poe in a famous essay.[46] "The story is told of an automaton constructed in such a way that it could play a winning game of chess, answering each move of an opponent with a countermove. A puppet in Turkish attire and with a hookah in its mouth sat before a chessboard placed on a large table. A system of mirrors created the illusion that this table was transparent from all sides. Actually, a little hunchback who was an expert chess player sat inside and guided the puppet's hand by means of strings" (693). But unlike his image of the angel in the ninth thesis, Benjamin adds to the interpretation of the image his interpretation of the figures as well:

> One can imagine a philosophical counterpart to this device. The puppet called "historical materialism" is to win all the time. It can easily be a match for anyone if it enlists the services of theology, which today, as we know, is wizened and has to keep out of sight (693).

How, then, do the dwarf and the puppet, theology and historical materialism, relate to one another?

Historical materialism and "theology, the genius which sets the apparatus of historical materialism in motion," are by no means *identical*. This applies neither to the historical materalism "to be discussed in the following theses,"[47] as Kaiser would have it, nor to *any* other form. Neither in the image nor in its interpretation is there identity between the separate figures. The puppet and the dwarf are and remain separate: one sits at the table in front of the chessboard, the other hunches inside the box below. The dwarf can think, analyze, and make combinations. He guides the puppet's hand which, for *its* part, is merely the object of manipulation: it can make no move which is not prescribed. It is no accident that the puppet wears Turkish attire: it is used to put up a facade (i.e. to "put up a Turk," as German slang would have it).[48] But it is the dwarf who guides the puppet's hand; he "holds the strings." Although the puppet is a lifeless thing, the dwarf is quite lively. In Benjamin's interpretation of the image these relationships seem to be shifted, but historical materialism and theology are by no means merged. Historical materialism "enlists the services of theology": it is in control. Theology is the servant who must do the work—who must take care of the thinking, so to speak. Although philosophy was once considered an *ancilla theologiae,* theology has now become the servant of historical materialism. Of course the tasks undertaken by thelogy are not prescribed to it; on the contrary, it is the expert. But it can only do anything when it is in the interest of its master: under feudalism the situation was not so very different in principle. In Benjamin's interpretation of the image, the living dwarf does not "enlist the service" of the lifeless puppet, as the image itself would lead one to expect. Instead the relationship between master and maidservant is reversed. This reduces the living being to a mere object of domination and reveals "the tangible" to be that which is living and active. This may be a reference to Hegel's definition of the transition from feudal to bourgeois society as a dialectic of domination and servitude as well as to Marx's definition of the developed capitalist means of production as ubiquitous reification.

The two figures so clearly separated in Thesis I do become unified, however, even if they are not altogether identical: they make up the image of the automatic chess player. The puppet and the dwarf *and* the chessboard and the table *all* are required to make up the automaton. Only when theology and historical materialism have joined forces can the game begin—"the quarrel over the true concept of history" (1247) still referred to in the preparatory note for the text, but above all, the real struggle of the real classes. Only as allies would the two be a match for any opponent on the field of history. Such a rather simple dialectic—A mediated by B to produce C—could no doubt have been made clear discursively.

As a matter of fact, it may have turned out to be less enigmatic. Instead, Benjamin chooses in image, and what is more, one that switches the two sides around: the dwarf (theology) does not remain what it was—alive. The automaton as a whole is just as lifeless as the puppet. Perhaps the automaton already represents the field of death and debris which is the history stretching out before the angel in the ninth thesis—a living thing can only become a component of a lifeless apparatus if it, too, is dead, a corpse. Did Benjamin perhaps want to express *that?* But in the image, the dwarf *is* alive. He plans the moves of the chess game in advance and really does guide the hand of the puppet. The same applies to the contents of the image: Benjamin seeks a form of cooperation between historical materialism and theology in which they can do more than take up the struggle, they can win. But at least at the outset of the fight, the opponents must be counted among the living.

In Thesis I, the image and its interpretation diverge. "Winning the game," which was a certainty in the image, is no longer so in the interpretation. "The puppet is *supposed* to win all the time." Who says so? Benjamin first, of course, who explicitly adds in a variant, "if it were left to me" (1247). There can be no doubt about the desired outcome of the class struggle for one who has taken up the position of the revolutionary proletariat. But if such a choice of standpoint is to be more than a voluntaristic decision, it must also be decreed by history itself. The decision must seek out thought as much as it is sought by thinking, and the victory of the proletariat must be *objectively* irresistible. But that is only the case—at least according to Benjamin—if historical materialism "enlists the services of theology." But historical materialism is in quotation marks in the first thesis, indicating no doubt the common variety dating back to Marx and since annexed and corrupted by the policies of the Soviet Union. Enlisting the services of theology is precisely what *this* historical materialism does *not* do, which seems to be an indication to Benjamin that the outcome of the match is in doubt. "Historical materialism is to win all the time." This sentence does not express something certain, but rather possesses a weighting which is suspended between imperative and optative meaning. As long as historical materialism scorns the services of theology, it will in any case no longer be able to "simply take on anyone." The question necessarily raised anew here concerns the necessary conditions for "winning" the historical match. With this question Benjamin implicitly already departs from the investigation of the mere "concept" of history. In the subsequent theses the inquiry after possible historical *praxis* is made clearly enough. The "historical materialism" of the first thesis no longer fulfills the postulate that theory and practice should form a unity, which has been espoused by historical materialism since Marx. The historical materialism without quotation marks, invoked in all subsequent theses, would then of course not be identical with the one meant in thesis I. Instead it would be its corrective. *Benjamin's* historical materialism would consist of the attempt to develop the theory of a different practice which might have a chance of winning the "match," the class struggle, even under altered historical circumstances. Indeed, this seems to be the intention of the "Theses on the Philosophy of History." Historical materialism once sought to realize philosophy by transforming it.[49] But in the meantime, it has lost for Benjamin its relationship to reality— "concrete truth" in the sense of the *Theses on Feuerbach*. A paradoxical situation is produced in Benjamin's theses regarding the relationship between historical materialism and theology. In order to be able to catch up with real history again, historical materialism must return *beyond* philosophy to *theology*. Granted, it is still historical materialism that "is to win," but to be *able* to win, it is to require the services of the most spiritual of all disciplines. The question remains, whether Benjamin's attempt was successful; whether the alliance of historical materialism and theology is actually able to produce a new unity of theory and practice.

7

Scholem reports that the "Theses on the Philosophy of History" represent the "completion of Benjamin's awakening from the shock of the Hitler-Stalin Pact." As an answer to this pact, he read them to his fellow exile and friend, Soma Morgenstern, the writer.[50] Indeed the theses are predicated on a political situation that had to seem increasingly hopeless; yet the arrival at a political alternative is demonstrably Benjamin's hidden intent in the theses.

As early as 1924, as Benjamin was just beginning to turn toward historical materialism, he found that "in the realm of communism [. . .] the problem of 'theory and practice' seems to be situated in such a way that, despite all the disparity which separates the two, precisely here is found a definitive insight into theory that is bound up with practice."[51] At first Benjamin's involvement was with the politics of the communist parties; at least until 1933 his interest in Marxist theory was strikingly low by comparison. But it was also only with reluctance that he would turn his attention to political praxis beyond the realm of cultural policy. While he was in Moscow for two months, from early December, 1926 until the beginning of February, 1927, the conflict between Stalin and Trotsky reached a peak. In the copious journals which Benjamin kept during his two months in Moscow there is hardly any reference to these confrontations. Yet their outcome—still by no means decided at that time—largely determined the politics of the communist parties in the years to come. In July, 1931, Benjamin still expected the beginning of a civil war in Germany in the autumn of that year.[52] It seems not to have occurred to him that the communists' policy directed against "social fascism" had long since been similarly corrupted by 'the conviction that *they* were swimming with the current" (698), a criticism Benjamin levels at the Social Democrats of the Second International in the 1940 theses. The writer had indeed deserted his own class, but he was not able to join the proletariat merely on this basis, since he remained dependent on bourgeois publishing for the reproduction of his life. Therefore he simply let his burning questions about political praxis be conjointly answered by the existence of the KP at home and a Soviet state next door. Benjamin had a stronger need for a secure relationship to political reality after the outbreak of fascism in Germany and the beginning of his emigration. In spite of all his reservations—some of which were extensive—regarding the representatives of the PCF and the KPD in exile (of course, again, questions of cultural policy were still of most importance to him), he was for a long time prepared to endorse the policies of the Soviet Union; and here in a certain sense he went very far. The Moscow trials found him for the first time somewhat at a loss. On August 24, 1936, the verdict had come down against Zinoviev and Kamenev and had been carried out the next day. On August 31 Benjamin wrote to Horkheimer, "Naturally I am following the events in Russia very closely. And it seems to me I am not the only one who has run out of answers."[53] At the end of January, 1937, he writes in another letter to Horkheimer, "I haven't a clue regarding current conditions in the [Soviet] Union."[54] The "purge" of the Red Army had taken place in 1937; in January, Pyatakov and Radek had been executed, in March of the following year, Bukharin and Rykov, after two further trials. After this, in response to a question about Brecht's political position, Benjamin wrote Horkheimer from Denmark:

> The last month has brought a series of discussions between us [Brecht and Benjamin] regarding this subject. And I now see as clearly as I think possible today in questions touching our position on the Soviet Union. It seems to me that I may be permitted to include Brecht in this "our," as long as we can see the [Soviet] Union as a power which does not determine its foreign policy on the basis of imperialistic interests, and therefore as an anti-imperialist power. Since we do this, at least for the moment and with the gravest reservations, then we still see the Soviet Union as the agent of our interests in a future war or in the postponement of such a war. Perhaps your thoughts run along similar lines. This agent is conceivably the most costly one possible, since it demands sacrifices from us as payment, which erode especially those interests closest to us as producers. Brecht is hardly likely to deny this, to the extent that he does not see that the present Russian regime, with all its terror, is the rule of one person.[55]

A note in which Benjamin criticizes his own commentary on the third "Städtebewohner" poem, probably written shortly after the leter to

ROLF TIEDEMANN

Horkheimer, speaks even more clearly (cf. II, 557ff.). Above all it directs
harsh criticism at the author of the *Lesebuch für Städtebewohner:*

> [Heinrich] Blücher very aptly pointed out that certain elements of the
> *Lesebuch für Städtebewohner* are nothing but a formulation of GPU
> praxis. This would confirm the prophetic character of the poems,
> which I suggested, but from the opposite analytical point of view.
> Indeed, the thematic sections of these poems reflect exactly that
> course of action which is shared by the worst elements of the CP and
> the most unscrupulous side of National Socialism. Blücher is right in
> his criticism of my commentary on the third poem in the "Lesebuch fur
> Städtebewohner": Hitler was not the first to introduce a sadistic aspect
> into the *praxis* described here by directing it at the Jews rather than at
> the exploiters. Instead, this sadistic element is already present in the
> "expropriation of the expropriators" as described by Brecht. And the
> sentence added at the conclusion of the poem—"This is how we speak
> to our fathers"—proves that this is not expropriation of the expropri-
> ators for the good of the proletariat, but for the good of stronger ex-
> propriators, i.e., the young ones. This added line reveals this poem's
> complicity with the attitude of Arnolt Bronnen's dubious expression-
> istic clique. Perhaps one can assume that contact with revolutionary
> workers could have prevented Brecht from producing this poetic glo-
> rification of the dangerous errors which the GPU *praxis* brought upon
> the workers' movement. In any case, the commentary in the form I
> gave it is a pious counterfeit, a concealment of the guilt Brecht shared
> for the thematic developments.[56]

Finally, two months before the outbreak of the war, Benjamin wrote
Horkheimer concerning "our cause": "Its contours are sharply different
from those of the *communis opinio* to the right and left with a clarity that
is almost frightening. Because it sets the standard for the isolation of
those who rely on their ability to think for themselves."[57]

On August 19, 1939, the Soviet Union entered into a trade agreement
with National Socialist Germany, on August 23 the non-aggression pact—
accompanied by the secret agreement on the partition of Eastern Central
Europe—and on September 28, the "treaty of friendship." Stalin ordered
the celebration of the German occupation of Paris in June, 1940, with
banners on public buildings. Benjamin's position on domestic politics in
the Soviet Union was clearly very similar to Brecht's: "He would sit in
exile and wait for the Red Army."[59] It would thus be too simple to accuse
Benjamin of cynicism for basing the shift in his position primarily on

194

Soviet foreign policy. In his essay on Bloch's justification of the trials, Oskar Negt has recently described the "identity problems" the revolutionary intelligentsia necessarily faced in the thirties as a result of Stalinist policies:[59] Benjamin seems to have been able to deal with these problems, at least superficially, in regard to the trials, but the alliance between Stalin and Hitler made it necessary for him to seek a personal way out for himself as well. The text of the Historico-philosophical Theses can confirm that they represent this attempt. In Thesis X Benjamin writes about the "thoughts" he had been developing "here"—in the Theses as a whole: "At a moment when the politicians in whom the opponents of fascism had placed their hopes are prostrate and confirm their defeat by betraying their own cause, these observations are intended to disentangle the political worldling [*Weltkind*] from the snares in which the traitors have entrapped it" (698). In the late 1930s, the opponents of fascism could logically only put their hope in the politicians of the Soviet Union and the communist parties allied with the Soviets. Although the Social Democrats are discussed in the subsequent three theses, they represented no source of hope as a political force at that time. Hope was dashed by the victories of the fascist states at the beginning of the war. The "betrayal of one's own cause," which the Moscow trials had already made clear to Benjamin at least, was clinched by the pact between Hitler and Stalin. Two of the three criteria named here—which are only "three aspects of the same thing"—do apply to the Social Democrats of the Second International: "the politicians' stubborn faith in progress" and "their confidence in their 'mass basis.' ''. But they also describe Stalin's policy of forced industrialization and compulsory collectivization of agriculture, as well as the creation of a "mass basis" through the murder of his opponents in the party leadership and the institution of an "industrial reserve army" able to recruit fully one-third of all the labor power in the Soviet Union from forced labor camps.[61] Finally, the third criterion for the politicians cited in thesis X clearly refers to the Stalinist bureaucracy: "their servile integration in an uncontrollable apparatus" (698).

In the Historico-philosophical Theses, Benjamin has understood "*the high price* our accustomed thinking will have to pay for a conception of history that avoids any complicity with the thinking to which these politicians continue to adhere" (698). Since this is precisely the intent of the theses, it was also clear how *far* they had led away from Marxism. Similarly, for Marx and Engels when they wrote the *German Ideology,* "independent philosophy" had lost "its medium of existence."[62] Afterward Engels would never tire of stressing that dialectical materialism had no more use for "a philosophy which stands above the other disciplines"[63] and that the Marxian view of history had "put an end to [. . .] philosophy in the field of history."[64] By contrast, Benjamin twice returns affirmatively to the concept of philosophy in the Theses. The very first thesis describes the relationship between theology and historical materialism as a "philosophical counterpart" (693) to the image of the chess player, thereby characterizing historical materialism as a philosophical discipline. The Platonic is even brought to bear in thesis VIII: "The current amazement that the things we are experiencing are 'still' possible in the twentieth century is *not* philosophical" (697). A demand for a *philosophical* amazement could hardly be made more clearly. Benjamin intends to "disentangle the political worldling from the snares" in which it had been "entrapped" by the official custodians of a Marxism that had degenerated into a science of legitimation for the policies of Stalin. The term "wordling" comes from an occasional poem by Goethe. The last lines of this 1774 poem were included in *Dichtung und Wahrheit:* "As though along Emmaus road,/ We stormed with paces keen;/ On either side the prophets strode,/ With worldling me between."[65] Compelled to sit through a debate between the religious zealots Lavater and Basedow on a trip on the Rhine, Goethe could make use of the ironic evasions of "rooster" and "salmon." But the "political worldling"—Benjamin himself— sees himself confronted with fascism and Soviet communism and takes the evasion of philosophy: "The themes which monastic discipline assigned to friars for meditation were designed to turn them away from the world and its affairs. The thoughts which we are developing here originate from similar considerations" (698). But Benjamin is too much of a materialist to be able to withdraw from "the world and its affairs" for long, or even to wish to do so.

8

The "Theses on the Philosophy of History" interweave a theory of historiography with a theory of the real course of history in the same way in which history itself is referred to its "making"—political *praxis*. "Politicians know best" (1250) is the phrase in one of the variants of Thesis XVI. This must be learned by historians, too, Benjamin believes. In order to do so, according to another variant, it is necessary to have a certain conception of the present that allows one to "generate" an "interrelationship between historiography and politics" (1248). The concept of history intended by the theses is concretely meant "to improve our position in the struggle against fascism" (697). Benjamin turns away from the politicians who have "betrayed" the cause of this struggle and from historical materialism in the process. In so doing, he immediately begins to develop the concept of an alternate political *praxis,* which would be suited to the pursuit of the cause of historical materialism.[66] The first failure of socialist policy in regard to fascism was that "in the name of progress its opponents treat it as a historical norm" (697). Its theory and practice have been formed by a conception of progress "which did not adhere to reality but made dogmatic claims" (700). Benjamin's critical revision of the theory and practice of historical materialism logically has as its starting point a "criticism of the concept of progress itself" (701).[67] In its place the Theses adopt an emphatic conception of the discontinuity of history.

History always encompasses both continuity and discontinuity. "The generally accepted presentation of history cherishes the production of continuity. It values those elements of past events which were already exhausted in their consequences" (1242). The parts of history that have preserved themselves are what remains *ex post facto:* world history as a Last Judgment. "The continuum of history is that of the oppressors" (1236); "all rulers are the heirs of those who conquered before them" (696). Just as the ruling oppressors blaze their bloody trail through real history, "the concept of a continuum" which rightly dominates the victors' historiography "levels everything in its path" (1236). A "new beginning" of history (1242), an end to *prehistory* and the *beginning* of history, are not in sight from this position. Therefore the historical materialist Benjamin "regards it as his task to brush history against the grain" (697) "even if he needs firetongs to do so," as the sentence originally went on (1241). The "commonly accepted" historiography "ignores the places where tradition breaks off. These are its rough edges and points that could offer a handhold to those who would like to get beyond it" (1242). In order to get beyond the history of the oppressors, the historical materialist must hold on to the history of the oppressed. But this "is a discontinuum" (1236): repeatedly starting over without consequence, "the anonymous toil" of those who did not prevail and about whom dominant historiography is silent at best. Still, the discontinuities of history "can offer a handhold." Just as the history of the stronger batallions is constituted by "the continuum of events," so also "is the concept of a discontinuum the foundation of true tradition" (1236). Of course "tradition as the discontinuity of the past" (1236) is not something that can be "recounted" (1240) in the way that history is "recounted" by historicists. The historical materialist must liquidate "the epic moment" (1240) of history and "construe" history as the discontinuum it has always been (702ff.). Historical materialism no longer reconstructs history by repeating in thought the battles of the victors. Instead it brings about the *freezing* of motion: "The task of history is not only to give the oppressed access to tradition, but also to create it" (1246). Benjamin calls this a "messianic cessation" (702ff.) brought about by historical materialism (means in a literal sense of the words as well) because it seeks a belated justice for the oppressed, their final release from the spell of history.

"The destructive or critical element in historiography is the exploding of historical continuity" (1242). Benjamin withdraws *for the moment* from political practice and even orients his thoughts toward a "meditative" attitude as prescribed by monastic discipline; but the concept of historical understanding he seeks to achieve in this way also serves to mediate between theoretical and practical procedures (or just theory and practice). The historian who appreciates this mediation no longer approaches historical events as detached objects, but becomes united with the people who "make" history: "The subject of historical knowledge is the struggling, oppressed class itself" (700). Historiography that has been modified in this way—in the *Arcades Project,* Benjamin says it has to undergo a "Copernican shift"[68]— possess its *fundamentum in re:* "The awareness that they are about to make the continuum of history explode is characteristic of the revolutionary classes at the moment of their action" (701). After the failure of the revolution of 1848, a construction of the course of history in terms of natural history becomes increasingly clear in Marx. According to this construction, the development of the forces of production inevitably leads to property relations being blown apart and thus to a higher social formation. And the action of the proletariat need finally only affix its revolutionary stamp upon this formation. In the Theses, Benjamin opposes *this* model with an *alternative,* which is to give a new meaning to revolutionary acts themselves. For him, the proletariat has been discredited as bearer of the seal of an inexorably progressing development—ever since it abdicated its role as historical subject to the Party and its apparatus and finally regressed to the "regime of personality" in the Soviet Union under Stalin. By contrast, Benjamin points out forgotten qualities of the proletariat: it is "the avenging class," which must only relearn its "hatred and spirit of sacrifice" (700). It is no accident that the name of Blanqui appears along with that of Marx in this context. Marx and Engels had renounced Blanqui as a mere "man of action" after the experiences of the Paris Commune. In 1874, Engels accused the Blanquists of having the "child-like naïveté to cite impatience as a theoretically convincing argument!"[69] But Benjamin is by no means free of such actionistic naivete in the theses of 1940. His "conception of history" seeks to finally "bring back into the field the destructive energies of historical materialism which have been immobilized for so long" (1240). Benjamin is inconclusive regarding the relationship of his concept of history to that of Marx. He sees his prefigured in Marx, as a precedent, to be sure, but does not ignore the fact that there are essential differences. In a curious note from the drafts of the Theses, he writes, "Strength of the hatred in Marx. The working class' pugnaciousness. To interconnect revolutionary destruction and the idea of redemption. *The Possessed*" (1241). This is an attempt to unite the irreconcilable. Sergi Netschayev was the Russian anarchist who, along with Bakunin, wrote the "Catechism of a Revolutionary" in 1869. His murder of a student in Moscow was one of the models for Dostoyevsky's novel *The Possessed*. Marx and Engels also dealt with Netschayev in their article "On the Affairs of Bakunin and the Alliance of Socialist Democracy."[70] Despair over the failure of the proletarian-party and the treason of its self-appointed leaders cannot invalidate this critique of anarchism, of revolutionary destruction for its own sake. Revolutionary impatience cannot skip "all intermediate stages and compromises"; these are "not created by them"—the impatient ones—" but by historical developments."[71] Similarly, "destructive energies" (1240), "destructive power" (1246), or the "destructive impulse" (1242) cannot be transposed into sensible political practice. The impulse which theory justifiably derives from practice is the memory of "revolutionary destruction" as the representative of the "idea of redemption." Reintroduced into direct action as *praxis,* this can only be regressive—in reality a part of that same "retrogression of society" that accompanies "progress in the mastery of nature" (699) up to the present day.

Benjamin has attempted to establish "the discontinuity of historical time" and its political and practical complement, "the destructive power of the working class," "at the foundations of the materialistic view of history" (1246). This attempt terminates in the concept of history as "one single catastrophe" which dominates the image in Thesis IX. "Catastrophe as the continuum of history" (1244) means an absolute, not a specific, negation of progress. "Catastrophe is progress; progress is catastrophe" (1244)—thus history becomes a mythical *nunc stans* which extends itself into the present. "The concept of progress should be based on the idea of catastrophe. That things 'just keep on going' *is* the catastrophe. It isn't that which always lies ahead, but that which always is given" (V, 592). The proposition that at some point it would not go on can therefore not be included in a teleology of history in the Hegelian sense. Nor can it be sought in the historical labor of humanity, which—in the Marxian sense—seizes upon the inherent contradictions of the present and propels them to a higher social formation. If "the 'state of emergency' in which we live is not the exception but the rule," [. . .] "then we shall clearly realize that it is our task to bring about a real state of emergency" (697). This "real state of emergency" which the revolution is to produce appears as the Other of history. It is not merely the end of the class struggle, but the end of history itself: *this* was not how Marx imagined the conclusion of the pre-history of human society. And *the* revolution which would bring about this state of emergency would also be far from the proletarian revolution Marx hoped for: it would be an apocalyptic destruction, an eschatological finish. The historical materalist who disguises himself as the "angel of history" may not be one after all. Historical materialism remains entranced by the mythical make-up of the world. It is totally unable to turn toward the future,[73] much less to aid in establishing the "true empire of freedom." Marx knew that this empire "can only blossom with the empire of necessity as its basis." Concerning its establishment he added simply, "The shortening of the work day is the first condition."[73] In the Theses, Benjamin is far removed from such sobriety. In his youth, Benjamin had urged a "spirit of social endeavor" as he perceived it to arise from "the ideas of the most profound anarchists and in Christian monastic communities" (II, 79). Later he sympathized with Sorel's theory of a general strike (II, 179-203) and even in 1929, long after he began to consider himself a Marxist, he sought to connect "revolt with the revolution." Such a revolt would bear the imprint of the "radical concept of freedom" that the Surrealists were the first "since Bakunin" to possess (II, 306). Much in accordance with all of this, Benjamin's idea of political *praxis* in the 1940 Theses has more of the enthusiasm of the anarchists than the sobriety of Marxism. It becomes a cloudy mixture of aspects of utopian socialism and of Blanquism, producing a political Messianism which can neither take Messianism really seriously nor be seriously transposed into politics.

This is especially true for Benjamin's concept of revolution. "Precisely in the interest of the revolutionary politics of the proletariat itself, the concept of the classless society must again be given its true messianic aspect" (1232). The revolutionary politics of the proletariat are not to be embarked upon in the interest of establishing the classless society, but rather the other way around: this is only a reason for bringing revolutionary politics back into play, to make revolution for its own sake. In another variant Benjamin does indeed maintain, citing Marx, that the "idea of the messianic age" must be *secularized* "in the idea of the classless society" (cf. 1231). But the instrument of this secularization becomes fetishized.

End and means—the classless society and the revolution—are reversed: Bakunin and Netschayev, and Blanqui even more so, seem here to win out over Marx.[74] "Marx says that revolutions are the locomotives of world history. Things are entirely different. Perhaps revolutions are the human race, who is travelling in this train, reaching for the emergency brake" (1232). Assuming that this is a desperate expression of an objective dilemma—namely that by 1940 Benjamin the historical materialist had to recognize that world history had taken a course to which those politicians in whom he had placed his hope were not only unable to control it, but were even actively helping it on its way—then reaching for the emergency brake—the revolution as apocalypse—is not therefore any better politics. It remains merely Münchhausen's attempt to pull himself out of the quagmire by his own pigtail. "In reality there is not a single moment which does not bring with it *its own* revolutionary opportunity" (1231). This is no analysis of reality, but rather the impotent proclamation that salvation is indeed at hand in spite of all the barriers presented to it by actual conditions. Thus revolution becomes the "leap in the open air of history," the "dialectical one which is how Marx understood the revolution." But this leap is not dialectical, nor is it how Marx understood the revolution. For Marx there is no "open" air of history. For him, history is "the history of the developing forces of production adopted by each new generation, and thereby the history of the development of powers of individuals themselves."[75] In the Historico-philosophical Theses, Benjamin is about to leap out of historical materialism into the realm of political Messianism where nothing can be done at all. Since he can no longer perceive in social reality the "material conditions of existence" for possible change, Benjamin concludes that "the classless society [. . .] is not the final goal of historical progress, but the ultimate success of the often-frustrated attempts to interrupt it" (1231). Therefore, "every second of time" should be "the straight gate through which the Messiah might enter" (704). The theologizing terminology of the Theses announces *both* claims: it attempts to preserve the content of the proletarian revolution within the concept of the Messiah, the classless society within the messianic age and class struggle within messianic power. *At the same time* the revolution which does not come is supposed to be standing at the gate at any moment, like the Messiah. There, in some historical beyond, it can quickly put together a classless society, even if it is nowhere to be seen around here. The retranslation of materialism into theology cannot avoid the risk of losing both: the secularized content may dissolve while the theological idea evaporates.

9

Benjamin's Theses are no less than a handbook for urban guerillas. Obviously the author is not recommending anarchistic *actes gratuits* or Blanquist coups as political methods in the middle of the twentieth century. The relationship of the theoretical contents of the text to political practice nowhere takes the form of practical "instructions." At least here, and not least here, Benjamin does indeed retain an authentically Marxist viewpoint. Marx's postulate of objective truth announced who would be the proponents of an absolute primacy of *praxis:* in reality, nothing is in truth more abstract than a praxis that "bursts theory through the arch-bourgeois supremacy of practical reason proclaimed by Kant and Fichte."[76] In taking Hegel literally, Marx was led beyond subjective idealism by its own self-reflection: the discovery of the practical *telos* contained in every theory which is more than a positivistic classification of blind actualities. The emphatic *praxis* intended by historical materialism does not put itself in the place of theory; it would be theory itself becoming practical—the opposite of pragmatism, the illusionary *praxis* in with both anarchism and Blanquism remain entangled. Theoretical elements of anarchism can be identified in Benjamin's Theses as just such an *immanent telos,* and not as a recipe for revolutions. Only those who would try to read the theses as "instructions," which they were never intended to be, could draw from them anarchistic *conclusions* for political *praxis*. Benjamin did not desire such conclusions: perhaps barely conscious of them, he was even unconsciously *afraid* of such conclusions. This could help to explain the game of hide-and-seek in Benjamin's text. Its political content is hidden in the last place one would look for it: behind the mask of its theological language.

But the incomparable significance of the theses for the state of Marxist theory in 1940 lies in what they are unable to accomplish as a reconstruction of revolutionary *praxis*. They represent a document of both the objective degeneration of this theory and the isolation of a theorist who still does not cease to "rely on his own ability to think for himself." Benjamin composed the Theses "with the greatest effort, perhaps already countenancing that ultimate threat."[77] These are more than theses in the literal sense of the word, didactic phrases which largely omit argumentation. Beyond that, they make use of a metaphorical language precisely in those lines of reasoning with the most problematic meaning which stubbornly resists translation into the language of discourse. All too much seems to have been gathered into the few sentences of the theses. They offer themselves for meditative contemplation and demand to be pursued further, but they rarely permit a completely consistent interpretation. The theses even lack a thetic quality of unanimity, and have more of the character of working hypotheses, perhaps also even an element of "as if." Benjamin had good reasons for not wishing to see the text published: not only did he wish to avoid misunderstandings, but perhaps more than that, he considered the work to be incomplete. Like the *Arcades Project* itself, the Theses remained fragmentary. They attempt to anticipate in concise form the "grounding" of the *Arcades Project* in a theory of knowledge. Even before he began, Benjamin knew that such an undertaking should follow the "material proof"—the completion of the *Arcades Project*—rather than go before it (cf. 1224). Furthermore, every interpretation will do injustice to the Theses because it must necessarily condense elements into a unified line of reasoning and thus homogenize them in a way. But many elements of the text stand beside each other without mediation, or at times oppose or contradict each other. Clearly Benjamin's theological language makes itself most vulnerable to such homogenization. The attempt to extrapolate a political content from that language can therefore not claim to have exhaustively analyzed the function of theological thought in the Historico-philosophical Theses. From another point of view it may be precisely Benjamin's recourse to theology that is the proven truth content of the theses.

After returning from a visit to the Soviet Union in 1936, Andre Gidé reported on it in the book *Retour de l'U.R.S.S.* The book intensively occupied Benjamin's attention in both agreement and disagreement. Gide describes the prevailing anti-religious struggle waged "against a teaching which, after all, had brought the world a new hope and the most extraordinary revolutionary stimuli conceivable in those times. [. . .] One ought not here to begrudge me a remnant of my upbringing, my early convictions. I would speak in the same way about Greek myths; in them, too, I recognize a deep and lasting formative power. It would seem absurd to me to *believe* in them. But it would be equally absurd for me to ignore the truth in them and to try to dismiss them with a smile and a shrug."[79] It was Horkheimer who wrote to Benjamin in 1937 that "in the past few years, religion again [figured] among the central problems of the moment." "Are you familiar with André Gide's remarks in 'Retour' [. . .] on the subject? I find them to be quite significant."[80] Benjamin answered, "I had just intended to read Gide's book when I received your mention of it. The passage on religion is outstanding, perhaps the best in the book."[81] It can also cast a light on Benjamin's attempt in the Theses, written three years later, to combine theology and historical materialism. The latter was no longer to refute abstractly the truth content of religion, but to begin again to secure its own. It should "enlist the services of theology" in order to regain a "revolutionary stimulus." Any such stimulus had long since disappeared from the calcified theory of official materialism, while the *praxis* of Soviet politics had replaced it with brute force and an apparatus of the most brutal domination, leading the masses on with the construction of heavy industry. Benjamin's insistence on the "true messianic aspect" of the classless society is *also* reminiscent, on the other hand, of Marx's insight that *"no* form of servitude [can] be broken without breaking *every* form of servitude."[82] An abyss still lies between history (including the chapter written by Stalin, in which necessity was only used as an excuse) and the prophesied Empire of Freedom. Theology hopes that the arrival of the Messiah would bridge this abyss. "The puppet called 'historical materialism' is to win all the time" (694). Regarding this, even in the latter theses, *nothing* has changed for Benjamin. In the meantime, however, historical materialism has become a "puppet" that is only "called" by that name; a strawman that has only a name in common with the materialism of Marx. But in addition, to borrow a phrase from Ulrich Sonnemann, it is a "parrot-like prayer" which invokes what Marx had demystifed. It is not Benjamin who in these theses revokes the critique of religion which Marx had considered "essentially complete" by 1844. The new Inquisition of the Moscow Trials and the pious gestures of affirmation from consenting Party functionaries are *objectively* subject to criticism. Benjamin's theses fully satisfy Marx's demand for historical specificity: they mark the position of thought in regard to the objectivity of a certain historical moment, but do not provide an ontology of historicity *per se*. Theology would well have been abandoned as long as its secular content was preserved in the workers' movement. But even theological ideas take on new relevance when the class struggle comes to a halt in the authoritarian state for the sake of the "original socialist accumulation" (the cruelly ironic phrase under Stalinism). Then historical materialism must again "enlist the services" of theology—as a reminder that the historical pile of debris does not continue to grow as socialism as well, that it does not grow as high as the sky. Just as true theology points toward materialism, so it is only true materialism that first brings theology home. At times historical materialism has to learn from theology that there is no redemption, unless it is complete.

Frankfurt am Main

Translated by Barton Byg,
Jeremy Gaines, and Doris L. Jones

NOTES

1 Bertolt Brecht, *Arbeitsjournal*, Vol. 1, ed. Werner Hecht (Frankfurt: Suhrkamp, 1973), p. 294.

2 Cf. *ibid.*, p.16.

3 Hereafter page numbers in the text which are not preceded by volume number refer to Volume I of Benjamin's *Gesammelte Schriften*. Other numbers refer to subsequent volumes of this edition. Quotations are on the whole taken from the English translation with emendations made when deemed necessary, although page numbers are not provided. Cf. Walter Benjamin, *Illuminations,* ed. Hannah Arendt, trans. Harry Zohn (New York: Harcourt, Brace & World, 1968).

4 Hans Heinz Holz, "Prismatisches Denken," in *Über Walter Benjamin* (Frankfurt: Suhrkamp, 1968), p. 106.

5 Heinz-Dieter Kittsteiner, "Die 'Geschichtsphilosophischen Thesen' " in *Materialien zu Benjamins Thesen "Über den Begriff der Geschichte"*, ed. Peter Bulthaup (Frankfurt: Suhrkamp, 1975), p. 38.

6 The present attempt does not claim to fulfill this task. It limits itself to one aspect of the Benjaminian text: that of the relationship of historical materialism and theology as well as the political content of the "Theses on Philosophy of History," insofar as they are determined by this relationship. Other aspects of the same—particularly Benjamin's critique of historicism and the ideology of progress—have already been treated by the author in an earlier work. Cf. Rolf Tiedemann, *Studien zur Philosophie Walter Benjamins,* 2nd ed. (Suhrkamp: Frankfurt, 1973), pp. 128-66.

7 The sole title attributable to Benjamin himself reads "On the Concept of History"; the well-known "Historico-Philosophical Theses" [or "Theses on the Philosophy of History"] is apocryphal. (Cf. 1254). Since, however, the latter title represents a successful circumlocution of the text, it will also be utilized in the present text as a characteristic description.

8 Engels, *Anti-Dühring,* in Karl Marx/Friedrich Engels, *Werke,* Vol. 20 (Berlin: Dietz, 1968), p. 264.—Hereafter this edition will be cited as MEW.

9 Friedrich Engels, Letter from January 25, 1894 to W. Borgius, in MEW, Vol. 39, p. 206.

10 Benjamin, "Über Das Grauen," VI 76f.

11 Kant was aware of that, for example, as he worked to overcome the heterogeneity of pure concepts of understanding with "empirical intuitions, indeed sensible intuitions in general" through a "schematism" (cf. Kant, *Werke in sechs Bänden,* ed. Wilhelm Weischedel, Vol. II (Wiesbaden: Insel, 1956), p. 187.): the abstract language of conceptuality would virtually make amends through an abstraction at a higher level.

12 Cf. Gershom Scholem, "Walter Benjamin und sein Engel," in *Zur Aktualität Walter Benjamins,* ed. Siegfried Unseld (Suhrkamp: Frankfurt, 1972), pp. 87-138.

13 *Ibid.,* p. 134.

14 Cf. *Ibid.,* pp. 132f.

15 *Ibid.,* p. 132.

16 Scholem, *Über einige Grundbegriffe des Judentums* (Frankfurt: Suhrkamp, 1970), p. 125.

17 Karl Marx, "Briefe aus den 'Deutsch-Französischen Jahrbüchern," in MEW, Vol. 1, p. 346.

18 Hermann Schweppenhäuser, "Physiognomie eines Physiognomikers," in *Zur Aktualität Walter Benjamins,* p. 152.

19 Gerhard Kaiser, *Benjamin. Adorno. Zwei Studien* (Frankfurt: Athenäum, 1974).—
Following the first printing of the present inquiry, Kaiser published a reply to this
author's criticism, which, however, did not persuasively meet the objections raised.

20 Kaiser, p. 32.

21 *Ibid.*, p. 34.

22 Cf. *ibid.*

23 *Ibid.*

24 *Ibid.*

25 Cf. *ibid.*, pp. 34f.—The conclusion of Kaiser's interpretation should not be dismissed if
only for its curiosity factor: "Benjamin's 'Historico-philosophical Theses' are an eschatological, messianic event."—Positivism has a fitting characterization of such events: to
confuse the map with the territory.

26 Regarding Benjamin's sources, cf. Scholem, "Walter Benjamin und sein Engel," in *Zur
Aktualität Walter Benjamins*, p. 138, Fn. 24.

27 Horkheimer repeatedly expressed such considerations: they buried his unmistakeable
tendency towards materialistic sorrow—in no way identical with the pessimism of
Schopenhauer, with whom he is constantly brought together. (Cf. Max Horkheimer,
Critical Theory, trans. Matthew J. O'Connell *et al.* (New York: Herder & Herder, 1972),
pp. 26f., 251, as well as the fragment "Vergebliche Trauer" in Horkheimer, *Notizen 1950
bis 1969 und Dämmerung*, ed. Werner Brede (Frankfurt: Fischer, 1974), p. 69.)

28 The particular significance Benjamin assigned this thought is already superficially evident from his reply to Horkheimer's letter of March 16, 1937, where he not only commented on behalf of the *Arcades Project*, but also enclosed excerpts from preliminary
studies for the Historico-philosophical Theses as part of his commentary.

29 Marx, *Der achtzehnte Brumaire des Louise Bonaparte*, in MEW, Vol. 8, p. 115.

30 *Ibid.*, p. 117.

31 *Ibid.*, p. 115.

32 Cf. above.

33 Those, of course, that are full of metaphysical implications, and through the use of the
concept of the monad refer back to *The Origin of German Tragic Drama*, as well as
Benjamin's reception of Leibniz; Cf. Rolf Tiedemann, *Studien zur Philosophie Walter
Benjamins*.

34 Marx, *Das Kapital I*, in MEW, Vol. 23, p. 27.

35 *Ibid.*

36 *Ibid.*, p. 28.

37 Such an exemplification of Benjamin's "methodology" through the Marxist procedures
in the critique of political economy is self-evidently not a *sufficient* characterization of
the latter—in the same way, it is certainly no *impossible* one.

38 Marx, *Das Kapital I*, p. 28.

39 In addition, "Messiah" appears in its substantive form in the so-called thesis B (704); an
interpretation of this passage can be dispensed with in this context, however, since
Benjamin left out thesis B in the version of the "Historico-philosophical Theses" most
precisely reflecting his intentions. This passage, and similarly thesis A (which is a
strongly modified version), are only integrated into the earliest and handwritten version
of the textual continuum. The subsequently composed version—and previous to the
appearance of Volume I of Benjamin's *Gesammelte Schriften*, the only published version—has the two theses as a kind of appendix, following the conclusion of the text. In
both of Benjamin's final versions, he left out theses A and B. (For the philological
details, cf. 1254, as well as 1255-59, which include extant variations of the historico-

philosophical theses.)—It represents a grotesque misunderstanding—one without familiarity with the circumstances of the theses' transmission: purely with regard to the *meaning* of the Benjaminian texts such a misunderstanding is hardly unavoidable—to treat the theses A and B as *sections* of the XVIIIth thesis, which is approximately what Kaiser does (cf. Kaiser, pp. 55-58).

40 Cf. above.
41 Cf. Scholem, "Walter Benjamin und sein Engel," pp. 132f.
42 Marx, *Das Kapital I*, p. 86.
43 Cf. above.
44 Cf. Moritz Friedländer, *Der Antichrist in den vorchristlichen jüdischen Quellen* (Göttingen: Vandenhoeck & Ruprecht, 1901).
45 It was attempted above to demonstrate this in exemplary fashion for three passages; the interpretation of all other instances theological motifs and terminology throughout the theses, in the opinion of this author, would lead to the same conclusion.
46 "Maelzel's Chess Player" belongs to those of Poe's essays translated by Baudelaire. The translations are found in *Nouvelles histoires extraordinaires,* which Benjamin repeatedly drew into his writings on Baudelaire.
47 Kaiser, p. 17.
48 This was also referred to by Kaiser; cf. *ibid.,* p. 16.
49 Cf. Marx, "Einleitung," *Zur Kritik der Hegelschen Rechtsphilosophie,* in MEW, Vol. 1, p. 384; Cf. also *ibid.,* p. 391.
50 Scholem, "Walter Benjamin und sein Engel," p. 129. Scholem appeals to remarks—in other respects exceptionally unreliable—in letters from Soma Morgenstern written from 1970-72; "News of the [Hitler-Stalin] Pact gave him an irremediable personal blow [. . .] More than once he mournfully repeated. 'Why should we also have earned it, that our generation should have experienced the solution to humanity's most important questions? [. . .] Later in the conversation it turned out that this act of Stalin had taken away his belief in historical materialism. I assume that in that week he had already conceived the plan of his theses, which he wrote down later, and which signify nothing other than a revision of historical materialism. [. . .] Now to return to my further conversations about the Hitler-Stalin Pact and its effect on Walter Benjamin. When he brought that up again, that this pact had destroyed his faith in Marxism-Leninism, I asked him if it had ever occurred to him that this belief has a relation to his Jewish belief in the redemption of the world through a Messiah. 'You could go even further,' he said—ironically, of course—'and maintain that Karl Marx and the whole of nineteenth century socialism is merely another form of messianic belief' " (Morgenstern to Scholem, December 21, 1972, unpublished). After the Hitler-Stalin Pact, Benjamin was so depressed that he came to me almost daily to seek consolation [. . .] After Benjamin had recovered from the shock, he invited me for dinner and read from 'Twelve Theses towards a Revision of Historical Materialism.' I recall the First thesis. It was about the chess machine, which defeated all chess experts" (Morgenstern to Scholem, November 2, 1973, unpublished).
51 Benjamin, *Briefe,* ed. G. Scholem und T. W. Adorno, 2nd ed. (Frankfurt: Suhrkamp, 1978), p. 355.
52 Cf. *ibid.,* p. 536.
53 Benjamin, Letter of August 31, 1936 to Horkheimer (unpublished).
54 Benjamin, Letter of January 31, 1937 to Horkheimer (unpublished).
55 Benjamin, Letter of August 3, 1939 to Horkheimer (unpublished): cf. Benjamin, *Versuche über Brecht,* ed. R. Tiedemann, 6th ed. (Frankfurt: Suhrkamp, 1981), pp. 167-69.
56 Benjamin, Untitled manuscript *Aufzeichnung;* W. Benjamin Collection, Bibliothéque

Nationale, Paris.—This notice, first discovered in 1982, is now printed in the supplement to Volume VI of Benjamin's *Gesammelte Schriften.*

57 Benjamin, Letter of June 24, 1939 to Horkheimer (unpublished).

58 Benjamin, *Versuche über Brecht,* pp. 167f.—This corresponds to Benjamin's earliest utterances about Gide's Retour de l'U.R.S.S.: "During my absence Gide's *Retour de l'U.R.S.S.* appeared. It was not only published in book form, but was disseminated in countless excerpts in the fascist press. I have not yet read it. [. . .] The indignation of those in the party knows no bounds. (As for myself, I disapprove of it without yet being familiar with it. Also, without knowledge of what it contains and whether it holds true and whether it is decisive. In that I impute the latter, I can in no way ignore the attitude of the man, who at this point in time, takes a course to indulge himself, to see how the thing actually appears, representing a duping. A political position cannot be aired unrestricted in public at every given moment. Such a claim is pure dilettantism: the result is pure mischief. This is the case under the assumption that Gide has no precise political aim, rather merely intends 'reform.' Besides, the precise political aim could only lie in the Trotskyist direction. That would have to be known, and as far as I know, that is not the case.)" (Benjamin, Letter of December 12, 1936 to Margaret Steffin (unpublished); cf. below, regarding Benjamin's revision of his judgement of Gide's book).

59 Cf. Oskar Negt, "Ernst Bloch—der deutsche Philosoph der Oktoberrevolution," in Ernst Bloch, *Vom Hasard zur Katastrophe. Politische Aufsätze 1934-1939* (Frankfurt: Suhrkamp, 1972), p. 433.

60 When Benjamin, in the Xth thesis, attributes "stubborn belief in progress"—which he criticizes as that of the old Social Democracy in theses XI to XIII— to *these* politicians (namely those *Communist* politicians meant in the Xth thesis), then that is an unmistakeable hint that the ensuing critiqe of the notion of progress can hardly be addressed to the Social Democrats *alone.*

61 Cf. Maximilien Rubel, *Josef W. Stalin* (Reinbek: Rowohlt, 1975), p. 82.

62 Marx/Engels, *Die deutsche Ideologie,* in MEW, Vol. 3, p. 27.

63 Engels, *Anti-Dühring,* p. 24.

64 Engels, *Ludwig Feuerbach und der Ausgang der klassischen deutschen Philosophie,* in: MEW, Vol. 21, p. 306.

65 Goethe, *From My Life: Poetry and Truth,* trans. Robert R. Heitner, ed. Thomas P. Saine & Jeffrey L. Sammons. New York: Suhrkamp Publishers, 1987, p. 456.

66 The following explanation of the political contents of Benjamin's theses does not rely by accident primarily on preliminary studies and *paralipomena,* which either were not present in the text's final version at all or only in a somewhat modified form. These preliminary studies offer one key—not to be disdained—for the decoding of the theses. In doing so, it should be less a matter of locating the hidden *intentions* of the author to find the right track—although this cannot be totally ignored—, than a question of depicting the *implications* of the text itself, or if one will, to construe, from which it can remain indeterminate, whether or to what extent they were present for Benjamin.

67 In thesis XI Benjamin would like to have Marx himself being exempt from the critique of the idea of progress, as the reference to the "Critique of the Gotha Program" demonstrates; however, Marx's confidence is implicitly criticized in the theses, insofar as the unleashing of the forces of production are to bring the final breakdown of the capitalist productive relations. Not only did Benjamin (in a note for his theses) explicitly refer to the necessity of a "Critique of the Theory of Progress in Marx" (1239); even clearer language speaks still, in that in thesis XI, which *against* Social Democracy appeals to Marx, *simultaneously* cites Fourier—derided by Marx—with approval, and in the thesis

immediately thereafter recalls the name of Blanqui with no less consent. Benjamin would hardly have gone as far as Karl Korsch in his 1950 "Ten Theses on Marxism Today"; yet the "monopolistic claim of Marxism to the revolutionary initiative and to the theoretical and practical leadership" (Korsch, *Politische Texte,* ed. Erich Gerlach & Jürgen Seifert (Frankfurt, 1974), p. 386) is also immanently put into doubt in Benjamin's historico-philosophical theses.

68 Cf. above.

69 Engels, *Programm der blanquistischen Kommuneflüchtlinge,* in MEW, Vol. 18, p. 533.

70 Cf. Marx/Engels, *Ein Komplott gegen die Internationale Arbeiterassoziaton,* in MEW, Vol. 18, pp. 327-471, esp. pp. 396-432.

71 Engels, *Programm der blanquistischen Kommuneflüchtlinge,* p. 533.

72 Similarly, Ulrich Sonnemann's uncommonly witty variation he assigns to Benjamin's angel: "He has to turn [. . .] around, turn his face away from the mountain of debris: the most simple aerodynamic consideration makes it clear, that he can only close the wings in this way, to his great fortune then eventually even use them, whereby a start against the wind, which a new turning back perhaps makes necessary, must by no means bar him in the face of that opposing crossing exploitation from determining the direction of flight himself. [. . .] What the angel of history now accordingly needs is a rear-view mirror" (Ulrich Sonnemann, *Negative Anthropologie, Vorstudien zur Sabotage des Schicksals* (Reinbek: Rowohlt, 1969), p. 277).

73 Marx, *Das Kapital III,* in MEW, Vol. 25, p. 828.

74 According to Habermas, Benjamin "slowly abandoned his early anarchistic tendencies" (Jürgen Habermas, "Walter Benjamin. Bewußtmachende oder rettende Kritik," in *Philosophisch-politische Profile,* 3rd ed. (Frankfurt: Suhrkamp, 1981), p. 371). Without a doubt many of the texts from Benjamin's middle period can be given such an interpretation; the late works—not merely the historico-philosophical theses, but also the texts on Baudelaire—demonstrate meanwhile that such attempts are failures.—Regarding the anarchistic, Blanquist elements in the later Benjamin's works, cf. above.

75 Marx und Engels, *Die deutsche Ideologie,* p. 72.

76 Theodor W. Adorno, *Gesammelte Schriften,* Vol. 10, 2, *Kulturkritik and Gesellschaft II,* ed. R. Tiedemann (Frankfurt: Suhrkamp, 1977), p. 761.

77 Adorno, *Über Walter Benjamin,* ed. R. Tiedemann (Frankfurt: Suhrkamp, 1970), p. 45.

78 Cf. above.

79 André Gide, "Zurück aus Sowjetrußland," trans. Ferdinand Hardekopf, in Gide, *Reisen* (Stuttgart: Deutsche Verlagsanstalt, 1966), pp. 377f.

80 Horkheimer, Letter of January 11, 1937 to Benjamin (unpublished).

81 Benjamin, Letter of January 31, 1937 to Horkheimer (unpublished).

82 Marx, "Einleitung," *Zur Kritik der Hegelschen Rechtsphilosophie,* p. 391.

83 *Ibid.,* p. 378.

EXPERIENCE AND MATERIALISM IN BENJAMIN'S *PASSAGENWERK*

RICHARD WOLIN

Walter Benjamin intended the *Passagenwerk* or Arcades Project to be the culmination of his lifework. In it he hoped to do for nineteenth century Paris what he had done for the seventeenth century in his 1925 study *The Origin of German Tragic Drama:* through an allegorical reading of the life-forms of the era, to allow the truth-content (*Wahrheitsgehalt*) of the epoch to emerge through the veneer of its material content (*Sachgehalt*).[1] This approach coincided with his unconventional epistemological ideal of attempting to extract noumenal knowledge from *within* the phenomenal realm; to reverse the terms of Western metaphysics by ceding pride of place in the field of philosophical inquiry to what had previously been merely derided and scorned: the ephemeral and transient aspects of the phenomenal world. The success of this project hinged upon discovery of a new concept of experience. Ideally, this new concept of experience would view conventional experience in a radically new light and in this sense pave the way for the *redemption* (*Rettung*) of a prosaic phenomenal world. In his metaphysical phase (roughly, 1914-1925), the neo-Platonic overtones of this epistemological course are still pronounced: through their arrangement of the detritus of the phenomenal world in philosophically formed constellations, ideas effectuate the redemption of phenomenal experience. By the term "experience," Benjamin alludes to the Kantian meaning of the word: the epistemological prerequisite for our having knowledge of the world. At the same time, in Benjamin's usage the term takes on a significant evaluative dimension as a result of having simultaneously absorbed the resonances of early twentieth century German *Kulturkritik*. In this view, experience has fallen in value in the modern world; for ours is an age in which the crude, materialistic values of bourgeois *Zivilisation* reign triumphant at the expense of the refinement and sublimity of *Kultur*. The early Benjamin unquestionably views himself as an aesthete, a *Kulturmensch*. And it is through the sphere of

210

culture alone that the prosaic experience of the bourgeois social order can be surpassed in favor of a new concept of experience, as a result of which life will once again become a repository of value and meaning. In this sense, Benjamin makes common cause with the Weberian thesis of *Sinnverlust*—loss of meaning—as the defining feature of a modern age in which scientism has shredded the sacred canopy of religious life. The labor of Sisyphus confronting Benjamin in the *Passagenwerk* was the following: how to make this theory of experience compatible with a materialist (Marxist) world-view so that in the end *all* would be redeemed rather than merely a cultural elite.

A reading of Benjamin's *Passagenwerk* immediately suggests two interrelated hermeneutic difficulties: 1) how would one begin situating the *Passagenwerk* in relation to Benjamin's earlier, avowedly metaphysical-theological studies? 2) how might one describe the central, overall theoretical thrust of the study? The answer to the latter question is especially complicated by the fact that, as is well known, the *Passagenwerk* or Arcades Project remains a torso; and moreover, one extremely difficult to reconstruct.[2] Many of the "Konvoluten" for the study consist mainly of citations; and in numerous cases it becomes a matter of sheer conjecture as to how Benjamin himself would have actually made use of the materials in question, owing to the remarkable dearth of supporting commentary (never Benjamin's forte in any event). The point is worth emphasizing, therefore, that in judgments about the *Passagenwerk,* one is perpetually on shaky ground. For not only is the work itself a torso—labored on with various degrees of intensity or neglect for a period of 13 years (1927-1940)—but it is also quite apparent that Benjamin himself significantly altered the methodological focus of the project several times during this period.

It is apparent that very early in his literary activity, Benjamin was searching for what he dubbed a "superior concept of experience," i.e., one untainted by the profane nature of "mechanistic" world views. It was at the doorstep of neo-Kantianism (the intellectual current which enjoyed theoretical hegemony at German universities in Benjamin's day) that Benjamin lay responsibility for this situation, insofar as neo-Kantianism—while claiming to rescue the concept of autonomous subjectivity from the clutches of 19th century positivism through its by now renowned distinction between the methodologies of the natural and social sciences[3]—relapsed into "mechanism" by virtue of its servile methodological respect for the infamous Kantian proscription against meanderings in the intelligible or supersensible realm—the only realm, according to Benjamin, where a superior, non-mundane concept of experience might be discovered. In brief, this scenario provides the background concerning Benjamin's pronounced distaste for all prevailing, conventional philosophical methodologies and his early flirtation with pre-Kantian, theological conceptions of truth. For the early Benjamin, whose theory of knowledge ultimately remained *individualistic,* theology seemed a viable route to restore *the lost totality of experience,* a pre-paradisiac condition of purity and community that had been dissolved amid the "fallen" continuum of history. Yet, he was hardly simple-minded enough to undertake direct recourse to any traditional or inherited conceptions of religious experience. Rather, these too were equally compromised by the taint of secular convention. Instead, it was toward the ideas of Kabbalah, the forbidden mystical undercurrent of Jewish religious tradition, that he was attracted. It was a theological heritage that surfaced only obliquely in Benjamin's published work; but for all that, it was nonetheless influential. Above all, it was the Kabbalistic conception of the well-nigh absolute chasm separating the profane continuum of history from the Messianic realm of redemption that impressed him and that appeared time and again in his work: from the early (circa 1920) "Theological-Political Fragment," where Benjamin depicts the relation between the two aforementioned realms in terms of the provocative image of the two arrows pointed in opposite directions, which nevertheless influence one another, inexplicably but slightly;[4] to the 1940 "Theses of the Philosophy of History," where an equally striking metaphor is employed: that of the Klee watercolor "Angelus Novus" where the wings of the "angel of history" are caught in a storm emanating from paradise, which "piles up ruin upon ruin and hurls it in front of his feet"; and whereas "we" perceive a *chain* of events, the knowing angel perceives unremitting disaster, the disaster that characterizes unredeemed historical life to date.[5]

It would be difficult to overestimate the significance of the foregoing two metaphors for Benjamin's lifework as a whole. For they constitute the foundation of his philosophy of history, upon which his theory of experience is ultimately based. The philosophy of history might be characterized as a *negative* philosophy of history: analogous to the conception of *Verfallsgeschichte,* or history-as-decline, that informs his understanding of *Trauerspiel.*[6] Whereas the theory of experience which derives therefrom assumes at base the same form in all phases of his development, it is characterized by three different, though essentially parallel concepts: monad (*Trauerspiel* book), dialectical image (Arcades Project), and *Jetztzeit,* or Now-time ("Theses on the Philosophy of History"). All convey the idea of the *singularity* or *uniqueness* of the precious few images of transcendence that grace the otherwise profane continuum of history. The construction of such images is the task of the critic—or later the historical materialist. This process facilitates the *redemption* of the phenomena incorporated into the image. The theory of experience based on these concepts seeks to recapture a sense of wholeness, an integral sense, which had been eclipsed owing to the omnipresence of historical fragmentation. Although originally Benjamin remained satisfied with a theological explanation for this state of affairs, in the mid-twenties, with his new found interest in historical materialism, he began confronting its actual material, i.e., socio-historical, causes.[7]

The dialectical image is the methodological cornerstone of the Arcades Project. Yet, it has an important precursor in the notion of "dialectic at a standstill" developed in *One-Way Street*.[8] Like the monads and constellations of the *Trauerspiel* book, the dialectical image aims at a redemption of phenomena from their degraded, immediate state. As a result of their being drawn up into the image, phenomena receive new life as it were. They are forcibly wrenched from the *Zuhandensein,* their sheer givenness, and viewed afresh as a result of the process of juxtaposition effected by the image itself. An important feature of the dialectical image for Benjamin was that it was to remain uninfluenced by the admixture of philosophical commentary. This was in keeping with his epistemological asceticism or anti-subjectivism. In this sense Benjamin remained a staunch foe of the primacy in modern philosophy of epistemology over ontology. Instead, for him truth was not a subjective additive, but something objective, lying dormant in things themselves. Truth was to emerge from an unmediated juxtaposition of material elements, insofar as it was something unobtainable through strictly discursive means. Hence, Benjamin's epistemological preferences bore strong points of resemblance with various irrationalist and vitalist theories of knowledge current in Germany during the inter-war years, many of which were of course espoused by later fascist sympathizers. He himself made no secret of the fact that his imagistic theory of knowledge was significantly indebted to the work of the German cultural historian Ludwig Klages. With Klages he shared the conviction that discursive reason was an insufficient means of capturing truth in its pristine, lived immediacy. Thinking in images (instead of concepts) presented itself as an alternative insofar as the sensuousness of the image retained greater affinities with the concrete character of lived experience itself.

It is on the basis of what might be labeled the materialist turn in Benjamin's thinking that a substantive shift in his theoretical self-conception may be grasped. Yet, this shift is in part misleading, since his central epistemological tack—variously expressed in the theory of monads, dialectical images, or now-times—remains essentially unchanged throughout. At issue in all three cases is the question of a philosophical approach capable of surmounting the "original sin" of all human ratiocination: the fact that all thought attempts to grasp the *non-conceptual* through *conceptual* means. Benjamin's solution to this apparent dilemma was to strive for a presentation of knowledge that retained as few affinities with traditional philosophical conceptualization as possible. Hence, the "image-oriented" approach to truth, whose basic principle was very much akin to the surrealistic principle of montage: renunciation of conventional philosophical narrative in favor of an approach that called for an *unmediated* juxtaposition of insights. Through this method he sought to lend an autonomous voice to that which is otherwise denied one, that which is otherwise conceived of as mere fodder of the conceptual will-to-knowledge": things themselves, objectivity as such. The theological resonances of this conception echo clearly in Benjamin's oft-stated desire to formulate a theory of knowledge capable of calling things by their proper names—an allusion to the biblical theory of creation. However, as Adorno pointed out with regularity, this technique, though salutary in many respects, inherently ran the risk, by virtue of its rigorous anti-subjectivism, of relapsing into the positivism it detested, of fetishizing facticity in its immediacy; a charge to which Benjamin replied that by virtue of its—albeit immediate—incorporation in the monad or dialectical image, facticity was itself thereby transformed.[9]

Through this method Benjamin hoped to formulate a theory of experience capable of surpassing the degradation of the present historical era. In the 1930s, the work of both Baudelaire and Nikolai Leskov became the subject of dialectical images: Baudelaire by virtue of the *correspondences* of his poetic imagery with a past *ur*historical stage of species life where nature was viewed fraternally rather an as an object of domination; and Leskov by virtue of the capacity of storytelling to recapture a means of conveying experience in which totality, continuity, and meaningfulness receive pride of place.[10] In both instances, his analysis, while probing and consequential, remains tinged by a romanticization of the past which also characterized some of the more politically unsavory thinkers of his generation.

The work of Kafka and Karl Kraus was also subjected to this mode of analysis. Both were viewed less as harbingers of reconciled life than as prophets in the biblical mode, unrelentingly lamenting the perdition of worldly affairs; however, such lamentation in no way served as an end in itself, but rather as a powerful spur toward the rectification of this situation. In the same way that the arrows traversing opposite directions in the "Theologico-Political Fragment" remain capable of exerting nevertheless a decisive influence upon one another, the work of Kraus and Kafka, by dwelling in the profane and pushing the latter to its furthest extent, seeks thereby to explode it and clear the path for redemption.

One way in which Benjamin's new preoccupation with materialist modes of thought manifested itself in his work has already been noted: a more pronounced concern with a socio-historical understanding of the unredeemed character of the present age. Yet there is another aspect, at least as important, that merits equal consideration: his desire that the truth content of his dialectical monads or images now be redeemed *exoterically* rather than *esoterically;* that they be made serviceable for a (still inchoate) *collective subjectivity* rather than, as before, a coterie of initiates. This change in what might be called "strategies of redemption" represents probably the most noticeable alteration in Benjamin's self-conception as a critic from his so-called early work to the materials comprising and deriving from the *Passagenwerk.* Yet, despite this marked change of attitude toward reception-theory (Benjamin had written in 1923: "No poem is intended for the reader, no picture for the beholder, no symphony for the listener"),[11] one would be hard pressed to conclude that the works which resulted took on a more generalizable, accessible character in consequence. The (apparent) discrepancy between intention and actuality is ultimately, however, not so contradictory as it may at first seem. Instead the insights of the *Passagenwerk* were destined for "exoteric redemption" only ideally and not immediately: Benjamin remained well aware that redemption was in truth hardly a purely theoretical affair, but a question of historical practice.

It was a reading of Aragon's *Le Paysan de Paris* in 1926 that provided Benjamin with his original inspiration for the *Passagenwerk.*[12] As such, Benjamin's interest in surrealism and his programmatic intent for the Arcades Project are integrally related: for it was the surrealists who had hit upon an, as it were, exoteric, secularized conception of experience that satisfied Benjamin's early longing for transcendence without transgressing the immanent domain of this worldly experience. And it was this conception that Benjamin developed at length in his "Surrealism" essay of 1928, above all, with reference to the notion of "profane illumination," which he defines as "the creative overcoming of *religious illumination* [italics added; here we are offered an explicit self-criticism of his own previous theological dabblings] . . . a materialist, anthropological inspiration, to which hashish, opium or whatever else can serve as the introductory lesson"—if a dangerous one.[13] What the surrealists had to offer was of no small importance as far as Benjamin was concerned: a technique for transforming the mundane into the sublime. Along with *Paysan de Paris,* it was Breton's *Nadja* that proved seminal for him. "The surrealists were the first to perceive the revolutionary energies that appear in the 'outmoded,' that appear in the first iron constructions, the first factory buildings, the earliest photos, the objects that have begun to ebb from them. . . . No one before these visionaries and augurs perceived how destitution—not only social, but architectonic, the poverty of interiors, enslaved and enslaving objects—can be suddenly transformed into revolutionary nihilism," he waxes rhapsodic.[14] This is the methodological approach that would prove decisive for Benjamin's own Arcades Project. It is consequently by no means accidental that Benjamin refers to the "Surrealism" essay in letters as a type of "prolegomena to the Arcades project" as an "opaque paravent in front of the Arcades study."[15] In a manner analogous to the surrealists, he too wants in the Arcades Project "to determine the most concrete qualities of an epoch as they present themselves here and there in children's games, a building, or one of life's random situations."[16] Such concrete traits, the particulars of an epoch, were to be compressed philosophically to the point where they yielded the universal—the character of the epoch in its historico-philosophical essence. For Benjamin, like the surrealists, "the eternal would be the ruffles on a dress rather than an idea."[17]

The surrealism-interpretation bridges the gap between the earlier avowedly metaphysical-theological studies in literary criticism and Benjamin's later concern with materialist principles of research. As should be apparent, the word "materialist" is interpreted by him in a highly nominalist sense. The mediating link between the two stages, assuming they can properly be represented as such, is the search for a superior, noumenal concept of experience which inspired his Kant-critique of 1918.[18] The difference between them lies in the fact that now redemption is conceived of predominantly as a secular, collective, socio-historical phenomenon, not the privileged affair of a metaphysically inclined, elite coterie of literati. However, one must be clear about the fact that this change of emphasis in no way signaled a permanent break with the earlier metaphysical modes of analysis. Instead, Benjamin always remained mistrustful of historical materialism as a world view (just as he remained mistrustful of almost all world views considered as such); and his initial suspicions came to the fore—in somewhat apocalyptical fashion—in the 1940 "Theses on the Philosophy of History"—Benjamin's theoretical last will and testament, whose theory of history remains integrally tied to the critique of the Western doctrine of historical progress (one of the *Passagenwerk's* chief methodological concerns), yet whose substance unquestionably remains closer to his "early period" (so much for the tidy but artificial distinction between the "early" and "late" Benjamin).[19]

There is an additional, as yet unnamed theme that links the "Surrealism" essay to the Arcades Project and in fact, in the case of the 1935 Exposé ("Paris, Capital of the Nineteenth Century"), would come to play a determining methodological function: that of dream-life. The dream for Benjamin becomes an autonomous source of experience and knowledge, a hidden key to the secrets and mysteries of waking life. In no uncertain terms, dreams become the repositories of the utopian visions of humanity whose realization is forbidden in waking life; they serve as the refuge for those desires and aspirations that are denied to humanity in material life. Adorno touches on this point when he observes that for Benjamin, "the dream becomes a medium of unregimented experience, a source of knowledge opposed to the stale superficiality of thinking."[20] The fact that dreams reorganize the images of waking life in a strange and unfamiliar context suggests pronounced structural affinities with his conception of the function of dialectical images. In dreams, as Adorno has felicitously expressed it: "the absurd is presented as if it were self-evident in order to strip the self-evident of its power."[21] As such, the dream represents the realm of the possible, the non-identical, it serves to contest the pretensions to "Being-in-Itself" of the dominant reality principle. It consequently becomes the point of departure for the construction of a *new reality principle* (a point that Herbert Marcuse was later to make much of)[22] that would foreshadow the transposition of the dream-images into reality.

The central role to be played by dreams in the Arcades Project was made overwhelmingly clear in the 1935 Exposé. There, after quoting Michelet's dictum "Chaque epoch rêve la suivante," Benjamin outlines the conception of dialectical images that was intended to serve as the methodological foundation of the *Passagenwerk:*

To the form of every new means of production which to begin with is still dominated by the old (Marx), there correspond images in the collective consciousness in which the new and old are intermingled. These images are wish-images, and in them the collective seeks not only to transfigure, but also to transcend, the immaturity of the social product and the deficiencies of the social order of production. In these wish-images there also emerges a vigorous aspiration to break with what is outdated—which means, however, with the most recent past. These tendencies turn the image-fantasy, which gains its initial stimulus from the new, back upon the primal past. In the dream in which every epoch

RICHARD WOLIN

sees in images the epoch that is to succeed it, the latter appears coupled with elements from prehistory—that is to say, of a classless society. The experiences of this society, which have their storeplaces in the collective unconscious, interact with the new to give birth to the utopias which leave their traces in a thousand configurations of life, from permanent buildings to ephemeral fashions.[23]

"Utopias which leave their traces in a thousand configurations of life, from permanent buildings to ephemeral fashions"—that is, in iron constructions, panoramas, barricades, exhibitions, interiors, museums, railroads, lighting, photography, and, last but not least, the *arcades*—in other words, in the central categories of the Arcades Project itself. What Benjamin had in mind by all this is not difficult to discern. His conception equates "prehistory" with the idea of a "classless society." The collective unconscious of humanity (Jung) has somehow preserved this memory of a classless society, which awaits the proper historical moment to be unleashed. This moment has arisen with 19th century industrial capitalism. Benjamin has elected in the Arcades Project to perform for the cultural superstructure of capitalism what Marx had achieved for its economic base. For Benjamin, the superstructure represented not the immediate *reflection* of the base, but was its *expression*—in the same way that what someone has eaten is expressed and not merely reflected in his or her dreams.[24] Thus it was only by way of a rigorous analysis of the cultural sphere that the great utopian potential of capitalism could be released and made serviceable for society as a collectivity. This is precisely how Benjamin saw his task as a historical materialist researcher. Yet, what made the 19th century especially ripe for the release of the utopian images of an (originally primeval) classless society was the tremendous and unprecedented unleashing of productive forces as chronicled by Marx. For the first time the *objective possibility* had emerged of humanity casting off the chains of domination which had hitherto enslaved it and creating history consciously and freely.

Yet, for Benjamin, the sign under which this new utopian potential manifests itself is that of "ambiguity";[25] the condition is deemed ambiguous insofar as the utopian promise remains fettered, unrealized, owing to the constraint posed by the retrograde character of capitalist relations of production. In this argument, Benjamin relies on the classical Marxian dichotomy between forces and relations of production.[26] However, he escapes the determinist standpoint of orthodox Marxism by recognizing the fact that the forces of production will never of necessity explode the lagging relations of production. As in Lukács, the chief obstacle to liber-

218

ation is reified consciousness. Unlike Lukács, however, for Benjamin the latter is not a phenomenon of the workplace per se, but rather a product of the trance-like stupor into which humanity is lulled as a result of the phantasmagorical character of commodity production. Humanity has both a dream to be realized and one from which it must awake. Hence, the inherent "ambivalence" of the cultural sphere under capitalism.

To be sure, there is much that is problematical—and outright fanciful—in the conception of dialectical images advanced by Benjamin in the Exposé of 1935. The Exposé was roundly criticized by Adorno for the attempt to conceive the problem of commodity-fetishism or reification as a "fact of consciousness"; whereas, in fact, as social disorder, reification is something produced *outside of* consciousness. Moreover, the surrealist-inspired attempt to conceive the dialectical image as akin to a dream inherently ran the risk of dissipating the materialist intent of the project in irrationalist categories. "If you transpose the dialectical image into consciousness as a dream you also deprive it of that objective liberating power which could legitimate it in materialist terms," Adorno prudently warns.[27] The so-called classless society of prehistory eulogized by Benjamin, if it ever existed at all, was an oppressive society of unfreedom, not a society one would want to employ as a model. And regarding the Jungian notion that the latter idea had been somehow retained throughout history by a mythical collective unconscious, the less said, the better.

In the concluding passage of the 1935 Exposé, Benjamin confesses his belief that the "utilization of dream elements in waking is the textbook example of dialectical thought"—[28] which shows the extent to which Benjamin, even when he thought himself to be operating most consistently according to materialist principles of research, remained incapable of parting with his earlier metaphysical, speculative manner of interpretation. Here too the degree to which Benjamin viewed dreams as the cornerstone of a new emancipatory theory of experience is quite evident. Yet, there is a crucial sense in which Benjamin's conception of dream experience differs from that of the surrealists and approaches that of Freud: viz., when he remained true to his original intentions for the Arcades Project, i.e., a study of the "prehistory of the 19th century"—which was less concerned with the way in which elements of prehistory manifested themselves in the 19th century than the way in which the latter itself regressed to prehistory—he was less inclined to fetishize the manifest content of dream experience in its immediacy—as the surrealists had done—than consider the latter as an *obstacle* to emancipation (if nevertheless, an "obstacle" that pointed in a utopian direction). According to this competing conception of dream experience, it was not so much the dream itself but the *awakening therefrom* that mattered above all. As Benjamin concludes in a note from the Arcades Project, echoing the remark from the Exposé cited above: "the utilization of dream elements in awakening is the canon of dialectics."[29]

It is clear that Benjamin was overly taken with Marx's famous saying in a letter to Ruge in 1843: "the world has long been dreaming of something that it can acquire if it only becomes conscious of it."[30] At times, however, such as in the conception of dialectical images advanced in 1935, the content of dream experience seemed to be accorded a unilaterally positive function: one need merely translate the dream-image into reality to achieve the desired utopian end point. In other cases, as I have already suggested, the dream is viewed as a type of collective delusion—or better still: a "spell"—from which humanity must be awoken in order to free itself. In such instances the employment of the category tends to acquire a predominantly metaphorical rather than literal sense—and a powerful one at that. It becomes an equivalent of, as indicated earlier, the Lukácsian category of the reification of consciousness; it connotes an attitude toward historical becoming that is unconscious, passive, nature-like, and blind.

The latter, more satisfactory, approach to understanding history—and especially history under capitalism—as a dream is consistent with Benjamin's new self-styled "Copernican turn" in history writing, in which the traditional (read: German historicist) method of conceiving of history is reversed: the past is no longer valued for its own sake (i.e., for the sake of the historicist "as it really was"), but only insofar as it is relevant to the present. At this point in his thinking, the requirement of *Aktualität,* or relevance, comes to occupy center stage, and this then becomes the new canon for understanding the meaning of past historical events. Or, as Benjamin himself expresses the significance of his new turn in historiography: "Politics receives primacy over history."[31]

In this connection, two additional categories come to occupy pride of place: the categories of awakening and remembrance. The functions of both are inter-related. For only insofar as the nature of history as a spell, a trance, a dream, is reflected upon and made conscious—the task of historical remembrance—can humanity hope to awaken therefrom.

It is not as though in this version of the concept of dream-experience the dream is degraded to the level of an epiphenomenon or false consciousness *tout court*. Rather the dialectical—or, to use Benjamin's preferred epithet, *ambiguous*—character of the phantasmagorical, dream-like character of commodity culture remains. Its immediate influence is the effective integration of passive spectators into the phantasmagorical spectacle it engenders. Its deeper meaning is the yearning for utopia embodied in its appearances—such as the promise of a society of comfort, well-being, and plenty suggested by the Arcades. Benjamin expresses this idea in the following passage:

> The youthful experiences of a generation have much in common with dream experience. The historical form of the former is that of the dream. Every epoch has a side turned toward dreams, a childhood side. In the case of the previous century this side emerged very clearly in the arcades. . . . The new dialectical method of history presents itself as the art of experiencing the present as a world of awakening (*Wachwelt*) in which the dream which we call the past is brought into relation to truth. To make over the past in dream-remembrance!—Thus remembrance and awakening are intimately related. Awakening is merely the dialectical, Copernican turn of remembrance.[32]

According to Benjamin, what distinguished the 19th century was the fact that individual consciousness becomes ever more acutely self-consciousness, whereas collective consciousness sinks more and more deeply into sleep. It is only a handful of extremely conscious individuals—Baudelaire, Proust, etc.—who are capable of perceiving the advent of modernity for what is in fact—a perpetual relapse into the always-the-same of myth. Hence, it falls due to historical materialism to reverse this trend so that the insight achieved by the acutely sensitive individual consciousnesses is diffused and generalized.

Architecture and fashion, for example, represent the externalized manifestations of the collective consciousness which, according to Benjamin, "remain the equivalent of nature processes, as long as they persist in the unconscious, unformed dream-form." They stand in the cycle of the always-the-same until the collective strengthens itself.

The question remains, however, why Benjamin decided to focus on 19th century capitalism when his main interest seemed to be in the historical present; that is, why did his project reject a more contemporary historical focus when it was, it seemed, the contemporary political and cultural situation in which he was most interested?

There are several ways of answering this query. First, and perhaps most importantly, a full knowledge of the present can only be attained through knowledge of the past. Thus, in order to understand the present historical crisis, familiarity with its origins remained essential. Secondly, there is little doubt that due to the intermingling of old and new, which manifested itself in the wish- or dream-images of 19th century capitalist

221

culture, this seemed the era when emancipatory possibilities were most replete; and that over the course of time, these possibilities—or utopian memory traces—were eroded as a result of the advancing process of capitalist rationalization. In no uncertain terms, this earlier epoch acquired a privileged status in Benjamin's eyes precisely insofar as it embodied the youthful, child-like phase of capitalist development; that side turned toward *dreams:* the dreams of a qualitatively new life which appear, for example, in the writings of the utopian socialists. In this connection, it was hardly accidental that Benjamin originally intended to devote an entire chapter of the *Passagenwerk* to Fourier. "The child can do what the adult cannot," Benjamin observes at one point; "he can recognize the new. . . . Every childhood discovers these new images in order to incorporate them in the image-store of humanity."[33] It was therefore to the store of utopian images, generated in the century that witnessed the definitive emergence of industrial capitalism, that Benjamin turned in the hope of revivifying the rapidly disintegrating capacities of the contemporary historical generation to imagine a form of life qualitatively different and "other." As Adorno remarked once in a letter to Benjamin, "All reification is a forgetting."[34] Through the historical rescue or redemption of this forgotten wealth of 19th century utopian images, Benjamin sought to inspire a collective awareness concerning the possibilities for reconciled life that emerged at the dawn of the most recent historical period. For Benjamin, this act of remembrance represented a chance to awaken from the comatose sleep of a mechanistic civilization whose dreams were rapidly turning into nightmares. "For us," Benjamin explains, "the prehistorical countenance, both alluring and threatening, becomes clear in the beginnings of technique, in the lifestyle of the 19th century."[35] Hence for him, the 19th century represents, in its relation to industrial capitalism, a type of irreducible *origin,* in the sense of Goethe's *Urphänomene:* once one is familiar with this form in its monadic essence, one can extrapolate all subsequent phases of its development. Our historical distance from the 19th century alone allows its true nature to show forth; for as Benjamin remarks, "that which lies temporally nearer to us is not yet unveiled for us." And further: "just as (Sigfried) Giedion instructs us to discover the fundamental traits of contemporary buildings from the construction of 1850, we want to discover contemporary forms and contemporary life from the life and apparently inconsequential, forgotten forms of that time."[36]

"It can be seen as the methodological object of this work," confesses Benjamin, "to produce a historical materialism which has annihilated in itself the idea of progress. It is precisely on this point that historical materialism has reason to demarcate itself strictly from bourgeois habits of thought. Its fundamental concept is not progress, but actualization."[37] Herein lies an avowal of Benjamin's conviction that in and of itself historical materialism had become dysfunctional as a radical and historically adequate social theory. Yet, the dilemma penetrates even deeper than this level. For behind Benjamin's reasoning lies the belief that in its uncritical assimilation of the 18th century trust in linear, cumulative historical progress, historical materialism itself had become bourgeois. Fetishizing the theory of knowledge—and concept of experience—of bourgeois natural science, historical materialism itself had fallen victim to one of the primary illusions of modernity, and thereby lulled itself into a hopelessly false sense of security about the impending necessity of revolution in fatal disregard of the real historical and ideological obstacles facing the proletariat; which led in turn in Benjamin's day to a humiliating and ignominious defeat in face of the rise of fascism. It was precisely the awareness that, though it claimed to be a theory of liberation, historical materialism, in its proximity to "bourgeois habits of thought," had become in essential epistemological respects indistinguishable from the bourgeois ideologies it sought to vanquish, that led Benjamin to seek a new theory of the meaning of emancipation; one no longer grounded in the laws of economic necessity (for by definition, how could a condition of freedom emerge from a state of necessity—although this was precisely the solution to the problem of the possible "contingency" of freedom in the theories of "ethical life" of both Kant and Hegel), but rather in a new, non-profane theory of experience. And whether or not Benjamin's specific solution to this problem in terms of the theory of dialectical images ultimately proves serviceable for the historical materialist legacy, his formulation of the meaning of the latter in terms of a new theory of experience remains indispensable. For at the heart of this reformulation of the idea of materialism lies a recognition of the fact that "liberation" is not reducible to the question of merely changing relations of production per se; not is it simply a question of replacing private control of the means of production with state ownership. In fact Benjamin's relevance—his *Aktualität*—as a Marxist thinker resides in the fact that like his contemporary Ernst Bloch, he was capable of perceiving the meaning of emancipation in other than strictly economic terms.[38] Instead, for him the question became one of realizing a superior form of life, qualitatively different from past forms; and for that reason the theory of experience occupied center stage in his work.

In this connection, Benjamin's relevance for present attempts to reformulate a historically adequate conception of Marxism are quite apparent.

For since the early 1960s—and above all, since Paris, May '68—it has become an established fact of all reflexive discourse on the Left that the question of socialism must be one which far transcends purely political-economic considerations and instead places the totality of a way of life—from humanity's relation to nature, to sex roles, to modes of child rearing—on the agenda of the day. Walter Benjamin was one of the first thinkers on the Left to recognize the scope and importance of such concerns; and his attempt in the Arcades Project to render a surrealist-derived theory of experience serviceable for the ends of materialist historiography speaks precisely to this concern. Like Bloch, Benjamin sought to emphasize the spiritual and normative aspects of the struggle for emancipation, those aspects that had fallen victim to the occlusion of forgetting amid the historical preoccupation with "socio-economic determinants."

The a-conceptual principle of montage, the elevation of the trivial and everyday to a position of preeminence, the notion of dreams as the embodiment of an alternative, utopian reality principle, were the inheritances from surrealism that Benjamin attempted to incorporate into the theoretical foundations of his *Passagenwerk*. Yet, his suspicions concerning the viability of the materialist world view as an adequate hermeneutic key to understanding the relationship between historical past and present only reinforced his early conviction that the world could not be explained in secular terms alone; that the sense of wholeness and unity that he wished to restore to the world of historical fragmentation entailed of necessity recourse once again to the theological principles that had inspired his youthful work. To be sure, flirtation with the idea of a theological basis for the Arcades Project was a relatively late manifestation, one that seemed to go hand in hand with the worsening historical situation. But as Benjamin's trust in the ability of the secular forces of history to lead to a state of reconciliation increasingly waned, he found his historical thinking increasingly in need of theological supplementation. As he acknowledges in a terse but revealing simile: "My thinking is related to theology like a blotter is to ink. It is fully absorbed by it."[39] Horkheimer, in a detailed letter of March 16, 1937, tried to stay Benjamin's hand in this connection. "Past injustice has occurred and is done with. The slain are really slain. . . . If one takes the idea of openendedness *(Unabgeschlossenheit)* seriously, then one must believe in the Last Judgment. . . . The injustice, horror, and pain of the past are irreparable."

Yet, to a thinker as steadfastly devoted to questions of redemption as Benjamin, this verdict concerning the past remained radically unacceptable. Only a theory of history that provided for the *rectification* of past injustices and horrors, which somehow guaranteed that the dead would not have given their lives in vain, could satisfy his deep-seated longing for a form of reconciliation and fulfillment that would be total. His response (never sent) to Horkheimer reads as follows:

> The corrective to this way of thinking lies in the conviction that history is not only a science but also a form of remembrance. What science has 'established' can be modified by remembrance. Remembrance can make the openended (happiness) into something concluded and the concluded (suffering) into something open-ended. This is theology; however, in remembrance we have an experience which forbids us from conceiving of history fundamentally a-theologically, despite the fact that we are hardly able to describe it in theological concepts which are immediately theological.

It is this act of remembrance in relationship to past historical suffering and injustice that forms for Benjamin a quasi-theological guarantee or impetus for revolution. And thus he speaks of a "secret agreement" that the present generation has with the preceding generation; an agreement that establishes a "temporal index" between the two that serves as the basis for the redemption of the past by the present.[40] In this sense, the Arcades Project, as a labor of remembrance, seeks to resurrect, through the constellation of the dialectical image, those endangered and forgotten traces of utopian potential—now-times as Benjamin refers to them in the "Theses on the Philosophy of History"—discovered in the ruins of 19th century life, that provide a concrete, material basis for the hope for a reconciled existence. In want of its historical realization, the sublimity of the *telos* admits of depiction only as a distant, Messianic posit. For Benjamin, the unrealized semantic potentials of the past provide the essential signposts towards the surmounting of that-which-merely-is in the direction of what has never-yet-been.

Rice University

NOTES

1 For more on this distinction, see the Introduction by Hannah Arendt to Walter Benjamin, *Illuminations* (New York, 1969), pp. 1-58.

2 The *Passagenwerk* consists of the following materials: two early outlines from the late 1920s (when the work's title was "Pariser Passagen: Eine dialektische Feerie"), when it

was conceived of as merely as extended essay rather than a book; an unpublished essay from the same period, "Der Saturnring, oder etwas von Eisenbau"; 50 pages of notes for this early phase of the work; then (after a hiatus of about five years) the first formulation of the new, book-length version of the project, the 'Exposé' of 1935 ("Paris, Capital of the Nineteenth Century"); although he still referred to the work as the *Passagenarbeit* or Arcades Project at this point, the arcades themselves only figured as one of six parts of the work as a whole; a 1939 version of the 'Exposé' bearing the same title but composed in French (likely at the request of Max Horkheimer who had hoped to interest an American patron in publishing the work); and finally, the chief part of this work-in-progress, 900 pages of "Notes and Materials" whose compilation coincided with the later version of the project (i.e., from 1935 until Benjamin's death in 1940).

3 For an excellent discussion of this problem, see Andrew Arato, "The Neo-Idealist Defense of Subjectivity" *Telos* 21 (Fall, 1971), pp. 108-164.
4 Benjamin, *Reflections* (New York, 1978), pp. 312 ff.
5 Benjamin, *Illuminations,* p. 86.
6 Cf. Benjamin, *Origin of German Tragic Drama* (London, 1977), pp. 177-179 '*Trauerspiel*' means play of lamentation or sorrow.
7 In my book *Walter Benjamin: An Aesthetic of Redemption* (New York, 1982), I discuss Benjamin's transition "From Messianism to Materialism" in Chapter 4, pp. 107-137.
8 Cf. Benjamin, *Reflections,* p. 191.
9 See Benjamin's response to Adorno's criticism of his "Paris of the Second Empire in Baudelaire," in *Aesthetics and Politics* (London, 1977), p. 136. See also my discussion of their disagreement over this matter in *Walter Benjamin: An Aesthetic of Redemption,* pp. 198-207.
10 See the essays on Baudelaire and Leskov in *Illuminations.*
11 Cf. Benjamin, "The Task of the Translator," in *Illuminations,* p. 69.
12 Cf. Benjamin, *Briefe* II, p. 663.
13 Benjamin, "Surrealism," in *Reflections,* p. 179.
14 *Ibid.,* p. 182.
15 Benjamin, *Briefe* II, pp. 496, 489.
16 Cited in Theodor Adorno, Foreward to Rolf Tiedemann, *Studien zur Philosophie Walter Benjamins* (Frankfurt, 1973), p. 8.
17 Benjamin, *Briefe* II, p. 489.
18 Recently translated into English as "On the Program of the Coming Philosophy," *Philosophical Forum,* XV: 1-2 (Fall-Winter, 1983-84), pp. 41-51; this volume, pp. 1-12.
19 For a good indication of the considerable—though by no means unbroken—continuity between these two phases, one might compare the 1940 "Theses on the Philosophy of History" in *Illuminations* with the "Theologico-Political Fragment" (circa 1920) cited in note 4 above.
20 Adorno, *Über Walter Benjamin* (Frankfurt, 1970), pp. 53-54.
21 *Ibid.* p. 54.
22 Cf. Marcuse, *Eros and Civilization* (Boston, 1955).
23 Benjamin, *Charles Baudelaire: A Lyric Poet in the Era of High Capitalism* (London, 1973), p.
24 Cf. Benjamin, *Passagenwerk* I (Frankfurt, 1982), p. 495.
25 Benjamin, *Charles Baudelaire,* p. 159.
26 Cf. Karl Marx, *Contribution to the Critique of Political Economy* (Moscow, n.d.), pp. 20-21.
27 Adorno, *Aesthetics and Politics,* p. 111.

28 Benjamin, *Charles Baudelaire,* p. 176.
29 Benjamin, *Passagenwerk* I, p. 580.
30 Marx, letter to A. Ruge, in *The Marx-Engels Reader,* R. Tucker, ed., (New York, 1978), p. 15. Benjamin makes explicit references to this letter on p. 583 of the *Passagenwerk.*
31 Benjamin, *Passagenwerk* I, p. 491.
32 *Ibid.,* p. 490-491.
33 *Ibid.,* p. 493.
34 Adorno, *Über Walter Benjamin,* p. 59.
35 Benjamin, *Passagenwerk,* p. 571.
36 This volume, p.
37 This volume, p.
38 In this connection, see Bloch's incredibly prescient Marx-critique, "Karl Marx, Der Tod, und die Apokalypse," in *Geist der Utopie* (Frankfurt, 1923), pp. 291-346. English translation in Bloch, *Man on His Own* (New York, 1970), pp. 31-72.
39 Benjamin, *Gesammelte Schriften* I (3) (Frankfurt, 1978), p. 1235.
40 Benjamin, "Theses on the Philosophy of History," in *Illuminations,* p. 254. The citation in full reads as follows: "The past carries with it a temporal index by which it is referred to redemption. There is a secret agreement between past generations and the present one. Our coming was expected on earth. Like every generation that preceded us, we have been endowed with a *weak* Messianic power, a power to which the past has a claim. That claim cannot be settled cheaply."

WALTER BENJAMIN AND FRANZ ROSENZWEIG

STÉPHANE MOSES

As early as 1965, Gershom Scholem pointed out the influence of the German-Jewish philosopher Franz Rosenzweig and his work The *Star of Redemption* on Walter Benjamin's thought.[1] Since that time, however, the question of Benjamin's reception of Rosenzweig's work has not been reconsidered. This gap in Benjamin scholarship was probably due largely to the fact that Rosenzweig's work had long been studied only partially, and that until recently no fundamental delineation of his philosophy existed. On the other hand, thanks to the new edition of Benjamin's complete works, a considerable portion of the drafts, sketches, and paralipomena of his published works is now available, so that it has become possible to examine thoroughly the question of Rosenzweig's influence on Benjamin.

I

The Star of Redemption, which Rosenzweig wrote in the six months from the fall of 1918 through the spring of 1919, is based on the perception that the first World War refuted the central idea of Western philosophical tradition, viz. that the world is rational, that it obeys laws which are also the laws of reason, and that this logos-ruled universe assigns man his harmonious place in the general order of things. Rosenzweig belongs not to this philosophical tradition, which culminated in German Idealism, but to a system of relationships that seemed to him more firmly tied to experimental fact and human reality: religious thought, first manifested in the mythical world view of the ancient Greeks and later embodied in the belief systems of Judaism and Christianity. Although each of these three belief systems carried equal weight in the overall structure of *The Star of Redemption,* in the end it is Judaism which is the keystone and zenith of Rosenzweig's total system.

Mythical thought comprehends reality in its three fundamental elements: God, Man, and World. These elements, which reflect the immediate reality of human existence, are also the basis of Judaeo-Christian consciousness, which remains rooted in reality thanks to these three elements. At the same time, however, both Judaism and Christianity effect a radical negation of the pagan categories. Only this negation makes it possible to relate these three elements to each other. Comprehensible for mythical thought only in their original distinctness, in Judaism and Christianity each of these three elements goes beyond itself and becomes linked to the two others: God transcends himself for the sake of World and Man in the act of creation and in the moment of revelation; Man devotes himself to World, and this action, directed toward a radical utopia, signifies redemption.

For Rosenzweig, these three relationships constitute the real structure of human experience: *creation* is man's immediate experience that the existence of the world is good; *revelation* characterizes the experience of the divine word in prayer and ritual; *redemption* is that utopian effort upon which all human action is based.

These three relationships, unknown to classical philosophy, are immediately present in language. It is language—not abstract thought—which is the medium through which human experience is expressed. Through a close analysis of Biblical texts, Rosenzweig shows that narrative categories (symbolized by the pronoun *He*) correspond to the experience of creation, that the categories of dialogue (*I and Thou*) correspond to the experience of revelation, and that the categories of a communal language (*we*) correspond to the experience of redemption.

The idea of man outlined by Judaism and Christianity, a being open to a double Other—the world (his neighbor) on the one side, and God on the other—takes on an objective form in the two models of redemption, the two utopias, which are part of the two religions. Rosenzweig decodes the meaning of these two conceptions of redemption not through their theoretical doctrines but through their forms of community life, their calendars, liturgies, and institutions.

Both are characterized by the creation of a "holy time," which enables them to escape the vicissitudes and contingencies of history and live in eternity. Christianity, however, participates in both temporality and eternity; it is always "on the way to the Cross," for it is bound to the destinies of nations, accompanies them along the path of history, and attempts to bring them gradually to the Kingdom of God. This also means that Christianity must itself exist in the imperfection of history. The Jewish nation, however, lives outside history in the constantly renewed eternity of its

229

liturgical year, and it shows mankind an example of community life which is removed from the process of historical development. The relationship between Judaism and Christianity may also be described as that of a paradigm to its attempted historical realization; both belong to a total representation of truth.

II

In my examination of Benjamin's reception of Rosenzweig's work, I will consider three points: First, to what extent was Benjamin familiar with Rosenzweig's work? Second, which elements in Rosenzweig's thinking especially attracted Benjamin? And finally, how did Benjamin evaluate these elements? In what form does one find them in his own work?

These questions must be considered in reference to those passages in Benjamin's work that directly allude to Rosenzweig. But there are also certain themes in Benjamin's work that show a striking affinity to Rosenzweig's thought, even though direct influences can be ruled out completely for simple chronological reasons (in the case of Benjamin's early works on the philosophy of language) or are impossible to prove, as in the case of his late works on the philosophy of history. When lacking obvious proof, I will here attempt at least to compare the similarities of Benjamin's and Rosenzweig's thought.

In his autobiographical work *Walter Benjamin: The Story of a Friendship,* Gershom Scholem reports that he first told Benjamin of Franz Rosenzweig's religio-philosophical work *The Star of Redemption* in the June of 1921, several months after its publication.[2] Five months later, Benjamin wrote Scholem that he had "taken [Rosenzweig's book] up again" but hadn't yet "read it through."[3] A year later, on December 30, 1922, Benjamin wrote of a visit he had made to the failing Rosenzweig in Frankfurt. Here he remarked: "Conversation was very difficult, since I always had to take the initiative without knowing the book well enough."[4] Shortly after Rosenzweig's death, the *Frankfurter Zeitung* invited Benjamin to write on Rosenzweig's thought. Benjamin refused the offer, in part, as he wrote to Scholem, because at the time (January, 1930), "such an assignment . . . [lay too far outside his] present field of interest,"[5] but probably also because he did not feel confident enough to discuss a work which he did not know well. The pithy phrase, with which he attempted to summarize the content of *The Star* in 1929—" victorious breakthrough of the Hegelian dialectic into Hermann Cohen's *Religion der Vernunft aus den Quellen des Judentums'' (Rational Religion from a Jewish Source)*[6]—does not lead us to assume a very thorough knowledge of

Rosenzweig's work. Even in 1931, Benjamin referred to himself as *Am Hoorez* (Hebrew for a lay, ignorant person) in relation to Rosenzweig. Nevertheless, in 1935, he wrote that *The Star* had "much occupied him."[7]

Today it is possible to ascertain more clearly to what degree Benjamin actually was familiar with *The Star*. An examination of Benjamin's recently published notes and drafts shows clearly that all his quotations of Rosenzweig, both in his published and unpublished writings, are taken from two short passages in Part One and one passage, thematically closely related to the others, in Part Two. These are the China passages in Books II and III of Part One, from which Benjamin includes fragments in his Kafka essay of 1934 and the discourse on the metaethical self and the silent hero of Greek tragedy in Part One, which, along with the theory of modern tragedy from Part Two, Book Three, is important for *The Origin of German Tragic Drama*. All other allusions to Rosenzweig, for example in the first draft of his essay of Brecht ("What is Epic Theater?"), refer to these sections of Part One of *The Star*.

We can thus assume that Benjamin had most thoroughly studied Part One of *The Star*. He had probably read the other two sections, in which Rosenzweig develops his philosophy of language, history, and religion, but with the exception of the one section of Part Two just mentioned, he never alludes to them in any currently published text.

III

Benjamin's work which most clearly exhibits the influence of certain aspects of Rosenzweig's thought is undoubtedly *The Origin of German Tragic Drama,* written during the period (1923-25) directly following the time in which Benjamin had begun to study *The Star*. Benjamin proceeds from Rosenzweig's antithetical description of classical and modern tragedy, in order to set up the essential opposition between tragic drama and tragedy. Schopenhauer, writes Benjamin, "conceived of tragedy as *Trauerspiel*" and therefore misunderstood its essence. "This diffuse appreciation, inhibited by anti-historical metaphysics, needs only to be contrasted with a few sentences by Rosenzweig for us to realize what progress has been made in the philosophical history of the drama with the discoveries of this thinker."[8] For Rosenzweig, the hero of Greek tragedy embodies man in his original state, in his elemental self-assertion. Rooted only in himself, separated from the gods and his fellow man, the classical hero symbolizes tragic solitude and also the actuality of pagan man. Rosenzweig calls this primitive core of man his "self"; the self that wills only its own daemon, independent of every ethical norm, is "metaethical." It is silence, though, that characterizes the tragic hero as the embodiment of the metaethical self. Based on long scenes in Aeschylus' dramas in which only the chorus speaks while the hero is mute, Rosenzweig suggests that silence is the only language which completely suits the metaethical self: "By keeping silent, the hero breaks down the bridges which link him to God and the world."[9]

Benjamin speaks of the speechlessness and the infantility of the tragic hero. As a commentary to the passage in *The Star* in which Rosenzweig develops his thesis on tragic silence, Benjamin writes: "The speechlessness of the tragic hero, which distinguishes the main figure of Attic tragedy from every later type, has made Rosenzweig's analysis of 'metaethical man' a foundation of the study of tragedy."[10]

The theory of the infantility of the tragic hero had already been posited by Benjamin himself in his essay "Fate and Character" in 1919. There he wrote:

> In tragedy, pagan man realized that he is better than his gods, but this realization strikes him dumb . . . There can be no discussion that the moral world order will be reestablished, but rather that moral man, dumb and speechless—for as such can he be called hero—will arise in the quaking of that tortuous world. The paradox of the birth of genius in moral speechlessness, moral infantility, is the sublime element of tragedy.[11]

Even Rosenzweig's concept "metaethical man" seems to have been anticipated to a certain degree by Benjamin in this essay: "Establishing the concept of character will therefore also have to be related to a function of nature and will be as far removed from ethics and morality as fate is from religion."[12]

These parallels, to which Benjamin himself referred in a footnote to his book on German *Trauerspiel*,[13] probably explain the attraction which Rosenzweig's theory had for him. But even more intriguing for Benjamin must have been his discovery of Rosenzweig's concept of "modern tragedy." In Rosenzweig's system, classical and modern tragedy are as fundamentally opposed to one another as the two worlds of paganism and revelation, to which they belong and whose systems they symbolically represent. Revelation, i.e., the religious world of Judaism and Christianity, is for Rosenzweig the inversion of all ideas of paganism. Inversion here does not mean a revocation, or taking back, but rather an opening-up of that which is closed in the pagan world, an emergence of God, World, and Man from isolation into a relationship with each other. Through their relatedness to each other, they gain new meaning. The medium of this emergence is language, itself inherently an unlocking of that which is closed and thus an instrument of revelation. And so the mute hero of classical tragedy becomes the speaking hero in the world of revelation: "By disclosing himself as a whole man, man has then become directly visible and audible . . . No longer is he a rigid marble statue like the tragic hero of antiquity—nay, he speaks . . . This hero awakens to full vitality in the dialogue under the eyes of the spectator."[14]

Unlike the classical hero, the modern hero does not embody the metaethical self but always portrays a different aspect of man, thrown into the world and constantly in conflict with it. All characters of modern tragedy are "different from each other";[15] each of them expresses a special and therefore limited perspective on the world. In order to overcome this limitation of its characters, modern tragedy must necessarily aspire to a form that allows the hero to attain "a perfect consciousness of himself and the world."[16]

This is the point which may well have been of decisive importance for the development of Benjamin's theory of *Trauerspiel*. "Modern tragedy," writes Rosenzweig (and Benjamin quotes this passage in his chapter on "'Tragedy' old and new") "aims for a goal which is quite alien to classical tragedy: for a tragedy of the absolute man in his relationship to the absolute object."[17] Further: "Those tragedies where the hero is to all intents and purposes a philosopher—for antiquity a perfectly fantastic idea—these philosophic dramas are unanimously regarded by us as the heights of modern tragedy altogether: Hamlet, Wallenstein, Faust."[18] But in the philosophical tragedy, the hero "only confronts the Absolute knowingly"; the true modern hero "as a point of convergence for all tragic characters" would be one "who has experienced the Absolute and who now, out of this experience, lives within the Absolute." This hero "is none other than the saint. The tragedy of the saint is the secret longing of the tragedian. Perhaps it is a longing that cannot be fulfilled."[19] Here Benjamin remarks: "The 'modern tragedy', whose deduction from ancient tragedy is the object of these sentences, bears—it hardly needs saying—the far from insignificant name: *Trauerspiel* . . . The *Trauerspiel* is confirmed as a form of the tragedy of the saint by means of the martyr-drama."[20]

It should be noted that unlike this influence of Rosenzweig's *Star* on Benjamin's book on German *Trauerspiel,* which, though limited, was emphasized by Benjamin himself, the "Epistemo-Critical Prologue" shows no demonstrable influence of Rosenzweig in either the published version or the until recently unpublished portions of the manuscript ("the most esoteric text that Benjamin ever wrote"[21] according to the editor of his collected works). The concepts "elements" and "revelation" that appear here are indeed basic categories of *The Star,* but Benjamin uses them here in a completely different sense and in a context completely alien to *The Star.* "Elements," which for Benjamin represent the result of the dissolution of things through the concept, are used in *The Star* to describe the three basic objects of reality, i.e., God, World, and Man. The concept "revelation" is understood by Benjamin as the paradisial, original condition of language before its degradation to a profane medium of communication, while Rosenzweig, to whom the idea of a mystical decline of language is completely alien, explains the concept "revelation" in a narrower sense as the experience of God in the human soul, and in a broader sense as the religious worlds of Judaism and Christianity.

After the publication of his book on baroque *Trauerspiel,* Benjamin refers specifically to Rosenzweig's theory of the tragic hero three times, in the years 1928-1932, during his so-called "Marxist" period. In a review of 1928 of Julien Green's novel *Mont Cinére,* in which the heroine has fallen prey to a special form of tragic hubris—a frozen "pride of possession"—Benjamin cites a passage from *The Star.* In this passage, Rosenzweig speaks of that moment of personal development in which man ceases to be a mere "individual" (a part of the natural and social world), in order to be reborn as a "self." Whereas Rosenzweig (Benjamin calls him here a "great contemporary thinker") relates this "birth of self" to erotic experience,[22] Benjamin calls attention to the first stirrings of greed in the soul of the heroine.[23] In an article from 1932 on Andre Gide's drama *Oedipus,* Benjamin returns to the "muteness" of the hero of Greek tragedy[24] and mentions again the passage from *The Star* that he had quoted in the book on baroque *Trauerspiel:* "The tragic hero has only one language which completely corresponds to him: precisely keeping silent."[25]

The most interesting modification of Rosenzweig's theory of tragedy, however, appears in the first draft of Benjamin's essay "What is Epic Theater?" (1931). Here Benjamin attempts to characterize Bertolt Brecht's drama as a renewal of the tradition of baroque drama and to recognize in the Brechtian hero a re-embodiment of the "non-tragic hero," as he had appeared in the mystery plays of the Middle Ages and later in Gryphius, Lenz, Grabbe, and *Faust,* Part II. Benjamin defines this non-tragic hero as the "thinking one," a character who, unlike the heroes of Greek tragedy, attempts to understand his fate and imbue it with meaning or, as is the case with Brecht, who critically analyzes and takes issue with his environment. Benjamin himself acknowledges that this "thinking hero'' corresponds to Rosenzweig's ideal hero of modern tragedy, "who is for all intents and purposes a philosopher,"[26] and praises Franz Rosenzweig along with Georg Lukács as one of those thinkers—the "best of his contemporaries"—who recognized early that the "paradoxical existence [of the ideal hero] on stage is redeemed through our actual existence."[27] With Benjamin's recognition of the modern hero as individual man searching for the meaning of his existence, he restates Rosenzweig's idea that the conception of philosophical tragedy is possible only in the world of Judeo-Christian revelation, for only then does the hero break through to real language, i.e., dialogue, a form of language in which at least the possibility of an answer to every question exists, especially to those questions directed toward God. That Benjamin found it necessary in 1931, especially in an essay on Brecht, to refer to Rosenzweig, and that he mentions him together with Lukács, seems to indicate that he thought it important to stress, and perhaps not without a certain provocative emphasis, the continuity of his Jewish inspiration.

IV

The strangeness of the association of Rosenzweig and Brecht, of the world of Jewish tradition with that of Marxism, also characterizes Benjamin's inclusion of two quotations from *The Star* in his essay on Kafka of 1934. These allusions are peculiar in that they refer to an idea which is quite peripheral with *The Star* as a whole. In the first part of the work, Rosenzweig attempts to contrast the religions of the Far East as archetypes of an imperfect world view with the pagan perfection of ancient Greece. While classical mythology created a world view in which the opposed principles of being and becoming, the one and the many, affirmation and negation are united in a living reality, the religions of India and China stopped short: Brahmanism sees everywhere infinite, indeterminate being; Taoism, on the other hand, teaches the silent entrance into the multiplicity of appearances. In a series of notes made between 1928-1931 for a projected essay on *The Trial* and for a radio lecture on Kafka given in July, 1931, Benjamin quotes two passages from *The Star* in which Rosenzweig describes the Chinese world as exclusively material, particular, and concrete, a world in which the Greek concept of *logos* would be unthinkable and defines the Chinese—in contrast to the classical hero—as completely without character. Benjamin copied these Rosenzweig passages again as he prepared his Kafka essay for the *Jüdische Rundschau* in 1934 and actually incorporated them into his text. The striking thing about these two passages is that they perform no essential function in the extremely complex structure of the Kafka essay, so that their inclusion seems both unmotivated and arbitrary. The "China" theme to which they refer is brought in anyway, and far more convincingly, at the mention of Kafka's posthumous work (published in 1931) *The Great Wall of China.* If anywhere, then particularly here, Benjamin could have explained the relationship between Kafka's narrative technique—which he sees as dispensing with psychological analysis and describing each gesture with minute particularity—and the gestic character of Chinese theater, unless Benjamin were employing these references to Rosenzweig less for their content than for the name of their author and the connotations associated with this name.

Benjamin's study of Kafka was accompanied by a conflict on two fronts—with Scholem and with Brecht—as to the meaning of Kafka's works. The entire Kafka essay is dominated by the tension between these two interpretations, the metaphysical-theological and the materialistic-critical. Benjamin himself in a letter to Scholem characterized their dialectical interrelation as the "crossroad of the way of his thought."[28] That Benjamin should choose to appeal to Rosenzweig, who was for him so closely tied to Jewish theological thought, in order to introduce the Chinese themes of his essay, which unequivocally call Brecht to mind, is a paradoxical figure of thought used to emphasis this dialectical tension and at the same time hint at its possible solution.

On the other hand, however, Benjamin did not fail to notice that the connection he was trying to establish between Rosenzweig's *Star* and Brecht's epic theater was indeed somewhat forced and problematic. In the second section of his Kafka essay of 1934 "A Childhood Photograph," he cites the passage from *The Star* in which Rosenzweig attempts to relate the character so defined to the figures which appear in Kafka's "Nature Theater of Oklahoma." Kafka's work "harks back to the Chinese theater, which is a gestic theater." Benjamin introduces this observation with the comment "No matter how one may convey it intellectually, this purity of feeling may be a particularly sensitive measurement of gestic behavior,"[30] a qualification which lends a purely associative and hypothetical character to this entire train of thought. If we look at the thematic structure of the Kafka essay, the "elemental purity of feeling" which, according to Rosenzweig, characterizes the Chinese may well be associated with the figure of Karl Rossman, the young hero of the novel *Amerika,* and later with the fools, assistants, and students, the only ones in Kafka's work, Benjamin writes, for whom there is hope of redemption. In a later note (1935) to the revision of the essay, Benjamin emphasizes that the redemption motif has nothing to do with the subject of acting and theater. At this time he clearly dispenses with the relationship to the Brecht theme. Instead, Benjamin now interprets the action of the Nature Theater as a "play for redemption," by which he seems to refer again to Jewish mystic thought. Following the Rosenzweig citation regarding the "elemental purity" of the Chinese is here:

> Oklahoma appeals to this purity of feeling. The title "Nature Theater" conceals a double meaning. Its secret meaning is that everyone in this theatre plays himself. Dramatic talent, which we might think of as a primary concern, is of no importance . . . Here we are reminded of those playful characters in Kafka's work, who want nothing from middle-class society and for whom there is boundless hope. These are the assistants. We exist as they do, and as nothing more in the Nature Theater: assistants in a play which however is bound to a decision process in a strange way that Kafka only slightly defines. Who cares if it takes place at a racetrack. Much seems to hint that this is a play about redemption.[31]

V

Walter Benjamin's first work on the philosophy of language was written in 1916. This was his essay "On Language as Such and the Language of Man," in which he develops a mystical theory of language influenced by the German Romantics and the ideas of Hamann. He begins with an exegesis of the story of creation in the first chapters of Genesis. In this work, which remained unpublished throughout his lifetime and was written two years before *The Star,* Benjamin anticipates some of Rosenzweig's most important trains of thought. On the other hand, the possibly more important differences in the two theories of language hint at the real difference in inspiration that distinguishes Rosenzweig's thought from Benjamin's. The same is true for the two essays on the theory of translation, published almost simultaneously: Benjamin's "The Task of the Translator" (1923), which was the foreword to his translation of Baudelaire's *Tableaux Parisiens,* and Rosenzweig's afterword to his translation of *Sixty Hymns and Poems of Jehuda Halevi* (1924).

In his essay, written in 1917, "The Program of Coming Philosophy," Benjamin states, "All philosophical knowledge finds its only expression in language," and a rejuvenation of philosophy can "come about only through a relationship of epistemology to language."[32] This idea, according to which philosophical truth is not to be found in a pure system of abstract concepts but reveals itself rather in the structure of language, is the common background against which we can understand Benjamin's and Rosenzweig's theories of language. When Rosenzweig writes in *The Star,* "Where the world is, there is language, the world is never without the word—it exists only in the word. Without the word, the world would not be,"[33] he is expressing a thought which appears as a central intuition in all Benjamin's early works on the philosophy of language, albeit in many forms.

In Benjamin's first essay on the philosophy of language and in Rosenzweig's *Star,* language becomes the medium through which truth reveals itself—its very nature is revelation. In other words, the structure of reality is identical with the structure of language. As a guarantee of this identity, Benjamin and Rosenzweig refer to the Biblical story of creation. The basic thought common to both of them is that God created the world through the Word: the world of things and the world of man spring from the same source, and a structural identity exists between them. But the narrower interpretation of the story of creation is very different for each of them. Firstly, Rosenzweig bases his theory on a general concept of creation on which the first chapter of Genesis is based, whereas Benjamin supports the idea of creation as a process, whose stages are described in the first three chapters of Genesis. In the process of the development of language, Benjamin differentiates between three distinct stages: first, divine creation, when the world is created through language and each physical thing is completely identical to its corresponding divine word of creation. This is followed by the stage in which Adam himself named things. This original language, while not creative as is divine language, is in no way arbitrary. Quite the opposite, this paradisial human language is the exact translation of the mute language of things. It is perfect as human language and possesses its own magic, which later reveals itself only in the most sublime poetry. But language loses its immanent magic at the moment of the Fall, which signifies "the birth of the human word."[34] From this point on, language no longer directly mirrors reality; it is debased to a mere medium of communication. "At the Fall," writes Benjamin, "immediacy in the communication of the concrete, the name, forsook man, and he fell into the abyss of the mediacy of all communication, the word as medium, the vain word in the abyss of idle talk."[35]

It is characteristic of the fundamental difference between Benjamin's and Rosenzweig's theories of language that the communicative function of language, which for Benjamin represents the main symptom of its degeneration, is for Rosenzweig identical with its quality of revelation.

For Rosenzweig, language is the organon of revelation, precisely because it mediates between individuals, because the act of speaking means the opening-up of the subject, previously locked in himself, to the Other. Language is revelation in so far as it is "the language of souls, the self-revelation of human inwardness."[36] The two ideas—Benjamin's language *of* revelation and Rosenzweig's language *as* revelation—are diametrically opposed. For Benjamin the revelatory character of language is set in a mythical past, while for Rosenzweig it is always present. This difference is deeply rooted in the metaphysical presuppositions of the two theories: basic experience for Benjamin as a young man was that of a devalued and degenerate reality, whose desolation was even more obvious against the background of an original, but now lost, perfection. The religious categories of creation and revelation are experienced here in their negativity, while for Rosenzweig, precisely in their religious positivity, they are two cornerstones of the experience of reality.

From a strictly linguistic analysis one could say that Benjamin sees language as a system of signs that conceals itself as a secret but ideal center behind the endless multiplicity of concrete utterances, while Rosenzweig begins with the concrete instance of speaking, in which language realizes its existing possibilities. The polarity is particularly evident in the different ways in which Benjamin and Rosenzweig treat the utopian dimension of language. Both see human language as imperfect but redeemable. Benjamin understands its imperfection as the break-down of the original correspondence between word and thing that has reduced language to an endless approximation, to a helpless groping that he calls "over-naming." Rosenzweig, on the other hand, does not attack the essence of language per se, but rather the existing proliferation of languages: "Nothing shows so clearly that the world is unredeemed as the diversity of languages."[37] But at the same time, both Rosenzweig and Benjamin point to the existence of a linguistic dimension which overcomes this principle of multiplicity—translation. Rosenzweig writes, "Language goes all the way back: man became man when he first spoke. And still to this day there is no language of mankind; that will only come to be at the end. Real language, however, is common to all between beginning and end, and yet is a distinct one for each; it unites and divides at the same time."[38] The diversity of language does not, of course, end with translation; translation actually presupposes this multiplicity. The "language of man," in the sense Rosenzweig gave to this phrase, can therefore not be a particular language but represents a limiting concept which expresses the ideal of universal communication. This ideal can be realized only on the other side of the multiplicity of languages—in silence.

This paradoxical thought, that the very essence of language is fulfilled at the point where it no longer exists—in silence—is key to Benjamin's theory of language. But in our concrete reality which is governed by speaking, communication without words is a non-attainable ideal, and so translation, which at least overcomes the claim to exclusivity that characterizes every linguistic utterance, is the only way to approach the utopia of a universal language. Tinged with mysticism, this theory of translation as the way to redemption is found both in *The Star* and in Benjamin's essay "The Task of the Translator," but its meaning is very different for each of them. For Rosenzweig, the utopian meaning of translation is that it makes communication possible:

> But this universal intelligibility cannot be attained in silence. It requires the intervention of speech. Through the miracle of language, speech overcomes the resistance of the Today that once was, and, though separated by language, still is as of today. It is the first effect of the spirit to translate, to erect a bridge between man and man, between tongue and tongue.[39]

For Benjamin, on the other hand, who sees the use of language as an instrument of communication as witness to its degeneration, the utopian function of translation is in no way that it aids communication, but that it attempts to recreate the original essence of language as magic. Behind every concrete text is an ideal meaning which is hidden by the linguistic utterance. It is the duty of the translator to free this hidden meaning, he writes in "The Task of the Translator." The utopian goal of all translations is then to unveil, in the course of history, the common world of meaning which is concealed behind all linguistic utterances. This truth should be understood less as content than as form: "a language of truth, the tensionless and even silent depository of the ultimate truth which all thought strives for . . . this language of truth is—the true language. And this very language, whose divination and description is the only perfection a philosopher can hope for, is concealed in concentrated fashion is translation."[40] This concept of a "pure language" which Benjamin could borrow from the theoretical linguistic texts of French symbolist Stéphane Mallarmé, but which originates in Jewish (linguistic) mysticism, shows how firmly Benjamin's early work in the philosophy of language is based on a systematic use of the three concepts of creation, revelation, and redemption—the three basic categories of Jewish theology, which also determine, albeit with very different presuppositions, the structure of Rosenzweig's *Star*.

VI

In Benjamin's last publication "On the Concept of History," one of his central themes is a radical criticism of the idea of progress. Benjamin proceeds here implicitly from the observation that European history in the 20th century appears as a succession of catastrophes which have made a naive belief in linear progress impossible and expose historical development as an unchecked process of destruction. Here he was probably thinking of the destruction of pre-war society, the break-up of society and state under the Weimar Republic, of Hitler's seizure of power, the horrors of the Nazi regime, and the war which had recently begun. Just as decisive for his rejection of the idea of progress in this text, written in 1940, was probably his despair at the signing of the Hitler-Stalin Pact.[41] In the years 1938-39, he had placed his last hope in the coming revolution. If there is no linear progress in history, however, true revolution can no longer be seen as the final moment in a constantly progressive evolution, but only as a sudden emergence of an infinitely higher and deeper form of life, which explodes the "continuity of history" and brings a radical upheaval of reality.

Gershom Scholem saw in this violent interruption of history "the secularization of a Jewish apocalypse."[42] It was Benjamin's explicit intention in this last meditation on time and history to portray the historical-political revolutionary utopia as the modern metamorphosis of the theological concept of redemption. For true revolutionary and theological thought, historical progress is nothing more than a tedious repetition of constant sameness, while redemption can only be experienced as a sudden standstill of history. The criticism of the idea of progress is based, for Benjamin, upon a fundamental rejection of profane temporality, which is experienced as form without content; every moment is as empty and meaningless as the previous or following one. "The idea of the progress of the human race in history," writes Benjamin, "cannot be separated from the idea of development moving through homogeneous, empty time. Criticism of the idea of this development must form the basis of criticism of the idea of progress *per se*."[43]

The recently published drafts to the *Arcades Project* show that Benjamin's criticism of the idea of progress was influenced decisively by Hermann Lotze's work *Mikrokosmos,* published in 1864.[44] But Rosenzweig had also developed-astonishingly similar patterns in *The Star*. There he relates the idea of progress to the concept of a homogeneous temporality, in which nothing radically new can happen, in contrast to Messianic time, which can be experienced only in the anticipation of the final goal (which Benjamin would have characterized as *sprunghaft,* constituting a break with what went before):

> Even if there is talk of "eternal" progress—in truth it is but "interminable" progress that is meant. It is a progress which progresses permanently on its way, where every moment has the guaranteed assurance that its turn will yet come, where it can thus be as certain of its coming into existence as a transpired moment of its already being-in-existence. Thus the real idea of progress resists nothing so strongly as the possibility that the "ideal goal" could and should be reached, perhaps in the next moment, or even this very moment . . . The future is not future without this anticipation and the inner compulsion for it, without this "wish to bring about the Messiah before his time" and the temptation to "coerce the kingdom of God into being;" without these, it is only a past distended endlessly and projected forward. For without such anticipation, the moment is not eternal; it is something that drags itself everlastingly along the long, long trail of time.[43]

Although Rosenzweig is not mentioned at all in the *Arcades Project,* we cannot exclude a continued influence of *The Star,* even during Benjamin's later years in Paris.

The ideal of an historical path to redemption, a sudden jump into utopia, which leads to the present moment a taste of eternity—as is the case for mystics—could also have been derived from Rosenzweig. In a note to the "Historico-philosophical Theses" Benjamin writes, "The Messiah interrupts history; the Messiah does not appear at the end of a development."[46] Later he writes, "The Messianic world is the world of universal and integral actuality."[47] This understanding of redemption as the realization of utopia corresponds to Rosenzweig's definition of eternity as a future which can already be experienced today:

> Eternity is not a very long time; it is a tomorrow that could as well be today. Eternity is a future which, without ceasing to be future, is nonetheless present. Eternity is a today which is, however, conscious of being more than today.[48]

Eternity, or redemption, for Rosenzweig, stands in opposition to historical development; it can be attained only through a radical break with historical continuity. This is the break which Benjamin describes as a "Messianic cessation of happening"[49] and which is alluded to in his concept of a "present, which, as a model of Messianic time, comprises the entire history of mankind in an enormous abridgment"[50] (p. 265). He speaks also of the "notion of a present which is not a transition, but in which time stands still and has come to a stop"[51] (p. 264). Rosenzweig had developed a surprisingly similar thought in a letter from 1917, in which he speaks of the opposition between "today which is only a bridge to tomorrow, and the other today, which is the spring board to eternity."[52] Since Rosenzweig's letters had been published by Schocken in 1935, Benjamin could have read them in Paris and might have been influenced by this idea, which in any case was close to his own thoughts.

Of course one could object that Rosenzweig's concept of redemption has a purely religious meaning, while for Benjamin, it is a question of the realization of a political utopia—the revolution. Such an objection would, however, ignore the central tenet of the theses "On the Concept of History." i.e., that theology is the hidden truth of history. The theological concepts which Benjamin uses are not to be understood as metaphors for political concepts; rather the political-historical is merely the outer appearance of a hidden theological dialectic. This is especially true for the function which Benjamin ascribes to the cult in the process of redemption. The sole hope that remains for us today, he writes, exists in the past. Redemption can come only when we dare to awaken suddenly the endlessly deep and rich experience of the past and experience it in the present as new. Benjamin calls these chosen moments "days of remembrance," "holidays," and also "monuments of the consciousness of history." In his Baudelaire essay he had written, "an experience which seeks to establish itself cyclically is possible only in the realm of the cult."[53] The ahistorical experience which interrupts and thereby subverts the hopelessness of historical temporality is precisely the ritual experience:

Even though chronology places regularity above permanence, it cannot prevent heterogeneous, conspicuous fragments from remaining within it. To have combined recognition of a quality with the measurement of the quantity was the work of the calendars in which the places of recognition are left blank, as it were, in the form of holidays.[54]

Even clearer is his reference to Jewish chronology in a note which follows the Baudelaire essay: "The Sabbath, the year of the Jubilee, are interruptions."[55]

Here the parallel with *The Star* is especially striking. Rosenzweig saw historical, profane temporality, in which nothing radically new can happen, as opposed to sacred time, which determine the experience of all religious social forms, but in particular those of Judaism and Christianity. Sacred time, which depends on the periodic recurrence of holy days, brings the endless procession of natural and historical time to a standstill and thus creates a sort of eternity in the middle of time:

> Only the stroke of bells establishes the hour, not the ticking of the pendulum . . . In the hour, then, one moment is recreated, whenever and if ever it were to perish, into something newly issued and thus imperishable, into a *nunc stans,* into eternity. . . . The cycles of the cultic prayer are repeated every day, every week, every year, and in this repetition, faith turns the moment into an "hour," it prepares time to accept eternity"[56]

For Benjamin, the emergence of these "monuments of the consciousness of history"—to be understood both as religious holidays and political revolutions—marks the process of Messianic redemption, in which "the broken will be joined together."[57] In a remarkable parallel to Rosenzweig's phenomenology of the religious time as the true dimension of redemption (*The Star,* Part III), Benjamin wrote in his Baudelaire essay that this poet has "assembled the days of remembrance into a spiritual year."[58] In the "Historico-philosophical Theses," he uses yet another image taken from Jewish mysticism: "sparks of hope" were concealed in the past, which modern consciousness of redemption pulls together and fans into a flame.[59] That "time of the Now," which is shot through with "chips of Messianic time"[60] is based on this experience of the present which suddenly refers back to the past. We may ask here whether it is merely a coincidence that Rosenzweig's letter mentioned above, in which he contrasts the "today which is only a bridge to tomorrow" with "the other today, which is the spring board to eternity," uses the same metaphor in his reference to spiritual attitudes in which "sparks of the Messianic Today may be scattered."

Translated by Deborah Johnson

NOTES

1 Gershom Scholem, "Walter Benjamin," *Judaica,* 2 (Frankfurt: Suhrkamp, 1970), p.219.
2 Gershom Scholem, *Walter Benjamin: The Story of a Friendship,* trans. Harry Zohn (Philadelphia: Jewish Publication Society, 1981), p. 101.
3 Walter Benjamin, *Briefe,* ed. Gershom Scholem & Theodor W. Adorno (Frankfurt: Suhrkamp, 1966), p. 281.

4 Benjamin, *Briefe*, p. 296.
5 *Ibid.*, p. 508.
6 Walter Benjamin, *Gesammelte Schriften*, III, ed. Rolf Tiedemann & Hermann Schweppenhäuser (Frankfurt: Suhrkamp, 1974), p. 170. Hereafter cited as *GS*.
7 Benjamin, *Briefe*, p. 670.
8 Benjamin, *The Origin of German Tragic Drama*, trans. John Osborne (London: New Left Books, 1977), pp. 111-12.
9 Franz Rosenzweig, *The Star of Redemption*, trans. William Hallo (New York: Schocken, 1970), p. 77.
10 Benjamin, *GS*, I, p. 286.
11 Benjamin, "Fate and Character," *Reflections* (New York: Harcourt Brace Jovanovich, 1978), pp. 304-11. *GS*, II, p. 175.
12 Benjamin, *GS*, II, p. 176.
13 *Ibid.*, p. 418.
14 Rosenzweig, *The Star*, p. 209.
15 *Ibid.*, p. 210.
16 *Ibid.*, p. 210.
17 *Ibid.*, p. 210.
18 *Ibid.*, p. 210.
19 *Ibid.*, p. 211.
20 Benjamin, *The Origin of German Tragic Drama*, p. 113.
21 Benjamin, *GS*, I, p. 925.
22 Rosenzweig, *The Star*, p. 71.
23 Benjamin, *GS*, III, p. 147.
24 *Ibid.*, p. 394.
25 Rosenzweig, *The Star*, p. 71.
26 *Ibid.*, p. 210.
27 Benjamin, *GS*, II, p. 523.
28 Benjamin, *Briefe*, p. 260.
29 Rosenzweig, *The Star*, p. 75.
30 Benjamin, "Franz Kafka," in *Illuminations*, trans. Harry Zohn, ed. Hannah Arendt (New York: Harcourt, Brace & World, 1968), p. 120.
31 Benjamin, *GS*, II, p. 1262.
32 *Ibid.*, p. 168.
33 Rosenzweig, *The Star*, p. 371.
34 Benjamin, *GS*, II, p. 153.
35 *Ibid.*, p. 154.
36 Rosenzweig, *The Star*, p. 185.
37 *Ibid.*, p. 295.
38 *Ibid.*, p. 110.
39 *Ibid.*, p. 366.
40 Benjamin, *Illuminations*, p. 77.
41 Scholem, *Story of a Friendship*, p. 221.
42 Scholem, *Judaica*, p. 223.
43 Benjamin, *GS*, I, p. 701.
44 Benjamin, *GS*, V, pp. 599-603.
45 Rosenzweig, *The Star*, p. 277.
46 Benjamin, *GS*, I, p. 1243.
47 *Ibid.*, p. 1285.
48 Rosenzweig, *The Star*, p. 224.

49 Benjamin, *Illuminations*, p. 265.
50 *Ibid.*, p. 265.
51 *Ibid.*, p. 264.
52 Rosenzweig, *Briefe*, ed. Ernst Simon & Edith Rosenzweig (Berlin: Schocken, 1935), p. 158.
53 Benjamin, *GS*, I, p. 1176.
54 Benjamin, *Illuminations*, p. 186.
55 Benjamin, *GS*, I, p. 1176.
56 Rosenzweig, *The Star*, pp. 290-92.
57 Benjamin, *GS*, I, p. 697.
58 Benjamin, *Illuminations*, p. 185.
59 Benjamin, *GS*, I, p. 695.
60 Benjamin, *Illuminations*, p. 265.

THE INTEGRITY OF THE INTELLECTUAL: IN MEMORY OF WALTER BENJAMIN[1]

LEO LOWENTHAL

Walter Benjamin ends his essay on surrealism with the image of "an alarm clock that in each minute rings for sixty seconds."[2] The essay appeared in 1929 and bore the subtitle: "The Last Snapshot of the European Intelligentsia." I can hardly find a better way to express the feelings that accompanied my preparations to make these remarks in memory of Benjamin. As I studied his work once again, it seemed indeed as if a clock were incessantly sounding an alarm: Benjamin's immediacy today set off uninterrupted shocks in my mind and demanded constant alertness.

Although I begin my lecture with similarities that link Benjamin and myself biographically and intellectually, I am quite conscious of the danger that by drawing such parallels I may appear to be placing myself on the same level as he. This is not my intention. Being only eight years his junior, I might be tempted to overestimate the value of mere survival and thus see things with which I myself am associated as more important than they are in the context of the fate experienced by a generation of German and German-Jewish intellectuals. When I speak of the past, i.e. of Benjamin's *Oeuvre* and the memory of his person, this past becomes entirely present. Benjamin's fundamental themes—and it is not by coincidence that I mentioned his essay on surrealism first—have accompanied me throughout my life.

While outliving someone cannot alone legitimize delivering a memorial address, I do not feel too uncomfortable with this task. In the relationship Benjamin and I had—direct or indirect—there was no discord. Elsewhere, I have spoken out with indignation against insinuations from some quarters concerning allegedly humiliating dependence and intellectual suppression in Benjamin's dealings with the Institute for Social Research. Gershom Scholem, who was to speak to you today, no longer lives. In his memory, I would like to read a few words from his long letter to Benjamin dated 6 and 8 November 1938. Scholem mentions a visit to our institute in

247

New York, and he reports: "I think the people of the institute have every reason to frame you in gold, even if only in secret. In our brief but harmless encounters, I had the impression that people like Marcuse and Lowenthal realize this as well." There could never be any doubt on that score.

The extent of my involvement with Benjamin's publications in our *Zeitschrift für Sozialforschung* is meticulously documented in the notes to his collected works. I will refer here to just one episode regarding his essay "The Paris of the Second Empire in Baudelaire," published posthumously by Rolf Tiedemann in 1969. As managing editor of the journal my main concern was to publish this essay—part of a planned book on Baudelaire and belonging to the *Arcades Project*—as soon as possible. There were repeated delays, due in part to Benjamin himself and in part to the complex correspondence between Adorno and Benjamin. On 3 August 1938, Gretel Adorno wrote to Benjamin from the Adorno's vacation address: "And now to the most important matter, to Baudelaire. Leo Lowenthal was visiting us here for a couple of days when your letter arrived. We thought it best to show him your letter right away. Lowenthal was beside himself (about the delay) and declared that he absolutely must have the essay for the next issue."

Then, when the essay arrived, Adorno and I had an argument, which I lost. In a letter to Benjamin dated 10 November 1939, Adorno wrote: "The plan is now to print the second chapter ("The *Flâneur*") in full and the third ("Modernism") in part. Leo Lowenthal in particular supports this emphatically. I myself am unambiguously opposed to it." At that point—and this played a role in the subsequent attacks on Adorno—the essay was not accepted for publication, undoubtedly under Adorno's influence.

He presented his objections bluntly, as the correspondence between him and Benjamin shows. Although Adorno's criticism upset him at first, Benjamin did put it to use very productively. On the basis of the revision suggested by Adorno, a new, independent essay emerged, "Some Motifs in Baudelaire," which we published in 1939, in the last German-language volume of the journal. In his essay Benjamin explicitly connected his themes of the crisis of aura and the loss of experience, which he had treated separately in his "Storyteller" and "Work of Art" essays. This decisive shift of emphasis in turn gives the first Baudelaire essay, whose publication I had supported, a weight of its own. Both essays are included in the edition of Benjamin's collected works.

No one who is familiar with the German intelligentsia in the Weimar Republic and in exile will be surprised to learn that my circle of friends and acquaintances overlapped extensively with Benjamin's, among them Adorno, Hannah Arendt, Ernst Bloch and Kracauer, Horkheimer and Lukács, Buber and Rosenzweig. These names also signify both definite identity and confrontation, for example in early relations with the *Jüdisches Lehrhaus* initiated by Buber and Rosenzweig. There was another almost tragicomic parallel between our two biographies: Benjamin's *Habilitation* for the University of Frankfurt in 1925 was rejected on the basis of objections by *Germanistik* Professor Franz Schultz and could not be rescued without the intervention of Hans Cornelius, philosopher and teacher of Horkheimer and Adorno. A year later the same thing happened to me. In 1926 my *Habilitation* as well—it was in the philosophy department—was prevented by Schultz in his capacity as dean, while Cornelius supported it most warmly.

As far as I remember, I did not yet know Benjamin personally in 1925, although the themes of our work already overlapped at important points. Benjamin was greatly interested in Franz von Baader, whose religious philosophy of redemptive mysticism and solidarity with society's lowest classes is evident in Benjamin's "Theses on the Philosophy of History." I wrote my dissertation in 1923 on Baader's philosophy of society. Today I gather from Benjamin's review of David Baumgardt's biography of Baader, and from his correspondence with Scholem, that the vanguard position of this conservative, Catholic philosopher of religion— particularly his political morality and his affinity to the suffering and to those who suffer in this world, to the "Proletärs", as he called them—had similarly attracted us both. Although at the time I was very radical politically, I did with a clear conscience write my dissertation about a conservative thinker. It strikes me as an additional confirmation that Benjamin had also been engrossed in this man's writings.

Another more important convergence of our intellectual interests lies in the unyielding critique he conducted in 1931 of the enterprise of literary history and criticism. My first essay in the first issue of the *Zeitschrift für Sozialforschung* in 1932 had borne the title "On the Social Standing of Literature." It passed judgment in its own way on then-current university and literary practices with its apolitical, *lebensphilosophischen,* and ultimately reactionary categories. It is hardly by coincidence that these same *Germanisten* Benjamin had taken to task were not treated gently in my essay either. I am ashamed to admit that I was not then familiar with Benjamin's essay, which had appeared in *Die Literarische Welt*. Otherwise I would certainly have cited it positively, if not considered my own essay superfluous. Benjamin was quite familiar with my later socio-literary work. I know for example that he was at first hardly enthusiastic

LEO LOWENTHAL

about my essay on Knut Hamsun, in which I analyzed Hamsuns's novels as anticipations of fascist mentality. But he did appreciate my study on the reception of Dostoyevsky in Germany. In these and other studies, I had practically begun formulating the now familiar questions of reception theory and *Wirkungsgeschichte,* admittedly with clear emphasis on the critique of ideology. That coincided with Benjamin's interests. He wrote to me from Denmark on 1 July 1934:

> In the few days since my arrival in Demark, the study of your Dos-
> toyevsky essay was my first undertaking. For a variety of reasons it
> has been extremely productive for me, above all because after your
> preliminary reference from Conrad Ferdinand Meyer, I have before me
> a kind of reception history that is precise and in its precision—as far as
> I know—entirely new. Until now such attempts have never got beyond
> a history of the literary material because a sensible formulation of the
> essential questions was lacking. An early and interesting venture,
> which admittedly has little to do with your observations, would be
> Julian Hirsch's "Genesis of Fame," with which you are probably fa-
> miliar. In many ways, Hirsch never gets beyond the schematic. In your
> work one is dealing with the concrete historical situation. One is, how-
> ever, surprised to learn just how contemporary the historical situation
> is in which the reception of Dostoyevsky has taken place. This surprise
> gives the reader—if I may infer from myself to others—the impulse that
> sets his own thinking into motion. . . . A certain continuity of class
> history right through the World War has been made visible for Ger-
> many, as well as its mythic apotheosis in the aura of cruelty. In addi-
> tion illumination came for me from a remote source, falling all the more
> revealingly on figures and trends from which literary history's usual
> point of view was able to derive but little. I found that the discourses
> on Naturalism confirmed what you had intimated to me in Paris; they
> met with my unqualified agreement. What you say about Zola is par-
> ticularly interesting. . . . To what extent has this German reception of
> Dostoyevsky done justice to his work? Is it not possible to imagine any
> other based on him, in other words is Gorky's the last word on this
> subject? For me, since I have not read Dostoyevsky for a long time,
> these questions are presently more open than they seem to be for you.
> I could imagine that, in the very folds of the work into which your
> psychoanalytical observations lead, elements can be found that the
> petit-bourgeois way of thinking was unable to assimilate.

My essay on C. F. Meyer and his reception as ideologue of the German

250

national *grand bourgeoisie* appeared to Benjamin of some importance in another context as well. In his efforts to place an article about our institute in New York with the culturally conservative emigré journal *Maß und Wert,* it occurred to Benjamin to stress the aesthetic contributions as politically unthreatening, and yet secretly to point out their political significance to those who knew how to read. As he informed Horkheimer on 6 December 1937, he wanted to try and introduce, through the back door so to speak, the radical critique of the present that informed the *Zeitschrift.* He wrote "The closest we might come to it [the sphere of actuality] would be to approach it in aesthetic disguise, i.e. by way of Lowenthal's studies on German reception of Dostoyevsky and on the writings of C. F. Meyer."

But the most profound contact between Benjamin and myself I see in reflection upon the dichotomy, which has never been resolved and resists resolution, between political, secularized radicalism and messianic utopia—Benjamin's concept of *Jetztzeit* [now-time], intended to explore the homogeneous continuum of history and the notion of unending progress. In this messianic-marxist dilemma, I am wholly on Benjamin's side, indeed I am his pupil. Like him, I initially came into close contact with the idea of the complementarity of religious and social motives through Hermann Cohen's school in Marburg. But exactly like Benjamin, I later realized that the way of Hermann Cohen's Neo-Kantianism leads into a bad infinity.

The Jewish assimilation into the liberal philosophical tradition (with or without socialist bias) was all the more futile since intellectual liberality remained something foreign in Germany. Just as the German university and later the fascist state drove him away, Benjamin was from the outset never at peace with the institutions of the cultural establishment. Was it prophetic instinct that the school desk, the first institution he confronted, suggested to him the law that would govern his life? In the section "Winter's Morning" from his book *A Berlin Childhood around Nineteen Hundred,* he writes ". . . There [in school], once I made contact with my desk, the whole tiredness, which seemed to have vanished, returned tenfold. And with it the wish to be able to sleep my fill. I must have wished that wish a thousand times, and later it was actually fulfilled. But it was a long time before I recognized that fulfillment in the fact that my every hope for a position and a steady income had been in vain."

In a letter to Scholem dated 13 July 1938, Benjamin says of Kafka: "In order to do justice to the figure of Kafka in its purity and its peculiar beauty, one must never forget: it is the figure of one who has failed." These words apply to Benjamin himself, not only in the tragic sense that

251

he took his life when he was not yet fifty years old (is this his childhood wish to sleep his fill being tragically fulfilled?), but also in the more positive sense that in Benjamin's life and in his work the suffering of the species—of which he spoke in his most significant book—is constantly reproduced. It is impossible to determine—and it makes no difference today—to what extent Benjamin consciously or half-consciously brought about his failure and to what extent it was determined by the historical space in which he had to live. World War I, inflation, expulsion, exile and internment in France—these facts outline the historical context clearly enough. But his integrity as an intellectual remains decisive in the motif of failure. He was never really able to decide upon a bourgeois profession. The educated bourgeoisie, and even the less well educated, could have asked maliciously: What in fact was Benjamin's profession? Even the attempts he made in this direction are not really believable, perhaps he did not quite believe in them himself. He certainly did not follow his father's wish that he establish himself in the business world. His *Habilitation* was turned down, he never held a steady position as editor for the *Frankfurter Zeitung* or for any publisher, and finally an attempt to secure a position at the University of Jerusalem went awry. The thought of leaving, by the way, was never free of ambivalence for him. And so from 1933 on, he repeatedly promised Scholem that he would move to Jerusalem and repeatedly put off going. He stayed in France until the last minute. In his letters to Adorno and to Horkheimer, it becomes clear that he conceived of the *Arcades Project* as a commitment that could be brought to completion only in Europe, in fact only in Paris. Would the only refuge he seemed once to have decided upon, the home that beckoned, namely membership in the *Institut für Sozialforschung,* the emigration to the United States that had been planned to the last detail, the move in with the rest of us in New York, would that have been a satisfactory solution for him? He did not live to see it. What a cruel allegory of failure!

Were there a Benjaminian fate, it would be that of the racial intellectuals of the Weimar Republic and that which followed. He himself was most aware, not only in terms of his own person, but also in his theoretical-political analysis of the intellectual, that there was no such thing as "free-floating" intellect—an idealized concept fashionable at the time in Karl Mannheim's coinage; no such thing as the so-called classless intellectual; no such thing as the "organic" intellectual à la Gramsci, nor even any such thing as the so-called intelligentsia. (Benjamin thoroughly disliked the word.) He knew that, in a bitter sense, the intellectual is homeless. As a German intellectual, he experienced that homelessness first-hand and paid tribute to France, in whose intellectualism he trusted. In a brief note in the *Literarische Welt* in 1927, he said the following about the French Association of Friends of the New Russia: "The problematic in the situation of the intellectual, which leads him to question his own right to exist while at the same time society denies him the means of existence, is virtually unknown in France. The artists and authors are perhaps not any better off than their German colleagues, but their prestige remains untouched. In a word, they know the condition of floating. But in Germany, soon no one will be able to last whose position [that of an intellectual] is not generally visible." In his programmatic essays about French intellectuals, for example in the essay on surrealism cited above or in the article first printed in our journal, "On the Current Social Position of the French Author," Benjamin criticized attempts to restore to intellectuals an independent status without commitment, stressing by contrast experiences of radical politization. One must grasp the paradoxical definitions together: "untouched" and "largely visible." The latter points to the necessity of taking a political stand, the former to maintaining the integrity of the intellectual. In the crisis, the intellectual remains "untouched" in his integrity when, instead of withdrawing into the ivory tower to timeless values, he takes a stand.

"Untouched" in the sense of *noli me tangere* is a fitting word for Benjamin's social stand as an intellectual. His urbanity concealed a willfulness of commitment that used even his urbanity as a weapon. In the genteel elegance of his manner and his epistolary style, Benjamin let his counterpart know that lines had been drawn, lines that would not allow an infringement upon his integrity. He had to pay for that. The intellectual marketplace in both Western and Eastern Europe understood Benjamin's intentions precisely. The *Frankfurter Zeitung,* in spite of its liberality and the occasional hospitality it showed the avant-garde, refused to publish the polemic essay "Left Melancholy," in which Benjamin settled accounts with pseudo-radicals. For him, their radicalism was nothing more than "leftist theater" for the consumption of the educated bourgeoisie, who used this radicalism-by-proxy to put distance between themselves and society's real political and moral problems whenever they paid their conscience money—which committed them to nothing at all—at the box office and the book store. Benjamin received similar treatment from the other side as well: the truncation—tantamount to rejection—by the *Great Soviet Encyclopedia* of his marvelous Goethe essay, the genuine radicalism of which was unbearable to the manipulative Soviet cultural policy, speaks volumes.

Was he a pariah? The ragpicker—no one wants to "touch" him—about whom Benjamin has a good bit to say, especially in the Baudelaire essay, knows no disguise, plays no roles. The ragpicker is as he is, stigmatized and yet independent. What he has given up, and what society would not allow him, is mimicry, playing up to the stronger of opposing forces, to those who dominate in society. Mimicry is, as I see it, one of the most perceptive categories for categorizing what is phony, false—false consciousness, false politics, cowardly attempts to find cover. Just think of that passage in his review of Kästner's volume of poetry, which sparked his essay "Left Melancholy," in which Benjamin in a single breath pinions both the feudal mimicry of the lieutenant in the Imperial Austrian Reserves and the "proletarian" mimicry of the disintegrating "leftist" intellectual: The reserve lieutenant of the bourgeoisie, crushed after World War I, who finds a futile resurrection in the Nazi empire; the leftist melancholic who fetches his tidy fees from the bourgeois press while trying to secure the sympathies of radicals internationally, and who ultimately disappears quite helplessly in the witch's cauldron of the nineteen-thirties—these are far removed from the failure of Benjamin with his Angelus Novus-like view of the ruins of history. Benjamin remains on the side of marginality, of negativity, he remains the figure on the fringe who refuses to take part. With his persistence in saying no—the "salt of refusal," as he called it in his essay on George—he becomes what I am tempted to call the esoteric figure of the intellectual. Most of what has been said about the definition of the intellectual—sociologically, anthropologically, and in terms of cultural politics—amounts to nothing before the figure of Benjamin, who is exactly what intellect should be: independence in a self-imposed exile. Hence every attempt to reduce him to a formula, in order to fit him into someone's convenient set of categories by rushing to label him messianic or Jewish or marxist or surrealist, was bound to fail. To use a fitting expression of W. Martin Lüdke's, what remains is the "difference," the idiosyncratic, the endless searching; what remains is the unrelenting, sorrowful gaze.

That can be seen precisely in his essay about Karl Kraus. In less than flattering terms, Kraus rejected the essay as a psychological portrait of himself. In reality, Benjamin's essay is autobiographically inspired: testimony for marginal existence and against mimicry, testimony of the relentlessness of the ever-watchful court of judgment, daily a Last Judgment. What a shame that Karl Kraus did not understand it.

The following words on Kraus appear in that essay: "Kraus accuses the law in its substance, not its effect. His charge is the betrayal of justice by law."[3] The linguistic tensions between *Recht* (right) and *Gerechtigkeit* (justice), *Recht* and *Gericht* (court), that perpetually convening "Last

Judgment" are decisive for Benjamin. Perhaps I can make that clearer with two quotes. The first is Schiller's sentence, which has been quoted to death: "World history is the world's court of judgment." The other is by Ibsen: "Writing means holding a day of judgment, judgment over oneself." Neither Schiller's nor Ibsen's formulations could have been acceptable to Benjamin; they are overcome dialectically. If history is the world's court of judgment (and Hegel agrees that it is), then the victors have won not only the spoils, but they have declared themselves on the right side of the law. In Benjamin's great formulation, "History has always been written by the victors." Schiller's bourgeois idealism, according to which the world court will have the final word, but only as an "idea," has always been reconcilable—tragically, as they say—with the continued existence of bourgeois society. And that is what Max Horkheimer and Herbert Marcuse mean with their concept of affirmative culture. Surely Ibsen's phrase about holding a day of judgment is an indictment against the ideology of the individual in individualistic, bourgeois society, But since he assigns to writing and to the writer a role in which the writer preempts truly autonomous human existence and thereby the passive observer or reader as recipient of his guilt appears to be redeemed with him, the monadology of class society is neither converted nor overcome in revolutionary form.

Burkhardt Lindner, to whom I showed a first draft of this talk, wrote me, adding:

> Benjamin's use of "court" stands in radical rejection of "right" (law). He criticizes so-called positive right as a rationalization for dominance and violence; it lays claim to justice only erroneously. Justice must be applied to the individual, to the particular. Justice is the messianic emergence or the purifying, profane power of revolutions. Correspondingly, Benjamin also rejects the notion of world history as world court. Only the revolutionary interruption of history or the messianic cessation of history can disrupt the repressive continuum and pass judgment over what has been.

In the concept of "court of judgment" of which Benjamin becomes the advocate, the motifs of political radicalism and historical materialism are combined with the messianic element of Judaism. This constellation of political radicalism, messianism, and Judaism is characteristic of Benjamin. In the volume of material on his theses "On the Concept of History,"[4] one finds passages like this: "Each moment is a moment of judgment upon certain moments that preceded it." Or this: "Without some sort of test of a classless society, the past is nothing more than a jumbled collection of facts. To that extent, every conception of the present participates in the conception of the Final Judgment."

At this point, I would like to return once more to the association between Walter Benjamin and the representatives of critical theory. Sometimes it even extended to similarities in formulation. An example: in Horkheimer's programmatic article "Traditional and Critical Theory" published in the *Zeitschrift für Sozialforschung* in 1937, these words occur: "The intellectual is satisfied to proclaim with reverent admiration the creative strength of the proletariat and find satisfaction in adapting himself to it and in canonizing it. He fails to see that such an evasion of theoretical effort (which the passivity of his own thinking spares him) and of temporary opposition to the masses (which active theoretical effort on his part might force upon him) only makes the masses blinder and weaker than they need be."[5] Nearly ten years earlier, in 1929, Benjamin had written: "The intellectual adopts a mimicry of proletarian existence without this linking him in the least with the working class. By doing so, he tries to reach the illusory goal of standing above the classes, especially to be sure that he is outside the bourgeois class." And later, in his 1938 essay about our institute in *Maß und Wert,* he cites that passage from Horkheimer's essay, adding: "The imperial nimbus in which the expectants of the millenium have cloaked themselves cannot be dissipated by the deification of the proletariat. This insight anticipates the concern of a critical theory of society."

Benjamin, like the rest of us, had to go through the painful process of recovering, theoretically and emotionally, from the disappointments dealt us by the history of the soviet republic and the communist movement from the mid-twenties on. As I formulated it once before, we felt that we had not abandoned the revolution, but rather that the revolution had abandoned us. Thus arose the disastrous situation of which Jörg Drews speaks in a review of the Benjamin/Scholem *Correspondence:* "The cruel dilemma, namely through which categories and by means of which future-directed group the antifascist intellectual might find orientation, was the central problem for Benjamin after 1930." It was the central problem for all of us.

Here it becomes clear once again why Benjamin's original confidence in the Marburg Neo-Kantianism, which attempted to unite Kant's moral system with a socialist conception of progress, ultimately had to be disappointed. Since I underwent a similar development myself about ten years later, I am particularly moved even today by what Benjamin says about that. There is a passage in the drafts of the theses "On the Concept of History," from which I quoted before, in which Benjamin connects the critique of neo-Kantianism with his critique of social democratic thought—linking them in the concept of endless progress, the ultimately quietist attitude of the average socialist. By contrast, Benjamin holds up his certainty of the always-waiting presence of the messianic spark. It reads:

> In the notion of the classless society, Marx secularized the notion of the messianic age. And that was good. The trouble arises in that social democratic thought raised that notion to an "ideal." That ideal was defined in the neo-Kantian teaching as an "endless task." And this teaching was the school philosophy of the Social Democratic Party. . . . Once the classless society was defined as an endless task, then the empty and homogeneous future was transformed, so to speak, into an anteroom in which one could wait more or less sanguinely for the appearance of the revolutionary age. In reality there is not a single moment that does not carry with it *its own* revolutionary opportunity.

Benjamin had already spoken of the necessity of overcoming neo-Kantianism in his significant, short review, dated 1929, that he named "Books that Have Stayed Alive." He cites *History and Class Consciousness* by Lukács, among others, and about Franz Rosenzweig's *Star of Redemption* he says: "A system of Jewish theology. As remarkable as the work itself is its genesis in the trenches of Macedonia. Victorious incursion of Hegelian dialectic into Hermann Cohen's *Religion of Reason*."

Here we come once more to the third element I spoke of, in addition to the messianic and the political: the Jewish. Some of us long defined its essential role in our development. In retrospect this must be corrected. After all, Benjamin in his time and I in mine came into contact with positive Jewish influences as a result of our protest against our parents—Benjamin through his encounter with Scholem, I myself through the friendship of the charismatic Rabbi Nobel, the Buber-Rosenzweig circle and the *Jüdisches Lehrhaus,* which later became important for Benjamin as well.

The utopian-messianic motif, which is deeply rooted in Jewish metaphysics and mysticism, played a significant role for Benjamin, surely also for Ernst Bloch or Herbert Marcuse as well as for myself. In his later years, when he ventured—a bit too far, for my taste—into concrete religious symbolism, Horkheimer frequently said (and on this point I agree with him completely) that the Jewish doctrine that the name of God may not be spoken or even written should be adhered to. The name of God—it is not yet fulfilled—perhaps it will never be fulfilled. It is not for us to determine if, when, and how it will be fulfilled for those who come after us. I believe that the essential thing about practical socialism that so shocked us is the idea that one is permitted to plan for someone else. The notion of something perhaps unattainable, perhaps unnameable, but which holds the messianic hope of fulfillment—I suppose this idea is very Jewish; it is certainly a motif in my thinking, and I suppose it was for my friends as well—but quite certainly it was for Benjamin a shining example of the irrevocable commitment to hope that remains with us "just for the sake of the hopeless."

In the sixth of his "Theses on the Philosophy of History," Benjamin writes: "Only that historian will have the gift of fanning the spark of hope in the past who is firmly convinced that *even the dead* will not be safe from the enemy if he wins. And this enemy has not ceased to be victorious."[6] Now that the edition of Benjamin's collected works is completed, the publishing house and the group responsible for it can collectively regard themselves as the writers of Benjamin's history. It will remain a concern to all of us, especially those younger than we, to define his gift to us from the enemy (and Benjamin never made it easy for us—that, too, a gift). The enemy comes in many guises, such as the paltry accusation that the appearance of a classic-type edition is a burial ceremony that puts Benjamin firmly and finally into his coffin—and we all know that, particularly in Germany, while being considered a classic may mean hours of nostalgic leisure reading, it also means ritual quoting and being forgotten. Yet the philosopher of a negative theology, the architect of history as ruins in temporal and atemporal space, the thinker of the contradiction (whether intentionally or not, he himself not free of contradictions), the traveller on Hegel's path of positive negation is entirely safe from the fate of a German classic. This cannot touch Benjamin, and indeed he has already survived the enemy.

Berkeley, California

Translated by David J. Ward

NOTES

1 This essay was first presented as a lecture in July, 1982, during a colloquium in Frankfurt on Walter Benjamin, sponsored jointly by Suhrkamp Verlag and the University of Frankfurt. The essay has been re-translated especially for this volume.

2 "Surrealism," Walter Benjamin, *Reflections*, trans. Edmund Jephcott (New York: Harcourt Brace Jovanovich, 1978), p. 192.

3 "Karl Kraus," *Reflections*, p. 255.

4 Cf. *Materialien zu Benjamins Thesen "Über den Begriff der Geschichte*," ed. Peter Bulthaup (Frankfurt: Suhrkamp, 1975).

5 "Traditional and Critical Theory," trans. Matthew J. O'Connell, in Max Horkheimer, *Critical Theory* (New York: Herder and Herder, 1972), p. 214.

6 "Theses on the Philosophy of History," Walter Benjamin, *Illuminations*, ed. Hannah Arendt, trans. Harry Zohn (New York: Schocken Books, 1969), p. 255.

WALTER BENJAMIN IN ENGLISH:
A BIBLIOGRAPHY OF TRANSLATIONS

GARY SMITH

BOOKS

Illuminations, ed. Hannah Arendt, trans. Harry Zohn. New York: Harcourt, Brace & World, 1968. Includes: "Unpacking my Library," "The Task of the Translator," "The Storyteller," "Franz Kafka," "Max Brod's Book on Kafka," "What is Epic Theater? [Second revision]," "On Some Motifs in Baudelaire," "The Image of Proust," "The Work of Art in the Age of Mechanical Reproduction," "Theses on the Philosophy of History."

Illuminations, 2nd ed., ed. Hannah Arendt, trans. Harry Zohn. New York: Schocken Books, 1978. Excludes: pp. 141-44 of "Max Brod's Book on Kafka" from the first edition, retitling the remainder "Some Reflections on Kafka."

Charles Baudelaire: A Lyric Poet in the Era of High Capitalism, trans. Harry Zohn. London: New Left Books, 1973. Includes: "The Paris of the Second Empire in Baudelaire," "Some Motifs in Baudelaire," "Paris the Capital of the Ninteteenth Century" [Slight revision of trans. by Quinton Hoare, *New Left Review,* No. 48 (March-April 1968), pp. 77-88].

Understanding Brecht, trans. Anna Bostock. London: New Left Books, 1973. Includes: "What is Epic Theater?" [First Version], "What is Epic Theater?" [Second version], "Studies for a Theory of Epic Theater," "From the Brecht Commentary," "A Family Drama in the Epic Theatre," "The Country where it is forbidden to Mention the Proletariat," "Commentaries on Poems by Brecht," "Brecht's *Threepenny Novel,*" "The Author as Producer," "Conversations with Brecht."

Reflections: Essays, Aphorisms, Autobiographical Writings, ed. Peter Demetz, trans. Edmund Jephcott. New York & London: Harcourt

Brace Jovanovich, 1978. Includes: "A Berlin Chronicle," "One-Way Street (selection)," "Moscow," "Marseilles," "Hashish in Marseilles," "Paris, Capital of the Nineteenth Century," "Naples" [with Asja Lacis], "Surrealism," "Brecht's *Threepenny Novel*," "Conversations with Brecht," "The Author as Producer," "Karl Kraus," "Critique of Violence," "The Destructive Character," "Fate and Character," "Theologico-Political Fragment," "On the Language as Such and on the Language of Man," "On the Mimetic Faculty."

The Origin of German Tragic Drama, trans. John Osborne. London: New Left Books, 1977.

One-Way Street and Other Writings, trans. Edmund Jephcott & Kingsley Shorter. London: New Left Books, 1979. Contents same as *Reflections* except for "A Small History of Photography" and "Eduard Fuchs, Collector and Historian," both translated by Kingsley Shorter.

Moscow Diary, pref. Gershom Scholem, trans. Richard Sieburth, ed. Gary Smith. Cambridge, MA: Harvard University Press, 1986. First published in *October* 35 (Winter 1985). Supplemented by "Russian Toys" [trans. G. Smith], "Preface to a planned series for *Humanité*," letters to Gershom Scholem, Jula Radt, Siegfried Kracauer, Martin Buber, and Hugo von Hofmannsthal.

The Correspondence of Walter Benjamin and Gershom Scholem, 1932-1940, trans. Gary Smith and André Lefevere. Introduction by Anson Rabinbach. New York: Schocken Books, 1989.

ESSAYS

The essays listed here are not available in the books above. Included are differing translations of the same original text. Unrevised reprints of translations are not noted.

"8 Notes on Brecht's Epic Theatre," trans. Edward Landberg, *Western Review* 12, 3 (Spring 1948): 167-73.

"The Work of Art in the Epoch of Mechanical Reproduction," trans. H. H. Gerth and Don Martindale, *Studies on the Left* 1, 2 (Winter 1960): 28-46.

"From *A Berlin Childhood*," trans. Mary-Jo Leibowitz, *Art and Literature: an International Review* (Lausanne) 4 (1965), pp. 37–45. Includes: "Tiergarten," "Kaiserpanorama," "The Moon," "The Little Hunchback."

"The Task of the Translator," trans. James Hynd and E. M. Valk, *Delos* 2 (1968): 76-99.

"Paris, Capital of the 19th Century," trans. Suzanne Ruta, *Dissent* 17, 5 (September-October 1970): 439-47.

"The Author as Producer," trans. John Heckman, *New Left Review* 62 (July-August 1970): 83-96.

"A Short History of Photography," trans. Stanley Mitchell, *Screen* 13, 1 (Spring 1972): 5-26.

"Victory Column," trans. Keith Hamnett, in: Dieter Hildebrandt & Siegfried Unseld, eds. *German Mosaic. An Album for Today* ("Official Gift Book of the Organizing Committee for the Games of the XXth Olympiade, Munich 1972"). English ed., Christopher Holme. Frankfurt: Suhrkamp, 1972, pp. 118-19.

"Conversations with Brecht," trans. Anna Bostock, *New Left Review* 77 (January-February 1973): 51-57; also in *Aesthetics and Politics,* ed. Perry Anderson et al. London: New Left Books, 1977, 86-99.

"Program for a Proletarian Children's Theater," trans. Susan Buck-Morss, *Performance* 1, 5 (March-April 1973): 28-32.

"Haschisch in Marseille," trans. Richard Sieburth, *The Minnesota Review* n.s. 1 (Fall 1973): 133-39.

"From Benjamin to Adorno," trans. Harry Zohn, *New Left Review* 81 (September-October 1973): 74-80; same as "Reply" [to Theodor W. Adorno] in *Aesthetics and Politics,* ed. Perry Anderson et al. London: New Left Books, 1977, 134-41.

"Left-Wing Melancholy" (On Erich Kästner's New Book of Poems), trans. Ben Brewster, *Screen* 15, 2 (Summer 1974): 28-32.

"From the Brecht Commentary," trans. John Peet. In Hubert Witt, ed. *Brecht As They Knew Him.* London: Lawrence and Wishart; New York: International Publishers; Berlin: Seven Seas, 1974, 63-68.

"Eduard Fuchs: Collector and Historian," trans. Knut Tarnowski, *New German Critique* 5 (Spring 1975): 27-58.

"Walter Benjamin's Short History of Photography," trans. Phil Patton, *Artforum* 15, 6 (February 1977): 46-61.

"The Destructive Character," trans. Irving Wohlfarth, *Diacritics* 8, 2 (June 1978): 47-48.

"New Things about Plants," trans. Jill Hollis. In *Karl Blossfeldt Photographs.* Oxford: Museum of Modern Art, 1978, 18-19.

"Rastelli narrates . . ." trans. Carol Jacobs. In Jacobs, *The Dissimulating Harmony.* Baltimore: Johns Hopkins University Press, 1978, 117-19.

"Doctrine of the Similar," trans. Knut Tarnowski, *New German Critique* 17 (Spring 1979): 65-69.

"Theories of German Fascism," trans. Jerolf Wikoff, *New German Critique* 17 (Spring 1979): 120-28.

"A Radio Talk on Brecht," trans. David Fernbach, *New Left Review* 123 (September-October 1980): 92-96.

"Goethe: The Reluctant Bourgeois," trans. Rodney Livingstone, *New Left Review* 133 (May-June 1982): 69-93.

"N [Theoretics of Knowledge; Theory of Progress]," trans. Leigh Hafrey and Richard Sieburth, *The Philosophical Forum* 15, 1-2 (Winter-Spring 1983-84): 1-40. [Revised for this volume]

"Program of the Coming Philosophy," trans. Mark Ritter, *The Philosophical Forum* 15, 1-2 (Winter-Spring 1983-84): 41-55.

"Socrates," trans. Thomas Levin, *The Philosophical Forum* 15, 1-2 (Winter-Spring 1983-84): 52-54.

"Central Park," trans. Lloyd Spencer (with Mark Harrington), *New German Critique* 34 (Winter 1985): 32-58.

"Robert Walser," trans. Mark Harman. In Mark Harman, ed., *Robert Walser Rediscovered*. Amherst: University of Massachusetts Press, 1985, 144-47.

"Rigorous Study of Art," trans. Thomas Y. Levin, *October* 47 (Winter 1988): 84–90.